State of Peril

State of Peril

RACE AND RAPE IN SOUTH AFRICAN LITERATURE

Lucy Valerie Graham

OXFORD
UNIVERSITY PRESS

OXFORD
UNIVERSITY PRESS

Oxford University Press is a department of the University of Oxford.
It furthers the University's objective of excellence in research, scholarship,
and education by publishing worldwide.

Oxford   New York
Auckland   Cape Town   Dar es Salaam   Hong Kong   Karachi
Kuala Lumpur   Madrid   Melbourne   Mexico City   Nairobi
New Delhi   Shanghai   Taipei   Toronto

With offices in
Argentina   Austria   Brazil   Chile   Czech Republic   France   Greece
Guatemala   Hungary   Italy   Japan   Poland   Portugal   Singapore
South Korea   Switzerland   Thailand   Turkey   Ukraine   Vietnam

Oxford is a registered trade mark of Oxford University Press
in the UK and certain other countries.

Published in the United States of America by
Oxford University Press
198 Madison Avenue, New York, NY 10016

Library of Congress Cataloging-in-Publication Data
Graham, Lucy Valerie, 1973–
State of peril : race and rape in South African literature / Lucy Valerie Graham.
p.   cm.
Includes bibliographical references and index.
ISBN 978-0-19-979637-3 (cloth : acid-free paper); 978-0-19-025641-8 (paper : acid-free paper)
1. South African literature (English)—History and criticism.
2. Rape in literature. 3. Race relations in literature. I. Title.
PR9355.2G73   2012
820.9'3552—dc23   2011031973

I dedicate this work to the memory of my mother, Vivien Jane Prestwich, and my grandmother, Dorothy May Graham.

{ CONTENTS }

{ PREFACE }

This project began as my doctoral studies in English literature at Oxford University, and I owe an immense debt of gratitude to my supervisor, Robert Young, for his patience and willingness to read and comment on my work as well as for his general benevolence. I also thank my historical consultant and greatest friend, Hugh Macmillan, for his untiring help and support during this project. The Association of Commonwealth Universities (ACU) and the Patrick and Margaret Flanagan Trust provided the financial means to enroll at Oxford University. Lincoln College at Oxford was hospitable in providing an academic home for me and for contributing funding towards my studies. The Nottingham Trent University generously awarded me a research studentship in 2000–2001, and the School of Criticism and Theory at Cornell University kindly offered me funding to attend its 2004 summer school, where I was able to develop the theoretical perspectives used in the study. I am grateful to Stellenbosch University, where I am currently based as a Lecturer in English Literature, for support in finishing this work. I have been privileged to have had access to excellent libraries and archives during my studies. The librarians at Oxford and the National English Literary Museum (NELM) in particular provided personalized and efficient research support. At NELM I owe a debt of gratitude to Paulette Coetzee, who, through discussions many years ago helped me to shape formative ideas for this project. I would also like to thank the late Daphne Rooke for her generosity in agreeing to be interviewed, Jenny Maimane for her willingness to provide information and documents relating to the life and work of Arthur Maimane, and Frances Wollen for assistance in accessing the Victor Gollancz archives. Mark Behr and Matthew Krouse were delightfully frank in talking about their work, and Annari van der Merwe was helpful in sharing information about the life of K. Sello Duiker.

Very special thanks to the following people for their helpful comments, friendship and support during the evolution of this work: Chris Warnes, Joy Wang, Margaret Hanzimanolis, Justin Snell, David Attwell, Rita Barnard, Tanya Barben, Nosipho Mlomzale, Deon de Kock, Mark Sanders, Andrew van der Vlies and Patrick Flanery. I would also like to thank the monks of the Cape Town Meditation Centre for teaching "the middle way", and Pye, Zorro and Ashes for their company during days and nights of writing. Finally, a big thank you to my family: Joel, Adam, Hilary, Dallis, Robert and Janet, and my maternal and paternal grandparents as well as the *amakhosi* who went before them.

Sections of chapters first appeared in the following sources, from which permission to reprint is gratefully acknowledged. An earlier version of the section on Olive Schreiner in Chapter 1 was published as "Re-imagining the Cave: Gender, Land and Imperialism in Olive Schreiner's *Trooper Peter Halket of Mashonaland* (1897)", in *English Studies in Africa* 50. 1 (2007), 25–40. An earlier version of the section on Daphne Rooke in Chapter 3 was published as "'Consequential Changes': Daphne Rooke's *Mittee* in America and South Africa", in *Safundi: The Journal of South African and American Studies* 10. 1 (2009), 43–58. An earlier version of the section on *Tshepang* in Chapter 5 was published as "Save Us All: 'Baby Rape' and Post-apartheid Narratives", in *Scrutiny2* 13.1 (2008), 105–19. An earlier version of the section on J.M. Coetzee's *Disgrace* in Chapter 5 was published as "Reading the Unspeakable: Rape in J.M. Coetzee's *Disgrace*", in *Journal of Southern African Studies* 29.2 (2003), 433–444.

Cape Town, Summer 2011

State of Peril

Introduction

In April 2000, a critical reading of J.M. Coetzee's novel *Disgrace* (1999) was presented by the ruling African National Congress (ANC) to the South African Human Rights Commission (SAHRC) hearings on racism in the media. Anonymously authored by President Thabo Mbeki, the ANC submission noted that in *Disgrace* "a white woman . . . is gang-raped by three black men who afterwards also steal her car and household goods. The following then appears in the novel: it was so personal she says." Mbeki continued that "in this novel J.M. Coetzee represents as brutally as he can the white people's perception of the post-apartheid black man . . . without the restraining leash around the neck that the European had been obliged to place in the interests of both the native and society."[1] Since the word "represents" in this context could mean that Coetzee is unflinchingly portraying white attitudes to the rape or that Coetzee's perspective is representative of white racist opinion, whether the author of *Disgrace* stands accused of racism in the document is ambiguous. Two months later, however, a public spat erupted between Mbeki and a white journalist, Charlene Smith, whose chilling personal account of rape had been published in the *Mail and Guardian* in April 1999. Detailing the violation and documenting the shabby treatment she received from police and hospital staff, Smith's article captured the attention of the nation, and drew considerable notice from abroad such that she quickly became a spokesperson for South Africa on the subject of sexual violence. In an article in the *Washington Post*, Smith claimed that "rape is endemic" in South African culture, and that "the role of tradition and religion" in fostering a "culture" of rape needed to be understood.[2] Decoding this reference to "culture" as a reference to African culture specifically, Mbeki protested that Smith "was sufficiently brave, or blinded by racist rage, publicly to make the deeply offensive statement that rape is an endemic feature of African society."[3] In a live BBC webcast in 2000, Mbeki was asked what he was doing about the incidence of rape in South Africa. The President responded that although South Africa, like many countries, had "a rape problem," there was "a lot of misreporting about these things."[4] Mbeki's denial of sexual violence as a serious social problem in South Africa is undermined by international studies such as the 1996 International

Police Organisation (Interpol) report, which found that South Africa had the highest number of reported rape cases of all countries selected for a survey, and the *Victims of Crime Survey*, which confirmed similar statistics in 1998.[5] Nonetheless, it is useful to place Mbeki's objections in relation to a history where rape narratives have been deployed for racist ends. Despite inferences made during an interview with Smith in the United States in February 2001, she is not "one of the first women to speak out about rape in South Africa."[6] More significantly, she is not the first white woman raped by a black man in South Africa to have received extensive media coverage. As I demonstrate throughout this study, "black peril" narratives—sensationalized accounts of white women raped by black men—have a long history in South Africa, where they have fed white paranoia and obscured the fact that most rapes are intra-racial. Although "black peril" typically refers to the period of social hysteria prevalent in South Africa from 1890 to 1914,[7] earlier scares set in South Africa can be traced further back in time, and the deployment of "black peril" anxieties has been a recurring strategy in South African politics throughout the twentieth century and into the post-apartheid environment.

As I argue in chapter 5, there is no statistical evidence that rape has increased since 1994.[8] My argument is that rape statistics have remained high but consistent for at least two decades, and that rape was a major but hidden social problem under apartheid. This position differs from that of critics who claim that rape statistics are ascendant or that the post-apartheid era has ushered in a "new" war on women and children. I would like to suggest that discourse on rape—rather than rape *per se*—has proliferated in the post-apartheid context and this may be read not only as a result of greater aware-ness of gender issues, but also as an expression of complex anxieties about the new nation and the transition to black governance. Moreover, such anx-ieties have been exploited by right-wing political parties. Laden with adjec-tives of hysterical outrage, for instance, a 1999 election poster for the New National Party (a reinvented version of the apartheid-era National Party) states that women are raped daily, that the party is "deeply shocked" at the ANC's "unfeeling" attitude to this "state of emergency," and that the New Nationalist Party plans to institute capital punishment for rapists (Figure I.1).[9] This election poster, the Smith/Mbeki confrontation, and the ANC's reference to *Disgrace* during the SAHRC hearings demonstrate the need for critical analyses that recognize high levels of sexual violence in South Africa, but also examine the racialized inferences and assumptions implicit in repre-sentations of bodily violation. Focusing on literary texts that foreground questions of race and rape in South African literature from the colonial pe-riod until the present day, my study aims to offer a dialectical approach that acknowledges the suffering of those who are subjected to sexual violence, without losing sight of the ways in which certain rape narratives have been exploited for political ends in South African history.

FIGURE I.1 *Election poster for the New National Party, 1999.*

Broadly speaking, my project comprises a study of South African literature through the prism of narratives of gender violence. As noted throughout the investigation, the most striking aspect of South African literary representations of rape is their obsessive focus on interracial rape, a fixation that is not justified by the realities of sexual violence in a country where most violations are intraracial. While I have no interest in any prescriptive formulation that literary representations should match reality, my book aims to give serious attention to the hold that interracial rape has had on the national imaginary, and to the role these portrayals have played in the making of a national literature and of the South African state as an imagined community.[10]

The study is historical in that it follows a chronological framework and pays close attention to the contexts of the selected texts, and to trends in the representation of rape in the periods under analysis. In my endeavor to trace a literary history of rape portrayals, I take seriously Fredric Jameson's injunction to "[always] historicize" and his assertion that "cultural artifacts" function "as socially symbolic acts."[11] However, I do not intend to pursue what J.M. Coetzee has called "the colonisation of novels by the discourse of history," but rather follow Coetzee in seeing literature and history as different and autonomous kinds of discourse.[12] For instance, if one simply reads "black peril" novels as expressing the racist prejudices of a dominant group at a given point in history, it is possible to miss the ways in which such texts may double back upon anxieties of authorship, revealing complex contestations over not only political but also literary voice. In considering the voices and countervoices within literary texts, I have found it useful to bear in mind Mikhail Bakhtin's observation that the novel "is a phenomenon multiform in style and variform in speech and voice."[13] As pointed out in chapter 2, even classic "black peril" novels, which could be dismissed as crass expressions of white paranoia, may be read in a Bakhtinian sense as dialogic and heteroglossic, riddled with contradictory voices and impulses. Inspiring my approach are Bakhtin's injunction "to overcome the divorce between an abstract 'formal' approach and an equally abstract 'ideological' approach,"[14] and Theodor Adorno's theories of music and art, which recognize the autonomy of the work of art, but also the ways in which art may stand in relation to the antinomies in society.[15]

In considering how South African literary representations of rape relate to other discourses on race, sexuality, and class, I draw on Michel Foucault's notion of sexuality as "an especially dense transfer point for relations of power," one "endowed with the greatest instrumentality: useful for the greatest number of maneuvers and capable of serving as a point of support, as a linchpin, for the most varied strategies."[16] As demonstrated in the study, "black peril" discourse in South Africa has indeed been instrumental in a variety of racially oppressive measures, from justifying the momentous Natives Land Act of 1913 to maintaining a race and class-based system of oppression that denied education and full citizenship to members of the population deemed, in the negative parlance of racist ideology, to be "non-white." While some would surmise that "white peril" stories, narratives of the rape or sexual exploitation of colonized women by colonizing men, offer a progressive alternative to "black peril" stories in South African literature, the issues that inhere in all representations of interracial rape are complex, and one could argue that "white peril" representations have historically been used to argue for legislation against "miscegenation." As evidenced by a tradition of white South African women writing about "the white peril," and by the case of Sarah Gertrude Millin in particular, portrayals of "the white peril" have often been marked by a horror of "miscegenation," by a phobic inability to think of interracial sex in any other than violent and abased terms.

By keeping focused on the particular while remaining mindful of a global picture and the possibility of comparisons across place and time, this study aims to pay attention to transnational links and to be comparative as far as possible without homogenizing or oversimplifying the issues at stake. I am thus trying to recognize the specificities of context without positing South Africa as "a special case." Indeed, as demonstrated in comparisons between early South African literature and literature of the Indian Mutiny (in chapter 1), and in comparisons between the ways in which race and sexuality have been deployed across the contexts of the United States and South Africa (in chapters 2 and 3), narratives of rape have functioned in similar ways across different geographical contexts. Because of similarities in constructions of black masculinity, the culture of letters in the United States probably provides the most fruitful comparison with South African literary representations of sexual violation. As Jenny Sharpe notes, as opposed to the Oriental male, black masculinity in colonial discourse has traditionally been hypersexualized, rendered bestial and rapacious: "the myth of the black rapist presupposes even as it reproduces the Negro's lustful bestiality; the Oriental male, by contrast, is constructed as licentious rather than lustful, duplicitous instead of bestial."[17] The investigation also seeks to concentrate on the selected texts in an interdisciplinary frame, drawing on perspectives from gender studies, poststructuralist and postcolonial theory, and social and historical studies. Representations in the media, in cinema, and in the visual arts will be referred to and analyzed where relevant.

One of the main points of the investigation is to draw attention to the inextricability of race, gender, and class in representations of sexual violence. Like Judith Butler, I am wary of "theories of intersectionality," or of approaches that keep, for instance, "processes of gendering and racing radically distinct."[18] Rather, I am interested in the ways in which representations of race, gender, and class "work together" in the literary texts under examination. Paying close attention to processes of colonialism and apartheid, this study considers race, gender, and class in examining issues of authority, narrative perspective, and genre, as well as the depiction or elision of the scene of violence in the texts selected for analysis. Particularly, I aim to consider how literary representations of rape in South Africa lend themselves to overmappings of signification that can draw attention away from the body and register anxieties regarding the defilement and invasion of "sacred boundaries" of collective identity. In order to analyze the currency that discourse on interracial sexual violence has had in South African literature, the study draws together as theoretical underpinnings Foucault's account of sexuality and biopower, and Butler's speculations on race and melancholia. While each part of the investigation makes use of specific theoretical perspectives relevant to the internal logic of that section, the use of Butler and Foucault's theories enables the study as a whole to link the rise and instrumentality of narratives of interracial sexual violence in South Africa to the emergence of modern racism, and to interrogate the cultural and psychic conditions under which such narratives proliferate.[19]

In *The Will to Knowledge: The History of Sexuality Vol.1* and *Society Must be Defended*, Foucault outlines his notion of biopower, proposing that a power organized around "the task of administering life" emerged from the late seventeenth century, and that this took two distinct forms "linked together by a whole intermediary cluster of relations." Foucault refers to the first of these "two poles of development" as "*an anatomo-politics of the human body*" and claims that, "starting in the seventeenth century," this mode of biopower took as its object "the body as machine: its disciplining, the optimization of its forces, the parallel increase of its usefulness and its docility, its integration into systems of efficient and economic controls."[20] The second type of biopower emerged somewhat later—Foucault estimates its appearance in the latter part of the eighteenth century.[21] Rather than centering on the individual body, this "*biopolitics of the population*" took as its subject "the species body, the body imbued with the mechanics of life and serving as the basis of the biological processes: propagation, births and mortality, the level of health life expectancy, and longevity, with all the conditions that cause these to vary."[22] Because of its distinctive relationship to the reproductive function, Foucault notes that sexuality became a privileged discourse linking the individual body of anatomo-politics to the species body of biopolitics: "at the juncture of the 'body' and the 'population' sex became a crucial target."[23] Foucault goes on to argue that with the emergence of biopolitics came a concern with the health and purity of the collective, and racism "in its modern, 'biologizing', statist form"[24] took shape, with sexuality becoming a major field of attention in the discourse of eugenics, of racial purity and degeneracy. Although Foucault does not mention it, among the great racist states of the twentieth century, South Africa clearly occupied a prominent place, bearing witness to the ways in which mechanisms of biopower have "acted as factors of segregation and social hierarchization, exerting their influence . . . guaranteeing relations of domination and effects of hegemony."[25]

As noted in chapter 1, as early as the 1790s there were rumblings of mass hysteria in England about white women shipwrecked on the southern African coastline becoming sexual prey to "native" men. By this time, the white woman's body had became a cherished frontier, the guarantor of collective health and purity, with paranoia developing about its sexual safety in zones outside of colonial control. Foucault notes that the interaction of biopolitics with anatomo-politics around issues of sexuality led to the emergence, at the end of the eighteenth century, of "a dynamic racism, a racism of expansionism, even if was in a budding state, awaiting the second half of the nineteenth century to bear the fruits that we have tasted."[26] Significantly, the consolidation of this racism coincides with an increasing emphasis on a certain narrative of rape— by the mid-nineteenth century, stories about the violation of colonizing women by colonized men were seizing the European imagination across the breadth of the colonial world, from Jamaica, to India, to South Africa.

As Foucault mentions, sexuality has a class dimension, in that "sexuality is originally, historically bourgeois" and "induces specific class effects."[27] Controlling and regulating its own sexuality in the first instance, the bourgeoisie should be seen as being occupied in forming "a 'class body' with its health, hygiene, descent and race . . . the endogamy of sex and the body."[28] Of course the idea of a "class body" is complicated in contexts such as South Africa by overlappings of race and class. Instead of dealing simply with "a class body," under apartheid the ruling bourgeoisie bifurcated the world into the racialized categories of "white" and "non-white." More starkly than in most other contexts, the boundaries of endogamy were drawn up along racial, and not only class lines. In colonial and apartheid-era South Africa, sexuality came to be a field under severe surveillance and regulation, and in a medicalized discourse of slippage between the body of the individual and the collective, protecting the white body from sexual threats became synonymous with safeguarding the purity and health of the white nation.

While Foucault sees psychoanalysis as another form of regulatory discourse on sex, however, I follow Judith Butler in attempting to trace the psychic effects of social power. In particular, I propose that Butler's account of cultural melancholia is useful in understanding the obsession with narratives of interracial rape that has characterized much discourse on race and sexuality in South Africa. I would thus like to extend and develop Foucault's account of biopolitics to suggest that the strength of this mode of biopower lay precisely in its capacity to mesh with deeply held psychological anxieties about contamination, filth, abjection, and disease. In her study *Public Rape: Representing Violation in Fiction and Film* (2004), Tanya Horeck proposes that psychoanalytic theories of fantasy, and in particular of collective fantasy, are useful for understanding the ways in which portrayals of rape, through public circulation, play out socially-repressed communal desires and serve to instantiate sexual and social difference.[29] What I would like to argue, however, is that the notion of fantasy alone is inadequate to the task of making sense, for instance, of the most common "black peril" phenomena. Rather, paranoia and phobia account more convincingly than fantasy for the terror, tropes of infection and degeneration, false accusations, and delusions of enmity and persecution that characterize such anxieties. Moreover, I propose that the obsessive manner in which South African literature has returned to the theme of interracial rape may be read as a symptom of what Butler calls "culturally instituted melancholia,"[30] which I place alongside what J.M. Coetzee has aptly called "a failure of love."[31]

In an interview with Vikki Bell in 1999, Butler focuses on the ways in which culturally-forged foreclosures in the field of love give rise to collective melancholia. While she had previously used melancholia to understand "how the melancholic structure of heterosexuality encrypts the homosexual,"[32] in this interview Butler draws on the notion of melancholia to understand what happens in the case of race, when "cross-racial sexual relations have been foreclosed . . . not just prohibited but foreclosed—in the sense of [being rendered] unthinkable."[33] Here Butler is following Freud, who distinguished between processes of mourning and melancholia by claiming that, as opposed to mourning where loss is recognized, melancholia presents a state where the loss of a love object is not acknowledged, leading to all kinds of morbid symptoms. Taking Freud's account of melancholia into an analysis of discourse, Butler argues that melancholia is "love foreclosed by discourse" and that it can be "culturally instituted":

> I think there are cultural forms, culturally instituted forms of melancholia . . .
> It's not just a question of this ego not being able to love that person—it's not
> that model—it's rather what it means to have one's desire formed as it were
> through cultural norms that dictate in part what will and what will not be
> a loveable object, what will and what will not be a legitimate form of love.[34]

As she notes, "the history of miscegenation involves a history of melancholia in an interesting way," since, when interracial desire becomes unthinkable, this results in "certain types of love that are held not to be love, loss that is held not to be loss, that remain within this kind of unthinkable domain or in a kind of ontologically shadowy domain."[35]

Strikingly, the foreclosure "in the field of love" that Butler mentions here finds an echo in J.M. Coetzee's Jerusalem Prize acceptance speech of 1987, which was concerned with the ways in which "the masters in South Africa experience their unfreedom today."[36] "In the 1950s," said Coetzee, "the heady years when the great city of apartheid was still being built, a law was passed making sexual relations between masters and slaves a crime." The psychic origin and meaning of this law, Coetzee claimed, "lie in fear and denial: denial of an unacknowledgeable desire to embrace Africa, embrace the body of Africa; and the fear of being embraced in return by Africa." Noting that love for South Africa has been directed, not towards its people but at *the land*, "toward what is least likely to respond to love: mountains and deserts, birds and animals and flowers," Coetzee proposed that:

> The deformed and stunted relations between human beings that were cre-
> ated under colonialism and exacerbated under what is loosely called apart-
> heid have their psychic representation in a deformed and stunted inner life.
> All expressions of that inner life, no matter how intense, no matter how
> pierced with exultation or despair, suffer from the same stuntedness and
> deformity. South African literature . . . is a less than fully human literature,

unnaturally preoccupied with power and the torsions of power, unable to move from elementary relations of contestation, domination, and subjugation to the vast and complex human world that lies beyond them.[37]

Notably, Coetzee did not exclude himself as a writer from this critique. While for Butler the problem is a "culturally-instituted" foreclosure and for Coetzee it is that the love of the colonizers or "masters" has simply "never been enough," the observations of these two writers may be brought into conversation. It is obviously not my intention to propose that interracial love is necessarily unthinkable or unimaginable. Rather, I am suggesting the prevalence of narratives of interracial rape in South African literature could lead one to conclude that the more extreme the form of biologizing racism that infuses a society at all social, cultural, and psychological levels, the more interracial desire becomes unimaginable, subject to foreclosure, and representable only in the melancholy terms of rape. I would also like to add that a history of the representation of interracial love or fraternity in South Africa remains to be written.

If the compulsive return to narratives of interracial violation that has characterized South African literature may be read as a symptom of melancholia and disavowal, of an inability to imagine interracial desire in anything but debased and violent terms, are there cultural texts about interracial desire that would constitute acts of mourning or bereavement? As I argue in chapter 3, Dora Taylor's short story entitled "To Tell My Story" (1960) could be read as a literary expression of mourning as it acknowledges the possibility of interracial love, but also the impossibility of such love blooming in the desert of a racist society. While it remains outside of this study to examine this in detail, my argument is that mourning for interracial love manifests in texts that *acknowledge* interracial desire as a site of loss, whether this loss is imposed by law, as in Athol Fugard's *Statements After an Arrest Under the Immorality Act* (1972), or whether it results from the psychological internalization of racist ideology—as in Frantz Fanon's *Black Skins, White Masks* and Lewis Nkosi's *Mating Birds* (1983), in which interracial desire is acknowledged but simultaneously traced as a wound, shown to be distorted by the fetishizations of internalized racism.[38]

To those who would object that South Africa in the post-apartheid era has surely moved on from the "deformed and stunted" relations that have characterized the past, I would argue that while the transition to non-racial democracy has ushered in some fresh and interesting developments in social and cultural terms, we should nonetheless heed warnings from commentators such as Pumla Dineo Gqola and Thembinkosi Goniwe, who point out that "post-apartheid" is a misnomer when it suggests a total rupture with apartheid.[39] The confrontation between Mbeki and Smith mentioned above, for instance, indicates that, far from being locked away in the past, a history of problematic representation has continued to impact upon and shape the post-apartheid environment. Moreover, the beginning of democracy in South Africa has not meant the end of poverty and privilege or the demise of racist thinking.

While I have uncovered, within South African English literature, a compulsive return to narratives of interracial rape, and have sought to explain this by using the theories of Foucault and Butler, as well as by drawing on J.M. Coetzee's analysis of South African literature as marked by "a failure of love," my study is not only about representations of interracial violation. There are a number of South African writers who have scripted scenes of intraracial sexual violence. As I point out in chapter 3, although she did draw on "black peril" stereotypes, Daphne Rooke predominantly foregrounds intraracial sexual violence as endemic in the orders of colonialism and apartheid. In chapter 4 I discuss the ways in which black authors in the 1980s dealt with the politically volatile subject matter of black-on-black rape, and in chapter 5 I discuss, among other topics, post-apartheid literary representations of male rape and sexual violence against children.

Because of their dialogic structure, literary texts relate to dominant ideologies in unstable and unpredictable ways. While it is of value to examine the ways in which narratives of interracial rape, and "black peril" narratives in particular, have been engaged in "renewing and reinvigorating racist rituals," it is also important to trace how certain literature facilitates ways of exploiting these rituals, mimicking and "restaging" them.[40] Homi Bhabha's theory of mimicry is relevant here, and as Butler points out, racialization has a certain temporality in that it "must be reiterated again and again . . . it has a kind of ritual dimension and . . . its very temporal dimension is the condition of its subversion."[41] In fact, what I have found most fascinating in this study is the ambivalent potential of portrayals of interracial rape. Although "black peril" imagery has prevailed in racist public discourse throughout much of South Africa's history, there are also instances of South African authors who have reterritorialized the worn-out tropes of racist discourse in subversive ways that interrogate rather than confirm stereotypes. There are also cases of black women writers who have re-scripted "white peril" encounters, not in order to damn "miscegenation" like white writers before them, but to focus attention on the material ways in which black women may experience systems of hierarchy and exclusion.

Since the significance of a literary text may not be the same in different contexts, a large part of the analysis is concerned with the circulation of rape narratives, with the production, distribution, and reception of the literary works under discussion.[42] Where relevant I examine publication history, including reception history and issues of censorship. Underlying this concern with the life of the text, with the text as a material object, is the proposal that ethical responsiveness to rape in fiction requires an acknowledgment that the society in which the text is produced and disseminated is the realm of the corporeal, and, particularly in South Africa, that suffering bodies are never far away from the reader. Such responsibility is inseparable from the recognition that the literary critic is an embodied, living subject interacting with(in) a particular context. As suggested above, representations of sexual violence in South African literature necessitate two levels of consideration, namely, recognizing the suffering of those affected by sexual violence, and acknowledging the ways in which rape stories have served to justify oppressive laws that dispossessed, disenfranchised, and violently acted out upon the bodies of those constructed as racially other.

The focus of the analysis is on literature written in English. This is mainly because there is little or no documented reference to rape in literature in South African indigenous languages, and, perhaps surprisingly, in Afrikaans literature throughout the twentieth century (apart from N.P. Van Wyk Louw's allegorical poem, *Raka*, 1941, and Mark Behr's *Die Reuk van Appels*, 1993, which is analyzed in chapter 5) one finds little preoccupation with rape or with "black peril" as a sexual threat. The reason for this lack of interest in rape narratives in Afrikaans fiction would appear to be that fears about interracial rape simply did not take hold of the Afrikaner imagination at an early and formative time in South African history. As pointed out in the first chapter of my study, South Africa's earliest recorded internal "black peril" scare took place in the early 1870s in Natal, a colony politically dominated by white English-speaking settlers. Moreover, in the two decades after the South African War, anxiety about "black peril" as a sexual threat seems to have filtered into South African political and literary discourse from the British colonial imaginary and has a low profile in public statements by white Afrikaans politicians and spokespersons.[43] Part of the reason for this may be that, in the first decades of the twentieth century, white Afrikaners were not as proletarianized as their English counterparts, and would not have been in direct competition with black workers to the same extent as their English compatriots. When white Afrikaner politicians did begin to draw on the lexicon of "the black peril," this was in the late 1920s, when the National Party aligned itself with the white Labour Party, and the term was used to signify a demographic and political/economic threat, as in the rhetoric of Hertzog's Nationalist Party in the run-up to the 1929 election. This is not to say, however, that it had no sexualized dimension. Conjuring up an image of a feminized white nation threatened with *oorstroming* (swamping) by black hordes, the term "*swart gevaar*" ("black peril") drew on the psychosexual connotations that "black peril" had accumulated. As I point out in chapter 3, with the advent of D.F. Malan's "Purified" National Party in the 1930s one begins to see direct evidence of biopolitical discourse, of "black peril" as a biological and sexual threat, in Afrikaner politicking. Yet this did not translate into narratives of interracial rape becoming a major feature of Afrikaans literature. Of the novels examined in this study, only one is originally written in Afrikaans, namely Mark Behr's *The Smell of Apples* (1995, originally published in Afrikaans as *Die Reuk van Appels*, 1993), and it is a narrative about intraracial rape.

In the first chapter of this study, I trace the relationship between imperial romance and narratives of sexual violence in South Africa's contact zone during the colonial era. Captain Marryat's *The Mission* (1845) is brought into dialogue with novels of the Indian Mutiny to show that a certain script of rape was integral to the emergence of modern racism. The chapter then demonstrates how Olive Schreiner's *Trooper Peter Halket of Mashonaland* (1897) subverts the discourse of imperial romance and more than a century of rape narratives set in South Africa. Whereas writers such as Henry Rider Haggard cultivated a mythology in which southern Africa was a feminized site laid bare for the pleasure of the male adventurer, Schreiner's novel counters the dominant mode of imperial romance even as it marks the beginning of a long tradition of white South African women writing against "miscegenation" by damning "the white peril." I then move on to consider literature of the South African War (1899–1902), and specifically Rudyard Kipling's short story entitled "A Sahib's War," to demonstrate links between chivalric discourse, "black peril," and the scandal of non-European combatants in a "white war." As a conclusion to this chapter, I suggest the ways in which the "black peril" began to function, during the war and in post-war discourse of reconciliation and early nation-building, to unite the white races of South Africa against a common enemy.

In chapter 2, three "black peril" novels of the early twentieth century are examined, with a focus on the difference between a text written by a white woman, Francis Bancroft, and novels written by two white men, George Webb Hardy and George Heaton Nicholls. My argument is that "black peril" around the time of Union (1910) was a discursive phenomenon directly related to white anxieties about the emergence of black literary and political enunciation. As in other contexts, such as the United States, in South Africa racially inflected narratives of rape have provided an index for white anxieties at times of social, economic, or political instability. This chapter discusses the relationship between "black peril" rhetoric, the making of the South African Union (1910), and anxieties about black readerships and black political voice. Examining Bancroft's *Of Like Passions* (1907), Webb Hardy's *The Black Peril* (1912), and Heaton Nicholls's *Bayete!* (1923), I argue that these classic and foundational "black peril" novels are concerned with the politics of authorship and literary authority, and that the contests over political voice and textual authority staged by these writers have a bearing on later black authors who parody and restage "black peril" typecasts.

In chapter 3 the study moves on to consider the transition from segregation into apartheid, outlining the ways in which representations of "black peril" or "white peril" may be read as a symptom of a melancholic inability to imagine interracial love. Beginning with the work of Sol Plaatje, a writer I regard as a "possibilist" in the sense that he is able to imagine the possibility of harmonious interracial relationships, I trace Plaatje's *The Mote and the Beam* as a transnational "sex tract" that elaborates on the dilemmas around interracial sex. As Butler points out, a history of "miscegenation" is also a history of melancholy representations, and while Sarah Gertrude Millin, like Plaatje, is concerned with uncovering "the white peril," her exposé of the abuse of colonized women by colonizing men stems from phobia for "miscegenation" that was instrumental in consolidating Millin's own position as "white" in an increasingly racist state. The last section of this chapter examines sexual violence in the work of Daphne Rooke. Drawing on unpublished archival material, I discuss the differences between a scene of rape in two editions of Rooke's novel *Mittee* (1951–2), the edition first circulated in the United States and the edition first circulated in the United Kingdom and South Africa. As I argue, despite Rooke's inclination at times to draw on racist stereotypes, she is the only major white writer of the apartheid era to draw attention to intraracial sexual violence.

Chapter 4 focuses on the ways in which black writers in the apartheid years rescripted previously white-authored narratives about rape. Arthur Maimane's *Victims* (1976) is pivotal here, as he simultaneously mimics and destabilizes the idea, as Bloke Modisane put it, that "natives have a rape-utation."[44] Rather than subscribing to the view that *Victims* simply reiterates the logic of apartheid, I argue that it restages "black peril" stereotypes in subversive ways and that in its composition and subject matter it engages with the fear at the heart of classic "black peril" phenomena—the anxiety, figured in contests over white women's bodies, of black authorship, particularly black authorship about the white woman's body. I then turn to consider the ways in which women such as Lauretta Ngcobo and Farida Karodia script "white peril" narratives, previously the domain of white women writers such as Schreiner, Bancroft, and Millin. The final section of the chapter examines the emergence of a focus on intraracial rape in short stories of the late apartheid era. Njabulo Ndebele's "Fools" (1983) and the post-apartheid film adaptation of this story, Gcina Mhlophe's "Nokulunga's Wedding" (1983) and Baleka Kgositsile's "In the Night" (1988) are discussed in comparison with a short story by the white writer Matthew Krouse.

In the final chapter, the investigation scrutinizes representations of sexual violence in the post-apartheid transition and beyond by focusing on violence and memory in a context where gender rights are entrenched in law, but where sexual violence remains as a persistent hangover from a violent, racially divided, and patriarchal past. As demonstrated in public debates, the post-apartheid government has failed to respond adequately to sexual violence as a serious social problem in South Africa, partly because of a racist and problematic history of rape portrayal. Starting with an analysis of J.M. Coetzee's most famous novel, *Disgrace*, I demonstrate the ways in which this text and the dilemma that emerged around it within South Africa disturbingly bring into focus a history of representation in which rape and issues of race are inextricably enmeshed. While the stories of the women in the novel are hidden from the reader, the text foregrounds positionality and calls the reader into account, ambivalently drawing attention to the problems of representing sexual violence. As I demonstrate, the theme of unspeakable violations may also be traced in Achmat Dangor's *Bitter Fruit* and Zoë Wicomb's *David's Story*, though these two post-apartheid novels engage more directly with the mandate and processes of the Truth and Reconciliation Commission in that they explore the difficulties of revealing, within the post-apartheid transition, certain stories of rape perpetrated under apartheid. Published before the Sexual Offences Act of 2007, which recognized that men could be victims of rape, *The Smell of Apples* by Mark Behr and K. Sello Duiker's *Thirteen Cents* and *The Quiet Violence of Dreams* are *Bildungsromane* that challenge prevailing myths about rape, most notably the ideas that rape only happens to women and that male rape is homosexual. The study ends with a consideration of Lara Foot-Newton's *Tshepang*, a dramatic production based on the horrific rape of a nine-month-old baby that took place in 2001 in an impoverished area of the Northern Cape.

While it is disturbing to recognize that a focus on rape has shaped much of South African literature from its earliest colonial manifestations to novels and dramatic productions of the present day, the investigation seeks not to contribute to Afro-pessimism, but rather to unpack, demystify, and understand the compulsive return to certain narratives of sexual violence that has characterized the national imaginary. Literary histories of sexual violence have been traced in other national literatures (see, for instance, Sabine Sielke's important study *Reading Rape: The Rhetoric of Sexual Violence in American Literature and Culture, 1790–1990*),[45] but until the past decade Gareth Cornwell was the only literary critic to give rigorous attention to discourse on sexual violence in the history of South African literature, although his studies have been confined to "black peril" novels of the early twentieth century.[46] As I argue above and in the final chapter, rape statistics have remained *consistently* high in South Africa's transition to democracy, but post-liberation South Africa, particularly in the last decade, has been characterized by *increased* discourse on sexual violence, and this is evident in South African literature and literary criticism. My study contributes to this proliferation, but with the aim of demystifying a long and problematic history of racist representations, so that sexual violence may be more readily confronted as a social problem in South Africa. By acknowledging the ways in which this history constitutes part of our "unfreedom" as a nation, it is also my hope to clear space for imagining and tracing relations other than those marked by sexual violence.

Danger and Desire

RAPE AND SEDUCTION IN THE COLONIAL IMAGINATION

In 1897, Fisher Unwin published Olive Schreiner's *Trooper Peter Halket of Mashonaland*, a novel that described the rape of indigenous women by colonizing men, subverting the dominant discourse of imperial romance and more than a century of stories of sexual violence set in southern Africa. One of the key events that had precipitated these narratives had been the wreck of the *Grosvenor*, a British ship that ran aground off the southern African coast in 1782. Following on the heels of captivity narratives from North America, which became popular in England during the eighteenth century,[1] reports emerged that women who survived the wreck had been assimilated into indigenous communities. As Stephen Taylor points out, the possibility of Englishwomen being stranded under such circumstances generated public hysteria in Britain, with newspapers registering as rape or "prostitution" the loss of cultural capital incurred when white women's wombs were wrecked beyond the boundaries of empire: "By the Hottentots, they were dragged up into the interior parts of the country, for the purposes of the vilest brutish prostitution."[2]

The perceived fate of the *Grosvenor* women haunted the first era of British settlement in southern Africa, and in anticipation of the arrival of the 1820 settlers in South Africa, in an etching entitled "The Blessings of Emigration to the Cape of Forlorn Hope" (Figure 1.1), the British cartoonist George Cruikshank depicted a group of "Hottentots" attacking white settlers. Lifted off the ground by her cannibal captor, a white woman dressed in a virginal gown throws her arms upward in resistance. Similar to that of the doomed women in Poussin's *The Rape of the Sabine Women*, her pose signals her fate. Skinny white settlers are pitted against large and muscular male indigenes, the inference being that the latter are also better endowed.[3] Anxieties about the products of interracial couplings are staged in the background as a "Hottentot," trampling on the body of a white infant, jabs a settler woman with a long and phallic spear. The caption below the cartoon reads: "To be half roasted by the sun & devoured by the Natives!!" Recalling J.M. Coetzee's observation about white "fear and denial: denial of an unacknowledgeable desire to embrace Africa, embrace the body of Africa; and the fear of being embraced in return

FIGURE 1.1 *George Cruikshank, "The Blessings of Emigration to the Cape of Forlorn Hope",*
1819.

by Africa," here the horrors of cannibalism and "native" rape are revealed as
twin penetration anxieties: not only is the white settler threatened with engulf-
ment by the alien land into which he has thrust himself, but his women are in
danger of being penetrated and contaminated by the monstrous others who
inhabit this territory.

Historians have pointed out that "black peril" hysteria peaked in South
Africa from the 1870s through to 1914,[4] but as accounts of the *Grosvenor* survi-
vors suggest, images of European womanhood under threat of rape by black
men in southern Africa can be traced at least from the end of the eighteenth
century, corresponding with the emergence of what Michel Foucault has called
biopolitics. According to Foucault, biopolitics was a form of biopower marked
by a new concern with the "health" and purity of the collective, and may be
observed in obsessions with supervising and extending regulatory controls over
"births and mortality, the level of health, life expectancy and longevity" of the
population.[5] In its extreme forms, biopolitics would begin to manifest in eugenics and ideas about racial degeneration. Although Foucault does not examine the status of white women in settlement colonies, in the colony the presence
of white women was a constant source of anxiety. It was on the fringes of empire
that the white woman's sexuality had most to be regulated, as her body became
a cherished frontier on which the status and superiority of the settler race
depended. Where threats to racial hierarchies were intense, colonial societies
became panic stricken about controlling white women's reproductivity.

As I demonstrate in the discussion of Captain Marryat's *The Mission* (1845) and novels of the Indian Mutiny, those women who endangered endogamous boundaries in what were perceived to be perilous contact zones were considered better off dead. At the same time, however, it is clear that critiques of colonialism have drawn on images of the figurative or literal ravishment of the colonized by colonizing men. Although representations of European women threatened by "native" men had become the prevailing storyline of sexual violence in the colonial imagination by the late nineteenth century, in *Trooper Peter Halket of Mashonaland* Schreiner offers a counter-narrative in which British imperialism in southern Africa is criticized as a catalog of rape and mass murder. As I shall demonstrate, the prevalence of "black peril" narratives is nonetheless evident in the ways in which, during the South African War (1899–1902, also known as the Anglo-Boer War), chivalric discourses coalesced with descriptions of white women threatened with rape by black men, marking white anxieties about the scandal of black combatants in a war between two white races.

"Wild Savages" and "Treasure Chests": Rape and Romance in Southern African Contact Narratives

According to Achille Mbembe, in European thought Africa has prevailed as the sign of monstrous alterity, "the very figure of 'the strange.'"[6] Nowhere is this more apparent than in the figure of Adamastor in Luiz Vaz de Camões's epic romance, *Os Lusíadas* (*The Lusíads*), which was published in Lisbon in 1572, commemorating a journey that took place almost a century earlier, namely Vasco Da Gama's forging of a European sea route to India in 1497–8. The earliest written literary account of Europe's encounter with southern Africa, the Adamastor stanzas of *Os Lusíadas* were described by John Purves (who was beginning to forge a canon of South African literature) in 1909 as South Africa's "portion of the Renaissance."[7] Like the overarching structure of the poem itself, Adamastor's story is a narrative of attempted ravishment, with the actions of the melancholy Adamastor mirroring aspects of the Portuguese imperial contest.

In Camões's poem, as they round the Cape, Da Gama and his crew are filled with terror at an immense darkness from which the monstrous form of Adamastor materializes, anthropomorphizing the mountainous landmass of the stormy Cape into the form of a giant.[8] Adamastor curses the Portuguese for their daring violation of his realm, with the poet ventriloquizing through the speech of the giant a critique of Portuguese imperialism even as the poem celebrates the achievements of the sons of Lusus. On being commanded by Da Gama to make his identity known, Adamastor explains that he is a Titan who fell in love with the sea nymph Tethys, and that he threatened to take her by force if she did not comply with his wishes. But in response, he tells, the nymph laughingly drew attention to the disproportionate size of her would-be suitor, and sent an ambiguous reply that she would do what was unavoidable, while keeping her honor intact. Adamastor explains that during their arranged tryst, he found himself simultaneously clasping a rock and transformed into a rock, and that he was then exiled to the Cape where his form petrified into the shape of a mountain. In Ovidian fashion, Tethys herself undergoes metamorphosis, first into stone in order to elude Adamastor, and then into the tantalizing waves that surround him at the Cape.

As Carmen Nocentelli Truett argues: "The sixteenth and seventeenth cen-turies witnessed a widespread fascination—not to say obsession—with the pri-vate parts and private practices of non-European peoples,"[9] and as Peter Fryer points out, the European idea of a monstrous African sexuality is evident in the "naked figures of Africans on more than one fifteenth century map."[10] While early modern variants of the word "race" did not carry the connotations that the term implies today, modern ideas of racial difference are nonetheless prefigured in the Renaissance. Ania Loomba points out that in the early mod-ern period, the term race "was distinct from, and also laid the ground for, later deployments of the word, and of the concept."[11] Thus, although he is not ex-plicitly marked as black or African in his color or features (in fact his color/"cor" is described as pale/"palida"),[12] Camões's lustful Adamastor may be compared with figures such as Shakespeare's Caliban, whom Loomba sees stereotyped as a "black rapist."[13]

In their interpretative "translations" of Os Lusíadas, South African com-mentators focus almost exclusively on the Adamastor stanzas of the poem, straining to interpret these in "black peril" terms.[14] What such analyses fail to recognize, however, is Adamastor's place within the poem as a whole. A threat-ening and inhospitable male character, Adamastor contrasts with the alluring, feminine personifications of the East that appear in Cantos IV and V, and Os Lusíadas constitutes an early modern example of what Edward Said has fa-mously described as Orientalism, as it takes the form of a gendered quest, culminating in a scene where Da Gama and his companions are granted, in the final cantos, the earthly treats of the Island of Love, a fantastical destina-tion that floats in eastern waters and has distinctly classical but also oriental and sexualized features: "pomegranates gaped, exposing jewels/richer, redder than any rubies"[15] ("Abre a romã, mostrando a rubicunda/Cor, com que tu, rubi, teu preço perdes"). Among the vegetation the mariners catch glimpses of nymphs dressed in "fine wool and variegated silks"[16] ("Mas da lã fina e seda diferente"). Questioning whether these are "fantasies or flesh," the men hunt them down and then have their way with them. The scene, which draws on classical mythology, is presented in aestheticized vocabulary where the nymphs have been softened up by the arrows of Cupid, and are only pretend-ing to run away. Conspiring with their pursuers, they are represented as complicit in their own ravishment. As Nocentelli Truett observes in her study of "islands of love" in early modern literature, the events that take place on this island have a direct historical referent in the "conquest marriages" organized between Portuguese men and local women in the trade routes of the Indian Ocean, where racial mixing was celebrated "as a means to consolidate colonial penetration, ensure thorough acculturation and promote religious conversion."[17] What this suggests is that Adamastor in the original poem is not only the personification of the southern tip of the African continent, a figure enmeshed with the very soil of Africa,[18] he also could be read as a doppelgänger for the Portuguese themselves, reflecting the dark and thwarted side of a rapacious maritime empire that was swiftly, at the time Camões was writing, losing its power.

Noting Columbus's observation that the world "was shaped like a woman's breast," Anne McClintock points out that early European narratives of exploration were gendered and "mapped as a metaphysics of gender violence."[19] Although the earliest instances of interracial gender violence in colonial environments must surely have been between colonizing men and colonized or slave women (and there are a substantial number of literary texts that confront this fact), by the mid-nineteenth century "native-peril" narratives had taken a firm hold of the European imagination. Jenny Sharpe and Nancy Paxton have both demonstrated the importance of the Indian Mutiny of 1857 for tracing a narrative in which English women are threatened with rape by "native" men. Discussing as "allegories of empire" representations of white women in colonial texts about India, Sharpe proposes that fears of the rape of colonizing women by colonized men were linked to moments of counter-colonial insurgency in the period after the abolition of slavery.[20] Paxton, on the other hand, wants to know why, in the narrative that Sharpe chooses to analyze, "white women necessarily replace native women" as victims of rape.[21] According to Paxton, the original rape script in European colonial writing, is not, as Fanon suggests, a narrative of "the colonizing woman threatened with rape by a native man," but is rather more complex, encompassing Edmund Burke's critique of colonial governance in India, his formulation of the sublime, and Romantic negotiations of gender that took place through descriptions of Oriental femininity. Paxton points out that as early as 1772 Burke described the colonial relationship between England and India as potentially "poised between courtship and rape," and that by 1787, he had charged Warren Hastings, the Governor General of Bengal between 1774 and 1785, with the economic rape of India and for allowing the literal rape of Indian women by "native" agents of the colonial regime.[22] Burke's inflammatory accusations led to a trial against Hastings in England that lasted for seven years and was attended by large crowds of people.

As mentioned above, however, six years before the trial in which Burke introduced his spectacular narrative of ravishment, and more than half a century before the lurid accounts of the Indian Mutiny, sensationalist tales of European women shipwrecked on the coast of southern Africa appeared in

1782 newspaper reports which fused rape and captivity narratives in order to
detail ravishings by Hottentots, "the most barbarous and monstrous of the
species."[23] As Ian Glenn has demonstrated, the wreck of the *Grosvenor* gave
rise to search parties which led to the first published accounts of the southern
African hinterland, and driving these rescue operations was one major concern: whether there were still white women in the interior, at risk of becoming
sexual prey to the indigene.[24] Although evidence suggests that European
women such as Lydia Logie, Mary Wilmot and Eleanor Dennis, who survived
shipwreck on the southern African coast in the late eighteenth century, assimilated willingly into hospitable Xhosa communities as a means of survival,
people in England saw their fates as worse than death.[25] This is illustrated in
The Mission, a novel by Captain Marryat that draws on historical events to
present a fictional search for a female castaway of the *Grosvenor* who is feared
by her father to be "the wife or slave of some wild savage."[26] When the hero,
Andrew Wilmot, returns from his travels and assures the old man that his
daughter is dead, his relief is such that on his deathbed he exclaims, "Gracious
Lord, I thank thee that this weight has been removed from my mind,"[27] and he
can then die in peace.

Published in 1845, *The Mission* preempted themes that were to follow in
novels about the Indian Mutiny of 1857. In Edward Money's *The Wife and
Ward: Or, A Life's Error* (1859), one of the first Mutiny novels to fictionalize
events at Cawnpore, where British women were rumored to have been raped
and mutilated by Indian men, the hero of the novel, Captain Edgington, is
delivered the following request by a beautiful blonde Englishwoman, Marion
Paris: "If the rebels beat us; if they should storm the entrenchments, will you
promise me, that under no circumstances I shall fall into their hands?"[28] Samuel Richardson's *Clarissa* (1748–9), a narrative of captivity and rape published
almost a century before *The Mission* and *The Wife and Ward*, may be read as an
indictment of a society where a raped woman is better off dead than a disgrace
to her family. By contrast, *The Mission* and Mutiny novels such as *The Wife and
Ward* foreclose upon any critique of "civilized" society, leaving no doubt that
the Englishwoman despoiled (or about to be despoiled) by "natives" is such a
threat to civilization that she must be mercifully killed off for the sake of cultural containment.

On the basis of her recent dissertation on the Eastern Cape region, histo-
rian Elizabeth Thornberry claims that while precolonial "Xhosa communities
generally assumed that women who complained of rape were telling the
truth," colonial authorities were "extremely skeptical" of black women's stories
of sexual assault.[29] With reference to the Cape Colony in the mid-nineteenth
century, Pamela Scully notes that "sex in the colonies was a political act with
repercussions on which children would be included in the category of colo-
nised and which in settler society."[30] In Cape Roman Dutch Law, rape was
described as "both the forcible ravishing and the forcible carrying off of a

woman against her will,"[31] but was also specifically linked to reproduction. Whereas this law had fallen away in England in 1828, up until 1845 in the Cape the prosecution in a rape case had to show that there was "emission" or ejaculation, and this was perceived as particularly dangerous in cases involving white women and black men. Scully elaborates:

> The discrepancy between the colony and the metropole suggests the ways in which racial hierarchy depended on the control of sexual relations: illegal reproduction, particularly when it involved a black man and a white woman, threatened the foundations of colonial life.[32]

In order to illustrate this, Scully traces the case of a black or "coloured" ("mixed-race") man, Damon Booysen, whose sentence for rape in 1850 was commuted from death by hanging to a term of hard labor when the presiding Judge was informed that the woman Booysen had raped was not white but a "Bastard Coloured" person, whose "character for chastity was very indifferent."[33] Scully argues that the tightening up of racial boundaries and fear of the rape of colonizing women in the Cape emerged against the backdrop of emancipation, where "the possession of legal or customary title to whiteness also became more important to farmers who could no longer claim the right to domination through their status as slaveholders."[34]

At a time marked by the concretizing of racial categorization, strikingly similar versions of a certain sexual peril narrative gained currency in settler societies across the breadth of the globe: during and after the Indian Mutiny of 1857; in the public discourse surrounding the 1865 Morant Bay uprising in Jamaica;[35] in the southern states of America following the Civil War; and in the period of early nation-building in South Africa, from the 1870s onwards.[36] As Robert Young has suggested, events such as the Indian Mutiny "dramatically altered popular perceptions of race and racial difference and formed the basis of the widespread acceptance of the new, and remarkably up-front, claims of a permanent racial superiority."[37] The historical juncture at which mass hysteria about the "natives" rapist takes hold of the colonial imagination indicates that these narratives were instrumental in justifying barbaric measures that suppressed "native" insurgency, and that these narratives are intimately linked to discourses of modern racism.

Interestingly, in the southern African context, fearful accounts of white women set upon by monstrous bands of "wild savages" were rivaled by a strand of British imperial discourse that encouraged immigration to the colonies. Victorian women travelers, in particular, produced pro-immigration works such as Charlotte Barter's provocatively titled *Alone among the Zulus* (1866), which attested to European women's safety and contentment in prospective settlement colonies. As Dorothy Driver observes, the emigration of English-women to the colonies "served a variety of social and economic purposes" as women were encouraged to take on the roles of wives and governesses in the building of the Empire, which conveniently neutralized potential threats posed to patriarchal authority by changing gender roles, at a time when "the concept of 'woman' was threatening to explode its definition as the patriarchally constructed 'feminine.'"[38] Playing against narratives which suggested that the region was inhospitable and particularly dangerous for European women, accounts such as *Alone among the Zulus* sketched the colonies, if not as idyllic destinations, then at least as places of relative freedom and independence for the women of empire. In fact, the number of travel narratives generated by white women in nineteenth-century southern Africa increases proportionately alongside the most intense of the early "black peril" scares in this region.[39] Spine-chilling stories about barbaric and violent "natives" that gripped the colonial imagination, and the presentation of southern Africa as a desirable travel destination, thus emerge in the nineteenth century as twinned bipolar narratives of danger and desire, foreshadowing the ways in which South Africa would be presented to the world in the future.

In 1867 (the year after the publication of *Alone among the Zulus*), diamonds were discovered in Kimberley, to be followed by gold in the Transvaal in 1886. Immigration to South Africa boomed, and by the latter part of the nineteenth century the region had become the economic powerhouse of the British Empire. Under these conditions South Africa was transformed, in the European imagination, from a distant and uninviting extremity of the African continent to a site of romance. In Camões's *Os Lusíadas*, the Orient is feminized and alluring, while the stormy coastline of southern Africa is guarded by a forbidding male giant. By the late nineteenth century however, southern Africa was reterritorialized as feminine. As Edward Said has argued, the Orient, a site of exotic and prized commodities, had for centuries been feminized and sexualized for Western possession. In the case of South Africa, it took the discovery of gold and diamonds for anything akin to Orientalism to rear its head. In accordance with the imperial codification of desirable territory as "virgin land," the economic allure of South Africa figures sexually in the adventure stories of late nineteenth century. One finds in quest narratives such as Henry Rider Haggard's *King Solomon's Mines* (1885) the land famously portrayed as feminine, naked and supine, luring male adventurers into dangerous subterranean realms that are brimming with treasure.[40]

As has been well-documented, the Victorian era was characterized by a revival of romance narratives where agents of imperialism were cast as enlightened crusaders acting out a "holy mission" in the name of rationality, Christianity, civilization and commerce.[41] Adventure novels for the young men of Empire transmogrified the violence of imperialism into the language of seduction, and from the work of Sir Walter Scott to that of Haggard and Conan Doyle, where literary renditions of masculinity are bound to questions of race and national identity, chivalry is invoked in order to inscribe a regulatory sexual economy. A moralizing standard for masculine behavior, chivalry in the nineteenth century professed to have its origins in codes of medieval knighthood, but its reformulation in the Victorian era operated performatively to demarcate boundaries of race and gender. As I demonstrate in discussion of the South African War, where the entry of black combatants provoked a crisis in racial hierarchies, a discourse of chivalry was mobilized in order to differentiate between European men and their barbarous others, thereby conserving the boundaries of racial identity.

The impulse of imperial romance is towards quest narratives that often read more like sexual tourism, with white male adventurers in the environs of the seductively feminine, the dark, the mysterious and exotic. As a genre that sexualizes the colonized/colonizing attachment, imperial romance is related to at least two other narratives. The first of these, known in South African history as "black peril" narratives, sketch in the variables left out of the romance equation, figuring not the bond of seduction between the European explorer and his dark, feminine other, but rather the relationship between the colonizing woman and the colonized man. In the colonial imagination, this taboo relationship is thinkable only in the melancholy terms of sexual violence, and is moreover a triangular affair, since it necessarily involves the colonizing man who must act in defense of his women. Where they evoke a code of chivalry as white men are called upon to defend their women, "black peril" narratives conjoin with the romance mode.

The second narrative that sketches the colonizing/colonized relation as sexualized, however, runs counter to romance, presenting the colonized as violated by the forces of imperialism. Examples of the representation of colonialism as metaphorical rape would be Joseph Conrad's *Heart of Darkness* (1899), which describes colonialism as the plunder and conquest of a dark and feminized continent, or W.E.B. Du Bois's analysis of slavery and colonial-era exploitation, *The Rape of Africa* (1954). A similar critique can be seen in the anti-imperial rhetoric of Indian nationalists such as Nehru, who described British colonialism as sexual aggression perpetrated by colonizers upon the feminized body of the Indian subcontinent.[42] Edward Said reveals the link between romance and counter-romance when he describes the tropologies governing the hermeneutic relation between Orientalist and Orient as having been established through images of the "depth, secrecy and sexual promise" of the colonial other, as well as the Westerner's freedom to "penetrate" and "wrestle with . . . the great Asiatic mystery."[43] In Sara Suleri's view, much critical discourse continues "to replicate the Orientalist desire to shroud the East in a 'female' mystery," and "the geography of rape as a dominant trope for the act of imperialism . . . has been in currency too long for it to remain at all critically liberating."[44] What makes a counter-romance text such as Schreiner's *Trooper Peter Halket of Mashonaland* (1897) interesting, however, is that rape is here not a trope but a literal act that draws attention to the material and gendered violence of imperialism. Schreiner's text comprises an exposé of the misdeeds of empire, but she is also the first in a line of white South African women to write of "the white peril" in a way that couples this melancholy representation of colonial desire with "miscegenation."

"A Black Woman Wasn't White!": Race and Rape in Olive Schreiner's *Trooper Peter Halket of Mashonaland*

In *Trooper Peter Halket of Mashonaland*, a colonial mercenary named Halket stares into his campfire on a solitary *kopje* in the *veld*, and remembers perpetrating the abduction and rape of an African woman:

> Then he thought suddenly of a black woman he and another man caught alone in the bush, her baby on her back, but young and pretty. Well, they didn't shoot her!—and a black woman wasn't white![45]

Details of the violation are elided, yet there is little doubt what Halket means when he reminisces that they "didn't shoot" the woman. By stating what the men have not done with their guns, the text draws attention to an unmentionable deed of violence that likewise asserts phallic supremacy and forges bonds between male adventurers in the liminal zones of empire. Scandalously, Schreiner's novel was one of the first published accounts to focus on white imperialists as the rapists of black women. It was to be followed, within a few years, by Pauline Hopkins's *Contending Forces* (1900), which similarly represents rape as empire's "device of terrorism."[46] The statement, "a black woman wasn't white," is echoed in Hopkins's novel when a white man's rape of a "mulatto" woman is excused with the words: "What does a woman of mixed blood, or any Negress, for that matter, know of virtue?"[47] The critique, in both texts, is of a longstanding racist attitude that depicts black women as hypersexualized and less than human, such that their violation seems a contradiction in terms. Through a double negation or disavowal ("they didn't shoot her!—and a black woman wasn't white!"), Schreiner alludes to the double standards that inhere in colonial attitudes to interracial rape, and to the ways in which imperial violence is mirrored in an act of sexual violation. As such, her novel is directed against the poetics and politics of the essentializing discourse of imperial romance. Instead of propagating the romance myth of seductive "virgin" territory, ripe for colonization, *Trooper Halket* exposes an imperialist war waged on a civilian population, and a context where African women are gang-raped or bought for the price of a bottle of brandy and forced into sexual slavery. While the African women in Schreiner's texts ultimately remain shadowy figures, present only through the eruption of their stories into the discourse of men, the novel goes some way towards rewriting colonial tropes about women and land, clearing a space for representations of African women's roles in the anti-colonial struggle.

Historically, Schreiner's text refers to events that would have been fresh in the minds of its contemporary reading public, namely the 1896–97 suppression of the Ndebele (Matabele) and Shona in Cecil John Rhodes's fledgling colony, Rhodesia. In the early 1890s, Rhodes, "a white capitalist of imperial reach,"[48] had primed this area for British settlement. Tales of frontier exploration and conflicts waged in the name of civilization beckoned to the young men of empire, and thus it was that, following the "clearing" of the territory in Mashonaland in the early 1890s, white settlers seized cattle and land, setting up more than a thousand farms over ten thousand square miles in the middle of what had been Ndebele country. Commissioners were appointed to deal with "Native problems," the Ndebele were reduced to aliens in the land in which they had lived, and a hut tax was imposed on the Shona in order to press them into farm labor. Those who resisted were stripped and flogged, whole villages were burnt to the ground in punishment for the slightest offence, and Ndebele leaders complained that not only were they being treated "like dogs," but their wives and daughters were being systematically raped by white native commissioners.[49] In 1896 the Ndebele rose up against their oppressors, first killing African collaborators, and then turning their anger on settlers in attacks that left about two hundred whites dead. They were later joined by the Shona. Having directed his attention northwards after the abortive Jameson Raid in which he had been implicated and disgraced, Rhodes realized the threat to his new colony and sprang into action, ordering militant whites armed with Maxim machine guns to "do the most harm to the natives around you . . . kill all you can."[50] Notwithstanding the technologized killing that went along with it, this sort of expansionism was the stuff of romance. Eyewitnesses claimed that after the massacres that ensued Rhodes personally inspected the battleground, counting dead "rebels" with approval. Equipped only with assegais and a few elephant-guns, the Ndebele were hopelessly outmatched from the start, and yet their strategic retreat into the Matopo Mountains almost brought the situation to a stalemate. Realizing that it was in his interest to end the conflict and to establish "complete confidence between the two [white and black] races" in order that his colony might have a reservoir of black labor, Rhodes brokered peace with the Ndebele and the Shona late in 1897.

On its first publication in 1897, *Trooper Peter Halket of Mashonaland* opened with a shocking frontispiece that was suppressed in almost all subsequent editions,[51] a photograph depicting a scene of hanging. The corpses of three black men hang from a tree, while spectators in the background, with their eyes fixed on the camera, assume various poses of nonchalance or bravado. Almost exclusively, the onlookers in the picture are male and white, and yet a solitary black man, smoking, stands slightly beyond the group. The significance of his liminality is uncertain, possibly he is a manservant, or one of the African collaborators who joined forces with Cecil Rhodes's Chartered Company, but his relaxed stance and European-style attire—trousers, a white shirt, a waistcoat and hat—clearly separate him from the near-naked bodies suspended in the air before him. A verbal account by Frank W. Sykes, who served on the campaign against "rebels," matches the image of hanging:

> What rebel spies were caught were summarily tried and hanged. There is a tree, known as the hanging tree, to the north of [Bulawayo], which did service as gallows. Hither the doomed men were conveyed. On the ropes being fastened to their necks, they were made to climb along an overhanging branch, and thence were pushed or compelled to jump into space after "a last look at Bulawayo." Their bodies were left suspended for twenty-four hours.[52]

Notably, the photograph taken in Matabeleland is meant to be displayed. A trophy, the pornographic violence it flaunts does not merely bolster the power of the imperial "hunters," but also encourages scopophilia. Setting spectators who are perpetrators within the photograph, with their eyes on the camera and thus on the viewer, creates a suturing of identity, such that the act of viewing is infused with complicity. In this regard, the photograph that sets the tone for Schreiner's novel may be compared with lynching photographs, and also with other photographic trophies of war, such as the snapshots taken by American soldiers of their acts of rape and murder in Vietnamese villages or, more recently, the digital images recorded by members of the American military in Abu Ghraib prison in Iraq. As with lynching snapshots, some of which depict white Southerners picnicking under the bodies of lynch victims, or the Abu Ghraib images, in which smiling GIs stand over hooded victims of torture, the presence of spectators in the photograph adds banality to atrocity. Taken out of its context as a memento that was meant to be disseminated among men in the frontier zone of empire, the horrific image aptly sets the tone for Schreiner's novel, which deploys strategies of mirroring, reversal, and displacement in order to reflect the excesses, hypocrisy, and *topoi* of patriarchal imperialism back to itself.

The photograph that Schreiner chose as a supplement to *Trooper Halket* was one of many that existed from the Matabeleland campaign.[53] She was in South Africa during the uprisings in Matabeleland, and in order to research her subject she had interviewed and corresponded with men who had served with the Chartered Company, some of whom had sent her journals and photographs. Many snapshots from the campaign show casualties of the conflict, usually dead black bodies on the "battlefield" or everyday activities in the British camps. That Schreiner chose to use a scene of hanging rather than any other image as the frontispiece for her novel is worth some consideration.

In a comparative frame, the photograph that accompanies *Trooper Halket* sets up a relationship of historical contiguity, as the image evokes the format of lynching photographs taken in the United States at around the same time. By the 1890s, lynching had reached an all-time peak in the southern states of America, and from the 1880s until well into the twentieth century, photographs of black men hanged by the neck, most often following allegations that they had raped white women, were disseminated as part of a reign of terror in the Southern states. As Patricia Schechter notes: "Circulated in cheap postcards, doggerel verse and other lynching 'souvenirs', the resulting 'folk pornography of the South' was serious business."[54]

In her use of the image, however, Schreiner was clearly attempting to harness the influence of the Anti-Lynching Committee, which had been established in Britain in 1894. Sponsored by members of the public, including prominent editors and politicians, the Committee aimed "to obtain reliable information on the subject of lynching and mob outrages in America, to make the facts known, and to give expression to public opinion in condemnation of such outrages in whatever way might best seem calculated to assist the cause of humanity and civilization."[55] By the time *Trooper Halket* was published, Schreiner had traveled twice to England, where debates about racial hatred in America were surfacing in the public sphere, and women made up the majority of those involved in the campaign against lynching. As a white woman concerned with disseminating an image of black suffering, Schreiner was therefore not alone. In fact, in 1893, on the cover of her journal *Anti-Caste*, which was published in England but "devoted to the interests of the Coloured race" on both sides of the Atlantic, the British anti-lynching campaigner Catherine Impey had reproduced a picture of a lynching in Alabama, drawing attention to the white children posing beside the body of the hanged man.[56] Vron Ware points out: "Against the background of Empire mania in their own country, these [English] women, who came from different political and social backgrounds, were briefly united in an alliance with black people across the Atlantic."[57]

The anti-lynching movement facilitated transnational solidarity and traffic across the Atlantic—Ida B. Wells, for instance, had come to England in the early 1890s, presenting arguments against lynching to the British public. As Hazel Carby notes, in the last decade of the nineteenth century, Afro-American women intellectuals such as Wells, Frances Harper, Anna Julia Cooper, and Pauline Hopkins offered definitive critiques of racism and the imperialist impulse, and "theorised about the possibilities and limits of patriarchal power through its manipulation of racialized and gendered social categories and practices."[58] In her reproduction of the photograph, Schreiner was thus not only aligning herself with white Englishwomen, but also with those black American women who were mobilizing "against Jim Crow segregation and the terrorising practices of lynching and rape."[59]

Not surprisingly, in its day the frontispiece of Schreiner's *Trooper Halket* attracted controversy. Reviewers claimed that the inclusion of such an image was in poor taste and unsuitable for use alongside a literary text. In a damning review of Schreiner's book, Arthur Quiller-Couch (who was to become professor of English at Cambridge University) nonetheless conceded:

It would be in bad taste if the picture were an imaginary one taken for the purpose of illustrating a work of fiction; but the camera will not photograph imaginary objects. Or again it would be in extremely bad taste if Miss Schreiner had "composed" the actual group, strung up the natives and arranged the Englishmen around, for the purpose of getting a picture to illustrate her work of fiction. But of course she did not. "Bad taste" is not the question and nothing to do with the question. The photograph is evidence of fact. You may argue that the evidence has been produced in a wrong court; and I agree. But you gain nothing by saying that it shocks you. Blood-stained garments may be evidence of a crime; it does not diminish the weight of their testimony if the sight of them turns a juryman queasy.[60]

One negative commentator went on to defend the atrocities depicted in terms commensurate with those used in support of lynching in the southern United States. In America the Virginia-based novelist Thomas Nelson Page had claimed that the barbarity of lynching shocked the South, but that "a deeper shock than this is at the bottom of their ferocious rage—the shock which comes from the ravishing and butchery of their own children."[61] Similarly, the reviewer of Schreiner's "gruesome frontispiece" went on to protest that: "many equally gruesome things on the other side preceded it—such as the massacre and mutilation of defenceless white women, by no means paltry provocation to punishment, even to revenge!"[62] Thus, at the same time that the stereotype of the black rapist was making available a state of exception which would condone racist murder in a newly unified America, the forces of imperial capital were annexing territory in Rhodesia, perpetrating innumerable acts of violence against the indigenous people of southern Africa, and justifying this as retaliation for outrages perpetrated against white womanhood. While it is true that *Trooper Halket* appeared within a few years of some early "black peril" scares in South Africa,[63] alongside Schreiner's text the image goes some way towards suggesting that "black peril" is the illusory photographic negative of the violations perpetrated by the agents of empire.

Transnational in its inspiration, *Trooper Halket* was a response to a treatise on social ills in urban America, entitled *If Christ Came to Chicago* (1894), by the British journalist and social activist W.T. Stead, founder and editor of the *Review of Reviews*. While writing his book on Chicago, Stead had delivered an emancipation address to the African-American community on the subject of lynching and the importance of solidarity. Present in the audience was Wells, who had already published *Southern Horrors: Lynch Law in All Its Phases* (1892), and was greatly inspired by his opinions.[64] A year or two later, Stead was corresponding with Schreiner. In his later review of Schreiner's novel, Stead claimed that she had written to him with a suggestion:

When Olive Schreiner read my book on Chicago, she wrote me a little letter saying, "Why don't you come to Africa? What a book you could write on the theme, 'If Christ came to Africa!'" I have not been able to go to Africa, but the suggestion which Olive Schreiner then made has borne fruit in her own mind. In *Trooper Peter Halket of Mashonaland*, which was published last month, we have Olive Schreiner's "If Christ came to Matabeleland". . . .[65]

Stead went on to claim that Schreiner's new novel was "no Story of an African Farm; it is a Sermon on the Veldt." As Stead proposes, the story takes a moralistic and didactic form. Yet it is important to recognize the radical and incisive nature of Schreiner's critical vision. *Trooper Peter Halket of Mashonaland* may have little of the ambiguity, the layers of narrative meaning, of Conrad's *Heart of Darkness*, which was published two years later, but, as commentators such as Laura Chrisman argue,[66] Schreiner's insight into the interlacing of imperialist racism and gender violence with economic and territorial dispossession is strikingly singular.

The text of *Trooper Halket* comprises two chapters, the first a good deal longer than the second. In the first section, Halket is sitting alone "in the impenetrable darkness" beside his campfire on a *kopje*, when he is visited by a dark stranger who is never named, but who identifies himself as "a Jew of Palestine." The stranger listens as Halket brags of his exploits with "nigger gals" and of his approval for Rhodes's plans to turn Africans into slaves on the lands seized by the Chartered Company. In response to Halket's anecdotes, the stranger begins to tell a series of stories or parables which eventually reveal his identity as Christ himself. Halket repents and becomes a changed man, such that, in the second section of the book, he saves a black captive, at the cost of his own life. While the second chapter offers didactic closure and stays strictly in the realm of men's activities, the dialogue of the first chapter incorporates stories about African women that reflect and destabilize the homosocial discourse of imperialism.

The story of *Trooper Halket* is told in the third person, and in the early part of the novel, the narrative perspective shifts in and out of Halket's thoughts. As Halket stares into his camp fire, he remembers blowing up a cave and turning the Maxim guns onto the kraals:

> He saw the skull of an old Mashona blown off at the top, the hands still moving. He heard the loud cry of the native women and children as they turned the maxims on to the kraal; and then he heard the dynamite explode that blew up a cave. Then again he was working the maxim gun, but it seemed to him it was more like a reaping machine he used to work in England, and that what was going down was not yellow corn, but black men's heads; and he thought when he looked back they lay behind him in rows, like corn in sheaves.[67]

Early cinema had made an appearance by the 1890s, and in this passage Schreiner uses a flickering cinematic style of description to rupture the fictive, as the images are meant to refer to actual events in the realm of life. A subversion of the imperial endeavor to make the colonized land productive, the image of the Maxim gun as a reaping machine is a reminder of the violence that pre-dates, and makes possible, the colonial pastoral. As in J.M. Coetzee's *Dusk-lands* (1974), in Schreiner's novel imperial violence that enlists technology is presented alongside literal rape. Immediately after he recalls working his Maxim gun, Halket remembers the young African woman whom he and an-other trooper "caught alone in the bush."

When Christ arrives on the scene in *Trooper Halket*, he listens to Halket bragging about his adventures, which include purchasing and impregnating African women as young as fifteen.[68] In a lengthy interlude Halket details the story of two Mashona women (one "only fifteen," and one "thirty if she was a day"), who are not named. In a recent reference to Schreiner, Paula Krebs claims: "[as] Anne McClintock has pointed out, black women are granted no agency in Schreiner's fictional portraits."[69] Here Krebs is following McClintock's lead. In *Imperial Leather*, McClintock argues that "Schreiner's fictional portrayal of African women betrays an unresolved recognition of their anger and strength, as well as resentful memories of their power over her."[70] While these statements may be true of some of Schreiner's other writings, they do not stand up in a reading of *Trooper Halket*, a text that McClintock incidentally does not mention in *Imperial Leather*. Although *Trooper Halket* brings the sexual abuse of colo-nized women into sharp focus, it also draws attention to African women's resis-tance and solidarity. After "buying" the older woman for a bottle of brandy, Halket is surprised when she makes a garden and produces enough food from the land for him to sell off the surplus. It is here that Schreiner develops fairly complex ideas that were on the cusp of being incorporated into her greatest non-fictional work, *Women and Labour* (1911), a text that was to become one of the most influential of the feminist movement. This ambitious book traces the evolution of women's work from a time when women hoed the earth and reaped the grain, to an era where, due to technological progress, this "ancient" field of labor became diminished and women were reduced to a state of "sex-parasit-ism" upon men. In the light of Schreiner's ideas in *Women and Labour*, the agrarian labor of the Mashona women in *Trooper Halket* may be read as a rep-resentative incarnation of women's power, an association that is doubly subver-sive and doubly problematic. On the one hand, the text shows African women's labor in order to undermine the imperial argument, used to justify possession of land, that indigenous people were idle and incapable of making their land productive. As a corollary to this, the novel suggests that the success of African farming was due to the fact that women played a significant role in agricultural production. On the other hand, however, the image welds the Mashona women to agrarian labor through an evolutionary narrative that places their endeavors as the "ancient" origin of a gendered field. Within this schema, black southern African women are remnants of a primitive past, existing within the modern, industrial age. Here is a version of specular alterity—the other as an earlier form of the self.

In *Trooper Peter Halket of Mashonaland*, the stranger tells Halket the story of two women who were left alive in a cave after Halket and his fellows blew it up. The passage focuses on images of grain, and ends with an anti-colonial and gendered gesture of territorial possession, as the older woman remembers cultivating the land in her youth:

> "Every day the old woman doled grain from the basket; and at night they cooked it in their cave where you could not see their smoke; and every day the old woman gave the young one two handfuls and kept one for herself, saying, 'Because of the child within you.' And when the child was born and the young woman strong, the old woman took a cloth and filled it with all the grain that was in the basket; and she put the grain on the young woman's head and tied the child on her back, and said, 'Go, keeping always along the bank of the river, till you come north to the land where our people are gone; and some day you can send and fetch me.' And the young woman said, 'Have you corn in the basket to last till they come?' And she said, 'I have enough.' And she sat at the broken door of the cave and watched the young woman go down the hill and up the river bank till she was hidden by the bush; and she looked down at the plain below, and she saw the spot where the kraal had been and where she had planted mealies when she was a young girl—"[71]

At this point Halket realizes that the younger women whose story the stranger is telling is the same one he and his fellow trooper had raped: "I met a woman with corn on her head and a child on her back!"[72] Placing Halket as the focalizer of the novel, and thus situating the narrative within the consciousness of a rapist who initially lacks the ability to imagine the effects he has on his victims, the text reflects upon the psychopathic tendency of the colonizer to efface the subjectivity of the colonized. In the passage cited above, however, what is activated is precisely a process of counter-focalization, a strategy that we will later see beginning to open up in a text such as J.M. Coetzee's *Disgrace*. Here Halket and the reader are invited to imagine the violation, not from the position of the perpetrator, but from the perspective of the woman.

Many of Schreiner's contemporary readers were shocked by the incidents of sexual violence detailed in her novel, and there was considerable debate about whether such allegations might be true. Interestingly, as Peter Wilhelm notes, a similar debate erupted over the behavior of the Rhodesian Selous Scouts in the more recent Chimurenga leading to Zimbabwean independence in 1980.[73] Although *Trooper Peter Halket of Mashonaland* was widely circulated and within a few years translated into Dutch, German, and French, it did not fit into literary conventions of the day, and a number of critics accused Schreiner of pamphleteering, or questioned whether literature was an appropriate medium

for making a political critique.[74] The inclusion of a photograph within a work
of fiction, the novel's critical references to current events and contemporary
personages, and its use of literary technique for political critique seemed difficult for many contemporary commentators to accept. In southern Africa, the
novel was generally met with outrage. The *Rhodesia Herald* protested that it
was "altogether one-sided, and the bias is so obvious as to effectively hinder the
aim [Schreiner] has in view, which undoubtedly is the discrediting of Mr
Rhodes."[75] A critic for the *Cape Argus* stated that "the whole story is farcical in
its improbability, and will be resented throughout South Africa as a gross libel
upon the brave fellows who suppressed the Matabeleland revolt."[76] Schreiner's
detractors were quick to call her a woman of one book, meaning that *The Story
of an African Farm* (which was less overtly political) was her only publication
of literary worth. In his appraisal of *Trooper Halket*, W.T. Stead discusses "the
tragedy of the native women," but Schreiner's contemporaries who produced
negative reviews steered away from mentioning the African women in the
novel. This may have been because they found Halket's unabashed references to
the rape and sexual abuse of black women too scandalous to dwell upon. With
the exception of Chrisman's *Rereading the Imperial Romance*, which selects
Trooper Peter Halket of Mashonaland as a primary text for analysis, this novel
by Schreiner remains a relatively neglected text in studies of Schreiner and
southern African literature.[77]

    While *Trooper Halket* is unsparing in its critique of British imperialism, one
could argue that in Schreiner's text there is no room for interracial desire un-
tainted by violence or exploitation and that, as such, her fictional representations of interracial rape set the tone for the work of Sarah Gertrude Millin,
whose fiction catered for years of "separate development" by representing
sexual encounters between white men and African women as similarly
wretched.[78] As Ian Glenn points out, Schreiner was the first in a tradition of
white South African women who produced literary texts "explicitly or implicitly calling for legislation to prevent "miscegenation" and, in particular, to prohibit sexual relationships between white men and women of colour."[79]
Schreiner saw the "half-caste" population of southern Africa as a "problem"
and urged South Africans to "*keep [their] breeds pure!*"[80] While Schreiner's
ideas on race and gender were progressive for her time (for instance, she
resigned from the Women's Enfranchisement League in South Africa when
the organization refused to include African women in its demand for the
vote), her posthumously published novel *From Man to Man* (1926), which I
return to in my discussion of "white peril" in the work of Lauretta Ngcobo (see
chapter 4), exploits the notion of the black woman's sexuality as deviant and
promiscuous in order to critique sexual liaisons between white men and black
women. At the time Schreiner was writing, horror of "miscegenation" was not
limited to supporters of British imperialism.[81] In his review of Schreiner's
novel, Stead explains that it is not only in South Africa that "the womanhood

of black women is held so cheap by the pioneers of the white race," but also "in British India, where the problem of the Eurasian has attained proportions which, as a factor in the comparative evolution of human society, makes it one of the most appalling in the wide world."[82] The idea that people of "mixed race" constituted a "problem" was also adopted by many otherwise progressive black political commentators. Attempting to draw attention to the exploitation and abuse of people of African descent, and to recuperate an authentically African culture, Marcus Garvey makes a judgment against interracial mingling. Stanza 54 of his poem, *The Tragedy of White Injustice* (1927), states:

> Black women are raped by the lordly white,
> In colonies the shame ne'er reaching the light;
> In other countries abuses are given,
> Shocking to morality and God's Heaven.
> Hybrids and mongrels are the open result,
> Which the whites give us as shameful insult:
> How can they justify this? None can tell;
> Yet crimes of the blacks are rung with a bell.[83]

Emerging as counter-romance, "white peril" narratives are thus historically linked to an aversion towards "miscegenation," to fears about the birth of problematic and degenerate "hybrid" progeny.

"The Inexpiable Outrage Remains": Black Combatants, Chivalry, and the South African War (1899–1902)

The conflict that took place in South Africa between 1899 and 1902 has been described as "the last of the gentlemen's wars," and was for a long time perceived as a struggle between the two white groups who had settled in South Africa, for domination over the region's resources. The three bitter and bloody years of conflict, however, involved every sector of South Africa's population, and attracted colonial volunteers from all around the world. The war completed the British imperial conquest of southern Africa, leaving in its wake massive civilian suffering and anger. The most well-known and resented aspects of the war remain the British use of scorched-earth tactics (the same strategy that Rhodes had used against the Matabele and Mashona in 1896–7) and the deployment of concentration camps in which Boer women and children, as well as Africans, were interned. In justifying the camps, which received increasingly negative attention, the British stressed the vulnerability of Boer women left alone on their farms. In reality the camps were an essential part of a military strategy that aimed to break Boer resistance, as Afrikaner women on farmsteads supported the war effort by providing supplies to their men who were out on commando. However, the efforts of these women would not have amounted to much without farm laborers, and the Boer commandos made use of armed African and "coloured" spies. By removing laborers from farms and placing them in segregated labor camps, the British aimed to disrupt the network supporting the Boer war effort, and to harness black labor in the production of food and other supplies for their own soldiers. At the same time, the British appointed and armed as many as thirty thousand Africans and "coloureds," and deployed a further one-hundred-and-twenty thousand African, "coloured," and Indian men in reserve.[84] Although it was denied for decades afterward and remains a lesser known fact today, the war was therefore not a white war, and by arming black, "coloured," and Indian men against another white race, the British in particular created a scandal that threatened racial hierarchies. As I shall demonstrate, anxieties about this state of affairs were expressed in fears that bands of African, "coloured," and even Indian men would rape white women who had been left on their farms.

In a lengthy letter to W.T. Stead, Jan Smuts, who was a commander of the Boer forces during the war, emphasized how shocking it was "to employ armed barbarians under white officers in a war between two Christian peoples," both in view of the "numeric disproportion of the two peoples engaged in this struggle" and "from the point of view of South African history and public policy." Notable in Smuts's letter is the way in which anxieties about the "Coloured races" becoming "the arbiter . . . the predominating factor or 'casting vote' in South Africa" are displaced onto fears that white women will be violated by "Natives" and "Coloured boys":

> Dark indeed is that shadow! When armed Natives and Coloured boys, trained and commanded by English officers . . . [pursue] the fugitive Boer and try to pay off old scores by insulting his wife and children on their [lonely] farms . . . ; when to escape violation and nameless insults at the hands of their former servants, now wearing the British uniform, Boer women and girls seek refuge in the mountains of the native land, as I have seen them do—a wound is given to South Africa which Time itself will not heal.[85]

As Shula Marks has cogently argued, the image of defenseless Boer women threatened by armed Africans and "coloureds" seems to have haunted Smuts for the rest of his life, and thus the war played a formative part in consolidating a certain angst that may be seen in the eruptions of visceral racism into his otherwise liberal and moderate political discourse.[86] The image of a topsy-turvy world—of "former servants, now wearing the British uniform"—is particularly vivid in Smuts's account.

Kipling's short story, "A Sahib's War," presents the problem of men who participated and fought in the South African War, but who are seen as being located outside of the white sexual economy of chivalry. Even though the Boers adopted unorthodox and often controversial strategies during the war, prowar British commentators strained to describe them as enemies worthy of chivalrous combat. In *The Great Boer War*, Arthur Conan Doyle depicts the Boers as if he were publicizing a jousting contest in which "Imperial Britain" is confronted with "one of the most rugged, virile and unconquerable races ever seen on earth."[87] Even though there was doubt as to whether the guerrilla tactics of the Boers conformed to an honorable code of war, the point is that the Boers were expected to behave according to chivalric conventions. The introduction of African, "coloured," and Indian men into the war, however, presented the dilemma of participants who were situated outside of white templates of masculinity. Kipling's story draws on these anxieties, delivering an account in which hierarchies of race are put into disarray, but finally restored. Narrated by an Indian Sikh, Umr Singh, the tale traces the adventures of this character as he follows his English master, identified as "Kurban Sahib," from India into the thick of the war in South Africa. Although Singh is aware that "this was a Sahib's war," the boundary between his role as "bearer, butler, sweeper"[88] for his master, and his position as a participant in the war begins to break down, such that, at the climax of his story, he and Kurban Sahib's cook, Sikandar Khan, attack a Boer family in order to avenge the death of Kurban Sahib. The narration perpetually stresses racial hierarchies. Umr Singh protests twice "do not herd me with these black Kaffirs"; he describes Africans as "certain woolly ones—*Hubshis*—whose touch is pollution" but he is devoted and subservient to Kurban Sahib; and Sikandar Khan is described variously as a "dog," or "a Patan, a Mohammedan." Through Singh's narration Kipling suggests that the Boers are less than white, and that the introduction of fighters who were not considered white into the battle against them may perhaps therefore be justified. Asserting that the deceptive guerrilla strategies of the Boers made them more like the Burmese or "Afridis," Singh asserts that "the Sahibs should have sent *us* into the game."[89] In his description of the Boer family who are involved in the death of Kurban Sahib, Singh (and Kipling) draws on a discourse of racial degeneracy and bestiality. The old Afrikaner man has "a wart upon the left side of his neck," his wife is fat, "with the eyes of a swine and the jowl of a swine," and the tall young man is an idiot, "deprived of understanding."[90] Executing a revenge attack on the farm, Khan kills one of the Boers, and in Singh's contemptuous assertion that he will not "defile [his] sword" there is a suggestion that he feels himself to be racially superior to them. Along with the introduction of Asian men into the fray, however, comes a sexual threat to the white woman that cannot be assimilated within this paradigm. This threat is hinted at in Singh's statement: "I claimed her life and body from Sikandar Khan, in our discussion of the spoil."[91] The Boer woman is put on a chain, and in a strikingly sexualized scene of interracial sadism, Singh narrates that "she followed upon her knees and lay along the ground, and pawed at my feet and howled." Poised on the brink of hanging her son and proceeding further with the woman, however, Singh and Khan are confronted by the ghost of their white master, who warns them three times: "No. It is a Sahib's war."[92] Although conventional racial hierarchies are subverted by the description of Asian men as fighters for the British against another white race, the story flips over into a conservative idiom as soon as the white woman is threatened sexually by men who are not white.

The South African War was not the first context in which resentment and anxiety about non-European combatants entering a war between Europeans was figured as a sexual threat to white women, and James Fennimore Cooper's *The Last of the Mohicans* (1826) provides a useful point of comparison with Kipling's tale. Cooper's novel deals with the war between the English and the French in North America (c. 1754–1764), a colonial conflict over territory in which both sides were allied with various groups of Native Americans who participated as scouts and as combatants during the conflict. Written when chivalric ideals were in the process of being established (Scott's *Ivanhoe* was published seven years before *The Last of the Mohicans*), Cooper's novel suggests the predicament posed by the presence of white women in a colonial war, and the problem of non-European combatants who are outside of European modes of chivalry. In the novel the Mohicans, allies of the British, are "noble savages," while the Huron, who fought on the side of the French, are represented as cruel and bestial. Uncas (a Mohican) and Magua (a Huron) covet Cora Munro, the daughter of an English general, but by the end of the novel both native Americans, as well as Cora, are dead, eliminating the possibility of any dangerous acts of "miscegenation." In the climatic penultimate chapter, Cora is captured by Magua and given the choice between his wigwam (sexual intercourse with him) or his knife (death). She is temporarily saved by Uncas, but during the struggle between Magua and Uncas she is killed by one of the Huron. In Cooper's novel, as in Kipling's tale, the anxiety generated as a result of using "native" combatants in a war between Europeans climaxes at the point where the white woman is threatened by the non-white man.[93]

In the context of the South African War, however, the figure of the black, "coloured", or Indian potential rapist arises out of and deflects another rape script in which Boer women had become visible as victims or potential victims of sexual violation by British soldiers. As early as 1900 a satirical cartoon appeared in a German publication, which depicted a thirteen-year-old British soldier being decorated by English princesses, for having "raped eight Boer women" (Figure 1.2). An expression of the pro-Boer sympathies that characterized much of Europe, the cartoon exploits and sensationalizes rumors about British atrocities during the war. As Paula Krebs demonstrates in her study of the popular discourse of the war, the debate about whether or not British soldiers had broken the chivalric code and committed acts of rape against Boer women articulated itself notably in the writings of the anti-war propagandist W.T. Stead and the pro-war propagandist Arthur Conan Doyle, both of whom mobilized conventions of masculine honor to justify their positions.[94]

In 1900, Stop the War Committee in London published Stead's pamphlet, *How not to Make Peace*, which emphasized that the burning of farmsteads left

FIGURE 1.2 *German cartoon, 1900. The caption below the woodcut reads: "English prin-cesses decorate the youngest soldier in the British army with the Victoria Cross because he has, though only thirteen years old, already raped eight Boer Women."*

women and children vulnerable "in a country swarming with Kaffirs and sol-diery."[95] Stating on the one hand that he never claimed that there had been an "outrage of women by British soldiers," he suggests that Boer women may nonetheless be forced into prostitution through deprivation: "Surely it is not necessary at this time of day to ask what the result must be if you deprive a woman of all mean of subsistence and place her penniless and shelterless in the midst of a military camp. It is not outrage by force but degradation by famine." But Stead then comes close to suggesting that the conditions in South Africa are such that British soldiers may indeed have raped Boer women: "when we have a hundred thousand men liberated from all the restraints of public opin-ion, let loose to burn and destroy in an enemy's country, is it rational to believe that the Dutch women can escape untouched from such proximity?"[96] Knowing the volatile and potentially unpatriotic status of such inferences, however, he then deflects the script in another direction:

> . . . for the sake of argument, I am willing to admit that every British soldier in the Republics leads a life of virginal purity. The crowning horror and the worst outrage of all was not the violation of the Dutch women by English soldiers, but the exposure of these unfortunate white women to the loathly horror of compulsory intercourse with the Kaffirs. That this has taken place repeatedly is proved by the executions of the Kaffirs, which have been ordered in punishment of this crime; but although we may shoot the Kaffir for outraging the white woman, the inexpiable outrage remains.[97]

Although this is rape by proxy, as Stead holds the British responsible (albeit indirectly) for the rape of Boer women, the image of the sexually-rampant black man acting as an agent of the British war effort is a central figure in his argument. To his credit, Stead's subsequent journalistic investigations led him to change his tune.

In *Methods of Barbarism*, a pamphlet published in July 1901, Stead lets the testimonies of Boer women speak for themselves and concludes: "no war can be conducted . . . without exposing multitudes of women, married and single to the worst extremities of outrage . . . It is absolutely impossible to attempt any comparative or quantitative estimate of the number of women who have suffered wrong at the hands of our troops."[98] Such heinous acts, he claims, are hidden beneath "the veil of the censorship," and in support of his argument he included in *Methods of Barbarism* the transcript of the trial of J. Spoelstra, a Dutch journalist who was convicted by the British for breaking war-time censorship laws. The trial took account of statements by a number of Boer women, six of whom testified to rape or attempted rape by British soldiers.[99]

In response to rumors about the misconduct of British soldiers during the war, Sir Arthur Conan Doyle stepped in with a scathing critique of Stead's *Methods of Barbarism*. Entitled *The War in South Africa: Its Cause and Conduct* (1902), Doyle's defense of British chivalry during the war alters the narrative of rape so that it is black men, and not white soldiers fighting for the British Crown, who are raping Boer women.[100] Unlike Stead, for whom the African is a rapist by proxy, in Doyle's account the black rapist averts allegations of British misconduct, and simultaneously allows Doyle to endorse British strategies during the war. Whereas Stead had suggested that the dire circumstances that befell Boer women and children due to British strategies would force many women into a state of prostitution, Doyle protests: "It is impossible without indignation to know that a Briton has written . . . of his own fellow-countrymen that they have 'used famine to pander to their lust.'" In the chivalric code that Doyle draws upon, male honor ensures female chastity, and Doyle goes so far as to suggest that even if Boer women offered themselves, British soldiers would be honorable enough to resist. Doyle knew that his attempt to rescue chivalric ideals, not only for the aristocratic British officer, but also for the average Tommy Atkins, would be more digestible to his readers in Britain than Stead's denunciations and allegations had been, but his argument depended on finding an antagonist against whom to measure the chivalry of the British soldier, which Stead had so baldly discredited. As Krebs points out, for Doyle "black men became the locus of animal sexuality to be counterposed against the white man's controlled civilised sexuality."[101]

As the debate between Stead and Conan Doyle suggests, by the late nineteenth century chivalry had become a mode of gendered surveillance that functioned within a discourse on race, such that chivalric and "native peril" narratives were closely intertwined.[102] By the late nineteenth century, gender roles were changing rapidly and women were becoming increasingly vocal and visible in the public sphere. Neutralizing the effects of this "unfeminine" behavior, narratives of "black peril" and white chivalry depicted white women as potential victims, curtailing their ambits and aspirations. It is not surprising that Doyle, an arch-proponent of chivalry, despised the suffragettes, suggesting that they should be lynched,[103] and argued against the vote for women.

As exemplified in Doyle's pro-war writings, the image of the black rapist also offered a means of justifying the concentration camps. Around twenty-five thousand Boer women and children perished in these camps, and it is estimated that between twenty- and thirty-thousand Africans lost their lives in segregated camps. Of the thousands of lives lost in the war, most were lost in the concentration camps. While the detailed reports of humanitarian campaigners such as Emily Hobhouse made it possible to imagine the levels of disease, starvation, and desperation that characterized life inside the Boer camps, much less is known about the camps to which Africans were sent. In a recent historical study, Stowell Kessler asserts that, like the camps for Boer women and children, the African camps were formalized as a response to the guerrilla tactics adopted by the Boers, although the conditions were likely to have been a great deal worse in the African camps.[104] The justification for the Boer camps in particular was framed in terms of a discursive blending of the chivalric and the humanitarian, such that the British could maintain that they were guardians of the weak and defenseless. In Charlotte Moor's *Marina de la Rey* (1903), for instance, the omniscient narrator states: "Indeed but for the extraordinary generosity of their enemies in maintaining, feeding, clothing, nursing and teaching, at so tremendous a cost, the thousands of Boer women and children who filled the camps to overflowing, their fate would have been one of such tragedy as to make the world shudder."[105]

Not surprisingly, the possibility of Afrikaans women becoming victims of rape by English soldiers during the war is avoided in British literary texts about the war. In Moor's *Marina de la Rey*, the writer directs the narrative away from rape, as British soldiers entering a Boer household are intimidated and shamed by the presence of a naked Boer woman:

Fearful of some hidden danger, perhaps of explosives, the Captain ordered the door to be broken in, but the first man who entered fell back with an oath and scarlet face of astonishment.

Marina flew in, full of terror as to what might have happened.

There stood Hélène, with her defiant face, streaming black hair, and look of almost frenzied determination, perfectly naked, and perfectly unashamed, her magnificent figure drawn up to its full height. In her desperation, not knowing what other weapon to use, and feeling the instinct of the wild creature to tear itself when caught in a trap, she had rent off every shred of clothing, and stood defying the whole band of men, a beautiful Fury.[106]

As Michael Rice has pointed out, it may "stretch the credibility of the modern reader" to imagine "a hardened detachment of troops, who cannot have had any contact with women for at least six months or longer, being cowed by the sight of a 'perfectly naked . . . [female] figure drawn up to its full height.'"[107] Perhaps unwittingly on the part of the author, however, in this passage the intruder narrative evokes sexual violation. The door is "broken in" on Hélène's nakedness, the first man who "entered" has a "scarlet" and impassioned face, and the entire scene is sexually charged.

In Afrikaans literature, the possibility of English soldiers having raped Boer women is dealt with explicitly. Gustav Preller's short story, "Lettie," published in Afrikaans in 1923, references a sexual threat by a British soldier, with the story centering on the ways in which certain memories are erased in a discourse of reconciliation, or in Preller's words, "to please colourless politics."[108] Alone on the farm, the "fresh and delicate" Lettie is threatened by an English soldier who evidently covets her. Although he takes a teasing, jovial tone, his words suggest a more sinister threat: "'it's not sensible for such a pretty girl, especially,' he added with another ha-hm and an idiotic laugh, 'if her father's on commando and she's alone at home.'"[109] As with many narratives following cultural trauma, the story then becomes a revenge fantasy, with Lettie getting the better of the soldier. In André Brink's post-apartheid novel *Duivel's Vlei* (later published in English as *Devil's Valley*), the rape of a Boer women by British soldiers actually occurs, and, horrifically, the victim's father and brothers throw her body, injured but still alive, into a ravine, hiding the shame her violation has caused them.

Despite the debate that emerged about whether English soldiers had raped Boer women, "black peril" narratives in connection with the war have proved to be of long-lasting effect. As I demonstrate in chapter 4 with reference to the version of Daphne Rooke's *Mittee* published in the United States in 1952, the idea that black upstarts took advantage of the chaos of the war to rape white women had a long hold on the popular imagination, though fear in fact stemmed from anxieties over the use of black combatants in a conflict between two white races. Mobilizing chivalric ideals, narratives of black rapists deflected attention away from British soldiers as perpetrators and justified herding civilians into concentration camps. The case of the South African War thus demonstrates that sexually menacing representations of men of color are not only deployed during the colonial management of overt "native" rebellion. In the following chapter, I demonstrate the ways in which "black peril" novels published in the early twentieth century expressed complex contests over political and textual authority, and worked towards consolidating white supremacy and nationhood after the war.

"Like a White Man"

"BLACK PERIL," PRINT CULTURE, AND POLITICAL VOICE IN THE MAKING OF THE UNION

His eye caught sight of the day's newspaper. He held it up and held
it before him, upside down, and looked round with that egotistical
childish look which Kaffirs so often assume, and asked the world in
general: "Now, am I not like a white man?"

—GEORGE HEATON NICHOLLS, *BAYETE!* (1923)[1]

In George Heaton Nicholls's "black peril" novel *Bayete!*, paranoia about white
women as potential victims of rape by black men converges with fears about
black involvement in print culture, as the attempt of the "houseboy" Mukwasi
to force himself on his white employer is immediately prefigured by his attempt to be "like a white man" through reading the newspaper. Running parallel to this incident in the novel, the leader of a black resistance movement,
Nelson, simultaneously attempts to seduce a white woman and to use the black
vote against white supremacy. These connections between access to print
media and an image of the "black peril," and between the black vote and the
"black peril," are not accidental. In 1910 the Union of South Africa was formed
as a self-governing dominion through the unification of four colonies—this
meant the consolidation of white supremacy. Yet, as revealed by the first national census in 1911, whites were outnumbered in South Africa by almost five
to one, and the nation, which depended on the labor of a large black underclass, began its life in a precarious position. Benedict Anderson has famously
argued that both news media and the literary industry play a major role in the
creation of nations as "imagined communities," with *mise en abyme* scenes of
reading (scenes where a character in the text is reading) enabling readers to
construct national imaginings that are "confirmed by the doubleness of our
reading about our young man reading."[2] For South Africa around the time of
Union, however, the era was one of competing nationalisms and print culture
was a racially segregated and complex field that brought into relief all the dilemmas around exclusions from citizenship. In three "black peril" novels of
the early twentieth century, namely Francis Bancroft's *Of Like Passions* (1911),

George Webb Hardy's *The Black Peril* (1912), and George Heaton Nicholls *Bayete!* (1923), it is possible to trace the ways in which each novel figures the relation of "black peril" phenomena to gendered and racialized contests over political voice and a culture of letters.

As has been well documented, although they have no relation to statistics of actual assault, waves of "black peril" anxiety rocked Natal from the 1870s and the Transvaal from the 1880s, with some of the worst scares erupting in the period around Union, in the Cape, Natal, and Transvaal in 1902–1903, and in the country generally in 1906–1908, and 1911–1913.[3] However, because previous commentators have focused on "black peril" as a feature of white rhetoric, expressed above all in white newspapers, they have not commented on the connection between "black peril" discourse and black print culture in the emerging nation. The early years of the twentieth century in South Africa were a boom time for black newspapers, many of which had been set up in the nineteenth century. Such periodicals included *Imvo Zabantsundu* (*Black Opinion*), founded by John Tengo Jabavu in 1884, and *Izwi Labantu* (*Voice of the People*), which was established in 1887. In 1903 Mahatma Gandhi's "International Printing Press" published the first issues of John Dube's *Ilanga Lase Natal* (*The Natal Sun*), and Gandhi's *Indian Opinion* made an appearance in English, Gujarati, Hindi, and Tamil in the same year. In 1909 the *A.P.O.* was set up in Cape Town by the predominantly Coloured African Political Organisation, which was founded in 1902, and in 1913 *Abantu Batho* (*The People*) emerged as the political mouthpiece of the South African National Natives Congress (SANNC, later known as the African National Congress, ANC), which was established in 1912. As their titles suggest, these publications foregrounded opinions that challenged the perspectives offered in white newspapers.

As Isabel Hofmeyr observes, there was considerable anxiety at the turn of the century about printing presses in "non-white" hands.[4] When the machinery of Gandhi's press arrived in Durban Harbour it was greeted by a violent mob of white protestors. Moreover, as Jeff Peires has shown, printing presses in the first half of the twentieth century themselves became organized around the protection of white labor. The South African Typographical Union was a "whites only" craft union, and was in 1881 one of the first two trade unions established in South Africa. Africans were not permitted to become members of the Federation of Master Printers, which meant that no Africans were permitted to work as printers or bookbinders. An exception was made for presses such as Lovedale, which was allowed to apprentice Africans on condition that it only produced work of "Native" or missionary aspect. As Peires points out: "Segregation thus meant a division of labour between Lovedale (and similar presses in other areas) which published for "Natives" and the European press which published for everyone else."[5] It also meant that Lovedale could produce texts that were more cheaply available, since the press was not compelled to pay protectionist wages demanded by white worker's unions.

Although the early twentieth century saw the consolidation of racialized capitalism, the period was one of labor unrest. Labor segregation law sought to address concerns that white men of the working classes were increasingly being threatened with substitution by semi-skilled Africans, and labor disputes led to strikes on the Rand in 1907 and again in 1913. As Charles van Onselen has shown, "black peril" convulsions were linked to a syndrome of "recession–political uncertainty–industrial action,"[6] so that economic crises coincided with "black peril" scares.[7] Fears that white jobs would be usurped by black, "coloured", or Indian workers were expressed through images of contamination, and lurid accounts of white girls working alongside sweating Africans and Indians in factories were used to justify the Mines and Works Act, which was passed in 1911.[8] Indeed it was the white Labour Party that was most vociferous on the subject of "the black peril" in the early twentieth century, and it is also a fact that the major white newspapers of the day catered for the tastes of white working-class readers.[9]

Anxiety about educated black men competing for white jobs converged with reservations about black readers and writers within the realm of literary consumption. Setting the scene for later apartheid-era policies that subjected black children to "Bantu education," "black peril" rhetoric became instrumental in an argument about the corrupting influence of education on black men and women. It was popularly expressed that African men who could read would become intimate with inappropriate European literature, and that if there was no control over dissemination, such men would be able to access representations meant for white men's eyes only. Like alcohol, exposure to a liberal education and to certain publications was seen as corrupting to "the native mind." A "little knowledge" combined with access to inappropriate literature, it was claimed, would excite the passions of "natives," causing them to slough off any veneer of acquired civilization and revert to a bestial state of lust in which settler women would become targets for sexual assault. A newspaper article of 1912, entitled "Little Knowledge is a Dangerous Thing," included the following statement by a magistrate "who has had to deal with criminal natives for some 30 years":

> My experience has been, in by far the majority of these cases which you term Black Peril, that the native can read, and that he has made a nice selection of the most unhealthy British literature. Similarly a native woman who by reason of a little knowledge and an environment which is sympathetic towards her becoming superior to her compatriots, soon calls for the attention of the White Peril, and is subsequently the prey of men of her own colour. The native has the intellect of a child and the passions and savagery of a baboon.[10]

According to this man of the law, not only does the "native" man degenerate into bestiality when brought into contact with "unhealthy British literature," but the black woman educated above her station is such an abomination that she calls upon herself rape by both white men and "men of her own colour."

Reverberating with a biopolitical poetics of disease and contamination that was linked to the constitution of racial hierarchy and difference, the idea that certain texts could be "unhealthy" fed into a budding discourse of censorship. The 1913 Commission of Enquiry into Assaults on Women concluded that obscene publications played a part in encouraging sexual attacks,[11] and a public questionnaire compiled in 1912 by the General Missionary Conference commission on "the so-called black peril" includes a section asking whether "obscene" representations, "low theatrical performances," and "shady bioscopes" contributed to attacks on white women, a question to which many respondents replied in the affirmative.[12] Prefiguring the intensely vigilant censorship that would be instituted under apartheid, in 1931 the South African parliament enacted the Entertainments (Censorship) Act No 29 to regulate any films, pictures, or public entertainments that showed, among other things, "nude human figures," "white slave traffic" (usually this meant white prostitution), "scenes of intermingling of Europeans and non-Europeans," and "scenes of rough-handling or ill-treatment of women and children."[13] As a corollary to general queasiness about black consumption of "unhealthy" texts, there was fear that black men might begin to produce such representations themselves. This anxiety haunted the South African literary establishment well into the twentieth century, and as I demonstrate in chapter 4 with reference to responses to Arthur Maimane's *Victims* (1976), the black author who dwells too intimately on the body of a white woman was treated punitively by the South African censors.

At the time of South Africa's union, the literary marketplace had begun to change dramatically nationally, but also on a global level. In 1913, the Bengali poet Rabindranath Tagore, already celebrated in the British Isles, made history as the first Asian writer to be awarded the Nobel Prize for literature. In South Africa, black writers were taking the reins of literary production, and producing literary texts that challenged white ideology. Following the Bambatha rebellion in Natal in 1906, for instance, a number of poems by black authors memorializing the rebels were published in *Ilanga Lase Natal*. Figures such as the Xhosa poet S.E.K. Mqhayi bridged the divide between oral and literary forms, publishing both journalism and literary pieces in *Izwi Labantu*, *Imvo Zabantsundu*, and *Umteteli wa Bantu* (*Mouthpiece of the People*). In a paper on "Bantu Belles lettres" in 1921, D.D.T. Jabavu cataloged existing black South African literature, emphasizing a "race" towards a culture of "Letters."[14] To a considerable extent, the struggle to protect the body of the white woman in South Africa at this time can be mapped as both a political and economic contest over the body of the nation, as well as an exertion that aimed to recover white authorship and authority. As I point out, the anxiety and sexual jealousy over white women's bodies that one notes in a text like Webb Hardy's novel *The*

Black Peril may be read partly as textual jealousy, a deflection of the struggle over access to textual production.

Although the three novels under discussion in this chapter reveal complex tensions, they often resort to crude stereotyping, and are not, by any stretch of the imagination, great works of literature. In fact, while Bancroft's novel is probably more "literary" than the novels of Webb Hardy and Heaton Nicholls, in their representation of "the black peril," all three novels vocalize culturally dominant assumptions and are self-professed instances of political commentary, which complicates any liberal inclination to divorce them from the public sphere. Yet, as mentioned in the introduction to this study, and as Paxton points out in her reading of novels of the Indian Mutiny, the world of the novel is anything but unitary; rather, it is necessarily "ideologically contested"—in a Bakhtinian sense novelistic language is dialogic and heteroglossic, representing "unresolvable dialogues" and "the coexistence of socio-ideological contradictions . . . between different socio-ideological groups."[15] Although a text such as *Bayete!* was intended by its author to warn against "black peril," it became a source of inspiration for black resistance leaders who saw the action taken by its main character, an African anti-colonial leader, as exemplary.[16] In the novels of Bancroft, Webb Hardy, and Heaton Nicholls, unexpected and often subversive articulations coexist with "black peril" narratives, bringing to the fore sites of contestation, of doubling or splitting in dominant discourse. Running parallel to the "peril" narrative in the novels of the two male writers, Webb Hardy and Heaton Nicholls, one finds an anxiety-ridden script of sexual jealousy in which white women actively seek out the company, conversation, or writing of men of color. In Francis Bancroft's *Of Like Passions*, secret and coercive sexual relations between white men and black women, and the disenfranchisement of white women, are presented as instigating the violation of white women by black men.

"Wholly Bestial and Mad with Burning Revenge": Contesting Enfranchisement in Francis Bancroft's *Of Like Passions*

Written by a self-professed New Woman, and setting out in its dedication to serve "in the cause, and for the safe-guarding of the Daughters of Greater Britain—the white womanhood of our colonies," Bancroft's *Of Like Passions* claims in an epigraph to be "mirrored in its essence from events now exercising a direct bearing on life and legislation abroad."[17] Aimed at a reading public in "Greater Britain," and declaring itself a reflection of reality, the novel deploys "black peril" in order to hold up a mirror to another narrative, the story of the "white peril" and the perceived culpability of white men in provoking "miscegenation" and "the black peril." The novel, which reached its ninth edition by 1911, was praised for both its moral message and its realism in the *Times Literary*

Supplement, where it was described as having "gone to the very root of the danger at which [the author] is so justly alarmed." In a flattering comparison between Bancroft and Schreiner, the *TLS* reviewer had this to say about the vividness of Bancroft's depiction of South African life:

> It is a fine book showing sympathy and wisdom and it is not without deliberation that we say that since the story of the 'South African Farm' we have read no book on South Africa so startlingly true in its representation of South African humanity.[18]

If one shuttles forward to the final years of the twentieth century and compares this to some comments made about a novel like J.M. Coetzee's *Disgrace*—which has been praised internationally as a searing depiction of post-apartheid South Africa—one sees that "black peril" novels have played a role in the making and marketing of a distinctly South African literature for almost a century. Read in a realist manner, they have provided a sensationalist and readily consumable fantasy about South African society for overseas readers.

In Bancroft's novel, a young and delicate white woman, Kathleen Rooyen, is brutally raped and murdered by a vengeful "half-caste," Andries, who, acting in a drunken fury, has also killed his wife, Nichinette, thinking that she has pandered to the lust of Kathleen's husband, Phillip Rooyen. The theme of revenge is central to the novel. The rape and double murders are presented as retribution for the behavior of white men who indulge in sexual liaisons with those dusky women who live on the outskirts of the white settlements, and the vengeance exacted by Andries, in turn, justifies legislative reprisals on the part of settlers. As presented in Bancroft's novel, however, the public response to the rape and murders is erroneous, since whites have petitioned for stricter vagrancy and labor laws, rather than acknowledging "the real first cause of the murder," and instituting legislation against interracial sex. "The black peril" is thus placed alongside an exposure of its shadowy double, the world of "the white peril," a phrase that had currency at the time Bancroft was writing.

As with Schreiner before her, and as would be the case with Sarah Gertrude Millin, in Bancroft's novel interracial sex can only be the site of abjection, and the ill-effects of "miscegenation" are blamed on the moral frailty of white men, while white women such as Kathleen Trevanor are upheld as innocent victims. Book One opens with an epigraph by Victor Hugo, used by Bancroft to refer to white women: "The Sublime Summit of Abnegation! The Highest Pinnacle of Virtue!—Servitude endured, torture accepted, punishment demanded, by Souls which have never sinned that they may absolve Souls which have erred." Notably it is the innocent young wife Kathleen, rather than the autobiographically represented figure of the New Woman, Irene Mabille, who becomes a victim, sacrificed because of the errant ways of white men. As I shall demonstrate, this may be contrasted with novels by

white men such as Webb Hardy and Heaton Nicholls, where the indepen-
dent-minded New Woman is punitively silenced by becoming the victim of a
"black peril" attack.

Focalized through the consciousness of the agonized, swooning Kathleen,
the rape in *Of Like Passions* takes a full five pages to narrate. On her way to visit
a neighboring farmstead, Kathleen is startled by "a sound as of a tearing and a
rending," which she first supposes to be an animal in the undergrowth but
then realizes this is something far more sinister:

> She uttered a short swift cry on perceiving her mistake. This was no
> peaceful, harmless ox or horse making for the water pools of the sandy
> bed, but a powerful nude savage turned to madness and bestiality. His
> blood-shot eyes glittered fiercely, and his blistered, sun-blackened lips
> were drawn back snarling from his white teeth. His muscular, broadly-
> built body was scratched and torn with the thorny growths of the dense
> brushwood. . . . Even as Kathleen Rooyen, catching a glimpse of the hor-
> ror, cried out in her sudden shock and fear, turning to fly, his long sinewy
> arms with thews and muscles of iron, swung round her body and caught
> it in a grip that crushed life and breath out of the unfortunate daughter
> of Bryan Trevanor.[19]

Although readers today would dismiss such crass racial stereotyping, in its day
the novel was read as a kind of tragic realism, and the scene may be usefully
compared with a similar incident in Thomas Dixon's *The Clansman*, which was
published two years before *Of Like Passions* and was praised for its realism by
President Theodore Roosevelt in its cinematic form as *Birth of a Nation*. In
Dixon's novel, the following scene leads up to the rape of Marion, feminine
emblem of the white South, whose violation and murder justifies the retributive actions taken by the Ku Klux Klan:

> The door flew open with a crash, and four black brutes leaped into the
> room, Gus in the lead, with a revolver in his hand, his yellow teeth grinning
> through his thick lips. . . .
>
> Marion staggered against the wall, her face white, her delicate lips trembling
> with the chill of a fear colder than death.
>
> "We have no money—the deed has not been delivered," she pleaded, a sud-
> den glimmer of hope flashing in her blue eyes.
>
> Gus stepped closer, with an ugly leer, his flat nose dilated, his sinister bead-
> eyes wide apart gleaming ape-like as he laughed:
>
> "We ain't atter money!"
>
> The girl uttered a cry, long, tremulous, heart-rending, piteous.
>
> A single tiger spring, and the black claws of the beast sunk into the soft white
> throat and she was still.[20]

In both extracts a violent spatial intrusion prefigures and provides a metaphor for the actual rape. In *The Clansman* the door of a white Southern home is broken open "with a crash," and in *Of Like Passions* the pastoral idyll of the white-owned farm space is torn asunder when Kathleen realizes that before her stands "no peaceful harmless ox or horse," but the very embodiment of colonial horror fantasies, the naked and vengeful savage. As Sabine Sielke has pointed out in her study of rape in American literature, in Dixon's narrative sexual assault is represented as robbery, and "Dixon at the same time plays upon his literary antecedents, including Shakespeare's *The Rape of Lucrece*, the captivity narrative, and the Western."[21] Bancroft's novel in turn deals with images relevant to the South African context, as the "nude savage" is contrasted with domesticated animals ("this was no harmless ox or horse"), and both the farm space and the white woman's body become synecdochical figures for the white nation under attack.

Presented from the perspective of the victim who slips in and out of consciousness, the rape in Bancroft's novel is elided, described through periphrasis and innuendo. Through the lapses in Kathleen's consciousness, which read as surprisingly modernist aspects of an otherwise realist novel, the author self-censors any explicit description of rape. In one part of the chapter dealing with the rape, Kathleen is literally defiled, penetrated by dirt, when Andries forces sand into her mouth to stifle her cries for help:

> It was in a stupor that she knew sand was being forced into her mouth to stifle her unconscious screams and cries. Into her ears, into her nostrils and eyes it filtered, choking and blinding her. The murderous barbarian had cunning and intelligence—wholly bestial and mad with burning revenge and brutal cruelty, but there was in him the higher human quality of intelligence.[22]

As in the image of the tearing apart of the undergrowth from which the "nude savage" emerges, sexual violation is represented symbolically. The emphasis on silencing the victim, which may also be noted in the scene from Dixon's novel quoted above, focuses attention on the mouth and throat: in Bancroft's novel Kathleen is stifled, and in Dixon's novel "the black claws of the beast [sink] into the soft white throat." Partly this may be read as a euphemism for blackness "filtering" or "sinking" into the unspeakable location of reproduction, as the violation is displaced upward, from the sex organs to the organs of speech. By gesturing towards the site of reproduction, the question of the honor of the white woman and of the white race become one in a biopolitical sense, because at stake in the image is the health of the collective. In both *The Clansman* and *Of Like Passions* any possibility of offspring from an interracial union is quickly suppressed, as Marion commits suicide and Kathleen is not only raped but also murdered by Andries. While sexual liaisons between white men and black women usually result in "mixed-race" offspring in "white peril" narratives, the white woman raped by a black man is always killed off in typical "black peril" fiction.

Through examining Bancroft's political writings and the novel's context, however, it becomes apparent that the question of voice and silencing are linked not only to the absent site of reproduction, but also to political representation, to the question of enfranchisement. The emphasis on the mouth of the victim, on the stifling of Kathleen in the rape scene, offers a complex interplay between the silencing of an individual woman and what Bancroft, as a New Woman, perceived to be a form of disease within the body politic, namely the denigration of white women's political voices within the newly emerging nation.

As Gareth Cornwell has suggested, in Bancroft's political writings, there is evidence that the themes that surface in *Of Like Passions* are deployed not merely to promote racial purity and a legislative bar on interracial sex, but also to argue for the enfranchisement of white women.[23] At the time of Union in South Africa, a number of black and "coloured" men in the Cape were still allowed to vote but white women were not yet enfranchised. In an article published in 1911, Bancroft's criticizes this policy:

> The Kaffir is essentially and entirely a creature of logic, he reasons towards an end. . . . He sees today, as in the past, the spectacle of the white master standing above his woman, the white woman standing below her master. The Kaffir respects—up to a certain point—the white man's possessions, but he will occasionally take chances. . . . He sees too that he—the black man— has a vote, because he is a man. Woman, therefore is but an inferior, a possession. Her deprivation of the coveted power to vote amounts to a public proclamation of the fact that her status is on a par with the status of the ordinary black man, and *below* the par of the status of the black man voter.[24]

Thus "black peril" rhetoric becomes instrumental in an argument for the political demands of the New Woman, and white women's enfranchisement takes place at the cost of bestializing the black man, even if he is granted enough "logic" and "the higher human qualities of intelligence" to rationalize about racial and gendered hierarchies. As with the other "black peril" novels discussed in this chapter, the silencing of the black man corresponds with his transformation into a beast at the moment of the sexual attack. During the rape scene in *Of Like Passions*, Andries becomes a "snarling" and wordless "savage turned to madness and bestiality." Although after his vengeful murder of Kathleen he is given some powerful lines written in an archaic language that evokes the soliloquies of Othello, another misguided black murderer of a white woman, Andries is finally silenced by being sentenced to hang for his crimes.

The turn of the twentieth century saw a consolidation of black resistance in South Africa, but also a crisis in gender relations as white colonial women challenged their confinement to the domestic sphere and were increasingly vocal in demanding enfranchisement. For white men, fears about white women's demands for political representation merged with anxieties that the New Woman, who held liberal views and was no longer under white patriarchal sway, might choose sexual partners from outside her class or ethnic enclave. Speaking on public platforms, writing forcefully about political issues, and often outdoing men in the literary arena, the New Woman had to be muted. Thus, as I shall demonstrate, one sees in "black peril" texts by white men such as Webb Hardy and Heaton Nicholls an emphasis on suppression of women's organs of speech. In a gesture of sadism directed at the political voice of the New Woman, the black rapist typically seizes the throat or covers the mouth of his victim, becoming a fictive proxy for those who desired to stifle women who were becoming too liberal and outspoken in their opinions.

"Catching Her by the Throat": Political and Literary Struggles in George Webb Hardy's *The Black Peril*

While Bancroft blames white men's indiscretion and the lowly political status of white women for "the black peril," in George Webb Hardy's novel *The Black Peril* (1912) the liberal attitudes, folly, and "lasciviousness"[25] of settler women are held to be accountable for interracial sexual assaults on white women. In Webb Hardy's novel, the protagonist, Raymond Chesterfield, publishes in his newspaper what he refers to as a case of "the Black Peril." White schoolgirls at an elite institution have been initiating sexual liaisons with a black gardener. Approaching Chesterfield, the father of one of the girls has begged him to "tell the truth about the Black Peril," and with his mind "full of the Black Peril,"[26] Chesterfield composes an article which shocks his readers and results in his imprisonment for obscenity. As Cornwell notes, the anecdote has a rather bizarre autobiographical referent, as Webb Hardy himself was a journalist who published in 1904 a newspaper article entitled "The Black Peril" that offered a lurid account of sex between white schoolgirls and a black laborer at a girls' school in Durban. Enraging the citizens of Durban by throwing into doubt the purity and honor of the city's white womanhood, Webb Hardy was duly prosecuted and imprisoned for obscene writing.[27] In his novel, the town of "Mosquito" situated in the colony of "Zutal," is meant to portray Durban in Natal, and Chesterfield is a barely concealed self-portrait of the author himself. At stake in this text that hovers between fiction and autobiography is its relationship with reality, and the issues that Webb Hardy sketches are clearly meant to raise awareness about what he feels to be problems in the real world. Interestingly, Chesterfield's—and Webb Hardy's—choice of a site for contestation over access to white women's bodies is a white newspaper with working-class interests at heart, the circulation figures and political opinions of which would have begun to be rivaled by successful black newspapers at this time.

Musing on some of the pressing concerns that need attention in his newspaper, *The Argonaut* (which he fancies is modeled on Henry Labouchere's *Truth*), Webb Hardy's hero, Chesterfield, envisions himself as the one to expose the threat of "the black peril." This turns out to be a demographic as well as a sexual threat:

> Raymond saw the danger under which the white woman had to live in the country—a danger inseparable from a land that contained a mere handful of whites as against millions of blacks, the majority of whom were only in the first stages of human evolution.[28]

Chesterfield also notes that the crisis is caused in part by "a small minority of white women in the country who, to put it in plain words, encourage Kafir immorality."[29] In the novel the meaning of consensual interracial sex (the incident with the schoolgirls) all but blurs into that of the attempted rape of Mary Roseberry, an ambivalently represented New Woman, who becomes Chesterfield's sweetheart in the novel.

A self-professed radical and socialist fresh from London, Mary is astounded by the intimate relations between white families and their black "houseboys" that she witnesses in the colony. As expressed in Webb Hardy's novel, panic about black rape at this time often centered on a social relationship at the heart of the white home, the association between white women and their black "houseboys." In an exercise of finger-pointing that expressed a wider cultural phenomenon of sexual jealousy, white male politicians and writers commonly blamed "the black peril" not only on the savagery of the "native," but also on those white middle-class women who encouraged "familiarity" with their "houseboys." Lord Gladstone, the Governor General of South Africa, writing to Harcourt in 1911 on the subject of a "black peril" case known as "the Umtali affair," claimed that:

> In Rhodesia, Johannesburg and elsewhere it is the almost universal practice for white women to allow black boys to come to their bedrooms. In the Umtali case it appeared . . . that the lady in bed received her coffee daily from a black boy. . . . What white lady at home tolerates a manservant in her bedroom? Yet these people insist on bringing savages into quite familiar relations with white women, and when one of them breaks out they look upon the offence as the "black peril" instead of what it is—the inevitable result of their own folly.[30]

Although critical of women who treat their black male servants with insufficient distance, Mary herself encourages a friendly relationship with "Jim," a "kitchen-Kafir," to whom she attempts, unsuccessfully, to teach English.

In his depiction of "Jim," and particularly in the portrayal of "Jim's" inability (or unwillingness) to learn to read and write, Webb Hardy was drawing on prevailing wisdom about "the native mind." In *The Essential Kafir*, published in 1904, Dudley Kidd had claimed that while African children show an early ability to absorb knowledge, at puberty their energies were directed elsewhere, so that their mental character remained stunted. The Reverend Noel Roberts summed up the ideas of his time when he attested in 1917 that, in the case of "natives," with the onset of puberty "the wave of intellectual progress and development ebbs and is followed by an overwhelming wave of sexualism which in many cases, takes entire possession of their natures to the exclusion of every other desire."[31] Thus blackness is constituted as hypersexuality, and scientific racism propagates an image of the intellectually backward black man incapable of entering into competition with whites for skilled or semi-skilled jobs.

For Chesterfield in Webb Hardy's novel, the problem comes when Africans are corrupted by contact with civilization, or treated with too much kindness and familiarity, when, "as a raw and uneducated creature, [the black man] comes into the circle of men and women ennobled . . . by two thousand years of Christian religion." For her inability to recognize that "Jim" has the intellect of a child, but all the lower passions of the animals, Mary must learn a lesson "in blood in tears," and a few pages later, she has become the victim of an attempted rape at the hands of "Jim."[32]

Although she starts out as a strong opponent during the attack, Mary is quickly transformed into weak and helpless prey. Accosted by "Jim" on the road one evening, she initially fights back, matching his strength with hers, but finally succumbs and swoons, like Kathleen Trevanor, into the position of victim:

> He hesitated, then continued: "Missis! I like-a you! I kiss missis!" He grasped her hand quickly and bent over her. . . . The blood was rushing through her. She half lost her head. But pulling herself together, she raised her arm and, swinging it swiftly, struck the boy full in the face with the back of her hand. It was a terrible blow for a woman, and the Kafir slipped and almost fell to the ground. Then his whole nature seemed to undergo a change. His eyes stood out of his head and he glared fiercely at Mary—and she read him like a book as the light of the moon emerging from a cloud shone full and clear on the Kafir's face. She turned towards the house and began to run. But the Kafir, fleet of foot, desperate in his resolve, fell upon her, and, catching her by the throat, threw her heavily to the ground. Everything seemed to become blurred. She swooned.[33]

The illiterate "Jim" is represented here as an object to be read ("she read him like a book"), rather than a subject who reads. There is also an implication that, until this moment when he is illuminated by a "full and clear" light, Mary has "misread" him. As was the case in Bancroft's *Of Like Passions*, the attack in Webb Hardy's novel centers on the organs of speech: "*catching her by the throat* [my emphasis]." But whereas Bancroft's focus on rape as silencing of innocent victims can be related to her critique of white women's political voicelessness, in Webb Hardy's novel the black rapist channels an act of aggression directed at the body and political voice of the New Woman. In fact it is the attack on her "throat" that, severing her body from her intellect, marks the transition in

Mary from New Woman to feminized and helpless victim. As in *Of Like Passions* and also in American novels such as *The Clansman* and *Red Rock*, by demoting the black man to the level of the bestial and corporeal, at the moment of the "black peril" attack the text elevates the white woman into a figurative icon whose purity and vulnerability suggest the status of the white nation.[34] Finally beaten into a feminized and vulnerable position, Mary has to be saved by the alcoholic white pastor, Timothy Trelawney, who is subsequently remasculinized, rendered as the phallus: "drunk or sober, the Reverend Timothy was not a coward. And in a second the little man seemed to grow to a giant as, without saying a word, he strode towards 'Jim.'"[35] What follows is a strangely sexualized scene in which the position of attacker is reversed into that of victim, as "Jim" is not only bestialized, but also penetrated, feminized and silenced: "The Kafir howled in his agony, but the clergyman, now beside himself with passion, was on top of him in a moment, *burying his fingers in his throat . . . [my emphasis]*." Like Mary, "Jim" becomes feminized, symbolically castrated and impotent, and the "black peril" scene in Webb Hardy's book thus serves to mute the voices of both the New Woman and the black man.

Fortunately for Mary, she is saved from "Jim," and so, unlike Kathleen Trevanor, the victim in Bancroft's *Of Like Passions*, she is allowed to live. The killing off of a white woman who has been debased by a sexual encounter with a black man and the letting live of one who has retained her purity may work conveniently in the world of fiction, but as Webb Hardy knew, things did not work out so tidily in the realm of life. In the case of the schoolgirls who willingly had sex with their gardener, what appalls Webb Hardy is not the horror of "miscegenation" (as the girls have used contraceptives), but rather his perception that their degenerative behavior will somehow contaminate the life of the collective:

The turning loose into society of girls who have been defiled and have consented to be defiled, by the black wretches who are the most cursed things that God ever made? . . . Is that not a matter of public interest?[36]

Here the schoolgirls have been irreparably tainted by their intercourse with a black man, and even though their liaison may be non-reproductive, their corruption will spread like a contagious disease or a bad smell, leading to an erosion of whiteness. This biopolitical discourse of contamination is as much about policing gender as about race, and for Webb Hardy, the same women who are emblems of purity can also be potential bearers of pollution. Condemning consensual sex between white women and black men as "the Black Peril" and thus mirroring it with the near-rape of Mary, the novel reveals that intimacy between white women and black men, rather than the threat of rape, is the contagion against which white society must be defended. Indeed, the question of black men's access to white women leads Chesterfield from a position of opposition to segregation, to considering elements of segregation as an alternative to South Africa becoming "a veritable black man's land":

Raymond was led to modify his views regarding the native races. He abated not one jot of his passion for the cause of absolute justice to them, of political equality for educated men with coloured skins. . . . But when Raymond faced the idea of a Kafir kissing the girl he loved, and, with strong imagination, pictured that Kafir becoming an educated civilized being and capturing the soul of one who was dear to him, perhaps his own sister, his whole being revolted against intimate relations between black and white in any form.[37]

For Chesterfield, the moment the black man is educated is the moment at which he becomes a sexual rival, and it is at the border of the socio-sexual that intellectual racism provides support for Chesterfield's views. In a quick shift from affect to pseudo-science that is typical of liberal segregationist discourse, Chesterfield is encouraged by his friend Mark Shepherd (a character based on the segregationist John Shepstone,[38] who was Webb Hardy's acquaintance) to read the "anthropo-sociological superior race theories of Gobineau, Lapouge and Galton," and finds that "they bore for him a psychological interpretation under the peculiar sociological conditions of the land of the Southern Cross that he was compelled to acknowledge."[39]

As Chesterfield's affinity with racialist theory suggests, the unthinkability of sex between black men and white women was a fairly common feature of the European and colonial imagination. What is interesting about Webb Hardy's novel, however, is the way in which images of interracial romance and hierarchies of race and caste are linked to an anxiety of authorship. Although the idea of a black man kissing his sister nauseates Chesterfield, he and Mary form their first dinner-table alliance over the question of a marriage between "a highly educated Parsee and an English girl." Mary boldly declares "Why shouldn't she marry him if she loves him?," and Chesterfield feels that he can support her with "a perfectly clear conscience" as he believes in the "social equality" of the parties concerned.[40] In Chesterfield's opening manifesto for *The Argonaut*, he claims:

> . . . the colour of a man's skin has no more to do with a man's worth—social, financial, or political—than it had to do with the question of whether Ranjitsinhji ought to have played for Sussex. . . . We say, it will be observed, Prince Ranjitsinhji. We do not say a raw, uneducated Kafir from the kraals who might happen (although it would require a miracle) to be up to the standard of a Sussex cricketer. There are degrees of black men, in exactly the same way as there are degrees of white.[41]

This concession about an Englishman's social equality with an "educated Parsee" or with Prince Ranjitsinhji sets the scene for the reference to Rabindranath Tagore at the end of the novel.

After serving a jail sentence for obscenity, Chesterfield sails to England with Mary. In their early meetings, it is emphasized that Mary greatly admires his writing, and that she keeps a notebook and is also a writer of sorts. On board, however, Chesterfield opens her precious notebook, only to find a romantic poem by Tagore: "Early in the morning it was whispered that we should sail in a boat, only thou and I, and never a soul in the world would know of this our pilgrimage, to no country and to no end." Underneath, Mary has written and underlined: "By Rabindranath Tagore, India's great poet, who, because of his colour, would be treated in one British country almost as a pariah." On the one hand, the reference sets up an identification between Chesterfield and Tagore that is flattering to Chesterfield. Just as Tagore would be persecuted in South Africa for his color, Chesterfield (and Webb Hardy) feels himself to have been martyred in South Africa for exposing "truth" through his journalism. On another level, however, by virtue of his writing, Tagore has intruded into Chesterfield's relationship with Mary. The triad of Chesterfield, Mary, and Tagore echoes the only other romantic incident between Chesterfield and Mary that is described in the novel. In this previous romantic incident, after an erotically charged scene, Chesterfield touches Mary's hair and leaves her apparently asleep on a veranda. The bipartite structure of the lovers, however, is then intruded upon by a third party as we are told that: "A Kafir, wending his way homeward rent the midnight air with his unearthly music."[42] Unlike the black man who enters the scene through his orality, however, Tagore's interruption into a romantic scene between Chesterfield and Mary makes him a competitor, not only for Mary's admiration, but also for her readership.

The many references to class and caste that litter the novel could thus be read as an anxiety of authorship, a rationalization of a context where an Indian man such as Tagore could receive great literary acclaim. Webb Hardy is forced to concede that the high-born Indian man can indeed compete as an equal with an Englishman, in sport, in writing, and even for the love of an Englishwoman. What he cannot tolerate, however, is rivalry from black Africans, "the most cursed things that God ever made." If a white man should be outdone by "a Kafir from the kraals," if the lowest outdoes the highest, then the entire fabric of the racial and caste-based hierarchy disintegrates. Because she has tried to set "Jim" on a path towards competing with an Englishman by teaching him English grammar, Mary is punished when her student misinterprets her attention and tries to rape her. The fear of black Africans competing with white writers is quickly defused in Webb Hardy's novel, however, as the lustful "Jim" is reduced to a stammering creature who has no wish to learn to read or write and can only say "*Ikona*, missis! *Ikona* English—*Ikona* white man—'Jim' black—all-a-right black!"[43] Yet sexual and textual jealousy are nonetheless noticeably intertwined in the novel, such that the struggle for possession of the white woman is inseparable from a racialized contest over literary worth and involvement in a culture of letters.

"His Sonorous Voice": George Heaton Nicholls's
Bayete! and the Black Vote

For George Heaton Nicholls, who was, like Webb Hardy, a white male Natalian, racialized anxiety is most manifest in hysteria around the question of the black vote, and before beginning a discussion of Heaton Nicholls's "black peril" novel *Bayete!*, it is necessary to provide some information about this author's part in theorizing the segregationist legislation that was to underpin the later policies of apartheid. Shula Marks has observed that "of all the colonies of South Africa, Natal's policies in the nineteenth century were closest to twentieth-century notions of segregation," and that although "his role in the policies of segregation has been curiously underestimated," George Heaton Nicholls was "by far one of the most articulate proponents of segregation" and "one of the most influential in terms of the political power he achieved."[44] As a Member of Parliament for Zululand from 1920, Heaton Nicholls followed the policies advocated in nineteenth century Natal by Sir Theophillus Shepstone (Diplomatic Agent to the Native Tribes and Secretary for Native Affairs in Natal between 1845 and 1875), which meant that he supported racial separation through the setting aside of reserved land for African "tribal" occupation, and the administering of "Native" areas through "traditional" African forms of authority. Examining Heaton Nicholls as a key figure in the passing of the Hertzog Bills, which offered small land concessions to dispossessed and land-starved Africans in return for banishing them from the common voters' roll, Susanna Glouwdina Bekker notes that Heaton Nicholls, "more than anyone else, provided the theoretical base on which Hertzog's legislation could rest."[45] In 1935 Professor D.D.T. Jabavu at the All-African Convention attributed the Hertzog Bills and attempts to abolish the black franchise to "an Englishman"; Jabavu did not name him but this Englishman was Heaton Nicholls.[46]

In 1926, having defeated Smuts's South African Party in the 1924 elections by forming a "Pact" between the white Labour Party and his Nationalist Party, J.B.M. Hertzog, the South African Prime Minister and Minister of Native Affairs, laid four Bills on the table of Parliament. A year later, a Select Committee was appointed to consider and take evidence on these Bills, and its proceedings only ended in 1936, when two of the Bills became law. Heaton Nicholls was a member of the Select Committee on the Hertzog Bills, and in the period 1930 to 1935 he began to cooperate more closely with the Prime Minister, providing theoretical support for Hertzog's vision. For Heaton Nicholls and Hertzog, the main problem was that there was no common "Native policy" in the Union, and this was largely because of the Cape franchise, which extended to men of color, provided they received a minimum income or owned property to a certain value. In Natal, by contrast, the question of the franchise was more disingenuous. Although in principle Africans were allowed to vote, legislation in effect did away with the black franchise as black men were obliged to fulfill strict conditions relating to residency, property, and income, and also to provide recommendations from three white electors and undergo assessment by the Lieutenant-Governor. In 1907 there were 23,686 registered voters in Natal, and of these 23,480 (99.1 percent) were white, 150 Indian, 50 "coloured", and 6 African. Natal's approach to the black franchise was thus close to that of the Orange River Colony and the Transvaal, where Africans were granted "no equality . . . either in Church or State."[47]

Although some social commentators perpetuate the idea that apartheid stemmed simply from a continuity of Afrikaner racism, this premise has largely been discredited, and it is clear that Natal, a relatively small province politically dominated at the time of Union by white English-speaking settlers, played a major role in the formulation of strategies that laid the foundations for apartheid.[48] Given this fact, it is intriguing that the country's first internal "black peril" scare took place in Natal, and that this area was a major site in which "black peril" rhetoric proliferated. While Africans outnumbered European settlers no more than five to one in other South African provinces, in early twentieth-century Natal the figure was around ten to one, and this demographic aspect can be seen as linked to the prominence of "black peril" rhetoric. Labor issues in Natal also played a role. By the early twentieth century white farming activities had expanded rapidly in response to global demands for commodities such as cotton and sugar. Labor strikes organized by Gandhi in 1906, as well as the growth of black trade unions such as the Industrial and Commercial Workers Union (ICU), which had large numbers of supporters in Natal by the 1920s, threatened to disrupt a lucrative system of exploitation.[49] As a plantation owner and later as President of the South African Planters Union, Heaton Nicholls would have been directly affected by labor unrest in Natal, and a conflation of "black peril" rhetoric with anxieties about industrial action may be seen in his novel *Bayete!*

Historians studying the important role played by Heaton Nicholls in South African politics have scanned his autobiography, *South Africa in My Time*, for informative details, but have tended to gloss over the significance of *Bayete!*, despite the fact that Heaton Nicholls saw his novel as being a direct intervention in an historical sense. A collage of fictionalized events with direct and indirect historical referents, the novel invokes a prophetic realism as its standard: "Yet always there has been the thought that it expresses something that is true, something of experience, something in anticipation of events already history."[50] As a result of this perception about the power of his book to represent and anticipate history, however, Heaton Nicholls feared that the novel could encourage what it depicted, namely industrial action as a means of bringing white rule to an end. Although Nelson, the leader of a transnational black resistance movement in the novel, takes his African name, Balumbatha, from that of the leader of the Bambatha armed rebellion that shook Natal in 1905–7, Nelson's strategy of resistance follows the ideas of an Indian, who can

only be Gandhi. It should be remembered that Gandhi was opposed to the
Bambatha rebellion, and refined his idea of *Satyagraha* in South Africa by or-
ganizing labor strikes in the Natal coalfields and sugar plantations in the first
decade of the twentieth century. In Heaton Nicholls's novel, industrial strike
action by black workers, rather than armed resistance, is used by Nelson to
bring the country to a standstill and then to bargain for black enfranchisement, which eventually topples white power.[51]

As the reference to Gandhi suggests, although *Bayete!* emerged out of the
political environment of Natal, it references a wide transnational web of resistance to white dominance. Nelson becomes Chief of the Matabele in Rhodesia,
but his ancestry is not southern African, and he travels to America, where he
joins proponents of a church-based black political movement that is clearly
modeled on the African Methodist Episcopal (AME) Church. After his return
to southern Africa, Nelson holds council in Northern Rhodesia (later to
become Zambia), where he begins to set in motion his plans for ending white
control of South Africa and for initiating his political ideal of a black Africa.
Nelson is often referred to as a Bishop, an appellation that evokes leaders of the
AME such as Bishop Henry M. Turner, the "black Moses" who visited South
Africa in 1898 and inspired the most significant "back-to-Africa" movement
among Afro-Americans before Marcus Garvey's campaign after the First
World War. Apparently Turner considered expanding his political aspirations
beyond West Africa into the southern and central regions of the continent,
and like Horatio Scott, an AME missionary in Port Elizabeth, Turner was
greatly impressed by South Africa's possibilities.[52] *Bayete!* thus references white
fears that Afro-Americans, "hungering for a land of their own," would start
spreading in South Africa a message of "Africa for the Africans."

Because of his anxieties about the novel's "effect in the light of day," Heaton
Nicholls claims to have sought advice on whether to proceed with publication.
His first publisher advised him against publication, as did the leader of the
South African Party, Jan Smuts. Heaton Nicholls then received encouragement
from "a Dutch South African, a writer of repute, a public man whose name is
known throughout the land," who was none other than the Afrikaans nationalist poet C.J. Langenhoven (most famous for composing the apartheid-era
national anthem, *Die Stem*), who had the following response:

> If it does awaken the native it will, to more effectual purpose, awaken the
> Whites. We are up against factors which operate with the relentless doom of
> natural laws. . . . So far as that result may be counteracted, its avoidance will
> be accomplished, if at all, by white superiority.[53]

Although *Bayete!* was only published in 1923, in the foreword Heaton Nicholls
attests that he completed the manuscript in 1913, and, in a confession of multiple reluctance, professes that during the intervening years it had "lain in the
dust, partly forgotten, partly in doubt of its worth: but largely in fear of its

effect in the light of day."[54] Leaving aside for a moment his fear about the effect
of *Bayete!* in stirring up black resistance, one sees here a classic anxiety over
authorship ("partly in doubt of its worth") that links, as was the case with
Webb Hardy, anxieties about interracial desire between white women and
black men to a contest over textual authority and worth. Foregrounded in the
novel is the relationship between the eloquent Nelson, messianic leader of a
black resistance movement, and the New Woman, Olive Garth, a novelist,
radical, and "negrophilist" who is clearly modeled on Olive Schreiner. Introducing a text that displays profound anxiety about the emerging voice of black
resistance, and writing under the shadow of his great literary predecessor,
Schreiner, Heaton Nicholls excuses his novel as "very crudely told, perhaps,
and lacking the skilful touch of the accomplished storyteller,"[55] while he brutally silences both Nelson and Olive in *Bayete!* At the heart of this novel one
finds extreme apprehension about the political demands and potential of the
educated black man and the New Woman.

Importantly, Nelson's status as a "noble savage," as a semi-heroic figure, is
made possible by a foreclosure in his racial categorization. Although we see
him becoming chief of the Matabele in the Prologue, he is an Arab whose
education and composure set him apart from his black African followers. Nelson is thus necessarily Orientalized and contrasted with indigenous southern
Africans. What makes Nelson dignified is his resemblance to Europeans, and
his physical appearance becomes a way of negotiating the more radical other-
ness of southern Africans: "His classic features, lofty brow, thin lips, straight
silky hair, light brown skin, and the dignity of his bearing, were in marked
contrast with the curly-haired, thick-lipped, careless, credulous [Africans]
who sat at his feet."[56] Nelson is also contrasted with American "negroes" who
have "thick lips" and "squab" faces. Similarly, Nelson's wife is set apart from
black southern Africans, as she bears the Greek name Zena, has "light skin . . .
[which] proclaimed her also to be of Arab descent," and "had the manner and
bearing" of "a Greek lady."[57] Yet the character of Zena registers white anxiety
about the increasing role black women were playing in the battle against white
oppression.

In South Africa as in the United States, it was not only black men who
expressed resistance to white domination. Hazel Carby notes that in America
at the turn of the century African-American women intellectuals such as Frances Harper, Anna Julia Cooper, Ida B. Wells, and Pauline Hopkins produced
essays, journalism, and novels that "theorized about the possibilities and limits
of patriarchal power through its manipulation of racialized and gendered
social categories and practices."[58]

In South Africa too, white patriarchal oppression was denounced by black
women intellectuals such as Charlotte Maxeke (née Manye), who graduated
from Wilberforce University in 1905 under the tutelage of Du Bois, and then
returned to South Africa where she organized the SANNC's first anti-pass

demonstrations in the Orange Free State in 1913 and famously founded the Bantu Women's League, a forerunner of the ANC Women's League, in 1919. Like Maxeke, Josie Palmer (Mpama), who wrote for *Umsebenzi*, the journal of the Communist Party of South Africa in the 1920s and 1930s, was involved in anti-pass demonstrations. By the 1920s, the impact of educated black women was being felt even in remote rural areas in South Africa. In June 1926, for example, the secretary for Native Affairs, Major Herbst, speaking at a public meeting in the Herschel district, a large reserve bordering on Basutoland (now Lesotho), said that he was shocked to see women present and "even women taking notes." Reflecting the ways in which black women were voicing political dissent and initiating trading store and school boycotts, Herbst said that General Hertzog, the prime minister and minister of Native Affairs, had wished to come to see the situation for himself "as they are a topsy-turvy people here, and women take part in hostilities, he wanted to see these belli-cose women who frighten teachers and caused certain people to ask for more police." Herbst's refusal to allow women to speak at the meeting provoked further disturbances, and three months later the resident magistrate told an-other meeting that during the trial of twenty-seven women who were subse-quently arrested in connection with the schools boycott he had had to call in mounted police to control women who behaved "like wild animals." He went on to say that "if the men cannot keep their women in order I shall." Appar-ently challenging the men to demonstrate their masculinity and discipline their wives by customary and, possibly, violent means, he went on to indicate that it was not for him "to say how they must do it. They are heads of kraals and are responsible." Casting doubt on the ability of women to act indepen-dently, he added that "he had never heard before that women could interfere in such matters," and that he knew who the men behind the women's move-ment were.[59]

In South African "black peril" novels of the early twentieth century, anxiety about educated black women entering the political realm is resolved either by showing the black woman as sexually rampant and intellectually stunted, or else by demonizing the black woman intellectual. Although there is a certain amount of sympathy for black female characters in a novel such as Francis Bancroft's *Of Like Passions*, the black woman in Bancroft's novel is nonetheless reduced to her sexuality. On the other hand, the black woman intellectual haunts Heaton Nicholls's novel *Bayete!*, where it is Zena, doppelgänger to Olive, whose actions present a pivotal moment in the narrative as she attempts to destroy the white nation, with a pistol shot aimed at the heart of the white woman. Like activists such as Ida B. Wells in the United States and the South African-born Charlotte Maxeke, Zena is an educated black woman with access to a typewriter, and like dangerous radical women such as Haymarket widow Lucy Parsons, or the French revolution's Charlotte Corday, to whom Wells was often likened,[60] Zena is demonized as a murderess.

Olive concedes that she is "infatuated"[61] with Nelson, but Nelson, however, ultimately descends into barbarity when he reaches for the physical love of the white woman. After he tries to kiss Olive in the last few pages of the novel, an action that corresponds with the national uprising of black laborers and servants against their white oppressors, he is instantly bestialized in Olive's eyes:

> How was it that she had been blind to his character all these years? . . . Love for him! She hated him. The idol of years was battered into the dust. She had been defiled by contact with him. The sting of his hot bestial kisses still burnt her lips, and the thought of them, the thought of feeling again his strong arms about her, disgusted beyond measure.[62]

After this encounter, Nelson locks Olive in a room, and their previous friendship descends into a captivity narrative where she becomes the stereotypical image of a female hysteric who "has lain on the couch all the day and has eaten nothing."[63] As with the New Woman Mary Roseberry in Webb Hardy's *The Black Peril*, Olive is transformed, despite her previous strength and independence, at the moment of the "black peril" scene into the embodiment of hyper-vulnerable white femininity. The connection between this femininity and the status of the nation is emphasized by the fact that Olive has now become the wife of the Prime Minister, John Bowden, and as "queenly"[64] mother to the country, her potential defilement at the hands of Nelson suggests the imperiled status of the white nation.[65]

As is the case in Webb Hardy's *The Black Peril*, *Bayete!* registers unease about the relationship between the white madam and her "houseboy." The "black peril" scene between Olive and Nelson mirrors an account earlier in the novel where a white woman, Phyllis Stultz, is attacked by her houseboy, Mukwasi, with whom she has encouraged a "familiar" relationship by allowing him to assist her with intimate acts of dressing:

> She turned her back to him, the fine linen and lace of her undergarments all exposed. "Fasten up my dress," she said, eyeing his moving countenance in the glass. The Kaffir towered over her, his eyes wide open and burning with excitement. . . . His fingers rested on her warm white skin; his breath came hot upon her neck; her wavy scented hair brushed his face. For a moment he seemed to be intoxicated and fumbled at his task.[66]

When we next come across Mukwasi and Phyllis alone, he is literally intoxicated, with "the liquor [making] the animal dominant," and the meaning of his gaze and touch are read utterly differently by Phyllis:

> He lurched forward; and there was that in his face which filled her with sudden realization of his meaning. For the first time she thought of the manner in which she was attired. Her arm fell, and she feverishly gathered her arm around her ample bosom. . . . She watched him coming, saw the black hands

getting nearer and nearer. And then he touched her, as if to soothe her. The contact had the effect of a galvanic shock, and, for the first time, there rose involuntarily to her lips a piercing shriek. . . . She sent another chasing after it before Mukwasi crushed her to him with one hand, while he placed the other over her mouth with brute ferocity.[67]

As with "Jim" in Webb Hardy's novel, the illiterate black man is here an object whose meaning the white woman, to her peril, has previously misread, and the moment of illumination comes when she recognizes the irreducibility of his bestial nature. For having failed to see that Mukwasi's sexual drive is that of a man, "with a man's lustful purpose," Phyllis is, like Olive, subjected by the author to a sadistic act of disciplining and silencing: "Mukwasi crushed her to him with one hand, *while he placed the other over her mouth* with brute ferocity [my emphasis]." As mentioned in the beginning of this chapter, this "black peril" incident is prefigured by Mukwasi's attempt to be "like a white man" through an act of reading. Taking up the newspaper and holding it upside-down, he looks around as if asking: "Now, am I not like a white man?"[68] Here are registered white anxieties about black print culture and reading publics, as well as rivalry over access to the type of education that would enable black men to compete with whites in the public realm and the political arena.

This is furthered in the representation of Nelson, who is represented as educated and as a gifted public speaker. The prologue of the novel describes the power of his rhetoric as he presents a rousing speech to his followers in which he states that he will "go and steal from the Whites all the knowledge that has made them powerful." His desire for usurpation of this knowledge takes him to America, where he meets Olive and her father, and interestingly, the novel shows transnational links between southern Africa and the southern United States in terms of both white supremacy and black resistance. The first chapter opens with Colonel Garth's approval as he watches a group of laboring African Americans: "Well, well!" he says to himself, "One has to come to America to learn something about the Kafir." A few pages later, this happy image of black labor is overturned by a focus on black speakers who address their audience on the subject of resistance to white supremacy. The meeting begins with the words of a "benevolent keen-eyed negro, with a mass of white hair," who states that his black audience members have "their homes in Africa." Nelson, who speaks after him and hopes to use the evangelical movement to unify black Africans in his home country against their oppressors, further develops the notion of "Africa for the Africans" in his address.[69]

Throughout the novel the reader is reminded of the power of Nelson's oratory: there are numerous references to his "deep sonorous voice,"[70] to his phallic intensity as a public speaker ("he stood erect"[71]), and to the effect his speeches have on black audiences, who for the most part degenerate into a writhing, slobbering mob of worshippers.[72] Nelson's eloquence is contrasted with the speech of his African rival Sigananda, whose superstitious mouth is "full of medicine, rendering articulation difficult," and who encourages open warfare, rather than more strategic and sophisticated forms of insurgency. In the first meeting between Olive and Nelson in America we are told that Nelson has "spoken at twenty meetings during the past seven days," and he reveals his immersion in a culture of letters by telling her that he "sat up all the night reading" her novel. He then goes on to speak "without restraint," telling her "stories of lynchings in many States, of innocent negroes tied to oil boxes and set on fire, of others diabolically tortured in ways that would have disgraced the Spanish Inquisition." As Olive listens intently through the feminized organ of the ear, she receives Nelson's words and enters a state of arousal, and when her party drives away, she sinks "back in the cushions thinking of the wonderful man who stood in the roadway watching the car out of sight."[73]

The power of black political articulation is echoed in Nelson's plan for ending white dominance, which comes to fruition at the end of Book III, where he uses labor strikes to force through a Bill making allowance for black enfranchisement. In this respect he represents Heaton Nicholls's worst fears. Nelson uses black political voice, the black vote, in order to bring white supremacy to an end. After his victory, Nelson walks with Olive through the Edenic gardens of the Prime Minister's residence like a lover, and she thrills to the sound of his voice as they look out over Cape Town: "Under the inspiration of his sonorous voice she found a new beauty in the familiar scene, and abandoning herself to the influence of the moment, she pictured a magic city of peace and love."[74] In a narrative that draws heavily on Milton's *Paradise Lost*, Nelson is sketched as part Messiah, part Satanic seducer. While he begins as an heroic and even sympathetic figure, he is gradually debased, and, as a way of defusing eloquently-argued black political demands, the reader is eventually told that he has "all the subtlety of the devil."[75]

If Nelson presents the figure of the good-looking Satanic revolutionary, Olive is for most of the novel his more-than-willing Eve, who is seduced not only by the power of his voice, but also by the idea that she may have a higher destiny. By the end of the novel, she has contributed to the fall of white rule, and has betrayed her husband and kinsmen by telling Nelson of a plot against him. As with Nelson, foregrounded in Olive's character is her "fine intellect," her natural inclination to "struggle and revolt," and her strong political and literary voice, evidenced in the title of her utopian novel, *Voice of the Veld*. Like her namesake, Olive Schreiner, Olive in *Bayete!* presents the figure of the New Woman whose political opinions enter the public realm. Her status as a woman who speaks in public is displayed when she gives a report at an assembly of the "Native Girls Guild," where her somewhat lackluster performance is turned around when Nelson enters the room: "Her voice took on a richer tone, and even had a touch of gaiety in it. Her speech which followed was eloquent and witty."[76] Discrediting women such as Schreiner who were speaking out on behalf of the oppressed, the novel thus infers that Olive's passionate political commitment is driven by "negrophilist" inclinations, by her "infatuation" with Nelson. In this respect, the novel uses the same strategy that had been used to cast doubt upon Catherine Impey, the Englishwoman who visited America, collaborated with African American intellectuals such as Douglass and Wells, and published the anti-racist journal *Anti-Caste*. After disclosing her affections for a black man, Impey was discredited by other reformers who suggested that she was "nymphomaniac" and was "failing mentally." As Patricia Schechter points out, such a "taint of immorality could jeopardize this new cohort of women activists because a female's social authority was only as secure as her reputation for chastity."[77]

The "black peril" scene between Olive and Nelson that takes place in the last section of *Bayete!* signals the end of collaboration between these two characters, and by the end of the novel both are finally silenced, as Olive is shot by the jealous and enraged Zena, and Nelson receives a mortal wound in the interracial skirmishes that have broken out in Cape Town. Tensions are thus resolved in the novel by silencing the voices of the black man and the New Woman.[78]

In "Signs Taken for Wonders," Homi Bhabha draws attention to a scenario "played out in the wild and wordless wastes of colonial India, Africa, the Caribbean, of the sudden, fortuitous discovery of the English book." According to Bhabha, in the colonial context, the "emblem of the English book" becomes a "wondrous presence" that operates as "an insignia of colonial authority and a signifier of colonial desire and discipline." Inducting the "natives" in a tradition of English literature, turning them into educated mimic men, becomes a mode of asserting colonial power.[79] Yet there is another view of literature that emerges in the settler society of early twentieth-century South Africa, the notion of access to a culture of letters as a mode of contaminating the "native," of literature as a dangerous and corrupting force that leads, among other things, to the "black peril." In "black peril" novels such as *Bayete!* and *The Black Peril*, the educated black man, and the black public speaker in particular, is a figure whose prospect provokes immense consternation. For Heaton Nicholls, the erudite African simultaneously preaches the end of white rule and menaces the white woman, and Webb Hardy's novel reveals a desire to mute the threat posed by black political utterance, as the lustful "houseboy," "Jim," is reduced to a stammering creature who has no wish to learn English. As expressed in these novels, "black peril" fear was linked to the prospect of educated Africans in settlement colonies competing with white men, for jobs, for women, and also for political and textual authority. As I shall demonstrate in the chapters that follow, more sophisticated and self-conscious explorations of race and sex may be found in the work of writers such as Plaatje, and more complex engagements with the fraught and ambivalent relations between white women and their black menservants in southern Africa may be found in later novels such as J.M. Coetzee's *In the Heart of the Country* (1977) and *Disgrace* (1999).

Yet early "black peril" narratives are integral to any understanding of South African history and literature, as they have proved to be of long-lasting cultural effect. Not only did such stories, read at home and abroad, play a role in justifying the foundational legislations of segregation and apartheid, but they also set the tone for writers such as Arthur Maimane, who reterritorialized constructions of black masculinity under apartheid. It is worth noting that there has even been some reclamation and playback of "black peril" stereotypes in the post-apartheid cultural context, where a soccer team sports the name "Dangerous Darkies," and a duo of rappers have chosen to be known as "Zulu Mobb." Despite the subversive potential that inheres in such performativity, reports and readings of sexual violence in South Africa continue to be infected by the past, and it is vital to understand early twentieth-century "black peril" narratives as a frame of reference for representations of sexual violence under apartheid and in the post-apartheid environment.

"A 'Black' or a 'White' Peril?"

WRITING THE MELANCHOLY (ALTER)NATION

In July 1914, addressing the British House of Commons on the subject of the South African Natives Land Act, the Colonial Secretary, Lewis Harcourt, claimed that arguments for racial segregation in South Africa had been "reinforced by the occurrence of cases of Black Peril, which we have had to regret, and with which we have had to deal in recent years."[1] Thus it was that the Land Act of 1913, one of the first and longest-lasting of the segregation laws that were to harden into the backbone of the system known as apartheid, was justified with reference to "the black peril." Present in the visitors gallery at this House of Commons debate was Solomon Tshekisho Plaatje (1876–1932),[2] the writer and first secretary-general of the South African Natives National Congress (SANNC, later ANC), who saw in the Act a violent enforcement of dispossession: "Awaking on Friday morning, June 20, 1913, the South African Native found himself, not actually a slave, but a pariah in the land of his birth."[3] A member of the class of educated South African black men who were increasingly making themselves heard on political issues, and whose voices (as argued in the previous chapter) inspired "black peril" anxiety among whites within South Africa, Plaatje later toured the United States, where in 1921 he published *The Mote and the Beam: An Epic on Sex-relationship 'twixt White and Black in British South Africa*. In *The Mote and the Beam*, Plaatje directly challenges "black peril" rhetoric with the question "Is it a 'Black' or a 'White' Peril?" Taking the melancholic obsession with interracial rape that appears in South African literature as a starting point, this chapter examines alternating stories of "black" and "white" peril from segregation into the period of early apartheid. The texts that are the main focus of the analysis are Sol Plaatje's *The Mote and the Beam* (1921), the fiction of Sarah Gertrude Millin, which spans the period from the 1920s to the 1960s, and the novels of Daphne Rooke published in the 1950s and 1960s.

In 1927, two years after the publication of William Plomer's *Turbott Wolfe*, a novel that explores precisely the theme of "miscegenation," an immorality act prohibited interracial sex in the Union. Whereas an earlier law had made consorting between white women and black men illegal in the Transvaal, this new act outlawed sex between white women and black men as well as between white men and black women. The act did not legislate against sex between white, "coloured", and Indian people, nor did it forbid interracial marriage, yet the record shows that such marriages were extremely rare. Despite this fact that "mixed" unions were becoming increasingly infrequent, the period from the late 1920s to the introduction of apartheid in the late 1940s saw a dramatic increase in political rhetoric around "mixed" marriages, particularly in the idea that black and Indian men were preying on white women.

In his article "White Working-Class Women and the Invention of Apartheid," Jonathan Hyslop argues that the intensification of political discourse on interracial marriages in the 1930s was directly related to the proletarianization of Afrikaner women, who were leaving farms and seeking work in the factories and industries of the urban areas during and after the Depression. Hyslop points out that social hierarchies were upset by white women entering the workforce and that white patriarchal authority was challenged by the enfranchisement of white women in 1930. The result was that issues of class and gender were foregrounded in the election campaigns of D.F. Malan's "Purified" National Party and became vital to "the invention of apartheid." The rise of apartheid thinking, in Hyslop's analysis, has its social foundations in "shifting gender relations among Afrikaners which arose from the growing social and economic independence of women," and Hyslop's analysis is meant, as he himself claims, to challenge "post-structuralist" inflected accounts such as J.M. Coetzee's essay "Apartheid Thinking," which argues that apartheid was a phenomenon of collective insanity in which leaders themselves were ensnared.[4] By contrast, Hyslop attempts to show that apartheid had its roots in social and economic conditions, in "hard-line nationalists" consciously taking advantage of public antipathy to "mixed" marriages. Hyslop is at pains to argue that the Nationalists adopted their antagonistic stance to mixed marriages as a means of attracting the votes of a white Afrikaner electorate, yet, as he himself points out, initially voters did not prioritize this as an issue. Moreover, to say that hysteria around "mixed" marriage was instrumental in dealing with economic threats to white patriarchal authority does not prove that political leaders were any less caught up in what Coetzee calls the "phantasmic transaction" than the white voters whom they represented. As noted in 1937 by I. D. MacCrone, a critic of scientific racism and at that time professor of Psychology at the University of the Witwatersrand: "Economic factors, if they are to have any effect upon group prejudice, must presuppose the existence of the psychologically prior division into an in- and out-group. It is not because of their economic competition that Jews and Japanese excite hostility, but it is because they are Jews and Japanese that their competition is unfair, or underhand, or an offence to those who are neither Jews nor Japanese."[5]

MacCrone's *Race Attitudes in South Africa* studies the ways in which "the racial situation . . . has become almost an obsession in the minds of many both within as well as to some extent beyond, the borders of the Union."[6] Among other surveys, MacCrone records the following statements when anonymous white women were asked to describe any dream in which "a native or black appeared":

> I dreamt that as I walked home late one afternoon a native began to chase me—I woke up paralysed with fear; frequently a dream of a native chasing me with a gleaming knife in the one hand; dreamt that a native was chasing me and my legs would not move; I have often dreamt of natives and Indians—they have usually chased me with knives, &c., or burgling the house, and the dreams have been extremely terrifying; I have often dreamt—especially as a child, that a native man was chasing me and I was unable to run away; a native came in through my bedroom window with a knife—I fled pretending I didn't see him and wasn't afraid; . . . I once dreamt that a native was standing in my room—the fact that he was there caused me to shriek with fear; a very repulsive dream in which I was not able to escape from native who had me in a corner and was just about to touch me—I was powerless; I have dreamt that I was left at home alone and that a native entered and tried to choke me . . .[7]

A decade and a half later, Frantz Fanon would offer a similar investigation in which he "questioned some 500 members of the white race." Noting that more than half of the respondents associated "Negro" with "biology, penis . . . savage, animal, devil, sin," Fanon proposed that the racist world view is characterized by "Manichaean delirium" in which things are divided into "Good-Evil, Beauty-Ugliness, White-Black."[8] As suggested by typical "black peril" narratives and even some "white peril" narratives such as those scripted by Millin, the success of biological racism, the delusion of racial purity, has been its ability to resonate with deep-held affective phobias of contamination and abjection, and as Fanon notes, "In the phobic, affect has a priority that defies all rational thinking."[9]

Of the writers examined in this chapter, Sol Plaatje and Dora Taylor are the closest to being "possibilist," in that Plaatje imagines the prospect of "mixed-race" children being "born of true parental love," and Taylor's "To Tell my Story" (1960) acknowledges the love between a black man and a white woman. Plaatje's main focus in *The Mote and the Beam*, however, is on the wiles of white women in seducing their black menservants, and on the sexual coercion that black women suffer at the hands of white men. As I shall demonstrate, his retrieval of these hidden narratives is meant to give the other side of story to the "black peril," and appears within a transnational discourse of resistance to white supremacy. In the novels of Millin, on the other hand, images of the "white peril" are deployed in order to emphasize the undesirability of "miscegenation." Although there are elements in Millin's fiction that destabilize the author's racialist agenda, the ends to which she uses "white peril" stories suggest that these representations were easily commensurate with the liberal segregationist discourse that was complicit in laying the groundwork for apartheid. Interest-ingly, Millin's shift in the 1960s to becoming a supporter of Verwoerd's Nation-alist Party government corresponds with the movement in her creative output from "white peril" representations to classic "black peril" imagery. In its de-ployment of "black peril" stereotypes, her novel *The Wizard Bird* (1962) may be usefully contrasted with Taylor's "To Tell My Story" (1960). As I argue, while in Millin's view interracial desire remains profoundly debased, "To Tell My Story" could be read as a literary expression of mourning as it acknowledges interra-cial love while showing the ways in which the pressures of a racist society ren-der such love impossible.

With the onset of apartheid, literature came under increasing scrutiny by the state, and although the "black peril" imagery of Millin's *Wizard Bird* (1961) did not attract any attention from the censors, the banning of Rooke's *The Greyling* (1962) registers that "white peril" narratives, which questioned white men's obedience to apartheid laws of sexual segregation, were regarded as of-fensive. As in the case of Rooke, censorship led writers and publishers to prac-tice self-surveillance, to formulate and amend manuscripts before publication in order to avoid banning. In the last section of this chapter I examine discrep-ancies between two editions of Rooke's *Mittee*, one published in America and the other circulated in South Africa, and discuss the extent to which Rooke focuses not only on "white peril" or "black peril," but also draws attention to intraracial sexual violence.

A Transatlantic Sex Tract: Sol Plaatje's *The Mote and the Beam*

In May 1921, Sol Plaatje attended in Boston a public celebration of the banning by the city of D.W. Griffith's *Birth of a Nation*, the notorious film adaptation of *The Clansman* by Thomas Dixon, who is called by one commentator "the most famous propagator of the trope of the black rapist" in America.[10] Earlier in 1921 Plaatje had begun disseminating during his public appearances in America *The Mote and the Beam*, which evidently struck a chord with readers in the United States, becoming Plaatje's bestselling publication in his lifetime. Like the work of the African American civil rights activist and anti-lynching cru-sader, Ida B. Wells (1862–1931), *The Mote and the Beam* counters the myth of the black rapist that was used to justify racist measures and white supremacy. In its focus on interracial sex from the perspective of a black man, Plaatje's pamphlet also resonates with the work of Plaatje's "pro-miscegenation" Afri-can American contemporary, Joel Augustus Rogers (c. 1880–1966). Moreover, as in the story "The Black Peril" (1927), by a fellow South African writer, Wil-liam Plomer (1903–1973), Plaatje disputes representations of black men as lustful and depraved, offering accounts of white seductresses or "mesdames Potiphar."[11] While his evocation of "the white peril," those white men who "flood the country with illegitimate half-castes,"[12] points forward to the fiction of Sarah Gertrude Millin, who uses such representations to render interracial desire as abject and damned, in *The Mote and the Beam* Plaatje is able to document interracial desire beyond the melancholy options of either "black peril" or "white peril."

Born in the Orange Free State in 1876, Plaatje was an African of Barolong ancestry, who, as his biographer Brian Willan points out, was "in the forefront of the public affairs of the African people for the greater part of his adult life, one of their best known leaders and spokesmen and a prolific writer and journalist."[13] As well as being one of the founding members and the first secretary-general of the SANNC, Plaatje was a pioneer of the African press, working both as an editor and journalist, and was the author of numerous pamphlets as well as his major political tract, *Native Life in South Africa* (1916), and *Mhudi* (1930), the first novel written in English by a black South African. A polymath, he was an academic linguist and translator of Shakespeare into the Tswana language. Plaatje travelled twice overseas to represent the interests of black South Africans, once to Great Britain in 1914–17 as part of a delegation sent to protest against the Land Act, and then again to Britain and France in 1919–1920, and on to Canada and the United States in 1920–22. Heard and read in America as an outspoken critic of the conditions of dispossession and subjugation under which black South Africans were increasingly being forced to live, he spoke alongside W.E.B. Du Bois and Marcus Garvey, and stayed in Chicago with Ida B. Wells, who was by this time elderly, but one of the most respected black activists of her generation.[14] Published and distributed on the visit to America in which Plaatje stayed with Wells, *The Mote and the Beam*, which Willan describes somewhat dismissively as "a curious little pamphlet and unlike anything else Plaatje wrote,"[15] was, in fact, the first major attempt by a black South African to write about sexuality, and particularly about the vexed question of interracial sex.

The Mote and the Beam was printed on both sides of the Atlantic: as a pamphlet of about four by seven inches published by Young's Book Exchange in New York; and in *Tsala ea Batho*, the Kimberley newspaper that Plaatje had established in 1912. In the United States the slim pamphlet of twelve pages sold at 25 cents (or $2.40 per dozen), which was not cheap, but, by the time he left the United States, Plaatje claimed that he had sold 18,000 copies.[16] To some extent, the success of *The Mote and the Beam* in America could be attributed to its risqué subject matter, as well as to the currency that the myth of the black rapist and the sense of injustice that this generated among black readers (and some progressive white readers) had across the Atlantic.[17] Plaatje's pamphlet was reviewed in Marcus Garvey's newspaper, *Negro World*, which often printed material about Africa and South Africa, and in the same issue ran stories with the headlines: "Southern brutes lynch mother and son" and "Roughhousing of a black man acquitted of assaulting a white woman."

Indeed, although the reviewer, Hubert H. Harrison, thought the pamphlet too expensive, he emphasized that the topics Plaatje was addressing were directly relevant to an African American readership:

> ... the chief value of this pamphlet to African Americans is to demonstrate to them that their provincial notion of the unique character of race prejudice in this country is entirely wrong. Every feature of outrage and hypocrisy, of cruelty and legalised social injustice with which we are acquainted 'in the land of the free and home of the brave' is duplicated in the USA i.e. The Union of South Africa.[18]

The comparability to which Harrison alludes here was later to become the subject of pioneering historical studies such as George Frederickson's *White Supremacy: A Comparative Study on American and South African History* (1981), Stanley Greenberg's *Race and State in Capitalist Development* (1980), and John Cell's *The Highest Stage of White Supremacy: The Origins of Segregation in South Africa and the American South* (1982). However, these analyses do not engage in a sustained manner with the issue of sexuality and this lacuna has not been filled in more recent comparative studies. A special issue of the *Journal of Southern African Studies* published in 2004 offers a collection of essays "comparing race and labour in South Africa and the United States" from the late nineteenth century to 1950, without any contributions exploring the enmeshment of labor issues with white paranoia about black rape across the two contexts.[19] Issues that have been overlooked in historical comparisons of South Africa and the United States include the ways in which images of the black rapist and the mutilated body of the white woman came to symbolize threats to white authority and authorship in both contexts, and also the extent to which black writers in both countries engaged with these stereotypes. Given these omissions, I would like to draw attention to the importance of *The Mote and the Beam* as a southern African sex tract in America and to highlight the resonance between the pamphlet and the work of black American writers.

One of these writers, Ida B. Wells, was a black newspaper editor and journalist, as well as the author of political pamphlets. Although, like Plaatje, Wells had no tertiary education, by the turn of the century she was the leading civil rights activist in America and "was better known than W.E.B. Du Bois and more ideologically compatible with [Frederick] Douglass than Booker T. Washington—the two men who eventually became the main contenders to fill Douglass's shoes."[20] During her early career, Wells became a target of threatened violence when she published in her Memphis newspaper, *Free Speech*, an editorial disclaiming charges of rape that were used to justify the lynching of black men. Arousing the ire of Southern whites, Wells suggested that white women became sexually involved with black men of their own volition, only to cry rape when they feared exposure. Wells's graphic and deliberately shocking writings on lynching, which she produced tirelessly from the 1890s, and which

Plaatje would have read, resonate with the form and content of *The Mote and the Beam*.

Plaatje begins his tract with the statement that he does "not want to write about it," but justifies himself by claiming that he is giving "the other side" of the picture presented by "white contributors to the daily press." He refers to his subject matter as "painful" and expresses a "fear of wounding the susceptibilities of the more sensitive of [his] readers."[21] While intimating that he was addressing the topic with some trepidation, this opening page no doubt served to arouse the curiosity of readers, and contributed to the sales of the exposé. Plaatje's pamphlet opens with a paragraph in which the author eschews any prurient motivation in his choice of subject matter, and in the preface to *Southern Horrors: Southern Lynch Law in All its Phases* (1892) Wells similarly claims "It is with no pleasure I have dipped my hands in the corruption here exposed."[22] Like Plaatje's pamphlet, *Southern Horrors* combines the characteristics of politicized protest, journalism and charismatic sermonizing, and calls the reader into account through rhetorical questions.[23] "Has it a motive?," Wells demands of the silence in the press on certain racial issues. Similarly, Plaatje frames his conclusion as a question with the heading: "Is it a 'Black' or a 'White' Peril?" In their writings, both Wells and Plaatje draw attention to what Plaatje called "the white peril," the sexual exploitation of black women by white men. Wells documents instances of black women becoming victims of sexual assault at the hands of white men, and in a comparable way, *The Mote and the Beam* points to the white man who sexually exploits black women as a "moral leper" who "holds the destiny of our unfortunate country in the hollow of his unholy hands."[24]

In *Southern Horrors* Wells develops the idea that "white women willingly consorted with black men until someone in the white community discovered their liaisons; then to save their reputations, the women either screamed rape of their own volition or were forced to do so by the avenging mobs."[25] Documenting cases of consensual sex being reported as rape, she urges her readers to read newspaper reports of lynchings with a critical eye, arguing that the truth obscured by these narratives is something that "we owe it to ourselves to find out." Towards the end of *The Mote and the Beam* Plaatje claims that white women's intercepted attempts to seduce black men have often been reported "in flaring headlines, such, for instance, as 'Another black peril case', 'Outrageous attack on a white lady', 'The brute caught in the nick of time', 'Providential rescue of victim in a fainting condition.'"[26] One of the most notable points of congruency between *Southern Horrors* and *The Mote and the Beam* is thus that both are directed against white newspapers that peddle stereotypes of a rapacious black masculinity.

In his review of *The Mote and the Beam* in *Negro World*, Harrison praised the pamphlet as "nifty" in drawing attention to white hypocrisy, and particularly to the ways in which black men were blamed for the attraction felt for them by white women:

Mr Plaatje points out that the gist of the complaints made by white men as to black men's love for white women is really the fact that white women have begun to exercise on their own account the sexual mixing and mingling which has been for so many years an exclusive privilege of white men. In short, as Mr Rogers points out in "As Nature Leads," white women, when given a free choice to express their freedom of choice, do like to become acquainted, in more than one way, with black men.[27]

Like Plaatje, Jamaica-born Rogers was a pioneering black commentator on interracial sex, and his work, *As Nature Leads: An Informal Discussion of the Reason Why Negro and Caucasian are Mixing in Spite of Opposition*, was published in the United States in 1919. Written at a time when a wave of Jim Crow bills was sweeping the United States and many states enforced a ban on interracial marriage, Rogers's pro-"miscegenation" ideas are presented through the fictional conversations, letters, and notes of three black friends, and draw on social and natural science and evolutionary thinking in order to show that "Caucasians . . . mix and persist in mixing with the Negro."[28] *The Mote and the Beam* resonates with Rogers's text in its foregrounding of the prevalence of interracial sexual attraction despite prohibitive attitudes and legislation.

What is interesting about Plaatje's analysis of the taboo on interracial sex is that his rhetoric at once reasons alongside racist thinking, and simultaneously shows it to be not only hypocritical, but also historically determined, even temporary and out of date. Criticizing white South Africans for their double standards in legislating against white and black people living in the same street while white men sleep "in the bare arms" of black women, he claims that if South Africa is to legislate against interracial socializing this should be followed through to its logical conclusion:

There was a time when it was an abomination for a Basuto to have social intercourse with Shangaans, and when Bechuana custom forbade intermarriage with Matabele. They carried their prejudice to its logical conclusion and allowed no exceptions in favour of illegitimate unions with Shangaan or Matabele girls. But a white South African apparently finds no paradox in procreating illegitimate half-castes with the girls of the race he looks down upon.[29]

Here the phrase "there was a time" suggests that the ban on socialization and sex between different groups or races is a temporary "prejudice" rather than something that demands any weightier consideration. The passage can also be read as dryly ironic. Reversing the colonial myth of white progress versus "native" backwardness, Plaatje implies that the black races have evolved beyond bigotry, unlike whites who have not.

Within South Africa, Plaatje was not the only major literary figure to examine the "black peril" with a critical eye in the 1920s. Like Plaatje, Wells, and

Rogers (who mentions the "terrible penalty"[30] of black men's desire for white women), in his short story "Black Peril" William Plomer confronts the ways in which consensual sex between black men and white women is "read" as rape. In this story, a white woman seduces her black manservant, but confined to bed in the manner of a nineteenth-century hysteric, she expires dramatically, "her head hanging downwards, so that her earrings are hanging upside down."[31] Her death is followed by newspaper posters claiming: "Frightful Outrage in Town, Society Woman Victim, Dies of Shock." As with the work of Wells and Plaatje, Plomer draws attention to the hollowness of "black peril" stereotypes in white newspapers, but his story also foregrounds the melancholy symptoms of a foreclosure in the field of desire. In the opening paragraphs, the woman's husband is confronted by an unbearable whiteness: the "starched" clothes and "white veil" of the nurse's uniform, the "white suit of the doctor," the sun reflecting on "white walls," and his wife's "white face on the pillow." White endogamy, centered on the white woman's body as a fetishized and medicalized object, has become all-pervasive and claustrophobic, incapable of recognizing interracial desire. Turning the order of settler society on its head, the white woman who has acted on her attraction for a black man dies, not of shock, Plomer suggests, but of the irreconcilable contradictions of her position. Her lost love object has become, to borrow Judith Butler's words, precisely "the unthinkable, the unlovable, the ungrievable."[32]

The reception in South Africa of Plomer's novel, *Turbott Wolfe* (1925), offers a gauge for measuring public antipathy towards interracial relationships. Attempting to confront the theme of "miscegenation," the novel nonetheless exhibits some squeamishness in approaching its subject. The protagonist of the story, "Chastity" Wolfe, is deeply attracted to a black woman, Nhliziyombi, but, finally unable to integrate with Africa or Africans, he retreats to London. At the same time, a fellow member of the Young Africa movement, a white woman named Mabel van der Horst, maintains a relationship with a black man, Zachary Msomi. Sketching the environment that Mabel and Zachary are up against, Plomer scripts an incident in which a black man is caught by a group of white men in a white woman's room, and is accused of rape and brutally castrated. Praised in Britain and America, the novel had an entirely different reception in South Africa. Laurens van der Post recalls: "Supporting the angry editorials, the correspondence columns of the daily papers carried letters of 'Mothers of five', 'Pro Bono Publicos' and so on and 'Bookworm' moaned that *Turbott Wolfe* was 'not cricket'."[33] Van der Post tells how his editor at the *Natal Advertiser* reviewed the novel with "a discharge of feelings of disapproval almost too violent to be endured."[34] Yet, as Peter Blair observes, Plomer's confrontation of the "doubly taboo" subject of a relationship between a white woman and a black man "proves too radical not only for his audience but for his protagonist, so much so that the novel risks undoing its own indictment of 'anti-miscegenation' prejudice."[35] Although Wolfe admires Mabel van der

Horst's actions in principle, the reality of her relationship with Zachary fills him with unease: "It was one thing to talk glibly about miscegenation, to fool about with an idea, and another to find oneself face to face with the actual happening: it was the difference between a box of matches and a house on fire."[36]

Like Fanon, who observes that it would be a mistake to see relationships in which "a soldier of the conquering army goes to bed with a Malagasy girl" or "Algerian colonists go to bed with their fourteen-year old housemaids" as demonstrating "a lack of racial conflicts,"[37] Plaatje notes that sexual relationships between white men and black women are largely expedient and exploitative. Nonetheless, Plaatje also acknowledges the possibility of interracial love, albeit distorted by prohibition. The Transvaal law, he points out, "prevents men from marrying their wives and forces them, sometimes against their wish—to make harlots of good mothers, adulteresses of potential housewives and bastards of *children born of true parental love* [my emphasis]."[38] Like Wells (who defended Catherine Impey's relationship with a black man and Frederick Douglass's marriage to a white woman) and Rogers, Plaatje was prepared to accept and defend interracial marriages. Although he is critical of cases where "the white peril" leads to the procreation of "children who are neither white nor black," his attitude thus differs from that of Sarah Gertrude Millin, who offers a scathing critique of interracial sex by linking interracial desire to racial degeneration.

Afraid of the Dark: Millin, Missionaries, and "Miscegenation"

In her first autobiography, *The Night is Long* (1941), Sarah Gertrude Millin (1889–1968), sifting through childhood memories in order to speculate upon the origins of her life-long insomnia, remembers lying awake at night, fearing that a man "with a big round yellow face" would come in through her window. Later in her autobiography, Millin elaborates on this image of peril, describing the yellow man as "Fate . . . laughing toothlessly as he pointed a derisive finger."[39] As J.M. Coetzee points out in his essay on Millin, however, physical descriptions in her work are never accidental or disinvested, but always ethnically encoded. Who or what then, is this uncanny yellow bogeyman? In her description of the Vaal River diggings on which she grew up alongside an assortment of families, not all of which were entirely white, Millin comments on the "yellowish" offspring of a white man and a black woman, and notes that "casual white men had left yellow children" in the "native" compounds.[40] Just as the nightmare man with his yellow face haunted her childhood (evoking the dreadful and uncanny Coppelius with his face of "yellow ochre" in E.T.A Hoffman's short story "The Sandman," on which Freud drew in his discussion of the uncanny),[41] Millin's writings reveal an obsession with the theme of "miscegenation." Like the theories of her contemporary Geoffrey Cronjé, Millin's racialistic ideas can be understood with reference to Foucault's idea of biopolitics, as her visceral abhorrence for "mixing of blood" is shown in the biopolitical language with which she damns it. Unlike Cronjé, however, with the exception of her "black peril" novel *The Wizard Bird*, published in the 1960s when Millin's political sympathies had swung in favor of the Nationalist Party government, there is little paranoia in Millin's writing about protecting potential mothers of the white race from the sexual advances of black men. Rather, Millin's major novels indict "the white peril" as the cause of racial degeneration, and "Fate," in the form of biological determinism, is made to fall heavily upon the "coloured" products of interracial mixing. In 1924, Adolf Hitler claimed that missionaries "turn healthy, though inferior, human beings into a rotten brood of bastards."[42] Although Millin was a Lithuanian-born Jew who was concerned about the anti-Semitism that was sweeping through Europe and South Africa in the 1930s and 1940s, in many of her novels blame for "miscegenation" similarly lies at the door of white missionaries who preach racial equality and father "coloured" offspring. Millin's interest in "the white peril" aligns her with other white South African women writers who were anti-"miscegenation" (her literary foremothers Olive Schreiner and Francis Bancroft), yet her fiction is ambivalently interpenetrated by the unruly voices of "coloured" women at the same time as she mimics European racialist thought to distance herself from these uncanny others and to consolidate her position as "white" in a country increasingly divided along racial lines.

In his preface to the 1986 edition of *God's Stepchildren*, Tony Voss claims that for Millin, "race mixture" means that "weak and misguided white men have mated with idle and sensual black women."[43] This is true of the first part of *God's Stepchildren*, where generations of tragedy are precipitated when a missionary, Andrew Flood, rejected by the blue-eyed Mary Keeble and in order to prove "that there was no difference between black and white," marries Silla, a "Hottentot" woman whose people Flood has been trying in vain to convert. What critics have tended to overlook in Millin's fiction, however, is the extent to which sexual encounters between white men and black women are represented in her fiction as coercive or violent, forced upon the woman. In *The South Africans*, Millin claims that in the veins of the "half-caste" run, "on the one side, the blood of slaves; on the other side, the blood of the careless, the selfish, the stupid, the vicious."[44] Although it draws on a language of racial purity, this statement, like Sol Plaatje's *The Mote and the Beam*, acknowledges the unequal and often "vicious" power relations that have been a part of South African history. Millin's short story entitled "Why Adonis laughed," published early in her career in the periodical *The New Adelphi* (1929), is essentially a "white peril" narrative. In the story, Millin's domestic worker Alita tells how a black woman named Dinah worked for Mr. Jackson, the white owner of the farm across the river. After Dinah married another farm worker, she gave birth to a child clearly fathered by Mr. Jackson. The sympathies of Alita and of the narrator are with Dinah and her husband, yet the story elides the voice of Dinah, and Millin describes her simply as very young but "singularly ugly, even for a Kaffir of Griqualand West."[45] In her novels, however, Millin scripts the rebellious speech of women subjected to the "white peril."

In the third part of *God's Stepchildren*, the beautiful but ill-fated Elmira, great-granddaughter to Andrew Flood, finds herself abandoned by white suitors who discover that she is tainted by "black blood," and she is forced into marriage with Mr. Lindsell, the aged landowner of the farm on which her father works. Here, as with the story "Why Adonis laughed," Millin's text is profoundly anti-pastoral, portraying the farm as a feudal arena where women of the laboring class are reduced to property, and have no more say in their own destiny than slaves. When Elmira's father suggests that the age difference between his daughter and Lindsell is not appropriate, Lindsell threatens that it would be better for Kleinhans's future on the farm if he gave up his daughter. Elmira's mother shudders to think of her "pretty child" married to a "hateful-looking old man," but Millin elaborates that "there flowed in her the blood of submissive slaves and acquiescent Eastern wives."[46] Having inherited this "acquiescent" blood herself, Elmira submits to Mr. Lindsell. In a remarkable passage towards the end of their story, however, Millin's text ventriloquizes the suppressed rage of generations of colonized women. After Lindsell sends Elmira's family away because they are an embarrassing reminder of his wife's black blood, Elmira vents her fury:

> "And I live here like a servant to mend your clothes and cook your food."
>
> Mr Lindsell was unused to resistance.
>
> "You never told me you were dissatisfied," he protested with a weakness that surprised even himself.
>
> "Did you think all I needed to make me happy was to be married to a man that looks like a tortoise, and is old enough to be my grandfather?"[47]

Similarly, Millin's *King of the Bastards* (1950) and *The Burning Man* (1952), set in the late eighteenth to early nineteenth centuries, foreground the outbursts of colonized women forced into unions with white men. The ambivalently celebrated hero of *King of the Bastards*, the great adventurer Coenraad Buys, takes black wives but is not as heavily judged in the novel as the missionaries, Johannes van der Kemp and James Read, with their "Hottentot wives and miserable progeny."[48] For Millin, as opposed to the straight-talking Buys, the missionaries are aged hypocrites who, in order to satisfy their lust, marry underage "Hottentot" women in the name of promoting racial equality. Hearing van der Kemp speak of his bride, a Dutch Commissary notes on the missionary's face a look "not entirely religious," the appearance of "senile men smitten with their sex."[49] When van der Kemp later introduces Buys to his bride, "a small brown barefoot girl" who may have been as young as thirteen, Buys looks "from the bald old man with the sprouting white hairs to the little dark frightened girl" and calls van der Kemp a "*Verdomde* hypocrite" ("Cursed hypocrite"), expressing disgust at "a Christian minister teaching that the way of God is for an old white man to satisfy himself with a little black girl."[50] When Buys leaves, the girl, who has been silent thus far, runs after him and begs him to buy her from "the ugly old man," thus failing to distinguish between her marriage and slavery. Although van der Kemp releases her from slavery, his marriage thus echoes the actions of the white men who forced her mother, a "Malagasy" slave, to submit to their sexual desires.

The scene where Buys meets van der Kemp's bride became the kernel of Millin's next novel, *The Burning Man*,[51] which focuses mainly on the life of this missionary. In this narrative van der Kemp writes a letter to the Directors of the London Missionary Society, noting that:

> A female slave may give her heart to whom she pleases, but she is compelled, and that not infrequently, by the most cruel treatment to yield her person to any who desires it; and sometimes with no other wish than to increase the misery of the wretched woman.[52]

His words return to haunt him when he realizes that his wife loathes him and bears his sexual attention and his children under duress. He has married her despite her antipathy towards him, which is apparent in their first meeting, when she is no more than a child, with "big dark eyes, passionate with mutiny."[53] Asked to shake his hand, she recoils violently from his touch:

> He stretched out his hand and touched her shoulder and she suddenly sprang back and began shrieking: "No, no, no!"
>
> Her flat little nose quivered. Her eyes blazed like an animal's in the night. She raged:
>
> "He mustn't touch me. He mustn't touch me."
>
> Lady Anne said:
>
> "What is the matter with you, Sally?"
>
> "I hate him, I hate him, the ugly old man."[54]

As was the case with Elmira, the space afforded to Sally's voice here is deeply ambivalent. On the one hand, the colonized woman speaks out against colonizing culture in a "white peril" scene set against an historical backdrop shaped by the institution of slavery. As with Elmira's keenly articulated rage towards Mr. Lindsell in *God's Stepchildren*, this appears in a text where few women's voices are foregrounded. On the other hand, however, while the novelistic form allows the incorporation of the voice of defiant alterity, Millin's scripting of Elmira and Sally brings with it all the problems that Gayatri Spivak describes as characterizing the desire to give voice to the subaltern other, but also echoes nineteenth-century racial thought, and particularly Gobineau's idea of the "natural repulsion felt by the black . . . woman" toward the white man.[55]

In defense of Millin, Lavinia Braun has claimed that Millin's Jewish background, her "stepchild-like" status in South Africa, led to a deep understanding of and sympathy for oppressed people who were classified as "non-white," and Marcia Leveson has attempted to qualify Millin's attitude towards "coloured" persons by arguing that it is matched, in her unpublished writings, by a similar ambivalence towards the Jew.[56] I believe, however, that such positions have difficulty in explaining Millin's statement: "I have pain over the pro-Nazism of our present government, but I will not be dominated by a continent of cruel, diseased savages."[57] In her autobiography, Millin tells that when somebody at a dinner party that she was attending in America "compared the treatment of Jews with the treatment of Negroes," a Jewish refugee, with whose viewpoint Millin clearly identifies, replied indignantly that he would be obliged if "the world's most civilized people" were not thought of "in terms of a people just emerging from barbarism."[58] In a recent article Peter Blair claims that the liberal humanist tradition of the novel in which Millin writes facilitates sympathy towards her "coloured" characters. Yet it is important to note that, for the three decades in which Millin reigned as South Africa's major novelist (1920s to 1940s), she was not regarded as conservative or overly racialist, but as a liberal, which is to say that she supported Jan Smuts's South African Party, and later, the United Party, and was also a friend and ally of Jan Hofmeyr, who came to represent the liberal wing of the United Party.[59] Thus, Michael Wade uses anachronistic terminology when, in an article published in 1974, he describes Millin as "anti-liberal."[60] Indeed, rather than ameliorating an otherwise racialist agenda, the sympathy for "coloured" characters that one detects in Millin's novels is actually in keeping with her outlook as a liberal segregationist, and suggests just how deeply liberalism was implicated in ideas about race that laid the foundations for apartheid. With the exception of Dora Taylor, who accused Millin of building a monument to color prejudice,[61] South African critics in her day considered Millin's work quite palatable (certainly it seems that none of her other contemporaries took her to task for racialism), and her views on race were also deemed desirable abroad. *God's Stepchildren* was extremely well-received in America, where Millin was hosted by Eleanor Roosevelt and thanked by a member of the African American community for being "a friend of God's stepchildren."[62] She was friendly with Katherine Mansfield, who encouraged her to publish a series of stories in the *Athenaeum*, and when she visited England, Millin was welcomed into the company of prominent writers and thinkers. To her consternation, *God's Stepchildren* was also read in Germany as a *Rassen Roman* that made "a poetical contribution to Germany's racial doctrines" and "all young Germans were advised to read the book."[63]

As Michel Foucault points out, theories of degenerescence, which found arch expression in Nazism, resulted in the politicization of sex, such that the individual was placed "in a position of 'biological responsibility' with regard to the species."[64] Like her contemporary, Geoffrey Cronjé, who argued that "The individual is responsible to his community for all his activities,"[65] Millin's writings convey the idea that "half-castes" have a duty *not to breed* so that they may die out in order to restore purity and health to the collective. The message of *God's Stepchildren*, which ends with Barry Lindsell deciding not to procreate in order to stamp out a line tainted by black blood, exemplifies Foucault's observation that, in the logic of biopolitics: "'The more inferior species die out, the more abnormal individuals are eliminated, the fewer degenerates there will be in the species as a whole'. . . . that will make life in general healthier: healthier and purer."[66] Theorizing the rise of modern racism, Foucault traces the ways in which ideas about blood, as the aristocratic means of marking class difference, became transposed in a bourgeois obsession with sex. Yet a "thematics of blood" persisted:

> Beginning in the second half of the nineteenth century, the thematics of blood was sometimes called on to lend its entire historical weight toward revitalizing the type of political power that was exercised through the devices of sexuality.[67]

What is interesting about Millin is her evocation of the age-old belief in blood, traceable in the European aristocracy's desire to maintain caste and in modes of nineteenth-century racial science, within fictions of race played out in a settlement colony that was on its way to becoming one of the most infamously racist states of the twentieth century. J.M. Coetzee observes that Millin's currency is "a poetics of blood rather than a politics of race," and in her work, "blood distinguishes African from European, Englishman from Afrikaner, Hottentot from Xhosa, Gentile from Jew. Blood is thus race."[68] This emphasis on blood in Millin's work needs some elucidation in relation to her own position within South African hierarchies of race.

At the time Millin's family arrived in South Africa from Lithuania, Jewish immigrants posed a dilemma of racial classification, and Eastern European Jews in particular bore the brunt of racial discrimination. From the late nineteenth century, when they arrived in large numbers on the diggings in Johannesburg, these *Ostjuden* were labeled "Peruvians" (a derogatory term derived from the acronym for Jewish immigrants from the "Polish and Russian Union"), and were looked down upon, not only by Gentiles, but also by other Jewish immigrants. Milton Shain's *The Roots of Anti-Semitism in South Africa* quotes a Cape Town newspaper as saying that the Jews there "live in dirtier style than kafirs."[69] In *The Fox and the Flies*, Charles van Onselen notes that in the early 1900s there was some uncertainty about whether Russian and Polish Jews were "eastern" (Asiatic) or "western" (European). According to *The South African Jewish Chronicle* in an article published in 1905—when Millin would have been about sixteen—*Ostjuden* presented "the most prominent section of those who stand on the border-line between white and Coloured."[70]

Jews were in 1930 the main target of the discriminatory "Quota Act," which severely restricted immigration from the Baltic states, including Lithuania. Although they came to be recognized as white after the First World War, Jewish South Africans, and to a greater extent *Ostjuden* like Millin's family, who grew up alongside racially-mixed households on the River diggings, maintained an ambiguous, uncomfortable "not-quite" element in relation to whiteness.

Millin's life writing suggests that her ambivalent place within South Africa's racial hierarchies, and, in particular, her physical appearance were sources of of self-consciousness and even anxiety to her. While visiting Norway, Millin was described by an interviewer as having "the frizzy black hair, the flashing black eyes, and the golden brown skin of the typical African." Although photographs of Millin suggest that the description was not entirely inaccurate, in her autobiography she indignantly protests against this sketch of herself as "a Coloured person," and then provides a self-portrait emphasizing her European aspect: "I have light blue eyes, dark brown hair and the skin that goes with such eyes and hair."[71] On the River diggings where Millin spent her childhood, the family's neighbors were "a big ruddy Englishman who had a coloured wife and a daughter white enough to be admitted to our school."[72] Although she did not expose the daughter for "passing," Millin was nonetheless careful not to associate herself with her.[73] Her exaggerated imitation of European racialist thought, and her reiterated attempts to inscribe her own identity as white, suggest a desire to reduce her distance from the white community within an increasingly race-conscious society. Her ambivalence towards her "coloured" characters, as well as her repugnance for "miscegenation," should be seen in the light of her own precarious and ambiguous position within South Africa. In a context where she was in danger of being seen as "coloured", "miscegenation" presented a paradigm, and a bogeyman, that gestured by default to her (Jewish) "pure blood" as opposed to the "mixed blood" of the "coloured".

The horror for "mixing of blood" that one finds in her earlier work is continued in Millin's penultimate novel, *The Wizard Bird*, though here the focus is on "the black peril." Significantly, Millin's swing towards "black peril" representation corresponds with the period, late in her life, in which she began to support the Nationalist government that had come to power in 1948. While the offspring produced through sexual unions between white men and black/"coloured" women were the focal point of her previous novels, *The Wizard Bird* reveals just how unthinkable is the possibility of the white womb being defiled by a "mixed-race" child. In this novel, as in other typical "black peril" tales, the white woman raped by a black man is not allowed to live.

As was the case in the "black peril" novels examined in the previous chapter, in Millin's late offering there is apprehension about the political voice of the educated black man. The antagonist in the novel, Chibisa Mantati, a potent public speaker in the cause of "Africa for the Africans" is one of those men "universities everywhere are training to rule a free Africa."[74] Like Nelson in

Heaton Nicholls's *Bayete!*, Chibisa is "a great speaker, truly an orator," but the novel silences him. Sharing his fate with Othello, another doomed dark-skinned lover and murderer of a white woman, Chibisa kills himself at the end of the narrative, his self-immolation the author's fantasy by which *sati* is displaced onto the body of the African man. His dramatic death provides resolution by obliterating that ambiguous and dangerous figure, the educated black man who speaks publicly of African liberation.

The narrative of *The Wizard Bird* begins with two South Africans in London bemoaning the decline of "civilization," with one of them expressing reservations about the lack of social decorum at a Picasso exhibition where they had just seen "a very fair, dirty English girl, all in black, clutching a big black man with the monstrous face of Jomo Kenyatta."[75] The link between African liberation, personified in the reference to Kenyatta, and white women becoming the sexual targets of black men becomes a central theme that is developed in the novel, as an imminent reversal in political fortunes is registered as the black man trying to gain access to the white woman. Foregrounded in the novel is Chibisa's relationship with John's sister, Allison. In order to save her brother who is being held captive by Chibisa after witnessing a savage and murderous African ceremony, Allison agrees to marry Chibisa. Taking on the role of mediator between a barbarous Africa on the one hand, and white civilization on the other, Allison offers herself as a sacrifice in order to safeguard her brother, and by extension, the European presence in Africa. Allison and her family describe the arrangement as a "rape": "when a woman marries under threat and in horror and conceives a black child, one feels as if it were rape."[76] The text resolves the horror of this conception as Allison, with her unborn child, falls down a cliff to her death while running away from Chibisa.

It is useful here to contrast *The Wizard Bird* with Dora Taylor's "To Tell my Story" (1960, published for the first time in *Don't Tread on my Dreams*, 2008).[77] Not only was Taylor a direct contemporary of Millin, but this story, which also deals with the theme of "black peril," is contemporaneous with *The Wizard Bird*. After a brief introductory preface, half of "To Tell my Story" is narrated by a white advocate defending a black man on a charge of raping and killing a white woman, and the second half by the accused, with the latter narrative thus comprising an interesting precursor to Lewis Nkosi's *Mating Birds*, which is similarly narrated by a black man who takes up his pen while on death row for supposedly raping a white woman. As in *Mating Birds*, and in contrast to *The Wizard Bird*, the black man in "To Tell my Story," Siyolo, has been falsely accused of this crime. In Taylor's story, the advocate, Leon Roth, fails to "replace, in the mind of the court, the stereotypical image labelled kaffir-rapist-murderer, with one possessing distinct human features,"[78] but the text succeeds in undermining "black peril" narrative as scripted by white writers such as George Webb Hardy, George Heaton Nicholls, and Millin herself. Like Jim in Webb Hardy's *The Black Peril*, Siyolo is being tutored in literature/language

by a progressive young white woman, and like Nelson in Heaton Nicholl's
Bayete! and Chibisa in *The Wizard Bird*, Siyolo is "the most dangerous type of
kaffir, the educated kaffir" with "a resonant, flexible voice" and "an uncommon
love of book learning."[79] However, Taylor's story then subverts "black peril"
narrative by tracing a hidden story of interracial love between Siyolo and
Magda Theron, the daughter of the farmer on whose land Siyolo labors while
in exile from his community. Instead of Siyolo being the guilty party, it becomes
apparent that there was no rape, and that Magda's white fiancé accidentally
fired the shot that killed her in the scuffle that ensued after he found Siyolo and
Magda together. Significantly, the texts of Shakespeare's that are quoted from
and alluded to in this story of books, learning, love, and loss are *Hamlet* and
the sonnets, rather than *Othello*. Telling of a relationship "that struggled to be
born and that nourished itself even in the desert,"[80] Siyolo tells how they were
both "wrapped in the swaddling clothes of racist myth," and acknowledges
through the repeated negative enunciation "did not know" how the unthinkability of love between himself and Magda has resulted in profound loss: "I did
not know that I loved Magda Theron. She did not know she loved me. No gesture of love ever passed between us. We were a man and a woman and we did
not know it, till it was too late."[81] Again, in his description of their love as ne-
gated, homeless, and "fugitive," the text performs an act of mourning: "Our
friendship had no home, no resting place in this world. It was a fugitive, hunted
thing."[82] Resonating uncannily with J.M. Coetzee's later observation, in his
"Jerusalem Prize Acceptance Speech," of apartheid society as stunted by "a failure of love,"[83] Siyolo asserts that "it is lack of feeling that kills a man, it is killing
the nation" and that "we all suffer spiritual mutilation."[84] As opposed to the
melancholy disavowal of interracial love in Millin's novels, including *The Wizard Bird*, "To Tell My Story" foregrounds interracial love as "the first step
across a gulf separated by rigid law and custom."[85]

In his essay on Millin, J.M. Coetzee writes off *The Wizard Bird* as "a work of
the feeblest imaginative power, a mere transcription of the isolationist paranoia
and racial prejudices of the right-wing South African press of the times."[86] Yet
the novel actually resembles Coetzee's *Disgrace* in some key respects, even if
Disgrace doubles back on "black peril" stereotypes knowingly. In both texts,
one could say that the author transfers anxieties about the end of white rule
onto the body of a white woman, such that white women become silent and
sacrificial victims forced into unions with black men in a nation where the old
order is either in the process of falling away or else hanging precariously in the
balance. The setting of Coetzee's novel is the post-apartheid transition, and in
The Wizard Bird, the time is 1960, when cold-war independence struggles in
Africa were being registered with alarm in white South African society. However, while *Disgrace* breaks with traditional "black peril" narratives in that the
birth of a "mixed-race" child from the rape symbolically and ambivalently
carries the weight of the nation's future, Millin's text erases the occupation of

the white womb by the "yellow man" whose birth threatens to bring the racial order of the nation to ruin.

"Consequential Changes": Daphne Rooke's *Mittee* in America and South Africa

In the 1950s, Daphne Rooke (1914-2009) was the South African writer most popular in America. This was largely as a result of the triumph of her second and most successful novel, *Mittee*, which was widely reviewed throughout the United States, where it became a bestseller.[87] In February 1952 *Time Magazine* noted the comparability of Rooke's themes with those of American writers: "The US South used to be the main source of the world's supply of fiction plots about the clash of white and Negro; in the last dozen years, South African writers have moved into the market. The latest is Transvaal born Daphne Rooke."[88] In May 1952 *The New York Herald Tribune Book Review* listed *Mittee* in its top fifteen of "what America is reading," and a Cleveland reviewer that year compared her "heady novels of romance and suspense" with those of Daphne du Maurier.[89] In the country of her birth, South Africa, Rooke's reception was not as enthusiastic. Ian Glenn notes that early South African reviewers were generally "condescending and inaccurate," and although an edition of *Mittee* published by Victor Gollancz in London circulated in South Africa from 1951, as J.M. Coetzee observes, it was only in the late 1980s, when a South African edition of *Mittee* was published, that readers began to give credit to Rooke in her native land.[90] While an interesting phenomenon in its own right, this discrepancy in reception is not my focus here. Rather, I would like to examine an inconsistency between two editions of *Mittee*—the edition that first circulated in America and the edition that first circulated in South Africa—a difference that has not been remarked on in previously published criticism.[91] The "consequential changes" that were made to the one edition of *Mittee* involve a scene of rape. I examine the factors that led to the changes that were made to the one edition, and the consequences of these changes. In particular, I am interested in examining this incongruity in relation to other instances of rape in *Mittee*, and in the relevance of these scenes to South African history and society. Although her original script for *Mittee* suggests that Rooke was capable of drawing on stereotypes of race and rape, and despite the fact that she has been described as "not a serious writer" whose romances "seemed to have little relevance to the great issues of the day,"[92] I argue that the value of Rooke's work is her ability to draw attention to the patriarchal violence endemic in the orders of colonialism and apartheid.

In an afterword to *Mittee*, J.M. Coetzee writes: "To her credit, Rooke does not indulge in the *ne plus ultra* of colonial horror stories, the rape of a white woman."[93] Given his awareness of the problematic nature of "black peril" representations, it may seem strange or contradictory that Coetzee included in his post-apartheid novel *Disgrace* the gang-rape of a white woman by three black men. In chapter 5 I examine this apparent inconsistency in Coetzee's judgment and shall not dwell on it here.[94] There is, however, another level on which Coetzee's comment is incongruous. In the version of *Mittee* published in 1952 by the Boston-based publishing house, Houghton Mifflin, and in the 2008 Toby Press edition in which Coetzee's afterword also appears, the rape of a white woman by a black man *does in fact occur*. The setting is a farmstead during the South African War (1999–1902) and in these two American editions, it is Letty, a white woman, who is raped by one of a band of marauding black men, while the Boer men are out on commando. Within the most recent edition of *Mittee*, the Toby Press publication, there is thus a contradiction: Coetzee mentions Rooke's avoidance of a "black peril" scene, but the rape of Letty by a black man takes place in this very edition.[95] There is an explanation for Coetzee's erroneous claim. In the British first version of *Mittee*, which was published by Victor Gollancz in 1951 and circulated in South Africa, the woman raped during the war is Anna, a black servant, while Letty is saved in the nick of time. This is also the case in the 1987 South African Chameleon Press edition, and in the 1991 Penguin Classics version in which Coetzee's afterword originally appeared.

Looking back at the early editions of *Mittee*, there is therefore a discrepancy between the Gollancz first edition (1951), which was sold in the United Kingdom and South Africa and contains the rape of a black woman by a black man, and the first American edition (Houghton Mifflin, 1952), which contains a typical "black peril" scenario. The question to be asked is whether Gollancz asked Rooke to remove the "black peril" rape in revising the manuscript of the novel, or whether Houghton Mifflin requested on behalf of a prospective American readership that a sensationalist scene of black-on-white rape be added. Regarding the latter option, it is likely that the violation of a white woman by a black man in the Houghton Mifflin edition resonated with the American theme of "the clash of white and Negro" and contributed to the marketability of the novel in the United States. It should also not be forgotten that Doris Lessing's American publisher, Alfred Knopf, tried to pressure Lessing to revise *The Grass is Singing* (1950) to accommodate an explicit rape of the white female protagonist by Moses, a black man, "in accordance," as the publishers put it, "with the mores of the country." Lessing refused, but much to her dismay, Knopf published the paperback version of the novel with "a lurid picture of a blond cowering terrified while a big buck nigger . . . stood over her."[96] Correspondence with Rooke in the Gollancz archives reveals, however, that Rooke originally scripted a "black peril" rape in *Mittee*, drawing on myths passed down through decades about black looters violating white women left alone on farms during the South African war.

Counter-intuitively (since they were a liberal/radical press), the reason for Gollancz's request for Rooke to change her "black peril" script came not from unease with racial stereotyping, but rather from commercial motivation related to a fear of censorship in South Africa, where copies of the Gollancz edition of the book would be circulating. At the time *Mittee* was published, the South African Entertainments (Censorship) Act of 1931 was still in force. Among other things, this Act banned representations of "intermingling" of Europeans and non-Europeans, as well as scenes of "rough handling or ill-treatment of women and children." Importantly, 1950 had also seen the passing of the Immorality Act, which forbade interracial sexual relations in the Union. Narrated by Selina, a "coloured" woman, *Mittee* tells of Selina's love-hate relationship with her white mistress, Mittee, and of the jealousy that she feels as a result of the marriage between Mittee and Paul du Plessis, with whom Selina has an affair, and who responds to Selina's love for him with staggering emotional and physical brutality. In the pre-publication discussions concerning the novel, Edwin Lamberth, Gollancz's South African distributor, expressed concern that the sexual relationship between a "coloured" woman and a white man represented in the novel might result in it being banned in South Africa. Rooke's Gollancz contact, Sheila Hodges, had this to report to Rooke's agent, Margaret Macpherson:

> I was talking about the book last week to our South African representative, who happens to be in England for a few weeks, and he says he thinks there is a chance that MITTEE may be banned because of the relationship between Paul and Selina.[97]

A few weeks after conveying these initial reservations, however, Hodges wrote that Lamberth had had second thoughts, and now "felt that his original fears about the banning of the book in South Africa were unfounded" but that he was "still nervous on another score."[98] He was now worried about the rape of a white woman that took place in the novel. Writing to the London sales manager, Lamberth recommended publication, claiming that he was "tremendously impressed with this book which kept [him] keyed up right to the last page" and that "it has all the makings of a best-seller for it involves the very spirit of the voortrekking days" (somewhat strange praise, as the novel has nothing to do with the Great Trek). He was nonetheless concerned about censorship, and specifically mentioned the rape of Letty in relation to the banning of Stuart Cloete's *Turning Wheels* (1937), which was published in the lead up to the centenary of the Great Trek, and showed the Voortrekkers in a less than favorable light, portraying, among other things, an interracial relationship:

> Given the opportunity I am certain that the South African reading public would gobble it up but I am more than a little uneasy about the possibility of its being banned. The rape of a Boer woman (galley 82) would, I fear, be enough for them to stop it. TURNING WHEELS has been on the banned list for a long time so I see little hope for MITTEE.

It is quite possible that many copies would be sold before the Government got around to it but if it were banned we should have to credit all unsold copies.[99]

What Lamberth misjudged was that while Cloete's *Turning Wheels* was "damned as an insult to Boer heroes," for being "filthy, discourteous, inaccurate, misleading to foreign readers"[100]—and the authorities were no doubt thinking here of the sexual liaison between a "coloured" woman and a Voortrekker leader described in the novel—"black peril" representations of all descriptions, unless written by black men, had great currency in the apartheid era.[101] As noted to Miss Hodges in a letter from Lessing's Gollancz agent, Margaret Macpherson, who was also Rooke's agent:

> I do not believe that MITTEE will be banned in South Africa over the colour question. Another book which I handle, *The Grass is Singing*, by Doris Lessing, had the same theme and sold well there.[102]

Although *Mittee* was not embargoed in South Africa, the banning of Rooke's later novel, *The Greyling* (1963), was to prove that the apartheid authorities were then more worried about literary representations that suggested that white men could be attracted to black or "coloured" women, and represented white men in a negative light, than they were about "black peril" narratives.[103] Lamberth's initial instinct, that *Mittee* would be banned because of the relationship between Paul and Selina, was thus more plausible than the novel being banned because of a "black peril" scene. Nonetheless, on the basis of Lamberth's misgivings about the "black peril" rape, which she passed on to Rooke, Hodges suggested that Rooke change the scene:

> Do you think there is anything at all in his point about the raping of Letty? If this incident were altered it would mean other consequential changes, and you may feel that in any case Mr Lamberth's fears are groundless. On the other hand, if he is right then it would be a thousand pities not to do something to avoid any risk of the book's being banned in South Africa.[104]

Rooke was reluctant to make alterations, claiming that the sexual violation of white women by black men was still relevant in South Africa:

> It was good to hear that Mr. Lamberth has such high hopes of MITTEE. I think he is right when he says that the book may be banned because of poor Letty. On the other hand, the raping of Letty fits closely into the pattern of South African life not only during the Boer War but at the present day. As you probably know, rape by natives was the major hazard that confronted Boer women during the Boer War when they were left unprotected on the farms and for that reason I would prefer to leave the episode as it stands.[105]

Despite her disinclination, Rooke was prepared to change the scene "to make it more palatable to the South African government":

> This is what I thought of doing: The girl Anna whom Mittee had had in her employ for years could be attacked instead of Letty. In this way, few changes would have to be made and I could let you have the galleys back within a week of receiving them.[106]

Rooke knew that a rape at this point in the narrative was vital to the plot as it led to Mittee's final estrangement from Paul. After the incident, Mittee induces an abortion for the victim which later results in her being accused of having "evil knowledge" and of having prevented pregnancy in her own marriage. Paul then whips her cruelly and her marriage to him becomes irretrievable. The rape thus could not be erased without substantial revisions to the manuscript. With the innovative thinking of a *bricoleur*, Rooke came up with a solution that deployed the simple close-to-hand structure of substitution. Whereas the American Houghton Mifflin version, which was not intended to be circulated in South Africa, retained the rape of Letty, by virtue of an exchange Letty was replaced by the black servant Anna as rape victim in the British edition of *Mittee*, which was also to be sold in South Africa.

In the American edition, the rape of a white woman by a black man takes place on a solitary farmstead, with the corporeal vulnerability of the white woman pointing to the absence of white men, those who traditionally possess and can guard this body. Although Letty's uncharitable attitude and sharp tongue have until this moment in the narrative alienated other characters and the reader, the descriptive language of the attack elevates her to a figurative political icon: her "dark-gold" hair is a reminder of her race, and, lying like "a banner" on the grass after the rape, it becomes a sign, a collective cause around which her kinsmen may rally:

> We came to the trees as one boy rose from Letty. There was another crouched beside Pieter, pounding at his face though the little boy was unconscious.
>
> As Mittee raised the gun to her shoulder the boy who had raped Letty bounded off among the trees but the flat faced Shangaan beside Pieter did not move. He was from the Mission, not ill-natured but a little muddled in the head and now so frightened that he was dangerous. . . .
>
> "Fanie," I screamed. My voice let loose a hellish explosion from Mittee's wavering finger and she fell back from the kick of the gun as though she were dead, blood streaming from her nose. The Shangaan fled through the trees with a terrible cry though the bullet had gone far over his head.
>
> Vain and foolish little Mittee lay in the dust with the smoking gun beside her. "Go and see to Letty, it's only my nose that is bleeding."

Letty had turned her face to the earth, her unloosed dark-gold hair like a banner on the grass. "Nonna," I said, "sit up, Pieter needs you, he is hurt, nonna." But the shamed head clung to the earth.[107]

Suggesting the threat of "miscegenation," the attack on the white woman occurs simultaneously with the literal defacement of the white child as Letty's son Pieter has his face "pounded" by the "flat-faced Shangaan." Interestingly, the phrase that Coetzee uses in his afterword to describe "black peril" narratives, "*ne plus ultra*"—meaning in Latin "nothing more beyond"—not only denotes that such stories express the height of colonial paranoia, but could also be read as suggesting the erasure of reproductive "miscegenation" that typically accompanies "black peril" encounters in fiction. Although Letty is not killed off, the possibility of progeny from a mixed-race sexual encounter is expunged, in this case by way of the abortion that Mittee administers to the victim. Given the politically charged significance of the white womb in biopolitical discourse, the abortion that takes place in the Gollancz version after the rape of a black servant simply does not have the same currency as the termination of pregnancy that takes place in the American edition. Whereas in the American publication Mittee attends immediately to Letty with an unquestionable focus: "We'll have to do something in case there's a baby,"[108] in the Gollancz edition Mittee must qualify the need for a termination of pregnancy in Anna's case: "There might be a baby and the hardest heart wouldn't expect her to go through with that."[109]

In the Gollancz version, which was circulated in the United Kingdom and South Africa, it is Anna rather than Letty who is sitting under the peach trees with Letty's children Pieter and Petronella at the time of the attack. Although there is no rape of a white woman in this edition, the text still points to the vulnerability of white womanhood in the incident. In the American edition Petronella was "barricaded" inside the house, whereas now she is outside, adding to the precariousness of the situation. There is still a reference to Letty's hair, which as in the passage cited above becomes a marker of racial difference, emphasizing the intensity and significance of her imperiled status in the scene. While Letty is not raped, she is caught by the throat by a "Kaffir," an image which leaves a trace of the originally scripted rape by displacing euphemistically the physical site of attack upwards:

We came to the trees as one boy rose from Anna. There was another, with his left hand wound in Letty's beautiful hair while he fought with his right to take the hoe from her. Near them Pieter lay unconscious, his face beaten to a pulp. I looked anxiously for little Petronella . . . her thin voice was lost entirely in the raging sounds that came from Letty and the Kaffir. As Mittee raised the gun to her shoulder the boy who had raped Anna bounded off among the trees but the flat faced Shangaan who had hold of Letty did not let go of her. He shifted his hand from her hair to her throat and so stopped her screaming. He was from the Mission, not ill-natured but a little muddled in the head and now so frightened that he was dangerous. . . .

"Fanie," I screamed. My voice let loose a hellish explosion from Mittee's wavering finger and she fell back from the kick of the gun as though she were dead, blood streaming from her nose. The Shangaan fled through the trees with a terrible cry though the bullet had gone far over his head.

Vain and foolish little Mittee lay in the dust with the smoking gun beside her. "Go and see to Pieter, it's only my nose that is bleeding. And there's poor Anna."

Anna had turned her face to the earth. I said, "Anna, sit up. It's no use lying there, what's done is done." But the shamed head clung to the earth.[110]

In his 1952 review of the novel for the *Cape Times*, Jack Cope found the incident in the Gollancz edition unconvincing: "The 'Kaffers' are seen as nothing more than a vague menace . . . Illogically they express their revolt in the Wolkbergen by raping one of their own women employed by the settlers."[111] Cope's observation of the marginal presence of black characters holds true for the representation of the rape itself. What is immediately apparent in the revised edition is the lack of impact of Anna's rape: whereas in the Houghton Mifflin edition Mittee commands Selina to attend to Letty, in the Gollancz version Selina is told first to attend to Pieter, and the reference to Anna comes as an afterthought. This could be attributed to Rooke's accurate depiction of racialistic attitudes at the time. However, it is important to recognize that Anna is near to hand as a substitute not only because she is a woman, like Letty, and is thus defined by common understanding as "rapeable," but is also chosen through a negative circuit of logic. She is useful as a replacement victim in the edition that was to be sold in South Africa precisely because she is black, not white. In substituting Anna for Letty, Rooke was exploiting the relatively ungrievable status of intraracial rape in the South Africa imaginary and of the black woman as rape victim in order to evade censorship.

The elision of interracial rape in the Gollancz edition of *Mittee* has important implications for reading the novel. Firstly, since the amended manuscript now portrayed a black on black rape, this lessened the novel's representation of interracial sex, and the rape itself become less politically charged. Secondly, the representation of a black woman as a victim of rape reduced the impact of the portrayal of "rough handling or ill-treatment of women" which the Entertainments Act had also forbidden. The idea being traded upon was that whereas the rape of a white woman would be seen as outrageous, the violation of a black woman simply did not have the same potential to inspire shock and identification in readers. This manipulation of narrative with specific consumer attitudes in mind has by no means been specific to publishers imagining the ways in which the apartheid censors might conceptualize the reaction of South African readers. In her comments on the Hollywood film *The Accused*

(1988), Tanya Horeck shows that although the narrative was based on the infamous New Bedford rape, in which a Portuguese woman had apparently been raped by a group of Portuguese men in a bar named Big Dan's in Massachusetts, in the film the victim, played by Jodie Foster, was "whitewashed" in order to make her more sympathetic to viewers: "In the version of events offered in *The Accused*, the ethnic tensions that characterized the rape in New Bedford are omitted." Instead, Horeck argues, an Anglo American victim is used to tell a "universal' story" (though one of the rapists, who has a "swarthy complexion," seems to be ethnically ambiguous). What would happen, Horeck asks in relation to the film, "*if we attempt to substitute a woman of colour for the white woman?*" Her answer comes via the words of an English-speaking Caribbean woman who responded: "if I change that woman into a black woman . . . I know the whole line of the story would've changed . . . the verdict would have been different. . . . the sympathy would've been very different . . ." As Horeck notes, "this spectator's affective response to the film is uncannily accurate. . . . the verdict in the Big Dan's rape case was indeed different, as was the level of sympathy accorded the woman by the community."[112] Horeck observes that Joel Schumacher's *A Time to Kill* (1996) also contains "highly ambivalent substitutions," processes "in which one body is made to stand in for another," as the prosecuting lawyer in the courtroom scene appeals to the jury by describing the ways in which a young black girl was "beaten, urinated on, raped," and then asks the jury: "Now imagine she is white." As Horeck argues, "within the scene of a white woman being raped we witness a hyperbolic attempt to reassert the primacy of white legal and civic culture."[113] Blackening the victim as in Rooke's novel, on the other hand, has the potential effect of diminishing sympathy, resonance and impact.

In her Oxford Amnesty Lecture of 2002, Judith Butler starts with the question "What makes for a grievable life?," and claims that while "certain lives will be highly protected . . . other lives will not find such fast and furious support and will not even qualify as grievable." "Violence against those who are already not quite lives," Butler points out, "leaves a mark that is no mark."[114] The diminished status of the black woman as victim worthy of grieving over was compounded under the feudal-style relations on farms during the South African war and up until the time Rooke was writing. Comparable with the slave in the system of plantation slavery, where, as Achille Mbembe has pointed out, the oppressed "appears as the perfect figure of a shadow," the black servant on the farm incarnates the result of a triple unacknowledged loss: "the loss of a 'home', loss of rights over his or her body, and loss of political status."[115] The South African farm novel, notoriously blind to the presence and concerns of black servants, perpetuated this, and although *Mittee* foregrounds the experience of a brown or "coloured" woman, the black women on the farm in the novel do not receive much attention. Because of their peripheral presence, violence perpetrated against such shadowy figures becomes

less remarkable, and this lack of acknowledgment is not only registered in
works of fiction, but was also entrenched in the workings of the legal system.
At the time that Rooke was writing *Mittee*, variations in significance and
impact between different types of rapes were registered in the punitive workings of the law. It should not be surprising to learn that while a white man was
reprimanded in 1946 as a "disgrace to his European race" and given seven
years imprisonment and six strokes for raping "a native child nine years
old,"[116] "a Native," Izak Gajene, was sentenced to death in the same year for
raping a European woman.[117] The law in South Africa at this time made the
rape of black women less of a crime, less punishable, and of less consequence
than the rape of white women. Similarly, the focus in South African literature
and mediascapes on interracial rape has resulted in intraracial rape taking on
a neglected and diminished status.

To be fair to Rooke, the punishment of the perpetrator is the same in the
Gollancz and the Houghton Mifflin editions. In both versions the offender is
hunted down and castrated by a gang of white vigilantes led by Paul, a punitive
measure the novel actually condemns by maintaining its sympathy with the
missionary, Basil Castledene, who tries to prevent the brutal punishment from
taking place. Nonetheless, as seen in her letter above, Rooke defended her depiction of Letty as rape victim by an appeal to authenticity and realism, claiming that the rape "fits closely into the pattern of South African life not only
during the Boer War but at the present day." Rooke's statement here opens up
precisely the question of "who is considered true and real." Original and
authentic rape victims, she is implying, are white women, and realistic scenes
of rape are interracial. As mentioned in chapter 1 of my study, the rape in the
American version of *Mittee* transmits longstanding fears about the presence of
black combatants during the South African war. Ironically, however, since
intraracial sexual violation has been and is far more common than interracial
rape in South Africa, the intraracial attack that became a substitute for the
"original" script in *Mittee* was more authentic than the "black peril" account in
terms of its relation to actual rape statistics.

Rooke is in many respects a complex and contradictory author, and it would
be a mistake, on the basis of the farm attack in the Houghton Mifflin edition
and her statement about the reality of white women as victims of rape by black
men, to dismiss her simply as a "black peril"-purveying reactionary. Despite
the following claim made in a *Times Literary Supplement* review, which refers
to one rape in the novel, the violation that takes place during the war is not the
only instance of sexual abuse in *Mittee*:

> Miss Rooke, it might be said, bludgeons a reader almost into insensibility,
> and then rapidly revives him with flicks of a wet towel; or she rasps at his
> nerves with a consistently discordant file; there can be no doubt at least that
> she gains and holds attention in a narrative which includes three murders

(one of them the smothering of an infant), a rape, a whipping, and any
amount of incidental promiscuity and vulgarity.[118]

Perpetuating the myth that the rapist is a stranger to his prey, a dark beast
roaming the fringes of civilization rather than a member of the community
who knows his victim, this review overlooks the fact that, in addition to the
most obvious instance of violation in the novel (the rape during the farm attack), at least three other rapes are mentioned or can be read as taking place in
Mittee: an incident early in the novel when Selina is assaulted by the insanely
violent farm laborer, Jansie; Paul's rape of Selina when she sacrifices herself for
Mittee; as well as the "white peril" rape of the imbecile Rebecca, which is mentioned as having resulted in the birth of Selina's husband, Fanie. In spite of
Rooke's support for the veracity of "black peril" representations, *Mittee* thus
draws attention to intraracial violence and "white peril" encounters, refuting
the notion of the rapist as an outsider to respectable society, one of the pre-
mises of "black peril" discourse.

The scene in which Selina is attacked by the violent farm laborer, Jansie,
reads as follows:

> With one frightful gesture he ripped the dress from my body. I brought my
> feet up and kicked him in the chest, crooking my fingers to tear at his lust-
> crazed eyes when he came at me again. Above my screams, he yelled in ju-
> bilation. I will always remember those few seconds, I will always remember
> that hateful body from which the hot sweat trickled.[119]

Although there is no direct reference to physical penetration in this scene, it is
necessary to bear in mind Lynne Higgins and Brenda Silver's injunction, in
their study *Rape and Representation*, to listen to the text's silences, to recognize
the possibility of a violation without this having been mentioned directly.[120]
What is particularly shocking about the scene in which Jansie springs onto
Selina, causing her to miscarry the child she has conceived as a result of her
affair with Paul, is that Jansie actually wants to marry her. He sees himself as a
potential husband, not as a rapist or a stranger. In her novels, Rooke does not
shy away from representing all modes of intraracial sexual violence, including
white-on-white rape. This may be seen in *Diamond Jo* (1965), which focuses on
a migrant population of diggers and tradesmen during the diamond rush of
the 1870s, and places great emphasis on the violence of white men towards
white women. In this novel, the Jewish narrator, Mannie, ignores the rape of a
black woman by a white man, Tanguy, to the peril of his own family, as Tanguy
later rapes Mannie's wife, Leah.[121] In *Mittee*, the brutality that characterizes the
interactions between Selina and Jansie is echoed in the relationship between
Paul and Mittee. Paul is physically violent towards Mittee and, like Jansie who
kills Selina's unborn baby, Paul murders the sickly infant that he and Mittee
have produced. When Paul emerges from the room where he has been beating

Mittee with a *sjambok*, his face mutates in Selina's imagination: "it was not into Paul's face that I was looking. 'Oh God, it's Jansie' I screamed."[122] Despite their different skin color, the novel intimates that both Paul and Jansie are equally brutal.

In an exchange that brings to mind the solution that Rooke engineered in order to avoid the novel being banned, Selina then *substitutes* herself for Mittee when Paul falls into a drunken rage and is about to attack Mittee. Selina allows him to rape her instead: "It was for my little nonnie's sake that I took off my clothes and danced before him."[123] Although Selina and Paul have had consensual sex previously, that this is rape there is no doubt, as her words read in the Gollancz edition: "Then I knew what Anna had suffered," and in the Houghton Mifflin edition: "Then I knew what Letty had suffered."[124] In these two mirrored substitutions—the rape of Anna, which Rooke engineered in order to make the novel more acceptable to the apartheid authorities, and the rape of Selina—a black woman replaces a white woman as the victim of sexual assault. The original "black peril" narrative in the farm attack plays to images of white women as sacrificial victims in colonial encounters, with the substitution of Anna for Letty then dissipating the political significance of this rape scene in the Gollancz edition. In Selina's self-sacrifice for Mittee the novel points to an intraracial marital rape that has been deflected onto the body of Selina. The substitution of Selina for Mittee thus serves ambivalently to recognize and to cover over the possibility of a wife becoming the victim of rape by her husband, something that the law at the time that Rooke was writing did not acknowledge. Rape was an act of aggression between strangers, it was unthinkable that a wife could be raped by the husband whom she had no right to refuse.

Of course, the scene in which Selina is raped by Paul also draws attention to the reality of "white peril" encounters, where the white man in question was often a respected member of his community rather than a dark-skinned stranger. Similarly, Selina's husband Fanie is conceived through the rape of his mentally disabled mother by a white man, "yet," the novel tells us, "you could look at the men of Plessisburg over a hundred times and not see one capable of such an act."[125] In *Mittee*, the measure of a white man is his capacity to resist becoming an agent of the "white peril." When Selina spitefully tells the missionary Basil Castledene that he will "probably drink or take a Kaffir wife," she sees that he has "clear eyes . . . a deep inward conviction of strength" that put him "beyond the reach of temptation"[126], and make him quite unlike the missionaries who appear in the novels of Sarah Gertrude Millin. Nonetheless, in this play on "white peril" images, one might conclude that, like Millin's novels, *Mittee* contributes to representations that render unthinkable the possibility of interracial love. But there is something interesting about Rooke's representation of relationships between white men and "coloured" women. In his commentary on Rooke's novels, J.M. Coetzee asks: "what draws the half-caste

woman and the sadistic man so obsessively together?" His answer is uncharitable to the writer, as he claims that Rooke "dodges [the vexed question of interracial desire] by shifting into higher rhetorical gear."[127] I argue that while it
appears that Rooke cannot imagine the possibility of mutual desire between
black men and white women, in her representations of the relationships
between white men and "coloured" women she intuitively confronts rather
than "dodges" the issue of interracial desire in a racist society. In this respect,
the sexual violence in her novels is not simply a symptom of an inability to
imagine interracial love, as was the case with Millin, but rather, Rooke teases
out the psychic consequences of illicit love, a strategy that attributes the failure
of interracial erotic love not to biological determinism, but to the intimate
workings of what Butler has called "a culturally-instituted melancholia,"
defined as "racial foreclosures on the production of the field of love."[128]

Rather than subscribing to a theory of racial intermingling as causing degeneration, in her representations of the attitudes of the colonizing man
toward the colonized woman Rooke exposes what Robert Young has identified as "the ambivalently double gesture of repulsion and attraction that
seems to lie at the heart of racism."[129] After Paul and Selina are sexually intimate for the first time in *Mittee*, Paul touches her "with his foot," swears her
to silence and reminds her to call him "Baas Paul."[130] A few pages later he is
disavowing her, spitting at her with the words "Voetsak, you bastard."[131] In
The Greyling, arguably Rooke's most political novel since it has an apartheid-
era setting and criticizes overtly the psychologically internalized and damaging effects of the Immorality Act, Maarten is unable to resolve his advocacy
of apartheid with the attraction he feels for a "coloured" woman, Bokkie, and
he is vicious in his treatment of her even as he is drawn to her. Bokkie remembers their intimacy as a brutalizing act that treads a fine line between seduction and violation: "he broke into me as if he wanted to smash me up for
life."[132] As Maarten's mother points out: "he considers it a worse sin to love her
than to take her as if she were a whore."[133] By the end of the novel, Maarten
has killed Bokkie in order to hide his "crime" of "miscegenation," just as the
narrator's husband, Ray, murders a white woman, Hester Adraanse, who
belongs to a family of *bywoners* and is therefore of a lower class, with the
words "a woman like you is only for a man's convenience."[134] These scenes afford a chilling sense of characters enmeshed in a melancholy field of interaction inflected by race and class, with the punishment meted out to the two
murderers—Maarten is sentenced to death, while Ray is given life imprisonment—
suggesting that "miscegenation" was seen as a greater crime than intraracial
inter-class liaisons.[135]

All of Rooke's major novels contain obscenely violent, even demonic, male
figures: Jansie and Paul in *Mittee*; John, the narrator's father in *Ratoons*;
Maarten and Ray in *The Greyling*; and Tanguy in *Diamond Jo*. The horror is
that these men are family: husbands, or potential husbands, and fathers.

When in an interview I asked Rooke about this, she responded that these "dark-haired" men are based on stories she heard from her mother, Marie (to whom *Mittee* is dedicated), about her first husband, Knevitt, a violent, hard-drinking Welshman who savagely beat Rooke's half-brothers and her mother. Eventually one night Marie and her three sons ran away from home. As Rooke tells it, they heard Knevitt coming after them on horseback, with his two colt revolvers firing, and they hid behind a waterfall, a scene which became the inspiration for the final major incident in *Mittee*, which leads to the death of Paul. Rooke claims that she grew up on these stories, but presumably there were other stories, and one may well question the significance of Rooke's deep investment in these tales of a frighteningly violent man.[136] In *The Art of the Ridiculous Sublime*, Slavoj Žižek perversely argues that fictions of "enraged paternal figures," excessively violent phallic figures with their "wild outbursts of violent rage," are essentially a fantasy, such that even the most obscene *Urvater*, "the rapist father," is an invented defense against the suffocating and protective figure of parental benevolence.[137] If one were to follow Žižek and read Rooke's novels alongside details of the author's autobiography, it could be argued that Rooke's childhood, in which she grew up without a father in a house mainly of women,[138] shaped the writer's obsession with the fiery, violent, and threatening men that she returns to again and again in her novels. Like Charlotte Bronte's Rochester, Paul in *Mittee* is a dark and powerful Romantic character with a "passionate soul" who first appears in the narrative on horseback[139] and in certain key respects it would not be amiss to read *Mittee* as a rewriting of *Jane Eyre*. In a similar vein to Jean Rhys's *Wide Sargasso Sea*, which it predates by a decade and a half, *Mittee* is the story of a love triangle told from the perspective of the Creole woman, and in his demonic intensity and intertwined sadism and appetite for dark-skinned or ethnically ambiguous women, Paul certainly has much in common with Rhys' Rochester-figure. While some of the brutal men in Rooke's novels are seductively portrayed, an interpretation of such excessively "evil" male figures as fantasies would overlook their relation to the actual violence of the patriarchal order. Indeed, in her memoir Rooke not only remembers growing up in a feminine household, but also makes a link between apartheid and male "discipline" and "aggression."[140] As Zoë Wicomb notes: "Rooke is resolute in her exposure of the bullying male. The consoling words of an Afrikaner matron—'Don't be upset by the boys. All girls have to put up with it, Selina, probably he meant no harm' reveal to what extent sexual harassment is institutionalized in that society."[141] But Rooke's critique of patriarchal violence does not simply apply to white society, and as this citation from *Mittee* suggests, Rooke does not excuse white women from complicity in oppression. Through the portrayal of brutal husband-fathers (and the women who excuse their behavior) her novels reflect the patriarchal violence that was systemic at every level in the arrangements of colonialism and apartheid. In fact, despite the original "black

peril" scene in *Mittee*, which was erased in the version of the book that circulated in the United Kingdom and South Africa, Rooke is the only white writer
of the apartheid era to draw attention to sexual harassment and male violence
within circles of intimacy, and to intraracial sexual violence as a major social
problem.

Restaging Rape: Black Writing and Sexual Apartheid

What would it mean to restage it, take it, do something else with the
ritual so that its revivability . . . is really seriously called into question.

—JUDITH BUTLER, INTERVIEW WITH VICKI BELL[1]

In 2002, *Hate No More* (2001), the post-apartheid edition of Arthur Maimane's
Victims (1976), which was the first South African novel by a black writer to
deal with the rape of a white woman by a black man, was dismissed as feeding
"directly into the discourse that [Maimane] is trying to counter."[2] Taking to
task critics who claim that Maimane's novel remains trapped within apartheid
thinking, I propose that *Victims* restages "black peril" scripts with subversive
effect, drawing attention to the temporality and contingency of "black peril" as
a racist discursive ritual, and to the melancholy structure of desire in apartheid
culture. This chapter, then, deals with the ways in which black writers, most of
whom wrote from exile about apartheid, tackled representations of sexual violence that had been instrumental in racist discourse. In his novel, Maimane
confronts the fact that "black peril" has been one of the choice narratives of
racist discourse in South Africa, epitomized in Bloke Modisane's observation
that "Natives have a rape-utation."[3] As with Maimane, who doubles back on
"black peril" narratives, Farida Karodia and Lauretta Ngcobo are the first black
women in South Africa to write of "the white peril," previously subject matter
for white women such as Schreiner, Bancroft, and Millin. Rather than abjecting "miscegenation" like their white predecessors, Karodia and Ngcobo replay
"white peril" themes in order to foreground the gendered nature of racialized
abuse under apartheid. Moreover, while Maimane, Karodia, and Ngcobo scrutinize narratives of interracial rape, in the work of black writers in the 1980s
there emerges a focus on intraracial rape: in writing by Njabulo Ndebele, as
well as by two black women, Gcina Mhlophe and Baleka Kgositsile. As I demonstrate, this movement towards a focus on intraracial rape is profoundly dis-
ruptive of apartheid binaries.

In an interview with Janice Harris in 1994, Lewis Nkosi explained that the
liberation struggle in South Africa advocated "solidarity criticism" which
favored "socialist-realist type fiction as against texts that were seen as bourgeois,

experimentalist or elitist."[4] Black South African authors who used playful or ironic narrative strategies were denounced as irrelevant believers in art for art's sake. Because of its narrative indeterminacy, Nkosi's *Mating Birds* is not a novel about rape,[5] although, like *Victims*, it is about the iterability of "black peril" stereotypes, and was similarly an interloper in the historically "whites only" territories of literary avant-gardism and erotic writing. Both *Victims* and *Mating Birds* were criticized not only by white feminists for their sexual politics, but also by commentators speaking on behalf of liberation movements for placing too much emphasis on sexual encounters. In "The Rediscovery of the Ordinary" (1984) Njabulo Ndebele articulates dissatisfaction with protest literature as a category concocted by critics who deny black writing "any literary and artistic value,"[6] and as a mode of literature that unambiguously reveals "the spectacular ugliness of the South African situation."[7] In Ndebele's short story "Fools," an incident of intraracial rape confounds simplistic moral positions and Manichaean notions of good and evil. Yet this is not to say that social realism was a bankrupt literary mode. While Ndebele deploys experimental narrative strategies to create resonance between intraracial rape and colonial violence, focusing thus on the implication of patriarchal and racist histories in black-on-black violence, a writer such as Gcina Mhlophe subversively uses the social realism advocated by the liberation movement to draw attention to gender violence and oppression within black communities.[8]

Most of the writers examined in this chapter faced harassment by the censors. When their work entered South Africa, it was embargoed or even banned, and in the cases of Maimane's *Victims* and Karodia's *Daughters of the Twilight*, South African editions (with different titles) only appeared years after the demise of apartheid. At the time they were writing, censorship was governed by two sets of laws, the Publications and Entertainment Act, No. 26 of 1963, and The Publications Act, No. 42 of 1974, which replaced the former Publications Control Board (PCB) with a Directorate of Publications, and removed the right of appeal from the law courts to hearings run by a Publications Appeal Board (PAB). In 1978, following the banning of Etienne Leroux's *Magersfontein, O Magersfontein!*, the act was amended again to provide the PAB with its own advisory "Committee of Experts," who now considered factors such as literary merit and likely readership in assessing whether a publication was "undesirable" or "not undesirable."[9] J.C.W van Rooyen stated that such experts were "appointed by reason of their educational qualifications and their special knowledge and experience in literature, language and art."[10] Despite this changeover to a supposedly more nuanced consideration of literary texts, the censors were typically more severe in dealing with the work of black writers. Moreover, as the banning of Maimane's *Victims* demonstrates, while the censors were only too happy for white writers to script "black peril" stereotypes, for a black man to write the rape of a white woman constituted an act of insurrection.

"A Rape-utation": "Black Peril" Mimicry in Arthur Maimane's *Victims*

In 1977, Arthur Maimane's novel *Victims* (1976), which begins with the rape of
a white woman by a black man in "a dank and smelly alley"[11] of Johannesburg,
was banned by the apartheid censors for being "dangerously explosive in the
South African context."[12] This banning took place despite the fact that "black
peril" narratives were among the stereotypes purveyed by the government.
Like his contemporary, Lewis Nkosi, Maimane was one of the black journalists
working for *Drum Magazine* who left the country in the late 1950s or early
1960s and found themselves in "a precarious divide between . . . cultures."[13]
Despite harassment by the South African censors, these writers had an ambivalent relationship with black nationalism and the idea of "political struggle."
Thabo Mbeki, in an interview with his biographer Mark Gevisser while president of post-apartheid South Africa, was scathing in his criticism of the *Drum*
writers, recalling what he called their "slave mentality": "Every week, every
month, [they] would be reporting black life, and it was drinking and rape. . . .
They themselves had a stereotype of life among the black urban population."[14]
As I shall demonstrate, although *Victims* received considerable acclaim on its
publication in 1976 and when a South African edition became available in the
post-apartheid era with the new title *Hate No More* (2000), there have been
negative critical views, which have taken two approaches. On the one hand
Victims was dismissed by politicized commentators, exponents of what Nkosi
has called "solidarity criticism," such as Mbeki's close comrade in the ANC,
Joan Brickhill, for dealing in racial stereotypes and for choosing sexual subject
matter over engagement with "the struggle." On the other hand, critics such as
Meg Samuelson have been disapproving of the novel's gender politics, particularly since the new edition appeared against the backdrop of proliferating
discourse on sexual violence in the post-apartheid context. I intend to argue
that neither "solidarity criticism" nor feminist arguments have been adequate
to the task of acknowledging the novel's dissident relationship with traditional
"black peril" stories, its experimental and shifting narrative perspective, and
the transgressive scripting by a black man of a white woman's sexual desire and
embodied subjectivity.

In *Victims*, Jean Ryan, a white English-speaking woman living in Johannesburg with her husband, Patrick, is raped by Philip Mokone in a Hillbrow alley
while walking home one night. Although her plight at first generates sympathy
among her white friends, this quickly changes to outrage when she decides to
keep the child she has conceived as a result of the rape. Abandoned by her
husband, she retreats to the "grey" area of Doornfontein where "coloureds"
and Indians live together with poor whites. Philip, a well-educated thinker and
township wit, eventually confesses to his wife, Betty, the act of brutality that he
has perpetrated. By coincidence, Betty has become Jean's housekeeper and a
nanny to her daughter, Beatrice. Betty and Philip offer to adopt Beatrice, but

Jean refuses and sends them away, with the plot thus revolving around the child born of interracial rape.

A decade and a half before the banning of *Victims* in South Africa, Sarah Gertrude Millin's *The Wizard Bird* (1962), a novel that similarly placed the rape of a white woman by a black man as its central structuring moment, did not raise the eyebrows of the South African censors. While the disparity in treatment meted out to these two texts may be partly explained by the passing of new censorship legislation in 1974 and by the fact that the censors were typically more severe in dealing with the work of black authors, it is important to recognize that, unlike Millin's novel, *Victims* was transgressive and scandalous in important ways. In contrast to conventional "black peril" narratives such as *The Wizard Bird*, where the possibility of the white womb bearing mixed-race progeny is erased by killing off the woman who has been defiled by intercourse with a black man, *Victims* is the first South African novel to represent a child born of a "black peril" rape. Like Lucy Lurie, the victim of interracial violation in J.M. Coetzee's *Disgrace* (1999), Jean Ryan in *Victims* chooses not to prosecute her attacker and does not opt for an abortion. Neither does she give up her child in order to return to the white areas of Johannesburg she once inhabited. In its original historical context, *Victims* subverted the Immorality Act by presenting "life after rape," a controversial and transgressive narrative in which the white womb is infiltrated by a "mixed-race" child.

Although there was no legislation forbidding interracial sex in the United Kingdom, where Maimane lived in exile while writing *Victims*, he left South Africa during the destruction of Sophiatown only to arrive in England in the wake of the 1958 Notting Hill Riots, which were sparked by an incident where a group of young white men attacked a Swedish woman when she defended her Jamaican husband from their insults after the youths had seen the couple arguing. The incident was followed by racist attacks, particularly on black West Indians living in Britain. According to his unpublished autobiography, when he arrived in England in 1961 Maimane was careful to differentiate himself from West Indians, as he "found a new fangled stereotype" in place and discovered that he had "high visibility." He also relates a number of "white peril" narratives, but with the gender dynamics reversed: a white widow offered him her spare bedroom promising to "tend to all [his] needs and requirements," a prospective married landlady appeared to be hinting that he take part in a *ménage a trois*, and white men cruised "looking for likely black studs whom they invited to their homes to service their wives."[15] According to his wife, Jenny, Maimane had a working draft of *Victims* as early as 1964.[16] Around the same time, Lionel Ngakane, one of his *Drum* contemporaries, who had arrived in London in the late 1950s and experienced the Notting Hill riots at first hand, tackled still-simmering racial tensions with his award-winning film, *Jemima and Johnny* (1964). Set in Notting Hill, the film deals with the friendship between a white English boy and a black girl from a West Indian family. One wonders whether the film would have been as highly acclaimed if it were made about a liaison that would have been more unsettling to white cinema-goers: the relationship that had actually set off the riots, between a black man and a white woman. To Maimane's credit, *Victims* tackles precisely this taboo subject.

In their decision to ban *Victims* in 1977, the apartheid censors cited section 47.2 (c), (d), and (e) of the Publications Act of 1974. Respectively, these clauses forbade any publication that "brings any section of the inhabitants of the Republic into ridicule or contempt," "is harmful to the relations between any sections of the inhabitants of the Republic," and "is prejudicial to the safety of the State, the general welfare or the peace and good order." Although the reader, Prof. H. van der Merwe Scholtz, was obliged to list relevant page numbers for each category of "undesirability," he simply listed pages he found to be objectionable in numerical order. The result is that it is difficult to see why the pages listed were regarded as objectionable. Moreover, the report on the novel was extremely brief, which suggests that not a great deal of time was spent on the assessment:

> This book is dangerously explosive in the South African context. The hatred
> of everything that is white, and especially white Afrikaans, is such an obses-
> sion that the writer is not in a state to get the distance that he needs to make
> sense of his subject.[17]

Anti-Afrikaans sections of the novel are in fact limited and relatively minor, but coming in the wake of the Soweto uprisings of 1976, when black school-children protested against Afrikaans as an enforced medium of instruction, the focus on this aspect of the novel was enough to have it banned. As Samuelson points out, in the novel the actual rape scene and the event of childbirth are elided: "rape and childbirth are relegated to the blank space between two paragraphs."[18] In the novel's encounter with the censors, this meant that the rape could not be isolated as an objectionable scene, and in his report Scholtz does not mention anything about the actual birth of Jean's child. Yet these aspects of the novel were clearly significant in the decision that the novel was "harmful" and "prejudicial to the safety of the State," as the novel was only unbanned in 1985, when the Immorality Act was repealed.

The application for unbanning *Victims* was motivated by the South African Public Library in Cape Town. This time, attention given to the text was more substantial. In line with the new emphasis on "expert opinion" and "likely readers" that had been in place in censorship legislation since 1978, the book was sent to two readers, J.C. Claassen and Prof. S. du Plessis, who summarized its content, both finding it "not undesirable." In their decision to unban the novel, the Directorate of Publications claimed that "the rape scene is merely alluded to and the author takes care to avoid an erotic, physical description." "The socio-political climate," they continued, "has changed considerably," and "the broader current outlook will justify release."[19] By this time, however, the novel was no longer in print. In 1986 Maimane attempted to negotiate a South African edition with local publisher Skotaville through Ezekiel Mphahlele, who was at this time the publisher's only reader for manuscripts, but they were concerned that a South African edition of the book might be banned and so these discussions came to nothing. It was only much later, well into the post-apartheid period, that Maimane successfully negotiated with Kwela Books for a South African edition of the novel, which was published as *Hate no More* in 2000.

While preparing the text for publication by Kwela, Maimane was warned by his new publishers "that the idea that a woman might enjoy being raped be very carefully handled."[20] The scene the publishers were uneasy about appears in *Victims*:

> But if only she'd fought back. Not to excite me, as Desmond says. Then I could really have hurt her, making her feel every single thing. Instead of lying there like a piece of wood. In a trance. And then what does she do? The Bitch! Responds. Oh still in her trance, but she shakes and grabs, moans. Like she's enjoying it! That ruined it. Yes, Desmond, they do enjoy it—even though they don't know they are, or don't want to.[21]

The implication that Jean was "enjoying" the rape is thus Philip's, as this part of the text is focalized through his perspective. Since the rape is motivated by Philip's desire to drag the white goddess of racist culture "into the muck," to "make her feel some loathing for herself," the phrase "they do enjoy it" should be read as racially encoded—Philip is referring to white women. As Maimane presents it, driving Philip's misogyny is the Fanonian notion of the black man's inferiority complex. In *Black Skin, White Masks*, Fanon wrote from his own painful experience about "a zone of nonbeing," "a feeling of nonexistence," "an inferiority complex" that "is the outcome of a double process:—primarily, economic;—subsequently, the internalization—or, better, the epidermalization—of this inferiority."[22] That Maimane consciously evokes this Fanonian idea becomes clear when Boykie points out to Philip: "That kind of hostile act is an attempt at assertion, and that doesn't result from a superiority complex. A superior being has no need to assert himself."[23]

Of course, the notion of a white woman harboring repressed desire for black men also appears in *Black Skin, White Masks*. Writing of the main character's desire for white flesh in Chester Himes's *If He Hollers Let Him Go*, Fanon makes one of his most controversial comments, referring to "That big blonde who was always in his way, weak, sensual, offered, open, fearing (desiring) rape."[24] Undeniably, Fanon has problematic theories about white women's desire for sexual violence, but as T. Denean Sharpley-Whiting points out, "To maintain that Fanon evokes a cultural stereotype of white women . . . ignores the context of his query."[25] What Fanon was tackling was white women's complicity in the axiom: "Whoever says rape says Negro,"[26] which has a parallel in *Victims*: "A rapist had to be a *Kaffir*."[27] For Fanon, the white woman's incessant sexual fear of the black man is a neurosis, "a racist cultural *affect* that cloaks desire."[28] When Philip echoes this implication that the white woman secretly desires to be seized by the black man, the novel becomes an intertext to Fanon's text, presenting a melancholic scenario whereby the black man attempts to transfer the internalized denigration that he experiences in a racist society onto the white woman: "If she knows—if she remembers those seconds—then she's going to hate herself."[29] In this way *Victims* exposes the complex enmeshment of racism, misogyny, and *ressentiment* in a system where white women are marked out as inaccessible to black men. A politically-motivated act of misogyny, the interracial rape in *Victims* is represented as a blow against, but also as a direct result of sexual apartheid and "Immorality" legislation.

As Maimane's Kwela editors suggested, however, Philip's inference that Jean "enjoyed" the rape would not be tolerated in the post-apartheid environment, which had seen the strengthening of gender-based criticism and become sensitized by the media to a high incidence of reported rape. At the prompting of his editors, Maimane revised the passage from *Victims* for the publication of *Hate No More* as follows:

> Yet if only she'd fought back. Just struggled a bit. Not to excite me, as Desmond claims is what rapists like to happen. Then I could really have made her feel every single thing. Instead of lying there like a piece of wood. Ice cold fish. In a trance like it wasn't happening to her. Not experiencing every single second of her degradation. But then if she didn't feel anything, it wasn't such a terrible thing you did.[30]

Meg Samuelson claims that "references to physical harm are expunged" in this version of the passage, and that this "is an important alteration in the novel's attempt to sketch the rape as a purely racial rather than gendered event."[31] Yet the revised version of the novel does not erase descriptions of bodily harm, in fact these are highlighted in references to Jean's "bruised hands and torn knees," and to the way she "rolled painfully on her side."[32] Leaving aside Samuelson's questionable use of Maimane's novel as a starting point in an argument about South African literary texts in the transitional period of 1990–2000, in constructing her argument that Maimane's "primary authorial impulse appears to be the exoneration of Philip" and that the author "glorifies" rape, Samuelson misreads the first paragraphs of the novel, inferring that the text privileges the perspective of a rapist by "open[ing] with the main protagonist, Philip, walking through the streets of Johannesburg."[33] The first chapter of each edition, however, begins with Jean's narrative point of view as she walks through the streets of Johannesburg. After the rape, the first perspective offered to the reader is Jean's, and the novel ends with her words to Philip and his wife, Betty: "Just go. Please." As C.J. Driver noted in a review of *Victims* for the

Guardian in 1977: "Maimane has done [something] which conventional wisdom would not allow him (a man and a black) to do: he has imagined himself into the mind of a white South African woman."[34] Although Jean's perspective is diminished in the Kwela edition by the addition of a prologue and epilogue set in the post-apartheid period and focalized through Philip's perspective alone, in both editions the main narrative works through a continuously shifting of point of view, through focalization and counter-focalization, emphasizing Maimane's observation that both Philip and Jean are injured parties, casualties of a brutal and humiliating system:

> The two victims who concern me most in the novel are a street-wise young black man and the young, white and middle-class woman he rapes without sexual passion. He is impelled by his frustrations to avenge himself on the apartheid that victimizes him and blights all his life. She becomes a knowing victim . . . not only of the act in the smelly alley but also of the system which turns against her because of her unexpected reaction to the consequences of the ravishing.[35]

The text can be read as critical of Philip's misogyny as it is of Jean's racism, drawing attention to the ways in which apartheid has induced Philip's sexism and "tough guy" masculinity as well as to the environment that has created Jean's prejudices. With authorial irony that questions the gender politics of the post-apartheid dispensation, the prologue and epilogue of *Hate No More* are set in the period immediately after Mbeki has replaced Mandela as President, and Philip has become "the elderly chair of the Equal Opportunities and Gender Equality Portfolio Committee on the Gauteng Legislature."[36] Pessimistically, the epilogue undermines the myth of the "rainbow nation" by sketching the post-apartheid state as a family founded on a nightmare of gender violence and incest: "Unknown daughters who're now mothers. . . . And sons who've also seduced and probably raped: like father like son. The difference being that they may have done it—seduction and rape—to their unknown half-sisters."[37]

Although both editions of Maimane's novel revolve around interracial rape, there is also an exposé of the everyday intraracial sexual violence in South African society. In both editions, casual gender violence finds a breeding place in South African township life under apartheid. Reflecting on his motive for raping Jean, Philip acknowledges that rape is not something from which to obtain pleasure: "Rape? Dammit, he'd refused an invitation once in Sophiatown because he'd known there would be nothing to enjoy. Some poor plaas-sheilas on their days off from slaving on the farm . . . ."[38] The incident has an actual referent in Maimane's experience of Sophiatown life recorded in his autobiography:

> . . . I was invited to partake in a rape without violence. Walking towards Thirteenth Avenue and the bus terminus with a friend—a Clever who held

down a job, not a tsotsi—against this tide of domestics hurrying towards the buses and suburbs, he put up the proposition.

"Let's pick ourselves one of these sheilas and take her to your place, Oupa." His eyes were already searching the bloom for an attractive victim. "She won't argue because they know the score; and she won't report to the police either."[39]

He critiques an environment in which sexual violence is commonplace, and where women are only safe from sexual assault because of their connections to men:

> For young women safety on the streets of the ghetto also depended on their connections with the wild side . . . At the opposite end of the sisterly scale were the comparatively decent women—ranging from domestic servants to teachers or nurses—who could walk the streets without fear of rape because they had a brother, cousin, uncle or some other young man within the ambience who'd be prepared to avenge their honour. . . .
>
> The rest walked the streets in fear and trepidation . . . even when accompanied by their boyfriends or brothers—if these men were not among those recognized as having their own connections. A young man lounging at a street corner shop could saunter up to such a couple and completely ignoring the man, say:
>
> "Hello, my sister. You shouldn't walk alone on these dangerous streets, you know. Come with me and I'll look after you, okay?"
>
> Some of these women were not seen for days afterwards. And their abductors did not have to use actual force, just the threat of it, for them to remain wherever they were taken for as long as the really real men enjoyed their company.[40]

Although Maimane's autobiography is unpublished, this sort of exposé, which drew attention to violence in a hard-drinking and male-dominated society, was precisely the sort of thing Thabo Mbeki found objectionable in the journalism of the *Drum* writers. In the ANC's statement to the Human Rights Commission (SAHRC) hearings on racism in the media in 2000 he lambasted the *Drum* journalists for having "consciously cultivated the notion that African news was necessarily about alcohol abuse, sex, crime, rape and corruption. The model African reporter was he/she who reported best on these subjects, and the best publication, the one that reported the most sensational scandals."[41] During the SAHRC hearings, Mbeki's ire towards the *Drum* writers was in fact more virulent and less ambiguous than his statements about J.M. Coetzee's *Disgrace*.

In the apartheid years, writers such as Maimane bore the brunt of the solidarity criticism advocated by the liberation movement. A classic example is a review of *Victims* by Joan Brickhill. A young white South African journalist and close friend to Mbeki in exile, Brickhill worked for the ANC's Department of Information and Publicity. In a review entitled "Self-indulgent/Unrealistic," published in the periodical *Africa* in 1976, Brickhill protests that "the author does not portray that resistance to oppression which was so evident in the fifties," and that the main character, Philip, "refuses to involve himself in the liberation struggle . . . and approaches life in a selfish individualistic manner illustrated by the futile act of raping a White woman in order to take revenge on the whole White nation." Like Samuelson, who wants the novel to reflect the social reality of South African life, Brickhill judges *Victims* by the standards of realism, claiming that Maimane's "portrayal of the main White character, Jane [*sic*], as typically racialistic and insensitive yet willing to sacrifice her privileged existence and successful marriage simply to keep the child . . . is so unrealistic in the South African context that it merely creates more confusion."[42] As I shall demonstrate, regulatory notions of realism are less suited to reading Maimane's novel than an approach which considers the text as restaging racist representations.

For Frantz Fanon in *Black Skin, White Masks* the black man's inferiority complex leads to an attempt to gain admittance to the white world through mimicry of white culture. One of the keys to whiteness is access to white women: "When my restless hands caress those white breasts, they grasp white civilization and dignity and make them mine."[43] The colonized man also becomes proportionately whiter, "elevated above his jungle status," in direct ratio "to his adoption of the mother country's cultural standards," which pivots on his mastery of the colonizers' language, an ambivalent gesture since "to speak means above all to assume a culture, to support the weight of a civilization" and this very "civilization" judges him by the colour of his skin. The result is a liminal state between cultures: "The educated Negro . . . feels at a given stage that his race no longer understands him. Or that he no longer understands it."[44] While for Fanon mimicry is profoundly melancholic, a symptom of the failure of a radical overhaul of both internal and external worlds, for Homi Bhabha it has ambivalent potential. In *The Location of Culture* Bhabha defines mimicry as "the signs of a double articulation: a complex strategy of reform, regulation and discipline, which appropriates the Other as it realizes power." Above all, mimicry hinges on the production of a certain spectrum of colonized subjectivity as "almost the same but not quite" (or "almost the same but not white").[45]

While Maimane's mimicry of "black peril" narrative leads Samuelson to claim that the author remains trapped within the "overarching logic" of apartheid, I argue that Maimane's text reterritorializes discourse on sexuality through the self-reflexive restaging of racist stereotypes. *Victims* can be read as "almost the same but not quite" like traditional "black peril" narratives, and it is with a focus on these "not quite" aspects that I would like to conclude my discussion of this novel. As mentioned above, *Victims* is the first South African novel to portray the birth of a "mixed-race" child from the rape of a white woman by a black man, with the text registering the scandal of this birth in Jean's constant references to her pregnancy. Eschewing the melancholic dimension of other narratives of interracial rape, *Victims* also details a love affair between Phillip and a white woman called Vivienne. Most importantly, the transgressive aspects of the novel are furthered by erotic descriptions of a white woman's desire and body in this text written by a black man. C.J. Driver commends Maimane for scripting Jean Ryan's inner life and subjectivity, but even more daring in the novel is the close-up focus on Jean's feelings about her naked, pregnant body and on her lusty sexual desire. At one point, she looks at her naked body in the mirror, her gaze echoing the author's: "It was a beautiful, desirable body, she decided after long, thoughtful moments. Any man would want it."[46] While pregnant with the child conceived during the rape, she aches with sexual desire: "Her breath came in gasps, her hands fluttered over her body."[47] As may be seen by the banning of *Victims*, for a black male writer in the apartheid era to linger on sexualized details of a white woman's anatomy was an extremely transgressive maneuver.

Rescripting "Miscegenation": "White Peril" in Fiction by Farida Karodia and Lauretta Ngcobo

Until the late 1980s, "white peril" narratives in South African literature had most frequently been the domain of white women writers such as Schreiner, Bancroft, and Millin, who used such narratives to denounce "miscegenation." As Ian Glenn points out in his article "Legislating Women," the fiction of three white women was called upon by Dr. T. E. Dönges, Nationalist Party Minister of the Interior, when introducing the Prohibition of Mixed Marriages Bill in 1949:

> I should have liked to have read to the House an extract from one of the writings of Olive Schreiner where she pays tribute to the Boer who in the middle of the desert and surrounded by barbarians preserved his racial purity. . . . It is striking that in our South African literature, two women writers, one in English, the other in Afrikaans, have chosen as the theme of their novels the disastrous results of mixed marriages. The one is Regina Neser, who wrote *Kinders van Ismael* and the other is Sarah Gertrude Millin.[48]

Glenn notes that there is a long tradition in South African literature of white women "explicitly or implicitly calling for legislation . . . to prohibit sexual relationships between white men and women of colour" in texts "marked by racial jealousy or rivalry."[49] Although Glenn does not mention it directly, it is clear that these white women deployed "white peril" representations specifically to this effect. In the final years of apartheid, however, one begins to see new departures in South African literary works that deal with relationships between white men and black women. In Farida Karodia's *Daughters of the Twilight* (1986) and Lauretta Ngcobo's *And They Didn't Die* (1990) "white peril" becomes a way of demonstrating the material brutality and gendered structure of apartheid.[50] It is useful to compare these two novels to a short story entitled "Bella," by Matthew Krouse, the first white male author in the apartheid era to publish a fictional account of "the white peril."[51] Exposing the potentially perverse environment of the white South African home, "Bella" deploys a voyeuristic, even pornographic, perspective on sexual violence. In the novels of Karodia and Ngcobo, on the other hand, the black woman's perspective of "white peril" rape is foregrounded. Karodia turns outside of a national tradition for her inspiration, and both the novels of both Karodia and Ngcobo can be read as doubling back on the writings of Schreiner and Millin, showing up the limitations of white women's perspectives on the sexual threats faced by black women, and rewriting white scripts of "miscegenation."

In Krouse's story, a domestic servant named Bella is violently raped by her employer's son and his friend, with the names of the rapists, Milton and Nathan (the latter resonating with "Satan"), metamorphosing the white home into a hellish environment. The story opens with a paragraph that parodies the style of Donald Barthelme's "Manual for Sons," which contains the following passage: "Some fathers masturbate because they fear women; some fathers sleep with hired women because they fear women who are free; some fathers never sleep at all, but are endlessly awake, staring at their features, which are behind them."[52] Like Barthelme's text, Krouse's style renders as strange and sexualized objects of scrutiny the role players in a "normal" domestic environment, with the text zooming in on the perversion of family life under apartheid: "Some children are stealing; some children are burning adults; some children are taking coke every ten minutes; some children will not restrict themselves to only one partner; some children are fucking their servants."[53] While the self-consciously avant-garde style seems inappropriately playful, creating a disjunction between form and content, "Bella" nonetheless has a serious objective. According to Krouse, the message of the story is that if an adult had sexual relations with children, this would be pedophilia, but with the warped environment of apartheid, there is no "ordinary" relation of power between child and adult.[54] In Krouse's narrative, white children are rapists, the black adult woman the victim. Like other "white peril" accounts in South African literary history, the story revolves around "miscegenation," caused in this instance by the failure of contraception during the rape as Nathan accidentally tears a black condom in his "wild frenzy."[55] At the end of the story, Bella leaves her job with the euphemistic excuse to Milton's mother that she must return home to look after her sister's children. Breaking with "the elision of the scene of violence in male texts about rape" mentioned by Higgins and Silver in their study *Rape and Representation*, Krouse's story was published in an anthology entitled *Porno*, which came out in a limited edition (allegedly printed by "Bobbejaan Press" in Grahamstown), and is shockingly graphic. Yet, this very exposure of violence may be read as registering what Higgins and Silver refer to as "masculine sexual anxiety and guilt," in this case the ambivalence of a white male author who evidently recognizes his own complicity in a race-, class- and gender-based system of oppression. Although representing a brutal violation, the story is told in the third person, creating a voyeuristic perspective that erases the victim's experience. In the novels of Karodia and Ngcobo on the other hand, women's perspectives reveal the enmeshment of sexual and racial domination under apartheid.

One of the questions critics have asked regarding narratives of interracial rape is the extent to which such accounts may be regarded as realistic in themselves, given the high levels of intraracial violence in South Africa. In her article "The Rainbow Womb," Meg Samuelson claims that the post-apartheid transition (which she classifies as the period from 1990–2000) has seen an increased emphasis on interracial rape in literary scripts, including those by Karodia and Ngcobo, where "the consequence of rape is measured in the birth of a mixed-race child." Such representations, Samuelson argues, are unrealistic, since rape in South Africa is most often intraracial and "the rate of conception comparatively low."[56] What this argument fails to register, however, is that the violations in *Daughters of the Twilight/Other Secrets* and *And They Didn't Die* take place under apartheid, where the sexual exploitation of black and "coloured" women by white men was a real but hidden phenomenon. As noted in *Daughters of the Twilight*, "white peril" rapes were not reported under apartheid because of "fear for a system of justice which punished the victim and not the offender."[57] Moreover, black women working for white families or living near white communities in this era often found themselves trapped in abusive situations where they had little access to contraceptives and safe abortion. Thus it is not possible to say that the birth of a child in "white peril" cases under apartheid was an unlikely outcome. If one is to judge the novels of Karodia and Ngcobo by the standards of realism, one could argue that these novels draw attention to the actual problems faced by women classified as "non-white" under apartheid, even though the intertextuality, and in Karodia's case, metafictional self-reflexivity, set up in each novel complicate any attempt to relegate this fiction simply to the realm of social realism.

Karodia was living in exile in Canada when she wrote *Daughters of the Twilight*, published by the Women's Press in London in 1986. In its plot and narrative structure, *Daughters of the Twilight* closely resembles *Two Virgins*, a novel by the Indian writer Karmala Markandaya (1973), and in fact *Daughters of the Twilight* could be seen as a palimpsest-type rewriting of this Indian text.[58] Both novels focus on the relationship between two sisters growing up in a small and marginalized town. In Karodia's novel, the setting is Sterkstroom, "a small dorp in South Africa . . . the type of town you drive through en route to some other place, happily forgetting that you've ever been there."[59] Similarly, the sisters in

Two Virgins spend their childhood in what Lalitha, the elder one, calls "this one-horse town, this backward place, this outpost of civilization."[60] The narrative perspective in each novel is limited to the experiences of the younger sister, as *Two Virgins* is focalized through the character of Saroja, and *Daughters of the Twilight* comprises the narration by Meena, who is in awe of the beauty and self-confidence of her more sexually-adventurous elder sister Yasmin. While these intertextual resonances suggest a deliberate tracking of Indian diasporic identity by Karodia, whose paternal family members were among those from the Indian subcontinent who migrated to South Africa in the late nineteenth or early twentieth centuries, differences between the novels are marked. In *Two Virgins*, Lalitha aspires to become an actress and runs away to Bombay where she is seduced by a film director whom she cannot marry because of caste inequality. Yasmin, in Karodia's novel, on the other hand, is brutally raped by the son of a local white farmer and National Party member of parliament, with the violation and its aftermath drawing attention to the precarious position of Indian traders in the interstices of territory designated "white" under the Group Areas Act. In *Two Virgins*, Lalitha has an abortion, but when Yasmin, in Karodia's novel, arrives at the clinic, her pregnancy is too far along for an abortion, and she is forced to carry to term the child whom she regards as a hateful reminder of the rape.

Daughters of the Twilight opens with an image of destructive invasion, as Cobus Steyn, the wealthy and influential white farmer's son, shatters the windows of Meena and Yasmin's home. Drawing attention to the vulnerability of the narrator's family space, the incident sets the scene for the many ways in which the novel shows the most sacred boundaries of self, family, home, and identity to be threatened by white men whose behavior is protected by the racialized and patriarchal structure of apartheid. Parallel to the story of Yasmin's rape is an account of the hardship inflicted on the family by the Group Areas Act. Because its members are not white, Meena's family is evicted and has to move to the remote and desolate settlement of McBain. Rather than becoming a mere symbolic extension of this assault on the home, however, the rape of Yasmin can be read alongside the forced relocation as among the most poignant of apartheid's intimate dehumanizations. In the second chapter, Cobus steals and dismembers Meena's doll, while fighting off Yasmin, who tries to retrieve it. The encounter leaves Yasmin disheveled, her "new pink organdie dress streaked with dirt" and her socks "around her ankles." Pre-empting the rape, Cobus tells Yasmin: "I'm your baas and I can have anything I want."[61] The "mutilated doll, tossed aside, the celluloid dented and fragmented" points to the metonymic ways in which apartheid was transferred onto the bodies of women such as Yasmin, turning them into trivialized objects, property to be pulled apart, emptied of voice and memory, a trend the novel reverses by remembering the voices and stories of women who were neither classified as "black" or "white" under apartheid and were able to slip fluidly between the classifications "Indian" and "coloured."

Despite the novel's recuperative project, however, neither the narrator of the novel nor her family are unreservedly sympathetic when Yasmin is raped by Cobus. The novel is thus ambivalent in its treatment of Yasmin's desire for independence. Before the incident, Meena watches her sister on horseback, claiming that she "was really proud of her, but [she] was also a little concerned about the situations she frequently got herself into. First it was Cobus, now it was Andrew Jordaan."[62] To some extent, it is implied, the rape is something Yasmin has "got herself into." When Yasmin fails to come home, Meena sets out to look for her and finds her, bruised and "dirt streaked," lying in a grove of trees. Yasmin's first word is simply: "Raped."[63] The emphasis, however, is on her endurance, rather than on victimhood. She says "I'll survive," and then narrates the rape to Meena. As if to refute the idea that she called the incident upon herself, she repeats over and over again that she tried to fight against her attacker. Yasmin tries to keep her violation a secret from the rest of her family, a strategy that succeeds only until it becomes clear that she is pregnant. She gives birth to a girl child whom she rejects, and after ongoing conflicts with her family, leaves home. Although Yasmin is often treated sympathetically in the text, the narrator and her family accuse her of attracting trouble "like a magnet"[64] and of being selfish and vain, portraying her departure as an abandonment of her child and family, with the text retaining some ambivalence about women's independence that continues in the post-apartheid reworking of the novel, entitled *Other Secrets*.

Daughters of the Twilight ends with the birth of the child of "white peril" rape and the disappearance of the child's mother, Yasmin. In the revised and extended South African post-apartheid edition, which came out with the new title, *Other Secrets* in 2000,[65] the story moves on as the first part, entitled "Daughters," comprises a subtly revised version of *Daughters of the Twilight* and the second and third parts, "Mothers" and "Other Secrets," trace the lives of the main characters further. *Other Secrets* differs from the story of *Daughters of the Twilight* by focussing on the life of the child born of the interracial rape. In this revised edition, after a doctor confirms that it is too late for an abortion, Meena refers to "the dawning of a new day, a new life," but rather than being, as Samuelson claims, the text's "slippage into the clichéd discourse of the South African miracle,"[66] the statement is metafictional, a deliberate reflection of Meena's naïve immersion in the cliché-ridden discourse of the romance literature that she reads and writes: "In *Desperate Moments*, Jennifer had said a tearful goodbye to Martin at the lake. It was sunrise then too. Sunrise. The dawning of a new day, a new life."[67] In fact the optimism that characterizes Meena's rose-tinted vision is undercut a few pages later when "weak rays" of sunlight are "dragged down, leaving shadows in their wake."[68] Like Lewis Nkosi's play, "The Black Psychiatrist" (1993), *Other Secrets* resists incorporating the child of "white peril" rape into a redemptive and reconciliatory nation-building narrative.

As Samuelson points out, in *Other Secrets* the name of Yasmin's child changes with the text's revisions from Fatima to Soraya, after the glamorous ex-Empress of Iran, Soraya Esfandiari Bakhtiari. A model of hybrid identity, Bakhtiari was born of German and Iranian parents and lived a cosmopolitan life between Europe and Iran. After divorcing the Shah of Iran, she had a relationship with the married film director, Franco Indovina, who left his wife to be with her but was then killed in an airplane accident. Following in the footsteps of Sarah Gertrude Millin's *God's Stepchildren*, *Other Secrets* traces generations of children born of "miscegenation," but aligning Yasmin's child with the beautiful and talented Bakhtiari clearly challenges the biological racism of Millin's novels, where the children produced by interracial sex are physically and intellectually degenerate. Rather than resulting from some biological flaw of the protagonists, the tragedies in *Other Secrets* are related to the novel's ambivalent representation of marriage. Although fond of each other, Meena's parents no longer have a fulfilling marriage. Like Bakhtiari, Karodia's women protagonists Yasmin, Meena, Soraya, and even, it is implied, Meena's mother, have sexual relations with married men, and all of these affairs end tragically. Thus, while not idealizing marriage, the novel could be read as offering a series of moralizing and cautionary accounts of women who enter sexual relationships with married men. Yet what is interesting about two of these relationships—Yasmin's relationship with Neville, and Soraya's affair with Douglas—is that they are interracial, focusing on, and rendering imaginable, genuine interracial love. Notably, both of these relationships develop outside of South Africa. Thus, although recognizing the brutality that underpins relations under apartheid, *Other Secrets* challenges the melancholic narratives of Schreiner, Bancroft, and Millin. In a melodramatic twist at the end of the novel, Soraya is killed in a car accident on a return trip to South Africa, leaving her body as a human incubator for the baby that will be born from her relationship with Douglas. Rather than simply relegating women to wombs within a nationalist framework, however, the novel draws attention here to the role of women's bodies and maternal lineage in forging diasporic identities as Soraya's child and Meena's remaining family, it is implied, will leave South Africa shortly and continue their lives elsewhere.

While the women in Karodia's *Other Secrets* escape South Africa, Lauretta Ngcobo's protagonist Jezile, in *And They Didn't Die*, exemplifies the status of the subaltern. This is despite the fact that like Karodia, Lauretta Ngcobo wrote her novel in exile, in her case due to her husband A.B. Ngcobo's political activities, his prosecution during the 1956 Treason Trial and his subsequent role as a founder and leader, both at home and in exile, of the Pan Africanist Congress (PAC). Ngcobo was forced to flee South Africa to Swaziland and Zambia before settling for twenty-five years in the United Kingdom, where she wrote *And They Didn't Die*, which was first published by Virago Press in London in 1990. A South African edition (Skotaville) appeared in the same year, and another edition, with an afterword by M.J. Daymond, followed in 1999. As Daymond explains in her appraisal of the novel:

> Ngcobo's fictional account of the effects of the 1913 Land Act and subsequent Land Acts pays tribute to the women of rural KwaZulu-Natal who have fought to retain control of their land and to keep their families alive while their husbands labor in the city. The land for which the women struggle is in the rural reserves . . . created by the policies of separate development and migrant labor, yet they are steadily being dispossessed even of this land.[69]

Despite her immense fortitude and resourcefulness, Jezile remains trapped within the exploitative and crushing environment of the apartheid Bantustan. According to Daymond, "[t]he novel which might have given Ngcobo the clearest indication of how a people's relationship to the land can be written is Olive Schreiner's *The Story of an African Farm*," but as she notes, when Ngcobo encountered Schreiner's work, she felt "utterly divided" from it.[70] While, as Daymond observes, Ngcobo paid a "moving tribute" to Schreiner later in her life, reading Schreiner's writings at university in South Africa Ngcobo felt "only disappointment as I kept meeting those nameless, shadowy 'wooly Kaffir maids.'"[71] Picking up on Ngcobo's "disappointment" and her engagement with Schreiner, I would like to suggest that Schreiner's unfinished life's work, *From Man to Man* (published posthumously in 1926) provides a more resonant intertext with *And They Didn't Die* than *The Story of an African Farm*.

As discussed in the first chapter of this study, Schreiner was concerned with drawing attention to "the white peril," what she called "that peril which has long overshadowed this country . . . one which exists for all dark-skinned women in the hands of white men."[72] In *From Man to Man*, Rebekah's philandering husband, Frank, who is associated with all the worst masculine energies, eventually over-strains the limits of his wife's tolerance when he has a sexual relationship with their black domestic worker. Unnamed in the story, the woman is referred to simply as "the girl" or "the servant girl." After Rebekah sees her husband visiting their domestic worker's room one moonlit night, she writes him a letter asking for either separation or divorce. She then attempts to confront the servant woman in person:

> Before the window on the side of her single bed the servant girl was sitting. She was half dressed: her short black wool, with difficulty parted, was combed out to stand in two solid masses on each side of her head; her small dark face, with its puckered forehead even a little blacker than the rest, was raised as Rebekah opened the door. She had on a red-striped flannel petticoat and a pair of crimson corsets, from a mass of frilled white lace, showed her puny black arms and bare shoulders; on the bed beside her lay a white nightdress heavy with bows: on the other side lay the serge dress she was just going to put on. The girl placed a closed fist on each of her hips, and raising her chin in the air looked at Rebekah through her half-closed twinkling eyes.

"Wat wil jij hé" she said, throwing her chin higher.

Rebekah stood silent; all she had determined to say passed from her. The girl threw back her head yet farther and burst into a laugh, intended to be defiant but with an undertone of fear; all her white teeth showing between her thick dark lips, as she sat with her fists on her hips.

Then, as Rebekah looked at her, Rebekah knew that it was with that girl even as it was with her that day.[73]

Here the "red-striped flannel petticoat" and "crimson corsets" are clearly not the undergarments of a respectable woman, and the black woman is the very image of promiscuous deviancy. The reference to the "nightdress heavy with bows" and the "single bed" tortuously compel the reader, with Rebekah, to rehearse the male gaze, to take on her husband's perspective as he would have entered the same room, seen the woman in her nightdress, and shared her bed. Bringing into relief racial difference, the "whiteness" of the servant's night-dress and "white lace" of her underwear create a stark contrast with her black-ness: her "puny black arms and bare shoulders." As explained in a footnote, the phrase "Wat wil jij hé" translates literally as "What do you want?," but "the pronoun 'jij' is in Cape Dutch, the only language of the Coloured people of the West, and is the most extreme insult when applied to a superior."[74] Through her speech and body language, the servant woman emerges here as a defiant, insubordinate subject, fearful, but also realizing that she is in a position to inspire shock and fear in Rebekah. A dark and anxiety-provoking figure, she has infiltrated the intimacy of the white home and usurped Rebekah's place in her husband's life. This mirroring is most evident in Rebekah's realization that the woman, like herself, is pregnant: "it was with that girl even as it was with her that day." Of course the shock value of the likeness plays off the fact that the woman's condition is due to "miscegenation," her pregnancy is an uncanny, literally "unhomely," physical signifier of a secret that threatens to undo the white domestic space.

There is another way of reading this scene, however, where the "single bed" draws attention to the curtailment, if not erasure, of black women's family life and sexuality in the system of migrant domestic employment. Moreover, the woman's "laugh with an undertone of fear" suggests her precarious and depen-dent position, which prompts the question of how much choice she has had in the relationship with Rebekah's husband. Unfortunately, though, the text fore-closes on exploring these issues further, with Frank soon finding that the woman has vanished, that her room has been literally whitewashed, purged of her presence:

> . . . he walked to the door of the servant's room and looked in. . . . the room
> held nothing but a bare iron bedstead standing in the centre, and there was
> a strong smell of fresh whitewash.[75]

While the reader should maintain some flexibility of judgment since the novel was not finished, the fact remains that whereas Schreiner plotted out the fates of her white women protagonists to the end,[76] the story of the servant woman remains untold. To what extent was the woman coerced into the sexual relationship with Frank? Did Rebekah dismiss her from her position, or did she leave the homestead of her own accord? Where has she gone? Her child, Sartje, suddenly appears in chapter twelve as Rebekah's adopted ward, who is "treated in all ways as her own child, except that it was taught to call her mistress."[77] Has Rebekah taken the child away from its mother to raise alongside her own white children? Or did the child's mother, finding herself without a home, deliver her to the home of the father? Is Schreiner implying that the mother abandoned her baby? The text evades confronting any of these questions, with such gaps and absences persisting as disturbing indicators of the limits of Schreiner's sympathetic imagination, and of the abyss dividing black and white women's experiences in South Africa.

With these problems of reading Schreiner's text in mind, I now turn to the ways in which Ngcobo's *And They Didn't Die* rewrites, from the perspective of the black woman, the theme of "miscegenation" that one finds in *From Man to Man*. In Ngcobo's novel, Jezile is forced to seek employment as a domestic worker, which takes her far from home to Bloemfontein where she is hired by Mr. and Mrs. Potgieter. Like the servant women in Schreiner's novels, Jezile is deprived of her name by Mrs. Potgieter (who calls her Annie). Although Mr. Potgieter is apparently kind to her, his activities bring into sharp focus the arbitrary power of white employers over black servants under apartheid. He treats Jezile with respect by communicating with her in Afrikaans rather than in Fanakalo, he agrees to a higher salary than his wife offers, he restrains his wife from subjecting Jezile to a punishing work timetable, and he brings Jezile small gifts that transform the meagerness of her living space: a lamp, a table at which she can write letters to her family, and a small pocket radio. His purpose, however, becomes clear to Jezile as he enters her room one night, claiming to love her, and deaf to her protests, rapes her. Ngcobo's text focuses on the physical and psychological effects of the violation on Jezile, and on her realization that she cannot tell anyone about what has happened. Whereas in Schreiner's *From Man to Man* it is only white women (particularly Rebekah's sister, Baby Bertie) who have reputations to be damaged by gossip, in Ngcobo's novel Jezile knows that if she returns to her village her life will never be the same: "Rape is a burden to its own victim. It was as though she had wished it on herself. She could predict all the lurid gossip. They would even suggest that she followed him to Bloemfontein because she had an affair with him."[78]

The shame and silence imposed on victims of rape are referred to earlier in the novel when Jezile is in prison. In contravention of custom, the young and old women are forced to strip naked in the prison yard and wash in cold water under the gaze of the prison guards, but when, after the naked parade, "some of the young women would be called out of their cells, sometimes for the rest of the day . . . No one dared speak out . . . they all pretended it was not happening."[79] Like the women who cannot discuss their rapes in prison, Jezile has no choice but to keep silent and to remain in her job with the Potgieters. However, Ngcobo's story then fills in some of the lacunae in Schreiner's text, foregrounding white women's complicity as Jezile blames Mrs. Potgieter for the rape: "If she had not treated her so harshly Jezile would have been less well disposed towards Mr. Potgieter."[80] Moreover, in Ngcobo's novel it is Mrs. Potgieter who finally sends Jezile away. As was the case with the servant woman in *From Man to Man*, Jezile discovers she is pregnant, but in a clear departure from Schreiner's novel, Jezile keeps her child, named Lungu (meaning "white"), on whom she "squandered all her love,"[81] resisting a white soldier who tries to lure him away "to live in town like all the white children did."[82] Although Lungu becomes paralyzed from the waist down after an uprising of schoolchildren against the police, he has been an avid learner and wins a scholarship to study medicine, thus overturning Sarah Gertrude Millin's representations of the intellectual degeneracy of "mixed-race" children.

Eschewing the victim status attributed to the black woman who is subjected to the "white peril," Ngcobo's novel tells of Jezile's life after the rape, inscribing the African woman within a framework of revolutionary and retributive violence described by Frantz Fanon in *The Wretched of the Earth*. In the final chapter of this, his last book, Fanon details "mental disorders which arise from the war of national liberation which the Algerian people are carrying on."[83] The first of these case studies is an account of impotence in an Algerian man after the rape of his wife while she was detained by French soldiers. What is problematic about the case study is not only the husband's pathological obsession that his wife and daughter have become "rotten" and his anger towards his wife for telling him about her ordeal,[84] but also the turn of phrase in Fanon's text: "she confessed her dishonor to him."[85] In her husband's eyes, and in Fanon's view, the woman is somehow responsible for what has happened to her, despite the fact that she was tortured because of her husband's political activities. However, it is also noteworthy that once the man reentered "political discussions" and the counter-colonial struggle, his symptoms decreased and he became willing to take his wife back.[86] Although Ngcobo presents a similar scenario as the marriage between Jezile and her husband Siyalo breaks down following her violation by Mr. Potgieter, it is the African woman, Jezile, who is finally afforded an opportunity for retributive violence directed at "the towering symbol" of apartheid power.[87] At the end of the novel, when her daughter is about to be raped by a white soldier, Jezile arrives in time to stab the attacker to death, an act that while not freeing her from oppression nonetheless transforms her into a powerful subject and reconciles her with her husband. Instead of rejecting her, Siyalo "held her hands in his and whispered inaudibly . . . 'Jezile life of my life.'"[88]

As this reconciliation between husband and wife suggests, in their work Karodia and Ngcobo faced the challenge of scripting "the white peril" from the violated woman's perspective, rewriting the lives, loves, and sexuality of women who are other than white bourgeois subjects. In her study of debates around interracial rape that have split feminists along racial lines, Valerie Smith points out that because black women were deemed by whites to be over-sexed and licentious, their rape seemed "a contradiction in terms."[89] As examined above, one of the starkest examples of this is Schreiner's *From Man to Man*, where the black servant woman emerges as a figure of aberrant hypersexuality. Circumventing the stereotype of the dark-skinned seductress, however, proves to be a precarious enterprise for both Karodia and Ngcobo. In *Other Secrets*, although Karodia's protagonist Meena has two erotic liaisons, which are described in the language of the romance novels she has been reading, both end tragically. Moreover, it is telling that it is only through Meena's identification with the white heroines of romance novels that her own sexual desire becomes legible. In an extremely subversive and risky gesture, on the other hand, Ngcobo brings into focus Jezile's sensuality by creating identification in the reader with her physical and emotional yearnings in the midst of deprivation and hardship: "Her body throbbed and ached inwardly, awash with longing . . . She turned her thoughts voraciously on herself, squeezing her body greedily as she wondered why she had not allowed herself the privilege of these deliciously painful and unfaithful thoughts."[90] Here the writing of sexuality takes on a political dimension, becoming an important part of rescripting narratives that had been for too long been in the hands of white women.

"When Victims Spit Upon Victims": Intraracial Rape in Short Stories by Njabulo Ndebele, Gcina Mhlophe, and Baleka Kgositsile

In Njabulo Ndebele's story "Fools" (1983), which deals with the aftermath of the violation of a schoolgirl by her teacher, the victim's brother addresses the perpetrator: "I hated you, as I had been hating you all these years, for the shattered dreams of my sister, and the shame you brought on us. . . . And when victims spit upon victims should they not be called fools? Fools of darkness? Should they not be trampled upon?"[91] Latent in the accusation is an acknowledgement of the intimate enmeshment of racial oppression and black-on-black violence. In the section that follows, I begin with "Fools" in an examination of intraracial rape as scripted by black authors in the apartheid period. Ndebele's story is discussed in comparison with its film adaptation, *Fools* (1997, director, Ramadan Suleman), and in relation to two stories by black women: "Nokulunga's Wedding" (1983) by Gcina Mhlophe, and "In the Night" (1988) by Baleka Kgositsile. The aims are to assess whether there are differences between the ways in which Ndebele represents rape and the ways in which Mhlophe and Kgositsile write of rape, and to examine the extent to which colonial history and apartheid are shown to be implicated in sexual violence in fiction by these black writers. Other objectives of the analysis are to find ways in which to read the gaps and absences in these literary texts dealing with intraracial rape, and to consider the extent to which political exigencies may have curtailed black authors from writing about intraracial sexual violence.

Ndebele's "Fools" is the story of a schoolteacher, Zamani, who has raped Mimi, one of his students. To summarize the text thus, however, is to reduce its many complexities. Narrated by the morally dubious Zamani, whose state of disgrace strangely elicits sympathy from the reader, much of the story revolves around Zamani's uncanny encounters with Mimi's brother Zani, an intellectually outstanding and impassioned young political activist whom Zamani first meets in the waiting room of a station. Compelled to make conversation with Zani en route to their mutual destination, the Charterston township, Zamani finds himself disrespected and insulted by the younger man for reasons that gradually become clear to him. "Are you really Teacher Zamani?,"[92] asks Zani, referring to Zamani as one of the "killers of dreams, putting out the fire of youth . . . expert at deflowering young virgins sent to school by their hopeful parents."[93] Evoking the doppelgänger figure in a text such as Dostoevsky's novella *The Double*, the narrative of "Fools" builds unsettling identifications between Zani and Zamani.[94] Not only are their names similar, but after Zani is stabbed Zamani feels a pain in his upper left arm. Finding himself within the dilemma of the educated black man who feels "that his race no longer understands him,"[95] Zani later tells Zamani that "Everybody here is a stranger now," and that Zamani is the "the only one he can talk to."[96] Despite their apparent antipathy towards each another, the two characters are drawn together, as Zani illuminates Zamani's disgrace, but also spurs development and change in Zamani's character. Appropriating the power of "science" and humanitarian ideals from his Western education, Zani has decided to return to Charterston from school in Swaziland in order "to bring light where there has been darkness."[97] His fiery arrogance soon gets him into trouble in the township, however, and when he is stabbed in a drunken brawl, the task falls to Zamani to take Zani home. Here Zamani is confronted, presumably for the first time since the rape, by Mimi and her family, including her son, conceived through the rape. Attacked verbally by Mimi's formidable sister Busi, he is nonetheless treated in a dignified manner by MaButhelezi, Mimi's mother, who reprimands Busi: "The man in there . . . is a disgrace. When you look at him you see disgrace. But he is in your home. Now do what I told you."[98] As I point out in the following chapter, in the extent to which it involves the rape of a student by a teacher (from the perspective of the rapist) and confrontation with the victim's family, J.M. Coetzee's *Disgrace* could be read as a rewriting of Ndebele's famously experimental story "Fools."

Set for the most part in Charterston in 1966, "Fools" balances subtle representation of interpersonal relations, such as Zamani's meetings with Mimi's family in the aftermath of the rape, Zani's conflicted love for his girlfriend, Ntozakhe, and the relationship between Zamani and his long-suffering wife Nosipho, with a focus on the political climate of a small and marginal township under apartheid. In "The Rediscovery of the Ordinary" (1984), Ndebele claims that in much protest writing there is no subtlety, the reader is faced with "the complete exteriority of everything," "dramatic contrasts" and stereotypical characters such as the good black victim and the bad white "baas" or "madam." Building on a simplified "moral ideology," protest writing "tends to ossify complex social problems into symbols which are perceived as finished forms of good and evil." Using Marcuse, Ndebele argues against the tendency to devalue interiority "as bourgeois subjectivity." Such devaluation, he claims, "permits neither inner dialogue with the self, nor a social public dialogue. It breeds insensitivity, insincerity and delusion. . . ." and as a result "not only fears are suppressed: the deepest dreams for love, hope, compassion, newness and justice, are also sacrificed to the spectacle of group survival."[99] These comments afford some background to Ndebele's attention to detail in scripting the interiority of the flawed but compelling character of Zamani in "Fools."[100]

Moralistic divisions of characters into categories of good and evil are not easy to make in reading this story in which there are few white characters. Instead, Ndebele draws attention to the internalization of racist thought. The black school principal who has a photograph of Verwoerd in his office and uses Afrikaans "at the slightest pretext"[101] and the black policemen who assault Zani mimic the authoritarian modes of apartheid, with the story recognizing the pathos and brutality of these imitations in a community now preying on itself. Not only is Zamani forced to repeat the psychological violations of apartheid by teaching a racist, state-dictated version of history in his classroom, but the final scene in which he is flogged by a "Boer" until he feels "as if [his] skin is peeling off,"[102] echoes his reputation as the teacher who "could beat a child until his skin peeled off."[103] Zani's accusation that Zamani is one of the "killers of dreams"[104] resonates with Zamani's description of the black policemen: "They were the destroyers of hope, for they knew nothing about hope; they were part of a world completely overcome with helplessness."[105] Although Zamani is gradually co-opted by Zani into political action, and in a drunken fury one night curses the "ominous history" of the Dutch Reformed Church,[106] his violation of Mimi as narrated from his viewpoint echoes the patriarchal tropes of colonial and religious discourse, and reflects a society where men's oppression, frustration, and symbolic emasculation propagates violence against women and children, rather than the gardens and crops Zamani has dreamt of in his fantasy of becoming "the township's model gardener."[107]

After Zamani leaves Zani's home, temporality is disrupted as the narrative incorporates a flashback to the rape, which has taken place years before. Shifting into the present tense, the text conveys here a sense of immediacy, making Zamani's recollection of the rape seem more real and close-up than the experiences he recounts in the rest of the narrative, which is written in the past tense (with the exception of another flashback later in the story, also relayed in the present tense). Drawing on the "stream of consciousness" literary mode, the flashback involving the rape begins when Zamani is prompted by his encounter with Mimi's family to remember the scene of his crime against Mimi. Sitting in his darkened house, Zamani is now "alone, enjoying the lingering heat of mid-January, in the late evening" when he is interrupted by a knock on the door. It is Mimi, she has brought a chicken as a gift from her mother, who wishes to thank Zamani for his part in helping Mimi to pass her final school exams. Claiming her success as his own—"she is the very reward of a teacher"[108]—Zamani without premeditation takes advantage of the situation and assaults her:

> We stand up at the same time, and I see her move towards me. I cannot see her eyes; I cannot see her cheeks; I cannot see her lips; I cannot see the bulge of her breasts beneath the dress; I cannot see the dress. But I can see her shape. She is there. It has grown darker now for it is finally night. I bump into the head of the chicken with my tummy. She has proffered it to me with both her hands. . . . And in my infinite gratitude, I squeeze the warm shoulders with a deep, inner certitude that I would never let go.
>
> I am talking to her, but I do not understand my words, for words have yielded more vividly to endless years of seeing. There is no end to years. . . . What is the meaning of years and years of water? Vast expanses of water? The beauty of steam hovering endlessly over the water? And the fresh perfume of sorghum fields? See, floating on the water, thousands of acorns, corn seeds, wheat and barley, eyeballs winking endlessly like the ever-changing patterns on the surface of the water, and the rain of sour milk pelting the water with thick curds. I want to come into the water, but I can't. I am trapped between screens of ice. I must break it down. I heave! And I heave! And there is a deafening scream of squawking geese. The pain of heaving! The frightening screams! And the ice cracks with the tearing sound of mutilation. And I break through with such a convulsion. And I'm in the water. It is so richly viscous. So thick. Like the sweetness of honey. And the acorns, and the corn seeds, wheat and barley, sprout into living things. And I swim through eyes that look at me with enchantment and revulsion.
>
> It is cold. It is cold. I know. Because I'm naked. And the door is open. And the darkness inside the house pours outside. And in the street is the fading cry of a woman. I close the door and return to the darkness of my house. I can feel a convulsion of weeping gathering inside me, for I know the words ringing in my mind: "I'm a respectable man! I'm a respectable man! I'm a respectable man! . . . And as I grope in the dark towards the kitchen to look for a match to chase the darkness away I stumble on Mimi's chicken. It flutters and squawks

like a voice of atonement. I have to find it. And after a long time of stumbling and falling and the breaking of glass and the scattering of books, I find it. And with tremendous force I tear its head off, and release the chicken to flutter to death freely in the dark.[109]

Some major shifts in language take place within this passage. Beginning with a description that acknowledges Mimi's physical presence in his house, Zamani's narrative shifts gear to detail his experience of the rape in abstract and poetic language that ambivalently aestheticizes the attack and effaces Mimi while suggesting violence. Images of "the beauty of steam hovering end-lessly over water" and of "the sweetness of honey" cover over violence, but there is simultaneously "pain," "heaving" and "a deafening scream." The narra-tive thus draws the reader into complicity with Zamani, but there are also words and phrases that offer the possibility of imagining Mimi's experience. Imitating the colonial myth of seductive "virgin land" ripe for seizure, Zamani draws on images of grasping and merging with the nurturing, feminized and fertile earth of Africa: "the fresh perfume of sorghum fields . . . corn seeds, wheat and barley [sprouting] into living things."[110] Images of "milk" and "honey" allude to the ways in which Zamani casts Mimi's body as his "prom-ised land," with the references to fertility and abundance calling to mind the lovers' dialogue from the "Song of Songs." In Zamani's memory of the rape, however, there is no dialogue, with the biblical allusion thus bringing into relief the elision of Mimi's perspective. After this abstract and psychologically impressionistic section, there is then another discursive shift as Zamani returns to the literally "cold" reality of the violation's aftermath. His refrain, "I am a respectable man," evokes both the Zulu "amarespectables," a somewhat mocking description of middle-class black people, and ironically also the no-tion of nhlonipha, usually translated into English as "respect," a core value of Zulu culture, having to do with respect between men and women, as well as between parents and children. Seizing the chicken in the same way that he has grasped Mimi, Zamani pulls off its head, with the text concretizing in sym-bolic terms the fact that a rape has taken place, as "chicken murder" is town-ship dialect for sex with a minor.

Although she is effaced in Zamani's account of the rape, Mimi tells her story in a letter to Zani. On the train, Zani berates Zamani:

I'm Zani Vuthela, the brother of the bright little girl whom you subdued with the story of your misfortunes. What girl would not give in, completely overwhelmed, to the passionate confessional of her legendary teacher? Tell me? What girl? What girl would not be flattered by this gift of recognition?[111]

Here the reader is afforded the possibility of imagining Zamani's verbal coercion of Mimi before the rape by telling her his life story, information that is elided in his flashback to the incident: "I'm talking to her, but I do not understand my words, for words have yielded more vividly to endless years of seeing."[112] Zani's knowledge of Zamani's life story comes from Mimi's letter:

> Do you see this briefcase, Teach? In it is her letter. I received it two years ago. A year after she bore your child. In it she was letting out to me, for the first time, the tragic poetry of her disillusionment. She has such a beautiful way with words. You did not completely destroy her. What a terrible lesson you are![113]

The reader, however, never sees this letter, which, in its "tragic poetry," apparently rivals and challenges Zamani's recollections. Pointing forward to Coetzee's *Disgrace*, "Fools" leaves offstage the woman's account of rape, but prompts the reader to imagine this hidden story. In *Rape and Representation*, Higgins and Silver demonstrate that such elisions in male texts about rape both reveal the male author's deep ambivalence in dealing with women's experiences of violation and suggest the possibility of making violence visible, as "the subversive presence of the O, the gap . . . for the critics, if not for the authors, provides a space to speak of women's violation."[114] As I shall demonstrate, the film version of "Fools," which represents the rape scene in the clear light of day, rather than through twilit abstract allusions, loses some of the subtlety and complexity of Ndebele's story while highlighting the physical violence of the rape and its effects on Mimi.

Released in 1998, the post-apartheid cinematic adaptation of "Fools" shifts the historical context of the story from 1966 to 1989. Moreover, the time period between the rape and Zamani's meeting with Zani on the train is compressed from years into months in the film such that, shortly after the meeting between the two men, Mimi aborts Zamani's child. Significantly, the film loses the first-person point of view. Partly this is a result of the transposition of the story to another medium, but apparently it was also the filmmaker's decision to move the perspective away from Zamani:

> There is the whole issue in the book where Njabulo talks about rape, but he does not deal with rape as the larger issue in the book. He deals more with the relationship and dilemma between the two characters Zani and Zamani. We had a problem in adapting this part of the book because the issue of rape is very important and needed to be addressed fully. [. . .] And how can the rapist be the moralist? Njabulo's examination of the issue in the novel was somehow surrealistic and narrated in a dreamlike manner. The book itself is wonderful literature, but we offered a different perspective by defining rape as a terrible crime.[115]

I would argue that rather than casting "the rapist as the moralist," Ndebele's story, like Coetzee's *Disgrace*, compels the reader to see and make critical decisions in dealing with the gaps and absences of the narrative. Nonetheless, it is these elisions that the film tries to fill in its attempt to emphasize the women in the narrative. Although Mimi is an almost entirely silent character in the text, and the words of her letter in Ndebele's story are left up to the reader's imagination, in the opening sequence of the film, as Lindiwe Dovey notes, Mimi's voice is the second voice that we hear in voice-over as "the camera cuts from a long shot of the train to a medium close-up of Zani's anxious expression, indicating that he is recalling the words of a letter Mimi has written to him."[116] The words Mimi has written to her brother express her suffering and disillusionment: "I have survived two months of hell; I am now frightened of men. Whatever it is they want, must it be built on our tethered souls? I cannot wait to see you. Your loving sister, Mimi." In their attempt to move away from Ndebele's focus on Zani and Zamani, the film-makers cut the conversation between these two men, such that Zani's reference, on the train, to Zamani's rape of Mimi does not take place in the film. The problem with this is that the tension in Zamani's meeting with Mimi and her family has to depend on the viewer's knowledge that Zamani has raped Mimi. This is resolved by altering the chronology of Ndebele's plot. Whereas the flashback in the book takes place after Zamani has delivered Zani to his home and has been forced to confront Mimi and her family, in the film the flashback occurs while Zamani is still carrying Zani homeward. From the darkness of that night, the film cuts to the bright interior of Zamani's house, with close-up soft focus on Mimi's face as she is speaking to him. After handing him the chicken, Zamani grabs her, and she responds with alarm. Juxtaposed with the rest of the film, in which the camera is steady and the average shot a few seconds long, the rape scene jumps very rapidly from the footage of one unsteady hand-held camera to another, creating a sense of urgency, precariousness, and violence, and showing the expressions on the faces of both Zamani and Mimi. Rather than effacing Mimi, which is what Zamani's account of the rape does in Ndebele's story, the film succeeds in showing Mimi's frightened face, and her struggle to free herself from Zamani's grasp. It does this, however, with some ambivalence. In their conversation before the assault, Mimi comes across as coy, even flirtatious, which is not the case in Ndebele's text. Moreover, after alternating between shots of Zamani and Mimi from the torso upwards, the camera focuses on the rape by shifting to a position immediately behind Zamani's naked left shoulder. While affording a close-up of Mimi's terrified face, this also unfortunately puts the viewer in a position where she/he is "behind" the rapist, forced into experiencing the rape from his perspective. Thus, although this post-apartheid adaptation of "Fools" strives to foreground the experience of black women and to condemn the violence of an intraracial rape, it achieves this aim only partially.

Published by Ravan Press in 1983, Ndebele's collection entitled *Fools and Other Stories*, in which his story appears, was embargoed by the censors in 1988. Upon scrutiny, the book was found to be "not undesirable," with the censors mentioning the only "possibly undesirable passages" as "describing the humiliation of blacks at the hands of whites."[117] No mention is made in the censorship report of the rape of Mimi, which suggests that intraracial rape, and especially the intraracial rape of a black woman, had less effect on the readers, and was of less consequence in the eyes of the state, than the interracial rape of a white woman as discussed, for instance, in the censors' 1985 report on Maimane's *Victims*. A corollary to this lack of recognition of the seriousness of black-on-black rape was that such accounts could be taken as evidence of the black man's natural predilection for criminality and rape, and of black society as depraved and amoral, by default riddled with violence. This problem is satirized in "Fools" when the white superintendent of the township responds to Zamani's reinstatement at the school after the rape with the condemnation: "You really are an immoral people, and that is as it should be."[118]

Like Ndebele's "Fools," Mhlophe's short story "Nokulunga's Wedding" and Kgositsile's "In the Night" both center on an incident of intraracial rape within a black community under apartheid. While Ndebele's narrative elided the woman's perspective of the rape, the stories scripted by Mhlophe and Kgositsile focus on the violation and its effects from the woman's point of view. Published in the same year as "Fools," Mhlophe's story is set in the rural Transkei and tells of Nokulunga's rape by Xolani, who is from a nearby settlement and aims to marry her. Seeing her among her friends at the riverside, Xolani shows off, and the next day returns with a group of men "dressed in heavy overcoats."[119] The men then abduct Nokulunga, with the destruction of her water pot a sinister premonition of the violence that will be inflicted upon her body. What is striking in this scene is the "helplessness" and passivity of the onlookers, and normalization of the abduction as the men carrying Nokulunga on their shoulders sing a wedding song. Challenging the male perspective, however, the story is focalized through Nokulunga's perspective, emphasizing, through realist details, her subjectivity and embodied experience. Beneath the heavy overcoats, she struggles to breathe, she feels "betrayed and lost," it is very hot and "she wanted to pee."[120] Rather than concentrating simply on her status as a helpless victim, however, the story foregrounds her agency, resourcefulness, and even her physical strength in her attempts to defend herself, which on the first night are actually successful as she evades Xolani. It is only on the second night when his male elders enter the hut with him and literally hold her down that the rape is accomplished.

Represented as weak and spineless, Xolani is goaded into the rape by his father and other male relatives:

"Xolani!" Malungi called to his son softly and angrily.

"Yes father," Xolani replied without looking up.

"What are you telling us, are you telling us that you spent all night with that girl and failed to sleep with her?"

"Father, I . . . I . . . "

"Yes, you failed to be a man with that girl in the hut. That is the kind of man you have grown into, unable to sleep with a woman the way a man should."[121]

The subjectivity of Xolani and his male family members, threatened with symbolic emasculation under apartheid, struggles to assert itself through the performative assertion of potency and power, in this case at the black woman's expense. Yet the story points towards an alternative, feminine vision of masculinity, whereby manhood is judged by the ability to protect rather than violate, as Nokulunga wonders sorrowfully: "Was [Xolani] the man she was supposed to look upon as a husband? How was he ever to defend her against anything or anyone?"[122] In a brutal bolstering of male authority and group identity, the men actually take pleasure in her pain and degradation. Attacking her "like a mob," they cheer and clap while "Xolani jumped high, now enjoying the rape." The men laugh at the blood on her thighs, and one of them says "he had had enough of holding the leg and wanted a share for his work."[123] At this point she faints, and the reader is left with the possibility that the incident is about to become a gang rape.

Although the men's behavior erases Nokulunga's subjectivity and humanity, the story brings her experience to the reader. Disjunctively, from the violence of the rape scene the narrative shifts to a wedding song and the preparations for Nokulunga's marriage to Xolani, emphasizing a situation where the sadism that would normally threaten societal structure is allowed to erupt and is in fact sanctioned through the performative ritual of marriage that takes place under so-called customary law. As Mahmood Mamdani notes, customary law was "how apartheid ruled its native subjects."[124] Rather than expressing precolonial values, customary law evolved as a peculiar hybrid, presenting, for the most part, the "piggybacking" of patriarchies on one another, and the reduction of women to currency, objects of exchange. Sketched by Mhlophe, the problem is largely economic. In the dire circumstances of the rural Bantustan, a great deal of emphasis is now placed on the *lobola* or "bride wealth," payable by the groom to the bride's family. Although Nokulunga has a lover, Vuyo, whom she would like to marry, he does not have money for *lobola*, especially after the rape, when "he would have had to pay a lot of cattle if he took Nokulunga with the unborn baby."[125] In *Changes: A Love Story* (1991), the Ghanaian writer Ama Ata Aidoo similarly represents intraracial rape within the context of marriage, as the protagonist, Esi, is assaulted by her husband who, despite her protests, "started to do what he had determined to do all morning."[126] Illuminating the concrete hardships experienced by contemporary African women, Aidoo suggests that there has been a lack of significant change in women's circumstances in the post-independence context. Yet, whereas Esi, who is clearly middle class, has access to contraceptives and is able to divorce her husband and move on to initiate a passionate love affair with another man,

Nokulunga's position epitomizes that of the subaltern. The hopelessness of her entrapment is indicated in the final line of Mhlophe's story: "There was nothing to be done."[127]

Like "Nokulunga's Wedding," Kgositsile's story, "In the Night," published in 1988 in *Rixaka*, the cultural journal of the ANC in exile in Zambia, foregrounds a black southern African woman's experience of intraracial rape. The story could also be read as an interesting companion piece to "Fools," in that it offers the woman's perspective, through a flashback, of being raped as a schoolgirl by her teacher. In fact, Kgositsile may indeed have been thinking of Ndebele's text when she scripted her story. The same shift in tense deployed by Ndebele, from the past tense of the framing narrative to the present tense in the flashback to the rape, is used in Kgositsile's story. "In the Night" begins with Nomathemba's "memories flashing through her mind in the dark bedroom," as she is about to tell her husband, Xola, of her childhood. Like "Fools," the narrative emphasizes frustration and brutality within a black community, and Xola's later reference to the rapist as "one fool I would like to kill in my life" could be read as an allusion to the "victims who spit upon victims," the "fools of darkness" referenced at the end of Ndebele's story.[128] Nomathemba remembers her father who beat her and "[crashed] her into a wall."[129] Her mother is also complicit in this domestic violence, either doing nothing or assaulting her just as viciously, and Nomathemba reveals to Xola that fear of her parents was a factor leading to the rape. When her teacher arrives at her family's home, "drunk and totally insensitive to her desperate pleas,"[130] she leads him away from the house so that her parents do not blame her for his presence. Mac Dubula, the teacher, then drags her into the bushes and rapes her. Even more so than in Mhlophe's story, the emphasis, with Nomathemba as focalizer, is on the victim's experience in an embodied sense: "She had never felt so much pain."[131] The text also highlights the ways in which the victim of rape internalizes a feeling of complicity and shame:

> She could scream, but she dared not at this point anyway. When everybody came out to see who was screaming and why, they would send for her parents. . . . she was evil; an evil ungrateful child who wanted nothing but to see them disgraced and dying of heart trouble. Screaming was out of the question. How could she face the world after that? She could hear the women sympathizing with her mother. "We are sorry for her; she did not give birth to a child, her womb produced rot."[132]

As Sabine Sielke points out in her study of sexual violence in American literature, work by African American women writers such as Toni Morrison, Maya Angelou, Ntozake Shange and Alice Walker that focuses on "plain black (gender) trouble" has been criticized for denouncing black men, for buying into the stereotype of the black rapist, for airing "dirty laundry" in front of an audience potentially "eager to use the fictional texts as evidence to support its own race prejudice."[133] According to Ramadan Suleman, director of the film version of "Fools," Ndebele "was criticized, even by black critics, for having dared to criticize the victims of apartheid."[134] The publication of Kgositsile's story in *Rixaka*, however, suggests that black nationalism and the liberation struggle against apartheid were not necessarily at odds with black women speaking out about instances of intraracial sexual violence, even if, as the passage above suggests, the bringing to light of such incidents in the public sphere had the potential to damage the life and reputation of the victim. Unfortunately, however, as demonstrated by the Jacob Zuma rape trial, in the post-apartheid context black women who have made allegations of rape against political figures within the ANC have occupied a precarious and endangered position.

"History Speaking": Sexual Violence and Post-Apartheid Narratives

It was history speaking through them, a history of wrong.

—DAVID LURIE, IN J.M. COETZEE, *DISGRACE* (1999)[1]

Historical memory, the term seems illogical, even contradictory . . .
yet it has an air of inevitability, solemn and compelling. . . . It explains
everything, the violence periodically sweeping the country, the crime
rate, even the strange 'upsurge' of brutality against women. It is as if
memory has a remembering process of its own, one that gives life to its
imaginary monsters.

—ACHMAT DANGOR, *BITTER FRUIT* (2001)[2]

Commenting on his novel *The Quiet Violence of Dreams* (2001), K. Sello
Duiker asserted that contemporary violence in South Africa "is a culture that
communicates a certain message," and that "we are part of a violent culture . . .
we never knew a period of rest."[3] As this suggests, while South Africa made a
peaceful transition to democracy by averting the major bloodshed that has
in other contexts accompanied revolutionary change, and while the processes
of the Truth and Reconciliation Commission sought to lay to rest the country's politically brutal past, violent behavior continues to extend throughout
society. Although it boasts progressive gender rights legislation, the country
remains marked by persistently high levels of sexual violence. The post-1994
Constitution upholds gender equality by forbidding discrimination on the
grounds of sexuality, and gender rights have been further developed through
legislative measures such as the Domestic Violence Act of 1998, which provides a legal definition of domestic violence and increases powers vested in
the court to protect women, and the recent Sexual Violence Act of 2007, which
extends the definition of rape and describes sexual violation in gender-neutral
terms. Yet as Lisa Vetten notes, "there is no necessary connection between a
progressive legislative framework and a reduction in violence against women,"
and "this state of affairs represents not so much a contradiction as an illustra-
tion of the contingent, conditional and contested nature of gender equality in

South Africa."[4] In a study of violence against women as a form of social control, Lillian Artz claims:

> Violence against women is still the most pervasive, yet least recognized – at
> least substantively – human rights abuse in South Africa. Every day, women
> are murdered, physically and sexually assaulted, threatened and humiliated
> by their partners, within their own homes and communities. The social, cul-
> tural and political structures and institutions in countries like South Africa
> continue to openly support gender inequality, despite political rhetoric to
> the contrary.[5]

According to Helen Moffett, studies have ranked South Africa as having the
highest reported incidence of rape for any country not at war.[6] Indeed, Gayatri
Spivak's observation, a response to the fate of women in post-independence
India as depicted in Mahasweta Devi's "Douloti the Bountiful," may be considered as having relevance to South Africa:

> . . . the event of political independence can automatically be assumed to
> stand in-between colony and decolonisation as an unexplained good that
> operates as a reversal . . . but . . . even within this space, the woman's body is
> the last instance, it is elsewhere.[7]

Below I argue that there is continuity between past and present gender violence in South Africa, and that a history entangling rape, race, and representation has thus far inflected and hampered an effective state response to the high
levels of gender violence that continue to plague the country. At the same time,
however, a factor that has characterized post-apartheid South Africa is a proliferation of media and cultural texts on sexual violence. From local news
media to novels, theatre, film, television drama, and the visual arts, rape is one
of the issues that has moved to center stage.[8]

Partly, this proliferation can be linked to an increasing and progressive
focus on gender rights. In an essay entitled "To Hear the Variety of Discourses"
Zoë Wicomb observed a tendency under apartheid to place "gender on the
backboiler while mighty matters of national liberation are dealt with,"[9] and as
Cherryl Walker notes in her 1991 preface to *Women and Resistance in South
Africa*, when the defeat of apartheid became a reality, more serious attention
was given to "the relationship between women's and national liberation."[10] The
propagation of rape stories in the media and in literary texts of the post-
apartheid transition also evokes, however, the specter of the "black peril" scares
that possessed South Africa at an earlier moment of nation-making, that is, at
the time of national unification around 1910. As explicated in Yunus Valley's
film, *The Glow of White Women* (2007), at the transitional time of 1990, Yeoville
in Johannesburg had begun to blossom into an area of racial integration, but
this was cut short when a number of white women were violated by a black
serial rapist. White commentators pronounced that the Yeoville rapist proved

that sex between the races was not a good thing and Teddy Mattera, the son of one of South Africa's most revered poets of the struggle, was wrongfully accused and detained before the real perpetrator was arrested. While most sex crimes in South Africa are intraracial, as noted in the introduction to this study, it took the dramatic media coverage of the rape of a white woman, Charlene Smith, by a black man in 1999 to draw attention to rape as a serious social problem in South Africa and the debate that ensued was clouded by racial issues. Writing of the "dated and incomplete" statistics on gender violence that are "inadequate to understanding and tracking the problem," Vetten draws attention to the ways in which "black peril" hysteria has obscured the realities of sexual violence:

> A comprehensive history of sexual violence in South Africa has yet to be written. Nonetheless, where snatches of such history may be glimpsed, they point to a long and ugly relationship between rape and race. . . . public outrage about rape has less often been motivated by pure concerns with women's rights than with efforts to control and regulate both black men and white women.[11]

Significantly, the spat between Smith and the ANC government turned into an extended debate about crime statistics as Smith's article in the *Mail and Guardian* had opened with the line: "Every twenty six seconds in South Africa a woman gets raped, it was my turn last Thursday night." A few weeks later, Steve Tshwete, Minister of Safety and Security, was cited as having said in front of a CBS television crew: "we've been standing here for more than 26 seconds and I haven't seen anyone raped, have you?"[12] While reported rapes are more correctly tabulated in total per annum or per 100,000 population rather than "per second" as suggested in Smith's sensationalist opening line, Tshwete's comment demonstrates that the state response to the question of sexual violence, shaped by a history in which black men have been cast as the rapists or potential rapists of white women, has at key moments been dismissive and inappropriate.

Tracing a continuity in which the past haunts the present, one of the characters in Achmat Dangor's *Bitter Fruit* (2001) ruminates on the ways in which "the strange 'upsurge' of brutality against women" is a "remembering process . . . that gives life to its imaginary monsters" (see epigraph above). Although my study is not sociological, I would like to scrutinize one of the assumptions implicit in this speculation, even while I concur with the other. The incidence of reported rape is unacceptably high in South Africa and is continuous with a violent past, but there is no conclusive evidence that sexual violence has been "ascendant" or that it shows an upward trend since the ANC government was voted into power in 1994.[13] In fact, statistics of reported rape have remained fairly consistent since surveys done at the time of the country's first democratic elections, suggesting that such violence was endemic under apartheid, and that South Africa has been engaged in an unacknowledged gender civil war for decades. While the current focus on rape as a social ill may be accounted for partly by the increasing emphasis on gender mentioned above, panic about crime statistics in the transition to a non-racial democracy often also expresses complex anxieties about governance by a historically-black political party. Like the outbursts of "black peril" hysteria in early twentieth-century South Africa, not only the media but also literary texts of the post-apartheid transition (such as J.M. Coetzee's *Disgrace*, Mike van Graan's play *Green Man Flashing*, Megan Voisey Braig's *Till We Can Keep an Animal*, Achmat Dangor's *Bitter Fruit*, Rachel Zadok's *Gem Squash Tokoloshe* and Zakes Mda's *The Madonna of Excelsior*) have continued to focus melancholically on "black peril" stories and/or their counterparts, "white peril" narratives. As mentioned in the introduction to this study, cognizant of a long and racist history, the ANC submission to the Human Rights Commission in April 2000 mentioned the rape of a white woman in *Disgrace* and responses to the rape by white characters in the novel as a preamble to a critique of representations of race in the media. In the following section of this chapter, I begin with *Disgrace* and argue that this literary text doubles back reflexively on the history of "black" and "white peril" narratives. I claim that the cinematic adaptation of *Disgrace*, which effectively reduces the novel to a "black peril" script, suggests why this novel by Coetzee has attained the status of "becoming classic." However, I argue that by drawing attention not only to hidden stories, but also to positionality, the novel ambivalently leaves a certain ethical responsibility with the reader.

The most important institutional event that has shaped the post-apartheid landscape has been the Truth and Reconciliation Commission (TRC), with debates that emerged during and after the Commission's hearings contributing to the idea of sexual violence as a "hidden" aspect of South African history. Founded by the Promotion of National Unity and Reconciliation Act of 1995, the TRC was mandated to investigate gross human rights violations that took place under apartheid. During its hearings, which ran from 1996 to 1998, the Commission gathered the testimonies of some 25,000 people. On the recommendation of feminist scholars from the Centre for Applied Legal Studies (CALS) at the University of Witwatersrand, the TRC recognized that many women who testified cast themselves as secondary victims, and it was thus arranged for special hearings to guarantee "a safe space" for women. As Veena Das points out, however, one must be wary where figurative language constructs rape narrative as waiting to be "unearthed" by the historiographer. Speaking with women who survived Partition violence in India, Das came across "a zone of silence," or "a code of silence" in the case of rape stories. Although some would surmise that it could be heroic to uncover these narratives, Das contends that they can become a "poisonous knowledge," damaging the lives of those who tell them.[14] During the TRC women's hearings, victims gave accounts of sexual violence, including rape, but although the CALS submission recommended that these hearings be held in camera and that steps be taken to guarantee privacy, the testimonies found their way into newspapers, into artworks and literary texts, and even onto the Internet. Even as the CALS submission called for the excavation of women's stories, the TRC's main objective, which was to make the testimonies public, was at odds with the creation of "a safe space," and there were pressing reasons why certain stories of rape and sexual abuse could not be told. As I demonstrate, Zoë Wicomb's *David's Story* and Achmat Dangor's *Bitter Fruit* foreground, despite the efforts of the South Africa's Truth and Reconciliation Commission (TRC), the unspeakability of certain aspects of the apartheid past in the post-apartheid transition.

One of the most interesting shifts of the post-apartheid era has been the end of official censorship, and as indicated by the slogan of South Africa's current Film and Publication Board, "We inform. You choose.," the 1996 Act endorsed a major shift from censorship to classification, though there are proscriptions in cases of child pornography or hatred based on race, ethnicity, gender, or religion. While the end of censorship has meant that graphic descriptions of sexual violence and previously taboo subjects have made their way into the public sphere, what is interesting is the ways in which the state and members of the general public have taken on censorious positions in relation to certain representations of sexual violence. As suggested by the ANC submission to the SAHRC hearings on racism in the media, one of the fields that has been scrutinized by the post-apartheid government is the representation of sex crimes, particularly in the media. Yet not only "black peril" representations have come under fire. In 1999 the South African-born film star Charlize Theron made an anti-rape advertisement in collaboration with Rape Crisis in which the actress stared directly at the viewer and stated: "Many people ask me what South African men are like." She then rattled off a series of rape statistics and concluded with an indictment of South African masculinity, claiming that it was "not easy" to say what men in South Africa are like. Following complaints that it discriminated against men, the advert was withdrawn by the Advertising Standards Authority, but after an appeal by Rape Crisis it was reinstated.

Where representations of rape have strayed from well-worn scripts, they have often come under attack. In the discussion below of K. Sello Duiker's novel *Thirteen Cents*, I demonstrate that Duiker's disturbing exposé of the life of a male street child in this novel proved to be too shocking for some readers. As I point out further, the representation of male rape in South African *Bildungsromane* of the post-apartheid transition challenges prevailing cultural myths and scripts about sexual violence, most notably the notion that rape is something that happens only to women, and the idea that male rape is "homosexual." Under apartheid, homosexual acts between men were outlawed, but their legalization after apartheid led to consideration of whether sex between men could be consensual (legal) or non-consensual (illegal). Gay-rights activists, among others, have criticized the fact that men could not legally be victims of rape, pointing out that this shortcoming in the law helped to hide the sexual abuse of young boys, and of men in prisons, where rape constitutes a horrific and persistent form of violence that is not new in the post-apartheid context. In 2007, following a case where a young girl had been anally raped, which meant that the perpetrator could not be convicted of rape, the Sexual Offences Act was passed, which extended the legal definition of rape to encompass any form of sexual penetration perpetrated without consent, regardless of the gender of the parties concerned.

One of the most disheartening events in the recent post-apartheid era has surely been the rape trial of Jacob Zuma, in which the complainant was harassed, given death threats publicly by Zuma's supporters, and finally dismissed by a white male judge as a liar and a madwoman on the basis of her sexual history (while Zuma's sexual history was not brought under scrutiny). Notably, in the year following the trial, the number of reported rapes in South Africa fell significantly. Since this is the first time that such a decline can be noted in the post-apartheid period, it suggests that less women felt safe in reporting rape, rather than that there was a decline in rape. As commentators such as Njabulo Ndebele and Pumla Dineo Gqola have noted, the trial, in which Zuma, who was later to become President of the ANC and of the nation, stood trial for the rape of a family friend, was a definitive national moment in that the events surrounding the trial foregrounded, in Ndebele's words, "webs of social and political relationships that may bedevil professional conduct."[15] In a newspaper article that was deeply critical of Zuma's bravado during the trial and of his apparent lack of concern for the ways in which the trial was inciting his followers to increasingly violent public displays of support, Ndebele claimed that Zuma was angry with the ANC as a "family," and that "as [Zuma] sang and danced with his supporters, images of South Africa's raped mothers, sisters, daughters (some, infants), nieces, aunts and grandmothers, raced through my mind, torturing me. Are their pain and the broad sense of public morality of little consequence in the settling of 'family' scores?"[16] Drawing on Ndebele's critique here and on his essay "Rediscovery of the Ordinary," Pumla Gqola went on to argue that "Ndebele's theorisation of the spectacular remains a powerful commentary on contemporary South African culture and gendered public life, and specifically the ways in which violent masculinities have taken centre stage since the Jacob Zuma rape trial."[17] Although Ndebele's essay was a critique of literary representation under apartheid, Gqola thus extends this critique of spectacle to public displays of misogyny present in contemporary South Africa. What is also interesting to remember, however, is that more than twenty years before the Zuma rape trial, Ndebele published a fictional narrative, "Fools" (examined in chapter 4), in which he describes the rape of a young woman by a male authority figure whom she respects as a father figure. Reading this story in the post-apartheid era, one is struck by the contemporary relevance of its careful examination of power and oppression. The rape in "Fools" disrupts any simple struggle history

FIGURE 5.1 *"The Rape of Justice"*, Zapiro, Sunday Times, *7 August 2008.*

evoked by Zuma's performative singing of the song *"Umshini Wam'"* ("bring
me my machine gun") during his trial.

On September 7, 2008 the *Sunday Times* newspaper published a cartoon
showing Zuma, who was at that time on trial for corruption and then-leader of
the ANC (though not yet the country's president), undoing his trousers and
about to rape a woman labeled "justice system" (Figure 5.1). Holding the
woman down are leaders of the tripartite alliance with Gwede Mantashe, the
ANC's secretary-general, telling Zuma: "Go for it Boss!"[18] The cartoon, which
bears a striking resemblance to an etching made by South African artist Diane
Victor in 2005 (Figure 5.2), provoked a national uproar. While many praised
the cartoonist Zapiro for his audacious gesture, some found the image too in-
cendiary. Pierre de Vos (Chair in Constitutional Governance at the University
of Cape Town) questioned whether, "by using the metaphor of rape, Zapiro is
not cheapening the horror of rape and—given our deeply patriarchal and sex-
ist society—is not helping to desensitize us to this scourge."[19]

Quickly, however, the debate about Zapiro's cartoon came not only to be
about the enmeshment of rape with metaphor, but also about race. Without
mentioning that Zuma had been on trial two years previously for the rape of a
family friend, a fact on which the cartoon obviously traded, parliamentary
Speaker Baleka Mbete-Kgositsile—who had in exile during apartheid authored
"In the Night," the short story of intraracial rape discussed in the previous
chapter—lashed out at Zapiro for implying that Zuma was a rapist of white
women. Mbete-Kgositsile was then accused of playing "the race card," and in a

FIGURE 5.2 *Diane Victor, "And Justice for All", Disasters of the Peace Series, Etching on Paper, 2006–2008.*

response that demonstrates the dilemma of how one decodes race in an artistic image without falling back on physiological stereotypes of ethnicity, Zapiro attested that he was shocked by Mbete's interpretation since the figure of justice in the cartoon was not white. As the spat between Mbete and Zapiro suggests, issues of race have persistently entangled and obscured a focus on sexual violence in the post-apartheid context.

One of the literary modes that have come to prominence in South Africa over the past decade is the crime novel. Many of these popular books deal with sexual violence, and specifically rape, but since this is an emerging genre, it has been beyond the scope of my project to examine it in any detail. It could constitute an avenue for future research, but at this stage I would like to observe that the prominence of crime fiction as a highly popular genre in South Africa corresponds with increased discourse on crime—including sexual violence as crime—and this may reveal complex anxieties about the nation, rather than correspond in a mimetic way with an increase in crime *per se*. In their forthcoming study of crime in South Africa, Jean and John Comaroff note that the middle classes who clamor the loudest about crime are in fact less likely to experience crime than those living in poverty, and contemporary discourse on social violence suggests more about the dilemmas of neo-liberalism and shifting boundaries of enmity in the post-apartheid transition than it does about actual crime. Yet, post-apartheid crime fiction also has its own complexities, and in fact often works to undo conservative ideas about the perpetrators of crime. As Christopher Warnes notes in a forthcoming study of such fiction, many contemporary South African thrillers knowingly engage with a history of "black peril" and "white peril" stories in politically-correct ways. Andrew Brown's *Cold Sleep Lullaby*, for instance, is "defined by a desire to develop a liberal postapartheid pedagogics which deliberately activates a colonial racist trope—the black peril—in order to reveal how it conceals the true source of violence."[20]

Although the focus on interracial rape that has characterized South African literature in the past has continued into the post-1994 cultural landscape, what makes the contemporary emphasis on sexual violence different, for instance, from the early twentieth century's hysteria about interracial rape, is that there has been an increasing focus in the post-apartheid transition not only on intraracial sexual violence but also on previously unmentionable acts such as male rape and the abuse of children within families and communities. This is not to say that these new narratives merely reflect social reality, however. Rather, as I demonstrate in the discussion of narratives about "Baby Tshepang" with which I conclude the chapter, coverage of even the most horrific narratives of sexual violence may be read as indices for anxieties about nationhood, citizenship, human rights, masculinity—and the disjuncture and continuity between a violent society and its dreams of wholeness and healing.

Reading the Unspeakable: Rape in J.M. Coetzee's *Disgrace*

Of Daphne Rooke's *Mittee*, J.M. Coetzee writes: "to her credit, Rooke does not indulge in the *ne plus ultra* of colonial horror fantasies, the rape of a white woman."[21] Since he is evidently aware of the volatile nature of this subject, what compels Coetzee to portray the rape of a white woman by three black men in *Disgrace*? One may well ask whether ethical scriptings of interracial rape are possible in a context where representations of sexual violence, under the old regime, supported racial injustice, and while Coetzee's novel has been widely acclaimed overseas, in South Africa *Disgrace* has been accused of being deeply implicated in racist attitudes, and of feeding national hysteria. I argue that *Disgrace* offers a self-reflexive scrutiny of "the black peril," and simultaneously reveals what Sol T. Plaatje referred to as "the white peril," the hidden sexual exploitation of black women by white men that has existed for centuries.[22] Examining the film of *Disgrace* alongside the novel, I discuss the ways in which interpretations of the novel have generally emphasized "the black peril" aspects of the narrative, and have focused on the violation done to Lucy, rather than Melanie. Notably, *Disgrace* is not the first of Coetzee's novels to examine issues of race and rape, and his earliest novels *Dusklands* (1974) and

In the Heart of the Country (1977) provide useful points of comparison with *Disgrace*. As I conclude, although the novel is focalized through David Lurie, it emphasizes positionality, such that the hidden stories of both Melanie and Lucy have unavoidable implications for the reader.

In *Disgrace*, the protagonist's daughter is gang-raped by three men on her smallholding in the Eastern Cape, but she chooses to say nothing about what happened to her. Reflecting on the triumph of the intruders, her father, David speculates: "It will dawn on them that over the body of the woman silence is being drawn like a blanket."[23] This stifling of rape narrative is a feature of the entire novel. The central incidents in both settings of *Disgrace* are acts of sexual violation, but notably, the experience of the violated body is absent, hidden from the reader. Although David acknowledges that his sexual encounter with a student, Melanie Isaacs, was "undesired" by her, the narrative voice, focalized through David, maintains it was "[n]ot rape, not quite that."[24] During the disciplinary hearing that ensues, Melanie's account never reaches the reader, and David, who refuses to defend himself, is accused of being "fundamentally evasive."[25] In the wake of the farm-attack, Lucy asks her father to tell only his story: "I tell what happened to me."[26] The irony is that *she does not tell*, she remains resolutely silent about her experience. Until she mentions having had tests, the inference that a rape has occurred is David's. He tells Bev Shaw that he is concerned for Lucy, about the risk of pregnancy, and of HIV, but in response he is told to ask Lucy himself.[27] An account of rape is completely elided in Lucy's report to the police. David pleads with his daughter to leave the Eastern Cape, or to tell the police, but she insists: "*You don't know what happened.*"[28] Bev Shaw reiterates Lucy's message: "But you weren't there, David. She told me."[29] When David confronts the word they have avoided, Lucy is not direct: "I think they *do* rape."[30]

The second part of Higgins and Silver's *Rape and Representation* focuses on "The Rhetoric of Elision" in a collection of essays that examine how rape may be read in its absence. Proposing that reading sexual violence requires "listening not only to who speaks and in what circumstances, but who does *not* speak and why,"[31] these critics concede that elision of the scene of violence in male-authored texts about rape could expose "the ambivalence of the male author caught in representations of masculinity and subjectivity he may question but that he ultimately leaves in place."[32] I intend to demonstrate, however, that *Disgrace* self-reflexively presupposes and doubles back on such "ambivalence," which is further complicated by issues of race.

As stated in the introduction to this study, the ANC submission to the South African Human Rights Commission (SAHRC) hearings on racism in the media alluded to J.M. Coetzee's *Disgrace*. Referring to the gang rape of a white woman by three black men in the novel, the ANC proposed that in *Disgrace* Coetzee illustrates the ways in which white South Africans still believe in

a stereotype of the African as bestial and uncivilized. Whether the ANC accused Coetzee himself of racism is ambiguous, but the submission stated:

> J.M. Coetzee makes a point that five years after liberation white South Af-
> rican society continues to believe in a particular stereotype of the African
> which defines the latter as immoral and amoral, a savage, violent, disre-
> spectful of private property, incapable of refinement through education and
> driven by . . . dark satanic impulses. To understand this phenomenon of rac-
> ism in our media we must start from this basic point that many practitioners
> of journalism in our country including the foreign correspondents carry this
> stereotype in their heads at all times.[33]

Countering the ANC's allusion, which he regarded as an accusation of racism
directed at the novel, Michael Marais proposed that by not reporting her rape,
Lucy in *Disgrace* rejects the narrative offered to her by a certain history, and by her
father.[34] Unlike the white women whose stories of rape by black men were sensationalized and exploited in South African history, the fictional white rape victim
in *Disgrace* refuses to report the crime committed against her, claiming that what
happened is "[her] business."[35] Readers may view Lucy's silence and passivity as
indicative of the impotence and abasement of whites in the new South Africa, but
in fact this character warns that her silence should not be read as an abstraction,
and that it signifies neither collective guilt nor personal salvation.[36] Rather, Lucy's
refusal to publicize an account of rape "in this place at this time" draws attention
to the very real and concrete ways in which rape narratives in South African history have justified oppressive laws that dispossessed those defined as racially
other. This said, most readers have found Lucy's silence after the rape one of the
most disturbing aspects of the novel. Moreover, it is interesting how many critics
have focused on Lucy and her passivity. In his essay "Very Morbid Phenomena:
'Liberal Funk', the 'Lucy-Syndrome' and JM Coetzee's *Disgrace*," Marais argues
against the "orthodox response to the novel" where Lucy's position has been read
as "exemplifying whites' acceptance of their peripherality in the 'new' South
Africa."[37] In an essay on "Ethics and Politics in Tagore, Coetzee and Certain Scenes
of Teaching," Gayatri Spivak reads Lucy's silence as "a refusal to be raped by
instrumentalizing reproduction" and Ian Glenn, in a discussion of *Disgrace* as an
expression of liberal Afro-pessimism, claims that Lucy, like Isabel in Henry
James's *Portrait of a Lady*, chooses to resist "interpretation, repetition, old familial
models."[38] Spivak notes that *Disgrace* urges "the active reader, to counterfocalize,"
but she only discusses the possibilities of "counterfocalization" in relation to
Lucy's story.[39] Most readers, from early reviews until recent overviews of the
novel, describe what happens to Lucy as rape, but what happens between Melanie
Isaacs and David Lurie as an "affair."[40] Although Meg Samuelson acknowledges
that one of David's encounters with Melanie is "indistinguishable from rape," she
nonetheless begins her discussion of *Disgrace* with reference to Lucy as the novel's
"raped character" and focuses mainly on the plight of Lucy in her analysis.[41]

Set in the post-apartheid context, *Disgrace* is "[h]alf campus novel, half anti-pastoral"[42] and central incidents in each case are acts of violation that reveal the power dynamics in the two settings, and in the respective literary modes. Immersed in a falsifying Romantic tradition, David speculates that "beauty does not belong to itself,"[43] and thus justifies his underlying assumption, as Melanie's educator, that she is somehow his property. This is revealed when he watches her in a play, claiming her achievements as his own: "When they laugh at Melanie's lines he cannot resist a flush of pride. Mine! He would like to say to them . . . as if she were his daughter."[44] By exposing institutionalized structures of power, Coetzee rewrites versions of the college novel, a genre that often masks the inequalities, gender harassment, and incidents of rape reported in campus life. In fact, the events that take place between David and Melanie in *Disgrace* invite consideration of David Mamet's play *Oleanna*, which dramatizes the vicissitudes of sexual harassment in the university environment. In *Oleanna*, however, the student who turns on her professor and accuses him of sexual harassment develops a shrill voice and strong opinions, whereas Melanie's words in *Disgrace* are few. Although the woman student in *Oleanna* is set up as possibly provoking the violence inflicted on her, in *Disgrace* there is a subtle critique of Mamet's play, articulated, significantly, via Melanie's script in a theatrical production: "*My gats*, why must everything always be my fault?"[45] Notably this statement is erased in the film version of *Disgrace*.

In viewing the film of *Disgrace* as an intersemiotic translation of the novel, I am not particularly concerned with the idea, although it may be true, that the film comprises a mediocre and unfaithful adaptation of Coetzee's novel. Rather, I am fascinated by Lawrence Venuti's observations that translation "contributes to canon formation by inscribing the foreign text with an interpretation that has achieved dominance in academic or other cultural institutions" and that translating "effects a more radical break than a relatively simple iteration such as a quotation because it simultaneously decontextualizes and recontextualizes the foreign text" within a new medium.[46] Taking my cue from Venuti's observations about translation and the making of the canon, I intend to examine the ways in which the cinematic adaptation of *Disgrace*, through representations of race and sexual violence, may reveal some of the criteria for this South African novel's status of "becoming-classic." The following questions are thus to be addressed: Are there ways in which the representation of sexual violence in the film of *Disgrace* reveals a consensus or dominance of certain interpretations of the novel? More specifically, how does the film of *Disgrace* suggest some of the criteria for this South African novel's status, and how does the cinematic version of *Disgrace* decontextualize and recontextualize the situations and settings of the novel?

In the novel of *Disgrace*, David translates Melanie's name as "the dark one,"[47] while Lucy's name has associations with light. Playing on tropes of darkness and light, the names of the two women expose "black peril" stereotypes and the residual threat of the "white peril" that prevailed under colonialism and apartheid. David has a history of desiring "dark" and "exotic" women, and assumes that he has the right to purchase or possess their bodies without being responsible for them or respecting the lives they live. As Plaatje observed, many white men in colonial South Africa exploited "Coloured concubines" without offering the women long-term security, or caring whether or not they became pregnant.[48] Moreover, rather than confirming "black peril" stereotypes, Lucy's name reveals that these have been based on upholding the "purity" of white women. The violation of Lucy further highlights a history tainted by racial injustice, by possession and dispossession, where, as Dorothy Driver has pointed out, white women have been "signs" of that which was not exchanged between men in different racial groups.[49] In David Lurie's opinion, "a history of wrong" was speaking through Lucy's rapists.[50] At the same time, Coetzee demonstrates that David is blind to the history of his own actions, and during the disciplinary hearing in *Disgrace* Farodia Rassool comments on David's refusal to acknowledge "the long history of exploitation of which [his treatment of Melanie] is a part."[51] Rassool's comment could point to gendered abuses of power in the academy that are as old as the academic profession, but it could also refer to "the white peril" and a history of slavery in South Africa.

Notably, the film erases three important and striking references to history that exist in the novel: Rassool's accusation that David has not acknowledged "the long history of exploitation of which [his behavior] is a part"; David's comment that his daughter's rape was "History speaking through [the rapists] . . ."; and Lucy's comment that "what happened to me is a purely private matter. *In another time*, in another place it might be held to be a public matter. But in this place, *at this time* it is not."[52] Eliding David and Lucy's comments about history and time, the film wipes out the novel's allusion to a problematic past in which the representation of rape has been entangled with racial stereotyping and oppression. Furthermore, by leaving out Rassool's statement, the film effectively expunges the history of "the white peril," and certainly this is the case from the first scene, where, although the focus is on the room in which David Lurie is exploiting a "coloured" sex worker, any "white peril" theme is deflected by the cinematography and dialogue. The film opens with a close-up shot of David's eyes visible between the slats of horizontal Venetian blinds, knowingly foregrounding the masked and predatory male gaze, yet reflected on the window from this outside perspective is traffic, a recognizably "third world" street, a place in flux, precarious, hazardous, somewhat chaotic. The bars of the blind both suggest that David is imprisoned and simultaneously give an impression of his vulnerability and imperilment, of a porous divide between inside and outside. Although the scene with Soraya is one in which a white man is paying a "coloured" woman for sex, in the film the opening dialogue is David talking to Soraya about his concerns for his daughter's safety:

DAVID: I haven't heard from my daughter.

SORAYA: Still living with the woman?

DAVID: Yes, still a lesbian, still on the farm, she thinks it's safer.

SORAYA: Nowhere's safe. Too many people with nothing to do but cause trouble.

This dialogue is absent in the novel, which begins instead by demonstrating David's appetite for dark-skinned women. There is but a fleeting reference to Lucy in the first chapter, and certainly there is no mention of her being in danger. Three pages into the novel, the text reads: "During their sessions he speaks to [Soraya] with a certain freedom, even on occasion unburdens himself. She has heard the stories of his two marriages, knows about his daughter and his daughter's ups and downs. She knows many of his opinions."[53] Moreover, in an encounter with the novel, the attentive reader learns to mistrust David's "opinions." David takes pleasure in Soraya, has affection for her, and wants to see her in her own time. He asserts to himself that "they have been lucky the two of them: he to have found her, she to have found him." By the end of the chapter, however, his complacency has been undercut by Soraya's evident aversion to his feelings of connection to her. He stalks her, and the chapter ends with a telephone call in which she says, "You are harassing me in my own house. I demand you will never phone me here again, never."[54] As Andrew van der Vlies notes, one of the problems with the film is that the focalization is not translated into a device such as voice-over,[55] so we do not, in the film, have an indication that David's perceptions might be flawed. In fact, the film suggests that the filmmakers have read the novel without much distance from David's viewpoint.

Bolstering David's judgment that his sexual encounter with his student, Melanie Isaacs, is "not rape," the film even goes so far as to alter the first scene in which David speaks with Melanie. In their first meeting in the novel, David makes a point of catching up with her. Here is the theme of pursuit, with Melanie as prey:

> He is returning home one Friday evening, taking the long route through the old college gardens, when he notices one of his students on the path ahead of him. Her name is Melanie Isaacs, from his Romantics course. Not the best student but not the worst either: clever enough, but unengaged. She is dawdling, he soon catches up with her.
>
> "Hello," he says.[56]

In the film, however, a very different impression is created as Melanie trips on the university stairs, and David, in a gallant gesture, helps her up, and the film works to exculpate David further in subsequent scenes that represent interaction between these two characters.

The novel of *Disgrace* has three scenes in which David "thrusts himself upon" Melanie. In the first, the text pulls an attentive reader in contradictory directions. Focalized through David, the act is referred to as "making love," yet

the text also mentions Melanie's passivity and the "frown on her face" afterwards:

> He takes her back to his house. On the living-room floor, to the sound of
> rain pattering against the windows, he makes love to her. Her body is clear,
> simple, in its way perfect; though she is passive throughout, he finds the
> act pleasurable, so pleasurable that from its climax he tumbles into blank
> oblivion.
>
> When he comes back the rain has stopped. The girl is lying beneath him,
> her eyes closed, her hands slack above her head, a slight frown on her face.
> His hands are under her coarse knit sweater, on her breasts. Her tights and
> panties lie in a tangle on the floor, his trousers are around his ankles. *After
> the storm*, he thinks, straight out of George Grosz.[57]

Clearly, Melanie's viewpoint is effaced in the description of the sexual act,
though there are clues that might, given the previously established unreli-
ability of David's opinions, cause us to suspect that she has experienced the
encounter very differently from David. The film is somewhat successful in
communicating Melanie's passivity in this scene, and as with the novel, which
is focalized through David, we experience the narrative from David's perspective, over his shoulder, literally. Subsequent scenes between these two characters in the film, however, are distinctly different from how they appear in the
novel.

In the second encounter with Melanie in the novel, David has just seen her
rehearsing, and has been turned on by her imitation of a *Kaaps* accent:

> At four o' clock the next afternoon he is at her flat. She opens the door wear-
> ing a crumpled T-shirt, cycling shorts, slippers in the shape of comic-book
> gophers which he finds silly, tasteless.
>
> He has given her no warning; she is too surprised to resist the intruder who
> thrusts himself upon her. When he takes her in his arms, her limbs crumple
> like a marionette's. Words heavy as clubs thud into the delicate whorl of her
> ear. "No, not now!" she says, struggling. "My cousin will be back!"
>
> But nothing will stop him. He carries her to the bedroom, brushes off the
> absurd slippers, kisses her feet, astonished by the feeling she evokes. Some-
> thing to do with the crude apparition on the stage: the wig, the wiggling bot-
> tom, the crude talk. Strange love! Yet from the quiver of Aphrodite, goddess
> of the foaming waves, no doubt about that.
>
> She does not resist. All she does is avert herself: avert her lips, avert her eyes.
> She lets him lay her out on the bed and then undress her: she even helps
> him lay her out on the bed and undress her: she even helps him, raising her
> arms and then her hips. Little shivers of cold run through her; as soon as she
> is bare, she slips under the quilted counterpane like a mole burrowing, and
> turns her back on him.

Not rape, not quite that, but undesired nevertheless, undesired to the core.[58]

Whereas the rape of Lucy remains off stage, Melanie's violation is thus luridly represented via David Lurie. The narrative point of view and aspects of description echo the father-daughter rape in Toni Morrison's *The Bluest Eye*, where the incident is distanced by way of a third-person narrative voice, focalized through the father-rapist, and the victim's experience is blanked out. In *The Bluest Eye* the victim faints, and in *Disgrace* Melanie "averts" herself, as if she had "decided to . . . die within herself for the duration." In Morrison's novel, Cholly nibbles his daughter's foot before he rapes her unresponsive body, and similarly, David kisses Melanie's feet before forcing himself upon her. Significantly, the perspective is destabilized in the paragraph beginning "[n]ot rape, not quite that,"[59] as the reader is plunged into an encounter where the distance between narrative voice and focalizer collapses. Melanie says "no" when David grabs her, she struggles against him as he picks her up and carries her to the bedroom, and there is an acknowledgement that for her, their intercourse is "undesired to the core."[60] But what, some might ask, was she doing in his home drinking alcohol before this incident? Why, if she was raped, does she later seek shelter at his home, and why does she have sex with him again? Since we have no access to Melanie's thoughts, we cannot know. Deliberately, it seems, Coetzee has invited a trial of sorts, where the reader is called upon to decide whether or not this encounter qualifies as a rape comparable to the rape of Lucy.

In their third sexual encounter in the novel, Melanie arrives at David's door, traumatized and in need of somewhere to stay. The reader is not sure what has happened to her, and David does not seem particularly interested in what has led to her arrival:

> He makes love to her one more time, on the bed in his daughter's room. It is good, as good as the first time; he is beginning to learn the way her body moves . . . If he does not sense in her a fully sexual appetite, that is only because she is still young. One moment stands out in recollection, when she hooks a leg behind his buttocks to draw him in closer . . . he feels a surge of joy and desire.[61]

Instead of reading her apparent lack of desire as reluctance or even as resistance, David tells himself it is because she is too young to have a sexual appetite that matches his, and in his recollection, he grasps at the one incident that showed some weak performance of desire on her part. In the cinematic version of *Disgrace*, however, the second and third scenes mentioned above from the novel are melded together, with the effect of representing Melanie's acquiescence rather than her passivity or resistance. We are shown David entering Melanie's apartment and that he grabs her, but whereas in the novel Melanie says "No, not now," the film script for Melanie's dialogue is simply a whispered

"Not now." The film then cuts to a scene in which a naked Melanie, somewhat reluctantly, gets into bed with David. Like Soraya who appears naked in the film in a sexualized and even Orientalized setting, Melanie is shown here as an erotic object. The viewer's eye is conflated with the desiring male gaze, with David's perspective, as the focus is on her breasts.[62]

Another significant shift in the film is the omission of references to WAR—the university organization Women Against Rape. In the novel, a note with the words "WOMEN SPEAK OUT" and "YOUR DAYS ARE OVER, CASANOVA," is slipped under David's door in the buildup to the disciplinary hearing in which he is accused of sexual harassment. David associates the note with WAR's "twenty-four-hour vigil in solidarity with 'recent victims.'"[63] In the film, however, the message is scrawled on the chalkboard in David's classroom, and there is no mention of Women Against Rape. Thus the film goes some way towards closing down the possibility—present in the novel—that the scenes between David and Melanie can be read, not as sexual harassment or an affair, but as violation and rape, and the film therefore works to undo any balance in the plot between "black" and "white peril." Most significantly, the erasure of history in the film of *Disgrace* means that the action that takes place is suspended in an ahistorical present where "white peril" is hidden and "black peril" may be played on endlessly, without regard for the ways in which such narrative has been used historically to justify dispossession, oppression, and disenfranchisement. Moreover, notwithstanding the film's failure at the box office, I would argue that the erasure of history in the cinematic version of *Disgrace* suggests a link between the success of Coetzee's novel and the global marketability of "black peril" narratives set in South Africa.

While the film disassociates the novel from history, it is difficult to read the silences of the two victims of sexual violation outside of a phenomenon of historical silencing. In spite of the Truth and Reconciliation Commission's "women's hearings," certain fragments of remembered history have had insignificant status in South Africa, and the climate of public exposure during the hearings failed to create "a safe space" for women. Like the Truth and Reconciliation Commission, which offered amnesty in exchange for truth, the disciplinary hearing in *Disgrace* is not a court of law, as it proposes to make a recommendation that amounts to a state of exception from the law. The disciplinary hearing thus offers "grace" ("pardon") in return for a confession and apology from David, but he forgoes this option and chooses "disgrace." Here, despite the focus on David's dilemma (to confess or not to confess), the reader could consider what has happened to Melanie, who is absent during the hearing. Evidently something has made her extremely unwell and distressed, to the point that she has not been able to fulfill her academic obligations and elects to drop out of university. While not oblivious to her distress, David has no desire or curiosity to know what is causing it, and seems blithely unaware that his behavior may have triggered her emotional and psychological decline.

In 1998, when Coetzee was writing *Disgrace*, he attended a public lecture by the philosopher Jacques Derrida, who was visiting South Africa, presenting lectures and workshops "On Forgiveness" and on his recent work, *The Gift of Death*. In "On Forgiveness," Derrida suggests that amnesty is akin to grace, "a law of exception,"[64] and his point here has relevance to an understanding of the Truth and Reconciliation Commission and the disciplinary hearing in *Disgrace*. In *The Gift of Death*, Derrida analyses the biblical story of Abraham and Isaac alongside a reading offered by Kierkegaard, and points out that responsibility to an absolute Other must inspire Abraham to hate that which he loves, his own family, and, as Derrida argues, humanity as a whole.[65] Examining Emmanuel Levinas's philosophy of the Other, Derrida observes "an aporia of responsibility" as there is no differentiation between *absolute responsibility* (to God, an infinite, unknowable Other) and *responsibility in general* (to embodied others with whom one shares mortality).[66] This split is played out in *Disgrace* as David Lurie's allegiance to an abstract ideal incites irresponsibility towards Melanie Isaacs. In obedience to and in the name of an Other, Abraham is prepared to sacrifice his son, Isaac. The story, Derrida maintains, is "monstrous, outrageous, barely conceivable: a father is ready to put to death his beloved son . . . because the Other, the great Other asks him or orders him without giving the slightest explanation."[67] A similar scenario is explored in *Disgrace*, as Melanie's family name, "Isaacs," and references to father-child-type bonds of responsibility between her and David, link David's violation of her body to Abraham's betrayal as he raises the knife over Isaac. No divine intercession, however, saves Melanie, and when Lucy finally speaks, indirectly, about her own rape, she implies that David's sexual exploit has been like "pushing the knife in . . . leaving the body covered in blood."[68] In the novel, Melanie Isaacs becomes David's sacrifice to Eros: "I was not myself . . . I became a servant of Eros," is all David is willing to offer in his defense.[69] In his apology to Melanie's father, David abnegates responsibility, claiming that he was serving an absolute, in this case fire (which consumes the burnt offering): "in the olden days people worshipped fire . . . It was that kind of fire that your daughter kindled in me."[70] Unlike Isaac, however, who was a blameless oblation, here is that most archaic and outrageous account of rape, where the "offering" is blamed for inciting the sacrifice. In the story of Abraham and Isaac, Derrida also notes that there is no room for women. "Does the system of sacrificial responsibility," he asks, "imply at its very basis an exclusion or a sacrifice of woman?"[71] He leaves the question unanswered. As mentioned above, in both narrative settings of *Disgrace* the central incidents are acts of sexual violation, but in each case the experience of the violated body is absent. During the disciplinary hearing in *Disgrace*, Melanie's interpretation of events never reaches the reader, and the charge brought against David is sexual harassment, thus stifling an account of rape. Melanie is not present in her family home when David makes his gesture of atonement in front of her mother and sister, and the uneasy encounter that ends Melanie's story in the novel is a telephone call between two men, David and Melanie's father. Lucy is adamant that what happened is "[hers] alone,"[72] insisting that David Lurie—and, by default, the reader—was not there. But if female silence in Coetzee's previous novels such as *Foe* (1986) could be linked to "the power to withhold,"[73] Lucy's refusal to speak about her experience certainly does not empower her and means that her story belongs to her rapists: "not her story to spread but theirs: they are its owners."[74]

Coetzee's choice of the rural Eastern Cape as a setting for the rape of David's daughter by three black men emphasizes complex historical relationships between race and gender in this "frontier" area. This set of historical associations is completely lost in the film as Lucy's smallholding is transposed to the Cedarberg, which has a very different history from that of the Eastern Cape. The preeminent meeting place of white and black, the Eastern Cape is a historically-fraught contact zone and evokes fierce past contestations over land. As mentioned in chapter 3, in *The Mote and the Beam* (1921), Sol Plaatje noted that the British Colonial Secretary, Lord Harcourt, justified the Natives Land Act as a means of stopping "black peril" cases.[75] The farm space is a violently contested boundary in post-apartheid South Africa and, as J.M. Coetzee demonstrates in *White Writing*, the South African pastoral, which presents a vision of the "husband-farmer" as custodian of the feminine earth, has been discursively implicated in the colonial appropriation of territory.[76]

At this point it is useful to examine and compare representations of sexual violation in *Disgrace* to those in Coetzee's earlier novels, *Dusklands* and *In the Heart of the Country*. In both of these texts, Coetzee demonstrates alertness to the ethical complexities of representing sexual violence. Mapping female bodies onto the landscape, colonialism propagated a myth of desirable territory as "virgin land," but *Dusklands*, Coetzee's first novel, follows in the tradition of Olive Schreiner's *Trooper Peter Halket of Mashonaland* in that it represents gendered violence literally inflicted on women's bodies in the project of territorial expansion. In the first section of the text, "The Vietnam Project," the narrator Eugene Dawn describes a memento, a photograph of an American soldier copulating with a Vietnamese woman who is "tiny and slim, possibly even a child."[77] Congruence with a real-life instance of captured reality adds horror to this fictive snapshot, as the gang rape and murder of Vietnamese women at My Lai in 1968 by Captain Ernst Medina's unit was photographed by one of the participants with his instamatic camera.[78] Rending the fictive, the chilling parallel draws attention to actual violation underpinning neo-imperial contest as the fictional photograph creates a *mise en abyme* such that Eugene Dawn's perusal of the snapshot, reducing violence to spectacle, echoes the reader's encounter with the text. Situated as voyeur, the viewer/reader is implicated in pornographic violence which, in this case, is not just fictive.

By describing political warfare and sexual violence as inseparable acts of penetration and domination, Dawn's narrative expresses a phenomenology of rape, as it becomes an expression of desire for transcendence, for proof that there is more than the self. In *Dusklands*, rape is violence directed at the body of an other, Oriental or African, that will not yield up its secrets:

> We cut their flesh open, we reached into their dying bodies . . . we forced ourselves deeper than we had ever gone before into their women, but when we came back we were still alone, and the women like stones. . . .
>
> For a while we were prepared to pity them, though we pitied more our tragic reach for transcendence. Then we ran out of pity.[79]

In this passage, an impulse towards transcendence is intimately linked to the penetration and effacement of the other, and this is echoed in *Disgrace* in the relationship between David and Melanie. In the second part of *Dusklands*, "The Narrative of Jacobus Coetzee," the protagonist dispassionately watches one of his men raping a "Hottentot" child, and his act of intercourse with a captured "Bushman" girl serves both to consolidate his power and to eliminate her: "You have become power itself now and she is nothing, a rag you wipe yourself on and throw away."[80] While in *Disgrace* the abuse of Melanie by David is more subtle, the impulse is the same, she becomes "nothing" as David's desire has not the capacity to imagine her embodied subjectivity.

While *Dusklands* uses "white peril" imagery in order to expose the violations of imperialism, Coetzee's second novel, *In the Heart of the Country*, like *Disgrace*, balances an image of "white peril" with scrutiny of "black peril" stereotypes. Set on a remote farm in the Karoo and narrated by Magda, a spinster coexisting uneasily with an authoritarian father and the servants on the farm, the novel mimics the farm novel genre in order to subvert it. *In the Heart of the Country* comprises a number of numbered fragments in a narrative characterized by shifts, ellipses, and an absence of temporal continuity. According to Magda, her mother has died and her father takes Anna, the young wife of the servant Hendrik, as his mistress, coercing her with sweets and gifts, while Hendrik is bought off with a bottle of brandy. Magda narrates a scene in which her father rides up to Klein-Anna: "perhaps he even smiles . . . Or: as Klein-Anna makes her way homeward in the heat of the afternoon my father comes upon her."[81] Here the use of "perhaps" and "or" warn the reader, however, that the meetings between her father and Klein-Anna might be Magda's imagination running wild. Similarly, there is uncertainty about the "black peril" scenes that follow later in the novel. In his reading of narrated incidents where Magda is apparently raped by Hendrik, Derek Attridge proposes that there are two rapes by Hendrik, and that the second should be read as "real" within the logic of plot. Claiming that "[a] responsible reading practice will keep the appeal to psychological explanations (like unbridled fantasising) to a minimum," Attridge proposes that the first rape should be read "as a product of Magda's fears, and the second, with its moments of ambivalence and its unexpected details . . . As real."[82] Attention to the novel reveals, however, that the so-called second rape splits still further into two alternative accounts, one in which Magda plunges a fork into Hendrik's arm, and the other in which she lies beside him and speaks to him with some tenderness. The narrative of the second rape therefore does not, as Attridge suggests, "flow on in a coherent sequence."[83] Complicating any realist reading still further, the numbered fragments in which Magda is raped by Hendrik are part of a narrative path that follows on from the second death of Magda's father, a trajectory that is disrupted by the end of the novel, where Magda's father reappears alive, albeit senile and drooling. The novel thus moves beyond the uncertainty of a modernist text like *A Passage to India* (where there is simply the question whether Adela has been assaulted in the Marabar Caves or whether the assault is a psychological hallucination on her part) and deploys a complex, splintered narrative configuration in order to scrutinize and undo "black peril" narrative.

Like *Disgrace*, *In the Heart of the Country* plays on a "black peril" trope, and reveals gender oppression operating within the farm setting and in the pastoral genre, where, as Coetzee notes in *White Writing*, we find women "imprisoned in the farmhouse" and "confined to the breast function."[84] After Lucy is raped by unnamed intruders, she is made a proposal of marriage by Petrus, the farmworker who claims kinship with one of her rapists and offers to look after her in return for her land. Although her decision not to terminate her pregnancy after the rape subverts classic "black peril" literature (in which there is no possibility of a biracial child being born), *Disgrace* seems to suggest that women's bodies may not fare better in the new order of post-apartheid South Africa, as after Lucy is raped and pregnant, she gives up her land and retreats into the house. In *Disgrace*, the anti-pastoral mode breaks with colonial mappings of the female body and land, depicting instead feudal systems of claiming and reclaiming where there is contempt for women as owners of property and land. Indeed *Disgrace* points to a context where women are regarded as property, and are liable for protection only insofar as they belong to men. As a lesbian, Lucy would be regarded as "unowned" and therefore "huntable," and there is even a suggestion that her sexuality may have provoked her attackers.[85] In fact, the dynamics of the attack even recall the spate of "corrective rape" incidents—the rape of lesbians by gangs of men—that have so horrified South Africa in recent times, since *Disgrace*.

While, as noted throughout this study, "black peril" imagery (unless scripted by black men) was acceptable within white racist political discourse, the subversive status of "white peril" literature is confirmed by attitudes of apartheid censors. As pointed out in chapter 3, records of the former board of censors reveal that in 1962 Daphne Rooke's *The Greyling* was banned in South Africa for portraying the ways in which white men abused certain women who were considered inferior in terms of race and class.[86] Similarly, although the censors in 1977 found Coetzee's *In the Heart of the Country* "not undesirable," with the chairman of the Committee, Professor H. van der Merwe Scholtz concluding that "sex across the colour bar takes place but the characters are situated historically and geographically such that it is completely acceptable,"[87] the novel was embargoed, partly for representing an apparent rape of a white woman by a black farmworker *as well as* the white farmer's coercion of a black female servant.[88]

Attitudes in the post-apartheid era have shifted, with the state now turning a suspicious eye on "black peril" narratives. What is disturbing about the ANC's submission to the SAHRC (as well as Marais's defense of *Disgrace*), however, is that rape as an actual fact of social life in South Africa is not mentioned. The complex enmeshment of race and rape in South African literature calls for critical wariness, but I suggest vigilance where reading strategies eclipse the significance of suffering within the reader's ambit. In an interview on "Autobiography and Confession," J.M. Coetzee warned against processes of textualization that render representation so powerless that "those represented in/by the text . . . have no power either."[89] Coetzee proposes that the body, with its frailty and suffering, is a counter to the endless skepticism that is a feature of both secular confession and textual analysis. In South Africa particularly, Coetzee emphasizes, "it is not possible to deny the authority of suffering and therefore of the body." Coetzee proposes that the suffering body claims authority "without having to speak," and looking back on his fiction in this interview, the writer professed to see "a simple . . . standard," and "that standard is the body."[90]

In *Disgrace*, Lucy insists that the violation she has suffered cannot be a public matter, and her failure to report the crime to the authorities may represent a rather extreme refusal to play a part in a history of oppression. This does not, however, explain the complete absence of her story in the narrative structure of *Disgrace*. Similarly, the reader never hears Melanie's story, and the accounts of the two women are noteworthy lacunae in each narrative setting. In a remarkable parallel with David Lurie's attitude during his disciplinary hearing, Lucy insists that she has "the right not to be put on trial,"[91] and in "The Harms of Pornography," Coetzee indicts a society where those who have suffered rape and sexual abuse may be perceived as "disgraced":

> The ambivalence of rape victims—particularly outside the West—about seeking redress from the law, and the surprising degree of suspicion or hostility with which the public, even in the West, treats such plaintiffs, indicates that in matters of honor archaic attitudes are far from dead . . . the system of justice of the modern state, based on notions of guilt and innocence has not entirely supplanted *the tribunal of public opinion*, based on notions of honor and shame.[92]

Even when sexual violence finds representation, this may signify disgrace, provoke further victimization, or fan the fires of political hate speech. When David imagines Lucy's story "like a stain . . . spreading across the district,"[93] he is imagining the "tribunal of public opinion" that will see her as tainted, disgraced. The dilemmas of Lucy and Melanie point to a context where victims are compelled to be silent, and thus collude with perpetrators. David tells Melanie to return to her work, but she stares at him in shock: "*You have cut me off from everyone*, she seems to want to say. *You have made me bear your secret*."[94] Similarly, Lucy's silence means that her rapists are "getting away with" their crime.[95]

In canonical literary narratives of the West, rape is often depicted as severed from articulation. Although Shakespeare's Lucrece names the one who has raped her, her account does not save her from perceiving herself as "disgraced," or from death. Philomela, in Ovid's *Metamorphosis*, is raped and has her tongue cut out to prevent her from naming the crime and the perpetrator. She sews her account into a tapestry, thus making it possible for her sister to discover the rapist's identity. In the workings of art, Philomela can thus convey that which is "unspeakable" in the realm of life. It is no accident that the names of Melanie and Lucy in *Disgrace* echo those of these two mythological rape victims, highlighting Western artistic traditions where rape has had a troubled relationship to representation. Amina Mama notes that the colonial cultures which imposed themselves on the African continent were steeped in gender violence,[96] and in my view this is revealed decisively in Western attitudes to the representation of sexual violence. In "The Harms of Pornography," Coetzee observes that the portrayal of violence is "deeply anti-classical," as the brutality of carnage and rape were typically represented euphemistically in classical representations.[97] Although sexual violation was a common enough subject in classical art, the violence of rape was both obscured and legitimized by representations that depicted sexual violation in an aesthetic manner.[98]

In Shakespeare's "The Rape of Lucrece," the distraught Lucrece stands before a painting of the war that ensued after the rape (typically represented as an "abduction" or "elopement") of Helen of Troy. The encounter, framed within the literary text, is between the artwork and the viewer, between representation and the realm of life, and *Disgrace* stages this confrontation, also via rape narrative, in a remarkably similar way. After the farm attack, David finds a reproduction of Poussin's *The Rape of the Sabine Women* in an art book in the Grahamstown Library and asks: "What had all this attitudinising to do with what he expected rape to be: the man lying on top of the woman and pushing himself into her?"[99] Thinking of Byron, who "pushed himself into" and possibly raped "legions of countesses and kitchenmaids," David speculates that from where Lucy stands, "Byron looks very old-fashioned indeed."[100] Here is a critique of the Romantic posturing that obscures, even justifies, abdicating ethical responsibility in the realm of life. And yet David, scholar of Romanticism, is guilty of "attitudinising" when he excuses his violation of Melanie Isaacs as an act motivated by Eros,[101] or inspired by "Aphrodite, goddess of the foaming waves."[102] Coetzee's novel thus assesses the disjuncture between allegiance to aesthetics and allegiance to the ethical, revealing Western artistic traditions that may condone unethical acts. David's attitude to Melanie is exemplified in his lecture on Wordsworth (Book 6 of *The Prelude*), where he describes the poet's disappointment upon seeing Mont Blanc:

> . . . *usurp upon* means to intrude upon or encroach upon . . . a soulless image, a mere image on the retina, has encroached upon a living thought . . . *the great archetypes of the mind, pure ideas, find themselves usurped by mere sense-images* . . . Like being in love . . . do you truly wish to see the beloved in the cold clarity of the visual apparatus? It may be in your best interest to throw a veil over the gaze, so as to keep her alive in her archetypal goddess-like form.[103]

Ironically, as David "usurps upon" Melanie a few pages later with thoughts of "Aphrodite, goddess of the foaming waves,"[104] there is a warning that veiling the other in sublimity may obscure abuse and permit one to behave unethically toward another body.

In "The Harms of Pornography," Coetzee attests that neither censorship nor the "delegitimization" of certain representations should stop serious writers from dramatizing darker aspects of experience.[105] In response to the campaign against pornography, led by feminist Catherine MacKinnon, Coetzee argues for the possibility of "a male writer-pornographer" who presents the following question:

> If I were to write an account of power and desire that, unlike yours, does not close the book on desire . . . if this hypothetical account were further to be offered, not in the discursive terms of 'theory', but in the form of a representation . . . if this representation were to share a thematics with pornography (including perhaps torture, abasement, acts of cruelty) . . . if this project were carried through and offered to the world, what would protect it from suffering the same fate—'delegitimitization'—as any work of pornography, except perhaps its *seriousness* (if that were recognized), as a philosophical project?[106]

Coetzee points to the moral blindness of an industry that profits from exploiting women but argues that an artist for whom "seriousness is . . . an imperative uniting the aesthetic and the ethical" should not shy away from problematic representations.[107]

Disgrace seems to suggest that imaginative empathy may not only prompt ethical responsibility for another, but also may reveal a dark kinship with those who commit violent acts. *Disgrace* presents mirror-like juxtapositions, creating disturbing likenesses. Petrus, the farm laborer, describes himself as "the dog-man,"[108] but Petrus's rise in the world corresponds, inversely, with the protagonist's fall into "a state of disgrace" such that David Lurie becomes "a dog-man."[109] Like the dogs, who are "too menny,"[110] David claims he cannot control his sexuality,[111] and similarly, the three men who rape Lucy are described "like dogs in a pack."[112] Resembling these men, David is also, albeit in different ways, a rapist and a dog-killer. By way of unsettling mirror-like concurrences, *Disgrace* draws the reader into a confrontation where she/he is called into account. Disturbingly, David claims he can become the three men who have raped his daughter, "inhabit" them,[113] and his treatment of Melanie, his desire to view her as a "goddess," is thus equated with the violent impulses of Lucy's rapists. As *Disgrace* demonstrates, the idealism and conventions of desire in the Western love tradition have a dark and violent aspect. Writing of Samuel Richardson's *Clarissa* in *Stranger Shores*, Coetzee proposes: "Lovelace the rapist-revenger is the dark side of the coin of which Dante the pilgrim-lover is the bright, ideal side."[114]

David is composing an opera about Byron's relationship with the young Teresa Guiccioli, but the rape of his daughter leads him to revise his artistic work.[115] Abandoning a Romantic tradition that has aided and abetted his misuse of Melanie, David shifts the focus of the opera away from Byron, scripting the voices of Byron's abandoned daughter, and of Teresa, "now middle-aged," asking whether he "can find it in his heart to love this plain ordinary woman."[116] Our last glimpse of the opera is where David, plunking away on a toy banjo, considers whether to include the "saying" of the non-human other: "Would he dare to do that: bring a dog into the piece, allow it to loose its own lament to the heavens between the strophes of the lovelorn Teresa's? Why not?"[117] Searching for counter-voices, David stumbles upon a stunted form of care, for the "plain ordinary" Bev Shaw, and for the dog he carries to its death in the final pages of *Disgrace*. Any notion that David has achieved personal reformation or redemption, however, is rendered ambivalent by the fact that towards the end of the novel, even as he is revising the opera to include Teresa's voice, on a return trip to Cape Town he goes back to seeking an encounter with a sex worker.

As in *Disgrace*, women's experiences of rape in Coetzee's most recent novels, *Diary of a Bad Year* and *Summertime*, are left offstage.[118] In *Diary of a Bad Year* Anya notes "Señor C'"s desire for her, and in the discussion that follows about dishonor and degrees of shame, she alludes to an incident in which she and a girl friend were gang-raped by three Americans, "three strapping young males." Notably, she declines to "go into the details."[119] Similarly, Julia in *Summertime* chooses to "draw a veil over what happened" when her husband finds out about her affair with John Coetzee and attacks her. Left out of sight here is a "shameful" and "shaming" scene of marital rape.[120] Although Coetzee is a writer known for his frequent deployment of women's voices and perspectives (he has written three novels where the first-person narrator is a woman, and substantial portions of *Diary of a Bad Year* and *Summertime* are written from women's perspectives), and although he writes about other somewhat taboo aspects of women's embodied existence,[121] with the exception of *In the Heart of the Country* (where Magda's accounts of rape read as fantasies or fears rather than as a part of the plot), Coetzee chooses *not* to script women's experiences of rape. Perhaps, like "Señor C" who feels that "dishonour descends on [his] shoulders,"[122] as a man, Coetzee is too aware of masculine complicity to articulate a woman's experience of sexual violation.

On the one hand, the stories of Melanie and Lucy in *Disgrace* are not offered to the reader and, perhaps, as Tessa Hadley argues (though only with reference to the rape of Lucy), in this way the text "preserves as inviolable the space . . . in which the actual rape happens."[123] At the same time, however, *Disgrace* does not merely draw attention to silence, it invites us to consider positionality in thinking about the absent stories of violation. Although Lucy's account of the farm attack is hidden from David and from the reader, David is haunted by possibilities, and mentally plays out the horrific scenario:

> . . . the men, for their part, drank up her fear, revelled in it, did all they could to hurt her, to menace her, to heighten her terror. *Call your dogs!* they said to her. *Go on call your dogs! No dogs? Then let us show you dogs!*
>
> . . . he can, if he concentrates, if he loses himself, be there, be the men, inhabit them, fill them with the ghost of himself. *The question is, does he have it in him to be the woman?*[124]

Through this imaginary "reading," the elided scene of violence is made visible, but David's question suggests that ethical responsiveness depends on experiencing the narrative differently, on "giving up" the viewpoint of perpetrator or voyeur. The novel may, as Spivak notes, "be relentless in keeping the focalisation confined to David Lurie,"[125] but the responsibility for an imaginative exploration that opens up space for alternative points of view is thus left with the reader.

The Limits of Testimony: Traces of Violation in Achmat Dangor's *Bitter Fruit* and Zoë Wicomb's *David's Story*

Reporting in the aftermath of South Africa's Truth and Reconciliation Commission, Beth Goldblatt and Sheila Meintjes claimed that violence against women "remains one of the hidden sides to the story of our past" and that this has serious implications for attempts to understand South Africa's history and for dealing with the country's present.[126] As noted above, while the women's hearings organized by the TRC were supposed to guarantee a secure environment for women to testify to abuses they had suffered under apartheid, for a number of reasons these hearings were not entirely successful in their objective. The Human Rights Watch report on rape and domestic violence in South Africa (1995) observed cases where women were targeted for rape as part of the political conflict,[127] but Jessie Duarte, a former activist, claimed that many women felt they could not say they were raped because "from the position of the people they worked with that was considered a weakness."[128] One of the fraught and controversial issues was the question of gender abuse within the training camps of the ANC. As the TRC report notes: "Where the sexual abuse was perpetrated by men within the liberation movements, there were further pressures not to speak."[129] The difficulty of speaking publicly at this transitional time in South African history about rape and sexual abuse perpetrated under apartheid is foregrounded in two novels, Achmat Dangor's *Bitter Fruit* (2001) and Zoë Wicomb's *David's Story* (2000). As I shall demonstrate, Dangor's text, which keeps the representation of rape at a remove through a *mise en abyme* scene of reading, comprises a "white peril" narrative that evokes Ariel Dorfman's *Death and the Maiden* (1991) in foregrounding the limits of Truth Commissions and the question of retributive violence. *David's Story*, on the other hand, deploys post-structuralist notions of *sous rature* in order to gesture to unspeakable questions about gender violence during the liberation struggle.

Opening in 1998 when the final report of the TRC is being prepared, *Bitter Fruit* contrasts public and private processes of remembering. In the first paragraphs of the novel, the protagonist Silas, who has a job in the new government "liaising between the Ministry of Justice and the Truth and Reconciliation Commission,"[130] encounters, in the banality of a supermarket environment, Du Boise, the apartheid-era policeman who raped his wife Lydia nineteen years previously. Silas's immediate impulse is to confront Du Boise, an effort that fails miserably. When he later tells Lydia about seeing Du Boise, they argue, Lydia drops the beer she is drinking and then dances on the broken shards of glass, which lands her in hospital. Forced into immobility, she takes on the status of a sacrificial and masochistic figure who, in her own words, has "crossed over into a zone of silence."[131] When Silas suggests that they go to the Truth and Reconciliation Commission, Lydia is scornful: "You think Archbishop Tutu has ever been fucked up his arse against his will?"[132] In an analysis of this novel, Meg Samuelson claims that Lydia speaks of rape "like a man."[133] What is striking, however, is that Lydia *does not* speak directly of the rape, but she does *write* about it in her diary. In her writing, Lydia explains that "Speaking about something heightens its reality, makes it unavoidable."[134] Foregrounding the "illogical" contradiction of the term "historical memory,"[135] the text demonstrates disjunction between public and private forms of remembering by focusing on an incident that cannot be told publicly.

According to Dangor, the novel's central event, namely the rape of Lydia, is based on the actual rape of one of Dangor's friends, whose marriage was destroyed following the violation. During the TRC proceedings, Dangor wondered if her friend's story, and that of her ex-husband, would ever be told.[136] Like the woman in Fanon's case study of an Algerian man's impotence following the rape of his wife in detention,[137] Lydia has been raped because of her husband's political activities and the rape has damaged her marriage. In Fanon's text, the rape is largely the man's dilemma, and *Bitter Fruit* remains within this paradigm, while foregrounding and critiquing its implications for the woman. When Silas claims that "we" had to "put up with those things," Lydia accuses him of making her pain his:

> "What did you have to put up with, Silas? He raped me, not you".
>
> "It hurt me too."
>
> "So that's it. Your hurt. You remembered your hurt."[138]

In her diary Lydia notes that the very mode of public confession as a patriarchal and performative ceremony would position her as a guilty party in talking about the rape: "Confess your sins, even those committed against you—and is not rape a sin committed by both victim and perpetrator, at least according to man's gospel?"[139] She also attests that she cannot speak to Silas or to her parents about what has happened, that once she speaks her experience becomes the property of others who do not want to hear it:

> I cannot speak to Silas, he makes my pain his tragedy. In any case, I know that he doesn't want to speak about my being raped, he wants to suffer silently, wants me to be his accomplice in this act of denial. I cannot also speak to my mother or my father. They too will want to take on my pain, make it theirs. . . . They will also demand of me a forgetful silence.[140]

In her diary Lydia is able to recount the rape, but it is through the eyes of her son Mikey—son of Du Boise through Du Boise's rape of Lydia—that the reader encounters the diary. While the novel begins with past tense narration, in the chapters where Mikey finds and reads the diary it shifts into the present tense, heightening the sense of immediacy as Mikey becomes a witness to the horrific primal scene that has resulted in his conception. Significantly, although the description of Lydia's diary account begins in the first person with Lydia's voice, "Three nights ago I was raped,"[141] the narrative slips into a third-person summary, mediated by Mikey, when the rape is described:

> Lydia's prose is clear, translucent almost. It has the transcendent quality of pain captured without sentimentality. She describes the rape in cold detail, Du Boise's eyes, his smell, his grunts, the flicker of fear when he reached his climax and, for a moment, was not in control. Silas's rage, his wild screaming, which did not lessen her terror but enhanced it, his fists hammering against the sides of the police van, giving rhythm to Du Boise's rapacious movements.[142]

Bringing forward the dilemma of the male author writing about rape, but also the problems of public access to women's words about violation, the text averts our eyes, focusing on Mikey's reaction to what he reads in the diary, even as it compels us to imagine Lydia's perspective. The rape is thus narrated indirectly through a framing device, creating a *mise en abyme* scene of reading that ambivalently aligns Mikey's reading of his mother's diary and the reader's encounter with the text, while placing the reader, unlike Mikey, at a remove from the narrated rape.

As noted by the Centre for Applied Legal Studies's submission, the TRC's focus on extraordinary violence "has a gender bias, as well as a racial one."[143] The question that follows is whether, by focusing on an instance of extraordinary violence—rape committed under torture—*Bitter Fruit*, like the processes of the TRC itself, can be said to neglect the "ordinary" workings of apartheid. Focusing on the universal disenfranchisement of black South Africans under apartheid as a violation not addressed by the TRC, Mark Sanders deploys Jacques Derrida's "Toward a Critique of Violence" to point out that such disenfranchisement "can be conceived as an instance of founding violence, not as instrumental violence," but that "each instrumental act of violence—be it a 'gross violation' or an act of 'ordinary' violence—inscribes and reinscribes this founding violence." Thus Sanders concludes that "there is no extraordinary violence, in this general sense of foundation, which can be rigorously opposed to ordinary violence."[144] I would like to extend and develop this insight by making the point that a consideration of sexual violence under apartheid undoes the TRC's focus on extraordinary violence by troubling any clear division between political crime and everyday sexual abuse. While the Commission recognized rape as "severe ill-treatment," that is, as a politically-motivated crime, what it had in mind were violations that took place in the context of torture or during specific instances of political attacks. Examining "ordinary" cases of rape clearly fell outside of the TRC's mandate, even though rape as a political crime was inseparable from a context where apartheid founded and extended patriarchal environments that were fertile soil for "everyday" sexual violence. The fact that not a single perpetrator during South Africa's Truth and Reconciliation Commission hearings came forward on account of rape to plead for amnesty suggests not only the shame associated with being a perpetrator of sex crimes, but also the tenuousness of the division between political crimes and everyday sexual abuse.

One of the pieces of music that Silas brings his wife to listen to while she recuperates in hospital with her lacerated feet is Schubert's *Death and the Maiden*, with this score and Lydia's question, "is the music you chose part of some sad and long-suffering image of me that you carry around in your head?"[145] summoning up the intertextual ghost of Dorfman's play *Death and the Maiden* and inviting comparisons between the South African and Chilean Truth Commissions. Like *Death and the Maiden*, *Bitter Fruit* is set in a newly democratic country still haunted by the past. Both texts use sexual violence as a way of bringing into relief the inability of respective Truth Commissions to address certain human rights violations and to deliver justice in a context where many felt that they could not forgive. While the TRC in South Africa had a mandate to investigate gross human rights violations, which included torture and rape, as noted above, this climate of public exposure was at odds with creating a safe space for victims of sexual assault to come forward and testify.[146] Shane Graham argues that South Africa's Truth and Reconciliation

Commission was "different from the cold, bureaucratic, and mostly in camera proceedings of similar bodies in Chile and other nations in transition from authoritarian regimes." Rather than "a blanket indemnity," amnesty in South Africa "was granted on an individual basis to those who gave 'full disclosure' of politically motivated crimes" and thus "amnesty was used as a tool for excavating the truth about the past."[147] However, there are similarities between the South African and Chilean Truth Commissions. As Mahmood Mamdani notes, the South African Commission "was the fruit of a political compromise whose terms both made possible the Commission and set the limits within which it would work,"[148] and similarly, the Chilean Rettig Commission was a compromise solution. A 1978 amnesty law enacted by the Pinochet regime restricted prosecution for prior crimes and Pinochet still had significant support in 1990, thus trials for political crimes were not an option when the Commission came into being a month after Patricio Aylwin became democratically elected President.

Moreover, the Rettig Commission was only given a mandate to investigate political crimes that ended in death or "disappearances." Thus, while the process gave many families some closure, it failed to bring to light a vast number of gross human rights violations. While Mark Sanders views the TRC as a "quasi-juridical body," an instrument of law,[149] I would argue that, because of its mandate to recommend amnesty in cases of full disclosure, the TRC was a quasi-legal or even *extralegal* body that acted in the interests of *exception to the law* rather than justice, becoming a channel for something more akin to the ancient power of grace, which, as Derrida points out in his essay *On Forgiveness*, is "a law which inscribes in the laws a power above the laws."[150] Since it was not a court of law and was examining political crimes long after the fact, the TRC did not have the capacity to hold trials that could establish guilt or innocence in accusations of rape. It could not, for instance, conduct a full investigation to determine whether a woman had been raped or a man had been penetrated by a broomstick during interrogation, or whether a woman had been violated by her comrades in the ANC camps. Sexual violation thus became one of the issues that for technical reasons could not be properly addressed, revealing a shortfall of justice in the workings of the TRC.

As Dorfman recalls, when he returned to Chile in 1990, it was to a country devastated by the Pinochet dictatorship, trying to rebuild itself when it had not dealt with its past:

> I saw victims and tormentors living side by side, drinking at the same bars, eating at the same restaurants, jostling each other on buses and streets—never acknowledging the pain and the guilt, not to themselves, not to anybody.
>
> I couldn't stand that silence, and the result was my play, *Death and the Maiden*. I wanted to look at the question of how we coexist in the same

country, even in the same room, with someone who has caused us grievous, perhaps irreparable harm. Would we be able to resist taking revenge, if that revenge were made possible?[151]

The protagonist of Dorfman's play, Paulina, claims to recognize a man who has by chance come into the home she shares with her husband as the doctor who arranged her torture and gang rape under the old regime. She conducts a trial, with her husband, who is working for a Truth Commission, acting as the doctor's "lawyer." The play ends with the audience thrust into Paulina's position, retaining ambiguity as to whether Paulina has shot the doctor or not. Like Paulina, Lydia in *Bitter Fruit* has a husband who is working within the processes of the Truth Commission. Yet, unlike *Death and the Maiden*, where the victim confronts the perpetrator directly, it is Silas who sees and recognizes Du Boise, and it is Mikey who finally pulls the trigger, "executing" Du Boise on his front lawn. Thus, whereas Dorfman stages the confrontation between the woman victim and the suspected male perpetrator within the fledgling democracy as open-ended and indeterminate, the encounter with the perpetrator in *Bitter Fruit* takes place via Lydia's male family members and provides closure by allowing for an act of retribution denied by the Truth and Reconciliation Commission. Indeed, one of the troubling aspects of *Bitter Fruit* is the way in which justice is handed over to men, and Lydia even casts herself as property exchanged between men. "Would you kill him for me?" Lydia asks Silas, "He took your woman, he fucked your wife, made you listen to him doing it. I became his property, even my screams were his instrument."[152]

As with the other "white peril" narratives examined in this study, the emphasis in *Bitter Fruit* is on the woman's womb bearing the "fruit" of the rape: "he had violated her womb with the horror of his seed."[153] Echoing the rape of Lydia is the sexual abuse of Mikey's "coloured" friend Vinu by her white Afrikaans father, which began during the apartheid years when the family lived in exile, a rape that slips into allegorizing the intimate violations of apartheid. As was the case with the retributive violence meted out on behalf of Lydia, Mikey passes judgment on Vinu's father ("he had imposed his ageing body on her, his stale lust")[154] and executes him after dealing with Du Boise. In fact the novel evokes a long and global history of "white peril" stories avenged by men, as it circles back to the story of Ali Ali, Mikey's paternal grandfather, who executed a British soldier in colonial India for raping Ali Ali's sister. While for Lydia, "nothing in any of their lives would change because of a public confession of pain suffered" and "nothing could be undone . . . it could not be withdrawn, not by an act of remorse, or vengeance, not even by justice,"[155] in the perspective of Moulana Ismail, who tells Mikey the story of Ali Ali, interracial rape is an ancient and unforgivable act of war that cries out for revenge:

> There are certain things people do not forget, or forgive. Rape is one of them. In ancient times, conquerors destroyed the will of those whom they

conquered by impregnating the women. It is an ancient form of genocide. [. . .]
You conquer a nation by bastardising its children.[156]

Notably, Mikey's murder of Du Boise corresponds with his adoption of an
Islamic name, Noor ("The Prophet's Light"), and his plan to leave South Africa
for India. Divided into three parts, "Memory," "Confession," and "Retribution,"
Bitter Fruit sets up a disjunction between the TRC processes, which drew on a
Christian model of confession and forgiveness, and an alternative model of
retributive violence.

In *Bitter Fruit* the reader is told that someone from the ANC government
"had accused Archbishop Tutu of naivety, saying that no one . . . should dare
to equate the inevitable excesses of the liberation struggle with the organised
murder of apartheid."[157] In its report the TRC notes that "while much of the
evidence related to abuse by government forces, women within the opposition
also faced abuse from colleagues."[158] As early as 1989, during an IDASA conference in which writers met with ANC delegates in Zimbabwe, the ANC was
asked to clarify "what the policy decision is concerning rape, regarding members." Pallo Jordan, who answered on behalf of the ANC, attested that "rape is
considered a grave crime in our code of conduct, punishable by all sorts of
terrible things."[159] While rape was thus punishable by the ANC in exile within
the camps, there were also, as attested by a number of women outside the TRC
hearings, gender abuses in the camps that fed off the silence induced by victims' fear and shame. With the exception of one case, these stories never
reached the TRC. Partly this was a result of the ANC having run its own internal investigation, the details of which were not made public. This investigation, presented to the TRC by Thabo Mbeki (then Deputy President),
"acknowledged that men in the camps had committed 'gender-specific offences' against their woman comrades" and claimed that the perpetrators had
been punished, though it "did not describe either the offences or the punishment in any detail" and "in the light of these silences, Commissioner Hlengiwe
Mkhize remarked that 'the submission fail(ed) women.'"[160]

In the 1980s a British-born director, Ingrid Sinclair, wanted to make a documentary about women's experiences in the camps of the Zimbabwean liberation movements. Beginning interviews with seven women, she found that
while some said that they had been raped in the camps, they were unwilling to
make their identities or those of their rapists known, which was not surprising
since the rapists now occupied prominent positions in government. As a result
of the women's reluctance to testify on camera, Sinclair decided to make the
film *Flame* (1996), a fictional narrative dealing with the story of two women
friends who leave their homes to join the liberation struggle, renaming themselves Comrade Flame and Comrade Liberty. Through fiction, Sinclair was
able to deal more openly with gender issues and the liberation movement,
although there was an attempt by war veterans to stop the film from being
made, and some of the women she interviewed were uneasy about the original

script. Basing revisions on their suggestions, Sinclair reformed the rapist, Che, into a benevolent paternal figure who by his own admission has only acted with inhumanity because of the war-time situation, a resolution that is by no means unproblematic, as after Che apologizes to Flame for raping her, she willingly becomes his lover and becomes pregnant with his child. Despite such revisions, however, advertising for the film reified its controversial content. Whereas the rape scene is a small part of the narrative of *Flame*, the cover of the home video version states in prominent but somewhat ambiguous lettering: "She went to war. She was raped. She fought back."[161] On its release in Zimbabwe, *Flame* was damned by former military leaders. Ironically drawing on a colonial discourse of chivalry, Bornwell Chakaodza, Director of Information for the Zimbabwean Defence Forces, claimed that: "The film's failure to balance the negative scenes of the freedom fighters with their resilience and values suggests an insidious attempt to make sure future generations will have no sense of their gallantry." Black Zimbabwean women themselves were divided in their responses to the film. One commented, "If the war had been about rape, we would not have fought or won it," but another woman supported the film testifying that she herself was raped and that: "A society which denies the truth cannot move forward."[162]

The South African cultural text that approaches the fraught question of gender violence and sexualized torture in the camps of the liberation movement is Zoë Wicomb's novel *David's Story*, which through its fragmentary narrative structure, marked by gaps, absences and unanswerable questions, draws attention to the difficulty of speaking out, or even writing, about certain events. Whereas a realist but fictional narrative enabled Sinclair to confront the issue of rape in the camps (though by no means unproblematically), *David's Story* eschews illusionistic effects that posit any simple "truth." On two occasions the issue of rape appears, only to slip out of focus. A nightmarish scene of torture is described by one of the apparent torturers as "not rape,"[163] and yet, as Meg Samuelson points out, even if torture does not involve penetration, the text here "redirects our focus to the myriad ways in which bodies are violated, and asks how we can distinguish between penetrative rape and the torture technique of attaching electrodes to genitals."[164] Later in the text one of the women who had spent time in the camps remembers an occasion when she had to subject herself to the "unspoken part of a girl's training." Acquiescence is her only path out of victimhood to agency: "And because she would not let him force her, lord it over her, she forced herself and said, Okay, if you want."[165]

Here the novel recalls evidence such as that of Thenjiwe Mtintso to the Truth and Reconciliation Commission's special women's hearings. She is reported to have said that "sexual violence is . . . used by those in power to destroy the identity of women who have rejected traditional roles, for example by engaging in 'masculine' roles in the struggle." Referring to the almost casual abuse of women by comrades in exile and to the pressure on women within the liberation movement

to be silent about sexual abuse, Mtintso described "how comrades who were con-
tacts within the country would come outside to report . . . They would put up a
comrade in a particular place and comrades would sleep with them. And that's
rape. That for me is rape." She also described how one of her own comrades had
said to her: "You know, it's going to get to the point that I am going to rape you.
And it's going to be very easy to rape you . . . and I know that there is no way that
you are going to stand in front of all these people and say I raped you."[166]

Highly metafictional and allusive, *David's Story* self-consciously takes up
from the work of Joyce and Beckett, whom it mentions,[167] and turns to decon-
structive strategies. In contrast to the social realism advocated by the liberation
movement in South Africa, the novel deploys experimental narrative modes to
double back on the history of this movement. Soweto Day, the writer reminds
us, is also Joyce's Bloomsday, "Day of the Revolution of the Word."[168] Written
by an anonymous amanuensis who claims to have put together and embroi-
dered upon the story told to her by the anti-apartheid fighter David Dirkse in
the transitional period after the release of Mandela, *David's Story* shifts between
different characters as focalizers of the narrative, between first- and third-person narration, between personal accounts and nightmares, collective stories,
and historical events. The narrative that is assembled is not a chronological
history. The present time of the novel is 1991, shifting in space between Cape
Town and Kokstad, but the narrative includes flashbacks to an apartheid past,
and the historical layering is further complicated as David, led by an interest in
the story of Saartjie Baartman ("the Hottentot Venus"), is compelled to construct a history of the Le Fleur family, the Griquas of Kokstad, from the late
nineteenth to the early twentieth centuries. Beginning the Le Fleur story as a
rewriting of Millin's *God's Stepchildren*, Wicomb initially gave up as she
"couldn't find a comfortable narrative voice."[169] She then wove this narrative
into the later project of *David's Story*. Although the Le Fleur narrative is not
compellingly linked to the rest of the novel, the strength of *David's Story* is its
ability to draw attention to "nuances of truth,"[170] to the hidden stories that sit
uncomfortably with nationalist histories.

Most significantly, *David's Story* centers on absence, on the seemingly irretrievable story of Dulcie, a woman guerilla who, according to David, has also
served in the armed struggle, but who remains a shadowy and insubstantial
figure: "a protean subject that slithers hither and thither, out of reach, re-
peating, replacing, transforming itself."[171] Like Dopdi, the woman guerilla
fighter in Mahasweta Devi's story "Draupadi" (translated into English by
Gayatri Spivak), a mythology has emerged around Dulcie, with the silences
and ambiguity of Dulcie's story contributing to her mystique. David will not
answer questions about her and when he is asked about "the conditions of
female guerillas" in the camps, he "barks" the predictable, programmed
response: "Irrelevant . . . In the Movement those kinds of differences are wiped
out by our common goal."[172] The novel evokes Dulcie's story as something that

has been erased or covered over, like the slave in a painting who became "unfashionable as an adornment [to his master] on canvas" and was thus "painted over."[173] As with the slave, Dulcie's narrative can only be glimpsed as a trace.

In *Of Grammatology*, Derrida demonstrates that "trace" (with this English word maintaining the notion of a "track" or "spoor" in his French text) is "the part played by the radically other within the structure of difference that is the sign," but is also "a word that presents itself as the mark of an anterior presence, origin, master."[174] Because of its associations with the problematic notions of "anterior presence," however, the term is made usable by Derrida by placing it *sous rature*, under erasure, which entails crossing it out on the page. In her Translator's Preface to *Of Grammatology*, Spivak points out that Derrida adapts the idea from Heidegger. Placing something under erasure, she explains, indicates that the concept is inaccurate or inadequate, and at the same time necessary. Like the "trace" that for Derrida is erased while remaining legible, Dulcie and her story are marked in *David's Story* by "the absence of a presence, an always already absent present."[175] As Wicomb notes: "The inchoate story, which for political reasons can't be told, threatens to fall apart."[176] Although the task of holding together "some sense of the events" rests with the reader, the text draws attention to Dulcie's fictionality. At one stage the narrator suspects that "Dulcie is a decoy. She does not exist in the real world . . . I believe in her fictionality."[177] In this sense, Dulcie's story cannot be retrieved precisely because this is fiction, there are no "real" events, and the text necessarily retains indeterminacy, resisting realist readings and the recuperative project of liberal humanist interpretation. *David's Story* thus adapts the notion of the Derridean trace to the realm of fiction as a means of figuring and drawing attention to untellable stories. As Wicomb notes: "It's narrative fiction that lends itself to questioning the notion of the truth, and has the capacity for showing truth as a complex, many-sided, contingent thing."[178]

"This text deletes itself" is a message that appears on the narrator's computer as she attempts to put the narrative together. Yet erasure is also shown as having violent overtones. Finding his name and Dulcie's on a hit list, David "scores her name out with a pen" but "when the name is completely obliterated, he shudders at what he has done."[179] Later the writer finds "a mess of scribbles and scoring out and doodling" by David that she knows is about Dulcie "because her name is written several times and struck out."[180] As the writer notes:

Dulcie and the events surrounding her cannot be cast as a story. . . .

David wants her simply outlined, wants her *traced* into his story as a *recurring imprint* in order to outwit her fixedness in time, in order for her to go on, to proceed. . . . But for Dulcie, whose life is swathed in secrets, such resolution is not possible; the thin anecdotes, the sorry clutch of hints and innuendos, do not lead to anything.[181]

One of the text's "hints and innuendos" is that Dulcie has been tortured, and although the identity of her assailants is not specified and the novel seemingly creates an amalgam between her torturers and the agents of apartheid, it does not rule out that she has been tortured by her comrades in the liberation struggle, possibly in the ANC's notorious Quatro Camp in Angola. The impossibility of telling this latter story in the transitional present is made clear in the words: "if on the edge of a new era, freedom should announce itself as a variant of the old—[herein] lies the thought of madness, madness, madness. . . ."[182]

In hallucinatory and fragmentary nightmares that are set in the post-apartheid transition but collapse past and present, men in black tracksuits and balaclavas come into Dulcie's room at night, inflicting horrifying injuries on her body. Suggesting that she (or the amanuensis who is trying to imagine her story) associates these "tortured night[s]"[183] with the training camps of the liberation movement, the black balaclavas are linked to David's account of an incident in the desert of Botswana, apparently narrated to him by Dulcie, when Dulcie raided a bee hive, "wearing only a balaclava for protection."[184] Looking for "the *trace* of her ordeal" [my emphasis] David claims to have seen only "a slight puckering of the eyelids, an excess of stretched skin" that point to the "savage attack,"[185] an incident that may or may not be another "innuendo," an extended metaphor for sexual assault. References to the marks of violence on Dulcie's body and to her recurring and ambiguous nightmares of being tortured by "the black hands, the white hands"[186] suggest the haunting of the post-apartheid transition by the traces of irretrievable narratives, despite collective attempts directed towards truth and remembering. Surveying David's scribbles, the writer of his story notes: "Truth, I gather, is the word that cannot be written."[187] Rather than colluding with what Lydia in Dangor's text calls, "a forgetful silence,"[188] *Bitter Fruit* and *David's Story* draw attention to the difficulty of telling stories of sexual violence in the politicized sphere of the post-apartheid transition.

"(Not) Like a Woman": Male Rape in *Bildungsromane* of the Post-Apartheid Transition

In K. Sello Duiker's *The Quiet Violence of Dreams* (2001), the protagonist Tshepo tells from within a mental asylum that he is bleeding "like a woman" and that "perhaps the distance between a man and a woman is not that far."[189] The incident echoes a scene in his childhood where he and his mother were both raped by gangsters and his later victimization and gang rape by three former inmates of Pollsmoor prison, one of whom refers to him as "*poes*", associating him with the derided and "rapeable" status of a woman. As I shall demonstrate, Mark Behr's *The Smell of Apples* (1995, published in Afrikaans in 1993), as well as Duiker's two novels, *Thirteen Cents* (2000) and *The Quiet Violence of*

Dreams, dispute the notion of rape as a gender-specific crime inflicted upon women and challenge prevailing myths about male rape, most notably the idea that such acts are "homosexual." Using Joseph Slaughter's insightful discussion of the *Bildungsroman* and its postcolonial subversions, I argue that these three novels, published before the legal recognition of male rape in South Africa, foreground sexual abuses as formative events in the lives of the respective protagonists, and that each novel can be read as a reworking and corruption of the *Bildungsroman*, with the depicted scene of rape having important consequences for the protagonist's relationship with all-male environments such as the military or the (prison) gang. While the coming-of-age process in the idealist *Bildungsroman* is resolved by the individual's harmonization with society, *The Smell of Apples* dramatizes, through the narrator's witnessing of a scene of male rape, the dilemma of a young white boy's acculturation into a perverse and authoritarian society structured on the military model. Foregrounding the question, if not of freedom, then of the individual's choice, this novel is a complicity narrative that examines the ways in which apartheid fostered, within the white home, the trans-generational reproduction of a violated and violating masculinity. In Duiker's novels, on the other hand, the rites of passage experienced by the protagonists are examined in the context of a nation undergoing its own transitional process. Placed under scrutiny through the representation of male rape are persistent forms of marginalization and informal group formation, including the mobility and flux of gang culture, with both of Duiker's novels focusing on the "gang" aspect of gang rape.

In his study of the *Bildungsroman* and human rights law, Slaughter analyzes these two modes of discourse as "mutually enabling fictions," with each "project[ing] an image of the human personality that ratifies the other's idealistic visions of the proper relations between the individual and society and the normative career of free and full human personality development."[190] As Slaughter notes, the *Bildungsroman* and the discourse of human rights law have been part of "the freight of Western colonialism and neo-imperialism over the past two centuries" and the *Bildungsroman* has an "ambivalent capacity to disseminate and naturalise not only the norms of human rights but also the paradoxical practices, prejudices, and exclusions codified in the law."[191] Referring to a scene in which a young boy is raped in *The Kite Runner*, Slaughter sees this particular *Bildungsroman* as endorsing the US-led "humanitarian" invasion of Afghanistan by "hypervilifying the Taliban as a gang of Nazi-loving, heroin-using, homosexual paedophiles intent on repressing the free and full development of the human personality."[192] While I would argue that what is represented in *The Kite Runner* is not "homosexual" rape, Slaughter's study is useful in that it draws attention not only to the *Bildungsroman's* collusion with the prejudices and exclusions of the law, but also to the ways in which postcolonial *Bildungsromane* may break with the idealist version of the genre. As Slaughter notes:

> Contemporary first-person post-colonial *Bildungsromane* tend to be novels
> of disillusionment, in which the promises of developmentalism and self-
> determinism are revealed to be empty, or at least exaggerated; *Bildung* thus
> becomes the process of recognizing the limits of personal development and
> the sociohistorically contingent condition of the idea and project of *Bildung*
> itself.[193]

While the idealist *Bildungsroman*, exemplified in Goethe's *Wilhelm Meister's
Apprenticeship* (1795), foregrounds the "image of man in the process of becoming" and traces the "progressive harmonization" of the individual and society, postcolonial (sub)versions often reflect critically on the process of
incorporation, on the state into which the individual is supposed to be incorporated, and on the equivocal tendencies of the *Bildungsroman* itself. In the
three novels I discuss, incidents of male rape reveal the abuse or neglect of the
individual by the state (rather than harmonious "incorporation"), and gesture
to the ways in which the disciplinary shaping of masculinity (whereby the
male individual is incorporated into institutionalized or informal all-male
groups) leads to violence that cannot be contained within situations of clear
enmity or within the walls of the prison.

Behr's novel, which originally appeared in Afrikaans as *Die Reuk van
Appels*[194] the year before South Africa's first democratic elections, is split
between two temporal settings, interspersing the narration of young Marnus
in 1973 with fragments detailing his later experience of fighting in the late
1980s for the apartheid state in its covert war in Angola. Connecting the two
narratives is the white protagonist's embeddedness in the masculine rituals of
a militarized society, which pivots on his unwillingness or inability, in the
childhood narrative, to react effectively against the rape of his best friend,
Frikkie, by his father, a General in the South African defense force. Like *The
Kite Runner*, *The Smell of Apples* portrays a scene in which a boy is raped in
order to suggest the perversion and violence of the patriarchal and authoritarian society into which the child is supposed to be inducted. As I shall argue,
however, while a text like *The Kite Runner* may be said to collude with imperialism, *The Smell of Apples* foregrounds precisely the notion of collusion. Marnus attains full citizenship by conforming to the intractable gender norms of
white society, though as the story suggests, this conformity makes him both
complicit in and a victim of apartheid.

Described as "a meticulous dissection of apartheid's moldy corpse," *The
Smell of Apples* was highly acclaimed nationally and internationally on its first
appearance in Afrikaans and English,[195] but as is now fairly well-known, many
commentators turned on Behr when, in an extraordinary public address in
1996 at a conference entitled "Fault Lines: Inquiries around Truth and Reconciliation," the author confessed to having been a spy for the apartheid security
forces while a student at Stellenbosch University from 1986–1989, after his military service in Angola. Apologizing in his confession, Behr attested that his

political sympathies changed as a result of his university experiences. During his time at Stellenbosch he served as chairperson of the progressive student organization, NUSAS, and in this portfolio he led student deputations to meet with the ANC in Lusaka in 1988 and 1989. He claimed that other intelligence agencies within the government were about to expose his "history of closeted gay experience,"[196] and finally a shooting incident, made to look like a right-wing assassination attempt, was arranged by the security police in order for Behr to leave Stellenbosch while keeping his apparently left-wing political reputation intact. In his confession, Behr went on to claim that in the two years after leaving the university he gave information to the ANC.[197] Speaking of his reasons for becoming a government spy, he said that the state offered to pay his student fees in exchange for his spying, and that "there could also have been a misguided design at imitating and becoming part of the masculanist [sic] codes which I since childhood, had both hated and adored."[198] What is interesting here is Behr's choice of the word "imitating," which contains an acknowledgment of the performativity of the acculturated gender roles to which he says he had an ambivalent relation.

Images of imitation and doubling are a vital part of the coming-of-age narrative of *The Smell of Apples*, suggesting Marnus's submission to masculine "codes" but also producing subversive textual effects. Punctuated by "Dad says" and "Mum says" as Marnus constantly ventriloquizes what is said by his parents, the text does not simply reproduce the banality of white paranoia, but restages the racist speech acts that echo in the white domestic space, a strategy that has an uncanny effect on the reader (particularly the reader who grew up "white" under apartheid). In a double gesture, racist stereotypes are recited and the reader drawn into a world where these are "home truths," and yet these speech acts, such as "the Communists will use pop music to take over the Republic,"[199] are simultaneously opened up for scrutiny and even ridicule. Cutting through such "truths," the rape of Frikkie is an "unhomely" act that, as witnessed and narrated by the young Marnus, exposes the duplicity of Marnus's domestic environment. Rather than representing harmonious integration between the human personality and society, *The Smell of Apples* portrays its young protagonist as ultimately submitting to the demands of an inflexible, anti-democratic and abusive culture that makes monsters of its others through projection.

For the young Marnus, who reproduces the rhetoric of his parents, sexual offenders are black or "coloured" men, and rape is something that happens to white women:

> Dad and Mum don't want Ilse and me to travel to school by train. In one week two white women were raped by Coloureds at Salt River station. It's the most dreadful of dreadful disgraces if a woman gets raped. Mum says it's even dangerous these days for young boys on the train, because you get exposed to all kinds of bad influences.[200]

Of course the text is deliberately ironic here, considering what happens to Frikkie. Rehearsing white cultural myths that the rape victim is a white woman and the rapist a dark-skinned outsider voracious for white female flesh, the passage places an account of rape in proximity but also in opposition to the dangers faced by young boys. The first part of the last sentence ("Mum says it's even dangerous these days for young boys on the train"), sets up the expectation that Marnus means that "even" boys can be raped, but the second part of this same sentence disavows this possibility ("because you get exposed to all kinds of bad influences"). A boy is thus, in Marnus's mind, not like a woman, who is defined by her potential to become the victim of rape. Later, in a scene that brings to mind the disturbing frontispiece of Schreiner's *Trooper Peter Halket of Mashonaland* (discussed in chapter 1), the images Marnus's father chooses to project in his home slide show are photographic trophies of his participation in the bush war in Rhodesia, where inhuman acts perpetrated on black bodies are justified as vengeance against "Ters" ("terrorists") who violate white women and dismember white families:

> "This is détente," Dad says. It's a soldier holding up a black arm with pink meat hanging out where it was cut from the body . . . The arm belonged to one of the Ters that murdered a white family on their farm near Gwelo. They first raped the mother and then forced her to watch as they chopped up her husband and two sons.[201]

Whereas Schreiner counters "black peril" imagery with "white peril" narratives, Behr attacks white values at a much more intimate level.[202] Foregrounding not only projection in the visual sense, but also in the psychological sense, set alongside the photograph is a horror story in which the white family and particularly the white mother are threatened from outside of the white social group, with the novel in its entirety exposing the ways in which the self through projection makes of the other an alien double, "unhomely" and demoniacal. Ironically, in *The Smell of Apples* it is not the white mother who is raped, and the white home is dismembered from within, as Marnus's mother has an affair with a visiting Chilean General, Marnus's father rapes Marnus's friend, and Marnus ultimately becomes complicit (through his silence and his imitation of his father's version of masculinity) in what happens to his "blood brother" Frikkie.

The Smell of Apples centers on the disclosure of sexual violation, on the unmasking of an "unhomely" truth whereby the authoritarian figure of the white household, namely the father, is split away from his place as seat of morality and revealed as the very figure of the monstrous. The narrated rape scene in Behr's novel is an ocular or even "peeping Tom" experience, marked by doubles and mistaken identities as under Behr's microscope the white home becomes a bifurcated space where morbid family secrets are covered and uncovered. Spying through the floorboards into the guest room below, Marnus watches the person he thinks is the Chilean General raping Frikkie:

> With my one eye shut, I look down into the bottom room . . . On the bed, right below me, the General is sitting next to Frikkie . . . I must go and call Dad! . . . Then he goes on to his knees between Frikkie's legs . . . He uses one hand to hold himself up on the bed. With the other he keeps the pillow down over Frikkie's head.[203]

Until he sees that the General no longer has a distinguishing scar on his back, Marnus does not comprehend that he is watching the other General, his father. Mistaken identity is repeated as the reader, drawn in by the first person account, "sees" what Marnus sees, and "watches" this primal scene. Marnus says he must "go and call Dad," but the person he tells is the reader, with this collapsing of identity implicating us, disturbingly, in what "Dad" is doing. The reader of the account is thus offered two positions, voyeur or rapist. In order to uncover the "secret," representation is necessary, and in Behr's novel the trajectory of confession converges upon telling this central incident. The episode demonstrates however, that there is a point at which bearing witness can lend itself to spectacle, to voyeurism and entrapment within a cycle of guilt and collusion.

While there have been commentators who have referred to the rape in Behr's novel as "homosexual rape," this entails making the assumption that the participants are homosexual in their affiliation (which is clearly not the case), and I would argue that neither is the term "bisexuality" appropriate when describing either Marnus's father or Frikkie.[204] What occurs in *The Smell of Apples* is the rape of a young boy by a man who regards himself, and is regarded by society, as heterosexual. The original Afrikaans text actually conveys this inequality of power—between a child and adult—in a more direct way. Whereas in the English edition Marnus observes that "the General" (who turns out to be Marnus's father), puts Frikkie's hand on his "mister" and touches Frikkie's "John Thomas," in the Afrikaans text the grown man's sex organ is a "*meneer*" ("mister") and the child's is the diminutive "*mannetjie*" ("little man"). It is possible to read the rape as the violent manifestation of repressed homosexual desire, and in this sense the novel may be compared with Oliver Hermanus's fascinating film, *Skoonheid* (2011), where a Free State farmer, unable to admit his homosexual desire publicly, stalks and then violently rapes a young man to whom he is attracted. Like *Skoonheid*, *The Smell of Apples* challenges the notion that male rape is a "homosexual" crime—committed by openly gay men. Yet the novel also scrutinizes rituals of induction into white masculinity, which center on the production of what Foucault, extrapolating from the figure of the soldier in the late eighteenth century, calls "docile bodies."

Between 1967 and 1991, conscription was compulsory for all white men over the age of sixteen in South Africa, and as in other racist and militarized states, the masculinity of the politically dominant group was formed by keeping homosocial bonding in tension with overt homophobia. When sex between men occurred in the army environment, this was covert, and most often the men involved regarded themselves as heterosexual. As noted in the shocking documentary entitled *Property of the State* (2003), medical science itself was harnessed in order to sanitize gender when the apartheid military forced more than 900 white homosexual soldiers in the 1970s and 1980s to undergo "sex-change" operations, and also used chemical castration and electric shock torture under medical auspices in order to "re-programme" these subjects. What one sees in such environments is a seemingly contradictory gesture whereby masculine, comradely love is celebrated in order to provide a sanitary barricade that keeps a homosocial space safe from feminizing elements. Within this space particularly, queerness presents as pollution, as the very figure of the abject. Of his own military service, Behr claims that he was not openly gay during these years,[205] though his comments about his ambivalence towards masculine "codes" could be read as implicating his queerness in his obedience to the state.

The morning after he is raped by Marnus's father, Frikkie picks up an apple only to complain: "These apples are rotten or something."[206] Of course what Frikkie is noticing is that his hand is tainted by the smell of the rape, with the text again deploying mistaken identification and displacement. The smell attributed to the apples is ironically echoed in the Chilean General's earlier comment: "Good military control, that's all you need to prevent the rot from setting in."[207] Rather than preventing corruption, "military control" is shown through the rape of Frikkie to be precisely the source of "rot." After they have washed Frikkie's hand, Marnus asks about the "sour" smell:

> "What did you think it was?" I ask.
>
> Frikkie's eyes fill with tears, and he looks down at his bare feet and shakes his head, and now I know what it is.
>
> "Let's go outside," I say.[208]

Earlier that morning Marnus had tried "not to look at Frikkie" while they were getting dressed,[209] and here he quickly closes down a discussion of what has happened. Although they have promised to keep no secrets from one another, Marnus is unwilling to acknowledge the rape, and it is at this point in the narrative, where he has a choice, that the reader is able to make sense of the intertextual references to Melville's *Moby Dick*—a fusion between a *Bildungsroman* and a tragic quest narrative—that have recurred in Behr's novel. In her illuminating account of *The Smell of Apples*, Rita Barnard deploys Althusser's notion of subjectification to trace processes of "becom[ing] submissive to a higher authority"[210] in Behr's novel but points out that the presence of *Moby Dick* in *The Smell of Apples* foregrounds "choice—a notion which complicates the novel's narrative of subjectification."[211] I would like to extend and develop this insight to point out that through this reference to another *Bildungsroman* that offers a microcosm for a range of masculinities, *The Smell of Apples* poses the question of individual choice and freedom at the center of the *Bildungsroman* itself.

On the morning after the rape, the image that Marnus sees on the cover of the book presents a dreadful return of the repressed: "there's a picture of Captain Ahab throwing his harpoon, and just in front of him, in the bloody water, is Moby Dick. There's a fountain of blood spurting from the little blowhole on Moby's head and his jaw is open as if he's screaming."[212] As Slaughter notes, many contemporary *Bildungsromane* that deal with colonial and postcolonial themes contain "*mise en abyme* scenes of reading" that "situate readers (both the novel's protagonists and its real readers) in an international imaginary, a translinguistic, intertextual order of *Bildungsromane* that places pressure on the parochial nation-statism of the traditional genre."[213] Like Ishmael, the narrator of Melville's novel, Marnus is the witness in a story about the marking out of masculine space, and beginning with the words "My name is really Marnus," *The Smell of Apples* echoes the famous opening lines of Melville's novel, "Call me Ishmael," but now with an emphasis on the narrator's enmeshment within his family unit as Marnus goes on to ventriloquize his parents' names for him: "my son," "my little bull," or "my little piccanin." Later in the text, Marnus's sister Ilse explains to the Chilean General that she has been reading *Moby Dick*, which in her view is about choice, because Ishmael has to choose between Ahab and Queequeg, who stand for "different things." Ilse then blurts out that the Chilean General and her father are "like Captain Ahab."[214] As an intertext in *The Smell of Apples*, *Moby Dick* points to the dangers of apartheid's monomaniacal aspects, but also offers a glimpse of alternative masculinity within a seemingly predestined national narrative of white male acculturation. In Melville's novel, the friendship between Ishmael and Queequeg, an indigene of a fictional South Pacific island, has been read variously as demonstrating white American culture coming to understand and love its other, and as an example of a barely veiled homoerotic relationship, symbolized in the "marriage" between these two characters that takes place in the bed at the Spouter Inn, and in their attachment to each other by a rope.[215] By the end of *Moby Dick*, however, it is not Queequeg, but Ahab and his obsession with the white whale that have attained center stage in Ishmael's narrative. In the final pages of *The Smell of Apples*, Marnus has a homoerotic dream about running along the beach with Frikkie who turns into "little Neville," the domestic worker's son who has been horrifically burned in a racist act, and here the novel inscribes a utopian vision of homosexual desire as non-violating, and also as potentially healing of racial divides. After witnessing the rape of his friend, Marnus acts out his disillusionment by refusing to have the Chilean General's epaulettes, left behind for him as a gift, screwed into the sleeves of his camo uniform by his father. His father flies into a rage and beats him, and at this point Marnus submits, yet it is not the physical assault that breaks down his resistance but his father's tears afterwards, and there is an implication that like his father, by acquiescing to the gendered codes of apartheid, Marnus becomes both perpetrator and victim. In *The Smell of Apples*, assimilation into apartheid society culminates in Marnus' death in Angola, evoking Foucault's claim that the most racist states are also the most "absolutely suicidal."[216] Foregrounding the tension between societal control and individual freedom through the dilemma that emerges around the rape of Frikkie, *The Smell of Apples* explores the issue of the individual's freedom to develop his/her personality—a theme central to the *Bildungsroman* and to international human rights law—in an environment where a young man's coming-of-age seemed inexorably predetermined, where he would leave school only to enter the army as part of his further education.

Whereas alternative affiliation remains a dream in *The Smell of Apples*, K. Sello Duiker places a variety of marginalized masculine subcultures as the focal points of his work. In contrast to *The Smell of Apples*, Duiker's *Thirteen Cents* describes a child narrator's failure to integrate into the social world (or rather, the failure of his social world to incorporate and protect him). In the extent to which it foregrounds a street child's complete marginalization within the nation-state, the novel is enough of a corruption of the traditional genre as to be read as an anti-*Bildungsroman*. While *The Smell of Apples* begins with Marnus's act of naming himself as a way of elucidating his relation to his family unit, *Thirteen Cents* opens with Azure asserting his identity in relation to his parents' absence:

> My name is Azure. Ah-zoo-ray. That's how you say it. My mother gave me that name. It's the only thing I have left from her.
>
> I have blue eyes and a dark skin. . . . I live alone. The streets of Sea Point are my home. But I'm almost a man, I'm nearly thirteen years old.[217]

If, as Slaughter notes, the opposite of full incorporation into society is "complete disenfranchisement" or the condition of being "nothing but a man" (as described by Hannah Arendt), by his own admission Azure is "almost" but not yet "nothing but a man," he is not even yet the "homo sacer" traced by Giorgio Agamben. Citing his experiences, which include a "primal scene" in which he witnessed a woman being raped by policemen, Azure nonetheless contests his "minor" status:

> A boy? I'm not a boy. I've seen a woman being raped by policemen at night near the station. I've seen a white man let a boy Bafana's age get into his car. I've seen a couple drive over a street child and they still kept going. I've seen a woman give birth in Sea Point in the beach and throw it in the sea. A boy? Fuck off. They must leave me alone. I have seen enough rubbish to fill the sea. I have been fucked by enough bastards and they've come on me with enough come to fill the swimming pool in Sea Point.[218]

In the transition to democracy South Africa may have avoided a race war, but Duiker's novel demonstrates that the most vulnerable members of society continue to be abused and exploited with impunity. As Duiker himself has noted, despite the demise of "an unjust and cruel political system," life is "harsh and confusing for many, particularly on the street, because despite our democratic system, not enough has been done yet for the poor and the homeless."[219]

Under apartheid, welfare for homeless children was segregated, which meant that whereas the state protected the interests of white children who could no longer live with their biological families (by moving them into homes and orphanages), it did nothing for the many black children who became homeless as a direct result of apartheid policies that devastated the home environment of the black underclass. If anything, however, the numbers of street children have increased in the post-apartheid context. The government currently offers meager social welfare grants to children, but obtaining these grants entails knowledge of the law and often a struggle with state bureaucracy. In its subject matter, *Thirteen Cents* could be read as foregrounding a global phenomenon, namely the ways in which the increasing presence of street children in developing countries is related to neoliberal economic policies and complemented by a long tradition of liberal and sentimental literature on street children.[220] Encouraging sympathy, these literary narratives typically portray the city's problems as embodied in the figure of the street child while erasing "the social relations that lie behind the child's condition."[221] Instead of presenting an opportunity for imagining a radical revision of social relations, the solitary street child in sentimental literature is "imaginatively up for adoption . . . She should hear kind words and become the rounded and happy child of middle class fantasy."[222] Veering away from the sentimentality that has characterized much writing on the subject from the nineteenth century onwards, *Thirteen Cents* offers an unsparing and harrowing account of the social world that has created the conditions for Azure's homelessness.

Unlike that classic *Bildungsroman, Oliver Twist*, in *Thirteen Cents* there is no happy final integration between the protagonist and moneyed society, but rather the child's vulnerability to an exploitative and market-driven society is revealed most saliently in his exposure to sexual abuse.

Thirteen Cents constantly stresses the meagerness of Azure's existence and of his body's value as a commodity. The resonance between his age and the title of the novel echoes the fact that thirteen is the average age of a child living on the streets in South Africa, but also suggests that Azure's exchange value is merely thirteen of the smallest South African currency (roughly equivalent to one US cent). Variously we see how Azure has to prostitute himself, how he is anally and orally raped in exchange for money by ordinary middle-class men, most of them overtly heterosexual, some married with families. After using his body, a man hands him money with words that parallel the clichés of commodity culture: "Great, it's been a slice of heaven but now I have to go."[223] In a social environment bifurcated into a gentrified compulsive spending class and impoverished sub-cultures dominated by gangs, Azure becomes an object for consumption or a rootless scapegoat. The gangsters who beat and rape him refer to him as *"gemors"* ("mess"),[224] suggesting their need to abject him and affirm at his expense their disciplinary codes modeled on the prison environment. When members of the middle classes are not sexually abusing him, they see him as a picturesque part of the cityscape, or damn him in biopolitical terms as the embodiment of social decay, blaming him for becoming a scapegoat: "he deserves what he got."[225]

Although this is a post-apartheid novel, the society depicted is marked by continuities with the apartheid past. The cycle of sexual exploitation suffered by Azure has racial and class dimensions, as the men who pay him for sex are all white and middle class, and in this respect the novel could be read as being situated within the tradition of "white peril" narratives. Shacks are constantly being demolished by the police, and race wars erupt on the streets between black and "coloured" gangsters, with the old racial hierarchies feeding into gang organization. Azure inadvertently offends a local "coloured" gangster, Gerald, who begrudges Azure his blue eyes, by confusing Gerald's name with that of Gerald's black henchman, Sealy. The incident results in a brutal beating after which Azure is told by his friend Vincent: "That's why people have beat you up all your life, because you're not black enough."[226] Azure is then incarcerated by three gangsters, operating as proxies for Gerald, who orally gang-rape him and call him "*poes*."[227] Gerald tells him: "You had to understand what it means to be a woman. That's why they did that to you. I know you understand what it means to be a woman already."[228] This "womanization" that Gerald forces upon Azure is intended as a "lesson" that Azure should not act "white," and hierarchies of race and gender are thus revealed in the novel as substitutable in conveying a message to the victim of sexual violence.

While the rape of women is generally regarded in South Africa as a social fact, male rape is a far more contentious subject. *Thirteen Cents*, which won the Commonwealth Writers Prize in the Best First Book category in 2001, is a prescribed text in the English departments of many universities in South Africa, but at Stellenbosch, where it is a set text in an undergraduate course, outraged parents and local religious leaders petitioned the head of department to have it removed from the curriculum. One parent complained: "My son read out to me a page of this book, of which not only was I repulsed but so was he." Another wrote: "Homosexuality is referred to as an Abomination to the Lord in the Bible. . . . A book of this nature goes against our very spirits . . . I regard it as nothing less than absolute filth regardless of any other qualities you may see." What "repulsed" these parents was clearly not the life Azure had to lead or the fact that he was raped, but rather what they referred to as the novel's representation of "explicit homosexual child pornography."[229] As in *The Smell of Apples*, however, the rapes that take place in *Thirteen Cents* are not perpetrated by homosexuals (except for one encounter with a gay white man who invites Azure to his home), but by men who regard themselves as heterosexual, and in this sense the novel dispels the myth that male rape is homosexual. Yet an outcry against homosexuality has repeatedly featured in complaints about the representation of male rape in the South African public sphere. Whereas the depiction of a schoolgirl being raped in the first series of the popular television drama *Yizo Yizo* raised no eyebrows, for instance, the scale of outcry following a prison rape scene, which takes place in episode four of the second season (screened in March 2001), was remarkable. In the scene, a gangster named Chester is forced to become the "wife" of another prisoner through sex. Outraged members of the public claimed that the show was corrupting South Africa's youth, and a flood of complaints led to a three-day debate in the South African parliament, where MPs claimed that the show was "a disgrace to the nation." As noted by *Yizo Yizo* writer and co-director, Teboho Mahlatsi: "That scene was on screen for 16 seconds. We didn't show any actual nudity. Everything was shielded. The heated response to it comes out of homophobia. We have had rape scenes but they were of girls. There was no criticism."[230]

According to an article written by Sasha Gear, a researcher in the Criminal Justice Programme at the Centre for the Study of Violence and Reconciliation, "the recent outcry over the screening of a prison rape on *Yizo Yizo* suggests widespread denial about the reality of sexual abuse in South African men's prisons."[231] As I shall demonstrate, Duiker's *The Quiet Violence of Dreams* is a "dissensual" *Bildungsroman* that foregrounds marginal subcultures in the formation of alternative masculinities and confronts a cycle of violence that spills out from disciplinary institutions.

"Have you ever raped anyone?," a gangster named Zebron asks his psychologist from inside a mental asylum in *The Quiet Violence of Dreams*.[232] In the same asylum is Tshepo, the novel's protagonist, who was raped by Zebron and other members of his criminal gang when he was a child. Zebron does not classify this as rape, however, and only tells his psychologist about raping women. What is interesting about the novel is its shifting narrative point of view, which incorporates the first person narratives of different characters, enabling the reader multiple perspectives on events, with one character filling in what is left out of the other's story. Although the novel traces the development of Tshepo's personhood, beginning and ending with his narration, it also contains sections narrated from the perspective of other characters, such that, for instance, we are given access to accounts of sexual violation from the point of view of both victim and perpetrator. Zebron confesses that he raped Tshepo's mother: "I got turned on by her fear. She looked so scared, so innocent. I liked that. I had to have her. We all had her."[233] He confesses that he has also raped his own sister, and he claims that he fantasizes about raping the nurses. Yet he says nothing of male rape, despite the fact that his rape of Tshepo happened immediately after the rape of Tshepo's mother. Tshepo on the other hand has witnessed his mother's rape and murder from his position as a child, and his narrative reveals the story of male rape that is hidden in Zebron's account. There are, however, also unfilled gaps even in his narrative. For instance, the novel suggests that Tshepo is being raped in the asylum, as he claims that he is "bleeding like a woman . . . at the other place," but he does not elucidate on this any further and there is no corresponding confession from any other character in the novel.[234]

In an interview with the Dutch journalist Fred de Vries, Duiker claimed that as an artist he has been interested in listening to violence as a language:

> I want to show that violence has a deeper meaning. . . . Without wanting to trivialize [its] seriousness . . . one can say that violence is a culture that communicates a certain message. . . .[235]

In the language of violence spoken in Duiker's novel, being raped relocates a man into the debased position of a woman, and similes become the vehicles that describe this transformation. When Tshepo is arrested and thrown into jail for a night due to possession of marijuana, one of the inmates, a Rastifarian, consoles him: "At least dey didn't lock you up with dem mens next door. Dey be chowing buttocks *like a woman's thighs* [my emphasis]."[236] Ironically, Tshepo is not raped within the prison, but outside of it, with the novel suggesting the ways in which the violence of the prison continues to circulate in the outside world. Tshepo is treated like a "wife" in the apartment that he shares with Chris, and he is later raped in this apartment by Chris and other members of the prison gang known as the Twenty-Eights. During the episode, Chris tells that Tshepo's voice is "shaking *like* a woman's voice [my emphasis],"[237] and that one of the gangsters perpetrating the rape is behaving "*like* he hasn't had a woman in a long time [my emphasis]."[238] Clearly, this is not homosexual rape but rape perpetrated by heterosexual men as a means of showing gang solidarity and hierarchy, as a disciplinary act against a man who is regarded as weak or feminine. Peeping into Chris's room the morning after Chris has locked him in the bathroom for spilling water on the floor, Tshepo sees evidence of his flatmate's immersion in a disciplinary culture:

> Bed immaculately done, military style but with prison vengeance. The pillow sits with authority on the bed and there is nothing lying over the desk and chair. His other pair of tackies sits neatly in one corner. Everything is where it should be, standing in the pristine order, stuffy with draconian discipline.[239]

Here "the military model as a means of preventing civil disorder"[240] is shown to persist after institutionalized racism, demonstrating continuity with modes of punishment instituted under apartheid. Like Azure in *Thirteen Cents*, Tshepo is not only called "*poes*" by the gangsters who rape him, but also "*gemors*" as he is thus feminized and rendered abject within their hypermasculine disciplinary code. For the gangsters, Tshepo has been taught a lesson through the rape, and Tshepo in turn experiences the rape as the killing off of the feminine: "I feel as though my mother died again."[241]

Readers of *The Quiet Violence of Dreams* might find it strange that after the brutal gang rape to which he is subjected, Tshepo becomes a prostitute in a massage parlor for men called *Steamy Windows*, and that he initially finds the experience liberating. Suggesting a splitting of identity rather than "the image of the unitary, monadic, self-possessed individual" of the traditional *Bildungs-roman*, Tshepo renames himself Angelo while working as a prostitute, and his narrative during this time takes place under the heading "Tshepo-Angelo." Like the central character Lucia in Liliana Cavani's controversial film, *The Night Porter*, Tshepo chooses to enter what would by bourgeois standards be considered an abased situation, presumably because this involves choice, a measure of agency or freedom, which is preferable to perpetual entrapment within victimhood. What is important about Tshepo's decision to work as a prostitute and his later movement towards homosexual encounters is that these serve to distinguish consensual sex between men from the rapes that he has endured as a child and adult. As in Behr's novel, which offers a utopian dream of homosexual desire, Tshepo initially believes that his work in the massage parlor will conjoin him with an all-male community that transcends the racial prejudices still shaping the post-apartheid environment. Yet he soon realizes his own delusion:

> I feel depressed and disillusioned, naïve for ever fooling myself that gay peo-
> ple are different. They are white people before they are gay, I tell myself bit-
> terly ... Someone just tore a beautiful image I had in my mind. It is offensive,
> even ludicrous, to imagine that a gay person can be prejudiced when we live
> with so much fear and prejudice. It is a rude awakening. You are black. You
> will always be black.[242]

By the end of the novel Tshepo has reinvented himself again, this time as Horus, Egyptian god of the Sky,[243] a name given to him by a gay lover, Nausib. Tellingly, unlike the rape to which he was subjected by the gangsters, his con-sensual sex with Nausib does not equate his position with that of a woman as Nausib tells him: "Your body is a receptacle but *not like a woman's*. One day you will give birth to your true self [my emphasis]."[244] Tshepo then moves from Cape Town to Johannesburg, where he rejects the niceties of black middle-class life and finds a place among vulnerable and marginalized groups. He gains a sense of community by working in a home for street children and living in Hillbrow among "illegal and legal immigrants, what black South Africans call makwere-kwere with derogatory and defiant arrogance."[245] In spite of what he has been through, Tshepo asserts that he believes "in people, in humankind, in personhood,"[246] and like many other contemporary *Bildungsromane* from the Global South, *The Quiet Violence of Dreams* may be read as a "dissensual" ver-sion of the *Bildungsroman* in that it does not entirely abandon an ideal of har-monious integration, but demonstrates the gendered, racial, ethnic, and class exclusions that are "constitutive of, rather than incidental to, the liberal public sphere's hegemonic functioning."[247] The novel finally unveils itself as a *Künstl-erroman* when Tshepo tells that he has an "easel" in his room and is "quietly . . . nurturing [his] talents."[248]

Written in a period spanning the breadth of the post-apartheid transition (from the early 1990s to the turn of the twenty-first century), *The Smell of Apples, Thirteen Cents* and *The Quiet Violence of Dreams* are *Bildungsromane* that confront the taboo subject of male rape without falling back on homophobic hysteria, on the myth that this is a crime perpetrated by gay men. Relevant to their work is the fact that Behr has openly declared himself to be gay, and that Duiker has demonstrated dissatisfaction with fixed categories of sexual orientation. As Slaughter notes, postcolonial *Bildungsromane* often refer "at least obliquely, to the law,"[249] and in the three novels discussed above, the subject that is foregrounded points to an exclusion in the law, a discrepancy between the post-apartheid Constitution, which supposedly guarantees rights regardless of race, religion, or sexual orientation, and statuary law, which up until very recently only regarded women as possible victims of rape. Because concern over rape has been driven by critics who assume that women are victims of sexual assault, and because of prevailing cultural myths (such as "real men don't get raped") that stigmatize male victims of sexual violation, male rape remains one of the most unacknowledged forms of sexual violence. In the three novels under discussion, male rape is foregrounded as a means of dramatizing the hyper-masculine and homophobic cultures and subcultures that continue to plague South Africa today.

"Save Us All": Tshepang and the New Nation

In 2003, a play entitled *Tshepang: The Third Testament*, scripted and directed by Lara Foot-Newton, premiered in South Africa. Although described as "fictional" in a number of reviews, the event at the center of the narrative is barely fictionalized, with the story closely resembling an unthinkably horrific incident, the rape of a nine-month old baby that had taken place in October 2001 in Louisvale, a small and desperately impoverished settlement in the Northern Cape province of South Africa. Seizing the attention of South Africa and the world, the rape became the center of a media furor that offered a dim view of the post-apartheid nation, which was presented as "on the brink of moral collapse."[250] In order to protect the child's identity, however, she was renamed and became known to the South African nation as "Tshepang," a word that has connotations of miraculous salvation and which means "have hope." Drawing on the redemptive impulse in this national act of renaming, in scripting her play Foot-Newton attempted to confront the story that had appalled South Africa and the world. Like the Truth and Reconciliation Commission, which, as Achille Mbembe notes, sought a way out of a cycle of "endless sacrifices," of

retributive bloodshed, through a discourse of forgiveness and reconciliation,[251]
Tshepang: The Third Testament draws on Christian iconography in an attempt
to foster an alternative model of dealing with collective crisis. Specifically,
Foot-Newton's drama demonstrates the problems of a sacrificial economy in
that it evokes the innocence of the victim as the violated child becomes "the
girl Christ." Moreover, unlike media accounts of the rape, the play exposes and
rejects scapegoating, showing the people of Louisvale, as well as the sexual
offender, to be victims of their histories. As I shall conclude, in the national
imaginary the child's incredible survival became conjoined with the very idea
of the body politic as the incident not only inspired a moral panic that came to
symbolize "the most fundamental political and moral challenges confronting
the newborn democratic nation,"[252] but also evoked the notion of South Africa's "miraculous" survival beyond the abusive history of apartheid.

At the center of *Tshepang: The Third Testament*, is the following image of
salvation:

> That's when they changed her name. Some people here in the village heard
> from the nurses that it was a miracle she had survived. So they decided it
> must be a sign. A sign maybe from God. That Siesie was the girl Christ. The
> saviour. That she had taken on the sins of the world, just like Jesus—and
> from now on all children would be saved. Tshepang, Tshepang—saviour,
> hope. That's what it means.[253]

Like almost all of the play, this is spoken by the protagonist, a black man
named Simon, played by Mncedisi Shabangu, who tells of an economically-
deprived town where a baby has been raped. As was the case with the Louisvale baby, Simon says that at first six men were accused of the crime, but that
later the mother's boyfriend was found to be the rapist. Kholeka Qwabe plays
the role of the baby's mother, who is named Ruth in the play, and is present on
the stage throughout Simon's narration, although she says nothing until the
end of the performance, when she utters the final word: "Tshepang." *Tshepang*
is not a Christian play, but rather draws on aspects of Christian theology as a
means of making sense of unthinkable violence. As Hugh Kirkegaard and
Wayne Northley point out: "The broken taboos that sexual offending, particularly those offences against children, represent, create a kind of 'holy fear.'"[254] I
would add that these "broken taboos" become even more scandalous and inspiring of "holy fear" when the case concerns a baby, who is by definition morally blameless.

Because of its focus on scapegoating and on the New Testament as exposing
and rejecting a sacrificial economy, the work of René Girard is useful in examining Foot-Newton's play. In *Violence and the Sacred* (1977, originally published
in French in 1972), Girard claims that societies have traditionally cohered around
scapegoating as a means of resolving the problems created by mimetic desire
(when one's desire imitates that of another, resulting in rivalry and jealousy).

Under conditions of crisis, sacrifice becomes "a deliberate act of collective substitution performed at the expense of the victim and absorbing all the internal
tensions, feuds, and rivalries pent up within the community."[255] Scapegoats are
"surrogate objects" chosen because they are "vulnerable and close at hand," especially when the real target of aggression is inaccessible.[256] These ideas are
taken further in Girard's later work, *The Scapegoat* and *I See Satan Fall like
Lightning*, where Girard turns to Christianity, and particularly the passion of
Christ, as exposing the injustice of the scapegoating process by focusing on
the innocent victim, Christ, "the lamb of God." Using Girard's idea that "scapegoats multiply wherever human groups seek to lock themselves into a given
identity—communal, local, national, ideological, racial, religious, and so on,"
one could argue that the "black peril" rhetoric that intensified during the
building of the South African nation in the early twentieth century was a form
of scapegoating that served to unite South Africa's white population against a
common enemy. As Leo Lefebure points out via Girard: "Every culture achieves
stability by discharging the tensions of mimetic rivalry and violence onto scapegoats. . . . The lynch mob is at the foundation of social order."[257] The story of
Tshepang is one of many scapegoats. Firstly the baby herself was a surrogate
victim as the act was one of drunken revenge directed at the child's mother, who
was absent. Secondly, the six men initially accused of the rape were treated in
the media as moral pariahs, despite the fact that they had not yet been found
guilty. As Nicky Naylor notes, media representations of the men convicted them
without trial, and traded in racist, class-driven stereotypes:

> Soon after the arrest of the six men in the Baby Tshepang case, the news-
> papers were flooded with headlines in which the men were referred to as
> "ill-educated, barbaric drunks" (*The Star*, October 30, 2001). Monsters were
> depicted, with newspapers even commenting on their "shabby clothing"
> (*Pretoria News*, November 14, 2001). They were all assumed to be evil, and
> more critically, guilty, long before the start of any trial. The words "sex per-
> verts" and "sadists" (*City Press*, November 4, 2001) were used contextualis-
> ing rape as a sexual act and not one of power and violence. These men were
> depicted as the dark monsters every South African would like to believe
> rapists are.[258]

Although this was an intraracial rape, the media typecast the suspected rapists
in accordance with "black peril" narratives, and prompted an impulse towards
retributive violence, as the community of Louisvale then called for the castration of the men. Yet the community itself became, in the eyes of the nation and
the world, a moral outcast. As Foot-Newton points out, "It felt like the village
was the rapist."[259]

Tshepang: The Third Testament and the animated film-adaptation of the
play, entitled *And There in the Dust*, which was scripted and conceptualized by
Foot-Newton with the help of the artist Gerhard Marx, expose these levels of

scapegoating, drawing on Christian imagery as a way of engaging the audience or viewer into communion with suffering and grace. *The Third Testament* in the title of Foot-Newton's play suggests that the violated baby is a Christ-figure who will usher in a new era, and this is referenced visually as Simon is carving a nativity scene. He calls the baby "Jesus's sister" who has come to take away the sins of the world, and in the published version of the play, the image that introduces the text is a small, iron-frame bed, laid over a cross. According to Gerhard Marx, who created the image, the bed was a central motif, and is meant to create an allusion to "the crib in which Baby Jesus lay."[260] Whereas there is a rigid societal proscription against an empathetic response to a child rapist, the play breaks with stereotypes of the dark-skinned rapist and with pre-Christian ideas about scapegoating in that the brutal behavior of the rapist, Alfred Sorrows, is given a context in which we see him also as a victim. During his childhood, Simon tells us, Alfred was beaten with a broomstick, and his presence in the play is symbolized by a broomstick handle thrust into a loaf of bread, suggesting the rape, but also Alfred's own victim status. With its eucharistic connotations, the loaf links the abused body of Alfred Sorrows to the damaged body of Tshepang, emphasizing the twin tragedies of both victim and perpetrator.

The film *And There in the Dust* shows "The Town of Shame" to be an ideal environment for the proliferation of scapegoats, opening with an image of the inescapable sun, as the voice-over of Mncedisi Shabangu tells "here the heat knows it's hot," and the camera shifts from sketches of the desolate town with its church to focusing, from above, on a close-up of Shabangu's sweating, resigned and resentful face. Here the people of Louisvale are no more able to address the source of their desperate economic and social circumstances than it would be possible to take up arms against the inaccessible sun, the "Makulu-baas" ("the big boss"). Shabangu breaks off a piece of bread, eats it, and the loaf he puts down disintegrates, in stop-animation, into communion-sized pieces. The story of Tshepang is then narrated in voice-over and etched visually into these crumbs. When he comes to fetch the body of Tshepang, what a white man from the ambulance gathers up are the little pieces of bread.[261]

In its stark focus on a man and a woman from a community dehumanized by apartheid, the play offers a deferential nod to Fugard's *Boesman and Lena*, but what is strange about *Tshepang: The Third Testament* is the almost psycho-pathic passivity attributed to members of the community in which the rape takes place. Simon's constant repetition that "Nothing much happens here" is meant, one would imagine, to be grossly ironic. Whereas Fugard's play constantly emphasizes the humanity of his two characters, in *Tshepang: The Third Testament* and in the film *And There in the Dust* it is not the community but the white ambulance man who becomes a register for the horror that has taken place. Following a trend in South African cinema where a white character is used as the point of identification for viewers,[262] this white man sheds the only tears in the play. Whereas news reports about the rape of the Louisvale infant gave a sense of a community devastated and angered by what had happened, in Foot-Newton's imagining it is only media attention and the subsequent small economic boom in the town that spur pro-active behavior on the part of the community:

> Then the police took action. They arrested six men. Six men had raped the infant. Six men! A gang rape!
>
> Now you want to see something happen? You want to see something happen? They all arrived. The press, the newspapers, television, film, cameras, USA, Britain, Johannesburg, Amsterdam. They all came here. What a story [*happily*]—six men raped a nine month old baby. You see! You see how shit you are? You see how shit we all are?
>
> Suddenly business was good. Sarah's mother at the shebeen started selling boerewors rolls and made a mint.
>
> Old Man Le Roux at the petrol station was beside himself, business was booming! "Lekker like a cracker!"
>
> People were smiling at the cameras, dancing, showing off!
>
> We had finally made it! "The Town of Shame!"
>
> "Town of Shame protests for Baby Tshepang!"
>
> Suddenly the town's people were motivated. Let's protest. Let's do something."
>
> "We must castrate them."[263]

On the one hand, representing the townspeople as opportunistic rather than pro-active is deeply problematic. Because they fail to register sufficient disgust and horror at what has happened, the townspeople are not sufficiently distanced from the rape. Yet the play demonstrates the media's commodification of suffering, and revealed in Simon's narration is the town's abjection in the world's eyes: "You see how shit you are? You see how shit we all are?" Like the dumbfounded mother, who carries a tiny bed strapped to her back as if carrying a baby (but also like Christ carrying his cross), the townspeople come to bear the burden of national guilt, the idea that "we did nothing." For Foot-Newton, who began the play as part of her doctoral research at the University of the Witwatersrand, and was assisted by Bheki Vilakazi, who interviewed the people of Louisvale, "it was important to bring the dishonoured town to life."[264] While the media presented the town as somehow implicated in what had happened, she believed that "the whole community had been violated—by colonialism, by apartheid, by poverty. It had lost its humanity."[265] The townspeople, it is implied in her play, have been brutalized and dehumanized by history, and this is meant to explain their behaviour and passivity. As Simon tells a white woman journalist: "Shame on all of you! . . . This town was raped long ago. This town was fucking gang-raped a long, long, long, long time ago."[266] What this enunciation risks is that it can fall easily into a racialized myth of symmetrical violation, arranged around the post-apartheid transition, that goes something like this: under apartheid black people were raped, literally or metaphorically, by whites; now the tables have turned and black men are potentially the literal rapists of white women or defenseless infants. Such anxieties, where unease over the transition of political power is translated into psychosexual terms, may be seen most blatantly in a play such as Mike van Graan's *Green Man Flashing* (2005), in which the rape of a black woman by a white man under apartheid is counterpoised with the rape of a white woman by a black man after apartheid, suggesting a false moral equation between post-apartheid democracy and the order of the apartheid regime. Rather than reiterating such an equation, however, Simon's comment in *Tshepang* about the town being "gang-raped a long, long, long, long time ago" stresses that in their behavior the rapist and the townspeople are being spoken by history.

In an interview Foot-Newton acknowledged that she had been inspired by the story of Tshepang, but also by "20,000 true stories":

> It was everywhere, and it wouldn't leave me alone. Who could do such a thing? It depressed me. I started reading about rape, talking about infant rape; I mean, who could tear an infant to pieces . . . How can a human being become that? And then I looked at the figures: 20,000 child rapes reported every year . . . and that's just the tip of the iceberg. Which is why I decided to write the play "Tshepang" to promote understanding.[267]

At the time Foot-Newton was writing *Tshepang*, a disturbing idea was beginning to emerge in the national and international media, namely that black men rape babies in South Africa because they believe that this cures HIV-AIDS. Alarm about supposed belief in the "virgin cure" was also quickly being transmitted to the rest of the world in a global media blitz that posed the issue of "baby rape" as a question of post-apartheid governance, and deepened international reservations about South Africa's new democracy.

Often cited as academic evidence of a widespread belief in "baby rape" as a form of "virgin cleansing" in South Africa is a study undertaken by Suzanne Leclerc-Madlala, an American anthropologist now based at the University of KwaZulu-Natal. In a published essay, Leclerc-Madlala claims that "according to the virgin cleansing myth (in southern Africa), a man can 'cleanse' his blood of HIV-AIDS through intercourse with a virgin, [and] sexual intercourse with a virgin is thought to provide inoculation against future HIV infection." Although her studies only focused on ideas about virginity and purity in a rural community in KwaZulu-Natal (an area of the country infamous for "virginity-testing" in young girls), Leclerc-Madlala shuttles quickly between the provincial and the national in her analysis, extrapolating that faith in "virgin-cleansing" is widespread in the country as a whole, and that it is linked to statistics of child rape: "Childline reports a 400 per cent increase in child rape in the past decade and a half. In KwaZulu-Natal there is hardly a community that is not discussing child rape and the idea that one can secure an AIDS cure through virgin sex."[268] South African journalist Charlene Smith, among others, proposed that the myth was not unique to South Africa:

> Many countries . . . are reporting the phenomenon of the rape of babies . . . One reason is linked to a myth in Africa, parts of India and the Caribbean that if an HIV-infected person rapes a virgin, he can rid himself of the virus. The myth is similar to one that prevailed in 19th-century England where some believed that sex with a virgin could cure a man of venereal disease.[269]

While the proposal was interesting in that it laid responsibility for virgin-cleansing myths at the door of colonialism, the "virgin cure" by this schema becomes one unfortunate symptom of an anachronistic mimicry that characterizes the post-independence context, and the narrative risks trading in yet another colonial myth, that of the bestial black rapist, hypersexualized and superstitious.

Considering what is at stake in such representations, it is important to acknowledge that claims about the resurrection of "virgin cleansing" myths in South Africa have not gone unchallenged. Disputing the extent to which belief in a "virgin-cure" for HIV-AIDS has increased rape statistics, researchers at the University of the Witwatersrand and the University of Cape Town argued in *The Lancet* that the incidence of child abuse in South Africa has remained high but fairly consistent since the early 1990s, and that the "virgin-cleansing" belief has not accounted for more than a few isolated instances of assault.[270] According to these researchers, the idea of the "virgin cure" circulating in the media is essentially a myth about a myth, and the causes of child abuse are more mundane. This critique was to some extent strengthened when DNA evidence indicated that baby Tshepang had not been violated by six men who believed in the "virgin cure," but rather by her mother's former partner, who committed the crime in an act of drunken revenge directed at the infant's mother.

Nonetheless, the idea that a myth of "virgin-cleansing" was spurring an epidemic of child rape in South Africa quickly found its way into local and global news reports, prestigious international medical journals,[271] and also cultural texts such as Deon Meyer's recent novel, *Devil's Peak* (2007), and the award-winning film *Beat the Drum* (2006), scripted by David McBrayer. In 2002 a documentary, "An Evil so Vile," which focused on the story of Tshepang, was screened on television in the United Kingdom. Commissioned by the BBC and directed by Clifford Bestall, the documentary inferred that an epidemic of child rape in the country was being fuelled by belief that sex with a virgin would cure a man of HIV-AIDS. The film was then criticized by members of South Africa's ruling party for "potentially devaluing [the South African currency] and portraying the country as 'the leader in all respects of bad things.'"[272] In a sensationalist program on violence against children, talk show host Oprah

Winfrey showcased South Africans speaking about infant rape and the myth of the "virgin cure."[273] Typically, African traditional healers were blamed for spreading the myth, and as a companion piece to the BBC documentary mentioned above, a report claimed that "witch doctors" were responsible for the "virgin cleansing" myth in South Africa, and that up to a third of the country's inhabitants now believe that sex with a virgin will cure AIDS.[274] South African spokespersons on right-wing American websites claimed that "in our Black ruled, sick South Africa, 961 child rapes occur every day . . . The tens of thousands of baby-rapes now routinely taking place in South Africa are also caused by the ongoing claims of so-called 'traditional healers' that raping virginal children would cure Aids-sufferers."[275] Reviewing Meyer's *Devil's Peak* for the British *Guardian*, Matthew Lewin writes that the novel "reflects the country's spiralling crime rate and particularly the dramatic increase in child rape, which is influenced by the pervasive myth that it can cure men of Aids."[276] In the film *Beat the Drum*, a schoolteacher with AIDS rapes a young schoolgirl and thanks her afterwards with the words: "I feel much better." A health worker in the film addresses a crowd of women, telling them: "Some of them say that if a man with AIDS has sex with a virgin he will be cured. That's not true. That's why so many young girls are being raped." *Sangomas* (African traditional healers) are rejected by the young protagonist who claims that they cure nothing, they only "kill cows."[277]

To her credit, in scripting *Tshepang: The Third Testament*, Foot-Newton avoided implying that "baby rape" is caused by a "virgin-cleansing" myth. Instead, the play itself takes on the form of *pharmakon* or remedy through its redemptive and conciliatory impulse. Although it stresses victimhood, it eschews a sacrificial economy by drawing on the imagery of forgiveness, atonement (at-one-ness), grace (miraculous salvation), and reconciliation. As Achille Mbembe points out:

> What the South African experience teaches us is that to make a fetish of the fact of having been a victim in world history often makes the person who has been prey to such a misfortune wish to shed blood, any blood; unfortunately, all too frequently, never that of the torturers but almost always someone else's, no matter whose. Because, in order to be able to function, the fetish requires endless sacrifices and thus fresh victims killed to appease the sacrificer-god. Central to the victimary economy is the desire for expiation: it takes the form of the spirit of vengeance—an eye for an eye and a tooth for a tooth—in line with the ancient monotheistic religions. Indeed, insofar as the transcendent is never grounded in one's own death, it has to be through the sacrificial killing of someone else that the sacred is established.

> That was what South Africa sought, through the Truth and Reconciliation Commission, to avoid, and what distinguishes the South African experience from that of a country like Israel. Indeed, those states which define

themselves mainly as victimary subjects often appear too as subjects filled with hate, that is subjects that can never stop miming death by sacrifice and inflicting on others all the acts of cruelty of which they were once themselves the expiatory victims.[278]

Simon explains that in the town there is nothing to do except "wake, wipe, eat, drink, *naai* [fuck], sleep,"[279] but he is ultimately redeemed by his love for Ruth. By the end of the drama, in a context where alcohol abuse appeared to have been one of the major factors leading to the rape, Simon tells Ruth "I will stay with you . . . I didn't really want to go to the tavern."[280] Ruth then breaks her silence by uttering the name given to the infant by the people of South Africa, her voice thus coalescing with a national cry for hope and redemption.

And There in the Dust opens with the following words appearing black against a lighter background: "In 2001 South Africa was devastated by the news of the brutal rape of a nine month old child by the name of baby Tshepang. Once the story hit the headlines, a scab was torn off a festering wound and hundreds of similar stories followed."[281] Here the rape of Tshepang is described as a "wound" in the nation itself. Yet, while no one can deny that the sexual abuse of infants is unthinkably appalling, it is also true that the recent alarm over "baby rape" in South Africa is matched by a lack of interest in the plight, for instance, of street children, who are more likely than any other group of children to be raped or otherwise sexually abused. It is common knowledge that sexual abuse is part of the daily life of street children, but it took the rape of a baby to generate moral outrage about child abuse in South Africa. Unlike Tshepang, who in Foot-Newton's play becomes "the girl Christ" who will "save us all,"[282] a morally blameless and sacrificial figure who comes to bear the weighty pressures of national angst, street children may be abused with impunity. For the most part, recent cultural texts about children who live on the street, such as the film *Boy Called Twist* (2005), leave the question of sexual violence offstage in a sanitized storyline. K. Sello Duiker's novel *Thirteen Cents* (which I examined earlier in this chapter) and to a lesser extent the film *Beat the Drum*, are the only fictional post-apartheid narratives to show an underclass of children who are constantly exposed to sexual abuse.

What seems to attract fascination, horror, and moral panic in the idea of "baby rape" motivated by "virgin cleansing" is that, in contrast with street children, who are perceived as the embodiment of moral decay, it is exactly the moral purity and sexual innocence of babies that supposedly immunizes or cures the rapist and makes the child a victim of rape. In an essay on "'Baby Rape' and the Politicization of Sexual Violence in Post-Apartheid South Africa," Deborah Posel claims that the "moral polarity" used in discourse about "baby rape" links the infant symbolically to aspects of the "newborn" post-apartheid nation. In the post-apartheid context, she argues:

... the sexual violation of babies produced a starkly binary opposition of moral good versus evil: the victim of sexual violence was unambiguously innocent, pure and fragile, as against the unmitigated and undiluted brutality of the actions of the perpetrator. This moral polarity in turn became a précis of the fledgling South African nation: its newborn good, fragile and unstable in the midst of destructive and predatory forces.[283]

Posel argues that concern about baby rape has taken the form of a scandal of manhood, which prescribes moral regeneration as its "cure," with men—and black men in particular—often taking the lead in calling for an interrogation of manhood and masculinity. Addressing the Moral Regeneration Movement National Consultative Meeting after the rape of Tshepang, for instance, the then-deputy president, Jacob Zuma, attested that "there is something seriously wrong in our society. We are still haunted by the news of six adult men having raped a nine month-old baby, and there are many other cases, which display barbarism and moral decay of the worst kind."[284] Although it is unclear what Zuma's brand of moral regeneration entails (perhaps it encompasses his support for virginity testing, and his alleged intention to marry a woman who accused him of rape), it becomes apparent that over the past few years, through the local and international media, black manhood in South Africa has come under public scrutiny in discussions of post-apartheid governance.

Posel argues that this perceived crisis in masculinity has been shaped by a new discourse on sexual violence that involves the myth of "virgin cleansing." Whereas previous discourse on rape (such as "black peril" discourse) figured the rapist as a stranger to civilization, a deviant sexual beast roaming the fringes of human society, the debate about "baby rape" and "virgin cleansing" led to a shift in the image of the rapist. Posel points out that as public health campaigns began to emphasize the extent to which the spread of HIV-AIDS was a feature of society at large, the figure of the HIV-positive man became positioned much more firmly within the social mainstream—a member of the community: "here, the source of the perceived threat to the moral order was at its very core: within the domain of the home, wielded by the head of the family and the father of the nation. . . . If men failed to don the mantle of responsible fatherhood, they jeopardized the possibility of responsible nationhood."[285] She quotes male journalists at *Drum* writing despondently: "With men raping their daughters and sodomizing their own sons, who can trust us?"[286] Focus on the sexual abuse of infants, then, has brought about a crisis in masculinity and nationhood—the potential rapist is a male figure most integral to family as building block of the nation, a father, uncle, stepfather, or, in the case of Tshepang, the mother's boyfriend.

Although representations of interracial rape in South Africa remain haunted by the hold that "black peril" narratives have exercised on the popular imagination, Posel is correct to observe that, because many of the instances of baby and child rape reported in the media were incestuous or familial in some way, they came to symbolize "the most fundamental political and moral challenges confronting the newborn democratic nation: the terms and conditions of the new nation's moral community, the manner of the national subject (who are we that we can do such things to our children?), and the meaning of hard-fought liberation and democracy."[287] In the Academy Award-winning post-apartheid film *Tsotsi* (2005), directed by Gavin Hood, a black gangster is reborn as a father-figure, as someone with the capacity to love, care for, and finally sacrifice himself for a child, and in this manner, the film assuages, for the benefit of local and global viewers, anxieties about black custodianship of the newborn democracy.[288] Partly, however, this is done by erasing, in the film, references to rape that may be found in the novel by Athol Fugard, on which the film is based.[289] By contrast, Lara Foot-Newton's *Tshepang*, which is similarly driven by a redemptive impulse, confronts the issue of child abuse in a narrative where a transformative sacrament, a eucharist of shared suffering, offers a path through horror and pessimism for the newborn nation.

Conclusion

When I began this project on rape narratives in South African literature, I had no idea how historically wide-ranging it would become, nor how a focus on stories of sexual violence would illuminate many aspects of South Africa's national and literary history. Starting with a focus on the representation of individual bodies, the investigation, which grapples with a fraught and complex history of rape portrayal from colonial times until the present day, became concerned with no less than the body politic and the national imaginary. Because I believe that a problematic history of discourse entangling race and rape has hampered an effective state response to sexual violence, I felt that it was vital to address the subject of rape and representation. The topic has been an extremely challenging one on which to work, partly because rape is an uncomfortable topic of conversation, and also because the enmeshment between race and gender that inheres in representations of sexual violence brings into relief all the fault lines in the troubled relationship between feminism and anti-racist commentary.

As Jonny Steinberg has noted in an article on the Jacob Zuma rape trial, discourse on sexuality "has achieved an extraordinary salience in South African politics,"[1] and gender has become one of the most crucial issues in the post-apartheid environment. Moreover, from the Charlene Smith-Thabo Mbeki confrontation to debates on Mbeki's AIDS denialism and the Zuma rape trial, references to sexual violence in particular have, at key moments, defined and shaped the post-apartheid political landscape. Sexual violence has undoubtedly become the most important subject of proliferating discourse on sexuality in South Africa. In order to tackle the insidious and deeply disturbing problem of sexual violence in South Africa today, it became apparent to me that what was needed was not simply a feminist call-to-arms, but a more complex response, which involves, partly, unpacking and demystifying certain narratives of rape.

Strikingly, as noted throughout this study, while intraracial sexual violence is the form of sexual abuse most prevalent in South African society, South African literature and media have been dominated by narratives of interracial sexual violence. Partly, as I have argued, this obsession with interracial rape may be read as a symptom of cultural melancholia, as a site of unacknowledged loss in a society obsessed with biopolitical ideas of race. Where racialist thought is most deeply entrenched, love for the other is unthinkable, and interracial sex becomes imaginable only in the melancholic form of violation. As I point out, "black peril" has been a dominant motif of sexual violence in South African literature, and yet to have focused only on such narratives would have yielded an impoverished study. The first chapter foregrounds the work of Olive Schreiner, who is writing, not about "black peril", but rather about the sexual violence inflicted by colonizing men on colonized women. In chapter 2, I do turn to focus exclusively on "black peril" novels, but precisely in order to sketch out and demystify the most typical features of "black peril" discourse, which has a direct relation, historically, to the emergence of black political and literary enunciation. While in a "black peril" novel by a white woman such as Francis Bancroft an attack on an innocent white victim is shown to be a direct result of "the white peril" and white women's diminished political status, in typical "black peril" novels by white male authors the liberal views of the New Woman are blamed for her becoming the victim of sexual assault by a black man. Moreover, whereas the white woman despoiled in a classic "black peril" novel is killed off to erase the white womb that has been contaminated, "white peril" stories by white women such as Sarah Gertrude Millin draw attention to the abuse of colonized women by colonizing men, but have the melancholic aim of abjecting interracial sex by showing the birth of a degenerate "mixed-race" child. In the extent to which they simultaneously mimic and deviate from a typical "black peril" script, Arthur Maimane's *Victims* and J.M. Coetzee's *Disgrace* may be read as returning to "black peril" motifs with subversive intent. Similarly, writers such as Farida Karodia and Lauretta Ngcobo in the apartheid years, and Achmat Dangor in the post-apartheid era, subversively rescript narratives of "white peril" and "miscegenation," which had previously been the domain of white women writers such as Schreiner, Bancroft, and Millin. There have, however, also been writers who have drawn attention to intraracial sexual violence. Although, as I point out in the final part of chapter 3, Daphne Rooke originally deployed "black peril" in a narrative about the South African war, her work is striking in that she is the only white writer of the apartheid era to foreground intraracial sexual violence as a serious social problem. In chapter 4 I examined the work of black writers who boldly address the question of intraracial rape: Njabulo Ndebele, Gcina Mhlophe, and Baleka Mbete-Kgositsile (who was in the post-apartheid period to become South Africa's deputy president and the speaker of the National Assembly).

In accordance with my aim of examining the literary text as a material object in the world, I have focused where relevant on the production, dissemination, and reception of the texts under examination. Using archival resources, I found that her publisher's fear of censorship led Rooke to change the script of *Mittee*, such that the original rape of a white woman was replaced by an intraracial black-on-black rape in the edition of the novel circulated in

South Africa. Also through using archival resources I found that the apartheid censors were intolerant of "white peril" narratives set during apartheid, such as Rooke's *The Greyling*. Moreover, while they had no interest in "black peril" narratives written by white authors, such as Millin's *Wizard Bird*, the censors banned a novel of the interracial rape of a white woman scripted by Maimane. Moreover, although the ANC government has been suspicious of and even antagonistic towards certain reports and representations of rape (and the Protection of Information Bill, could in theory enable government to prevent the press from publishing crime statistics), the falling away of censorship in the post-apartheid era has enabled writers to address previously taboo subjects, including male rape and the sexual abuse of children.

While post-apartheid South Africa boasts new and progressive gender rights legislation, this has not translated into a decreased incidence of sexual violence, and the country remains plagued by statistics of rape that are comparable to those in a war zone. Discussion of sexual violence and its representation thus remains an urgent matter, and some questions arise from my study. Is South Africa moving to a point where sexual violence can be viewed non-racially? Under what circumstances would sexual violence cease to be a literary concern? Instead of seeing post-apartheid sexuality synchronically, I would also hope that future scholarship will build on the work in this study by addressing the ways in which various patriarchies have become enmeshed and codependent historically, so that we may recognize the ways in which history speaks through the legacy of masculinities fostered by colonialism and apartheid. That said, as stated in the introduction to my study, I have focused on a taboo subject in order to clear space for imagining relations that are other than those marked by sexual violence. What would a literary history of friendship or of interracial love in South Africa look like?

{ NOTES }

Introduction

1. ANC, Statement of the ANC at the Human Rights Commission Hearings on Racism in the Media, April 2000. http://www.anc.org.za/ancdocs/misc/2000/sp0405.html.

2. Charlene Smith, "Their Deaths, His Doubts, My Fears," *The Washington Post*, June 4, 2000.

3. See: "AIDS: Mbeki vs. Leon," *The Sunday Times*, South Africa, July 9, 2000.

4. "Thabo Mbeki Answers Your Questions," live webcast, *BBC Talking Point*, June 6, 2000. http://news.bbc.co.uk/1/hi/talking_point/forum/746464.stm.

5. Ros Hirschowitz, Sebele Worku and Mark Orkin, *Quantitative Research Findings on Rape in South Africa* (Pretoria: Statistics South Africa, 2000), 28.

6. "Rape Survivor Speaks Out," transcript of live interview with Charlene Smith on "20/20 Downtown," *ABC News*, February 8, 2001. http://www.abcnews.go.com/onair/DailyNews/chat_CharleneSmith.html.

7. See: Charles van Onselen, "The Witches of Suburbia: Domestic Service on the Witwatersrand 1890–1914," *Studies in the Social and Economic History of the Witwatersrand 1886–1914: Volume 2, New Ninevah* (Johannesburg: Ravan Press, 1982), 45–54.

8. I am aware that this is a controversial claim, but it is nonetheless fact. Examination of reported rape statistics shows that *there has been no significant increase in reported rapes since 1994–5*. In that year there were 44,751 reported cases of rape or attempted rape, 115.3 per 100,000 of the population. In 1996–7 the incidence of reported rape or attempted rape peaked at 126.7 per 100,000. The highest actual number of rapes or attempted rapes reported was in 2004–5 at 55,114, but the rate per 100,000 was then lower, at 118.3, as the population had significantly increased. The 2006–7 figure, which was 52,417 cases of rape or reported rape, was only very slightly higher than the 1996–7 figure of 51,435, but the rate per 100,000 was lower. In 2007–8—the year following the Jacob Zuma rape trial—there was a noticeable *drop* in reported rapes with the number down to 36,190 or 75.6 per 100,000 (Institute of Race Relations, *South Africa Survey 2007–8* (Johannesburg: Institute of Race Relations, 2008), 556, 570). However, rape statistics are based on *reported* incidents, and an increase in the number of reported incidents does not necessarily mean that sexual violence is more prevalent; it may actually signify progress, as more women feel safe to come forward to report violation. Conversely, a decrease in reported rapes—such as the drop in the year following the Zuma rape trial—does not mean that violence has necessarily decreased; it may suggest that women do not feel safe in reporting rape. Estimates of the ratio between actual and reported rapes in South Africa vary from 2:1 to 9:1.

9. Dirk Bakker, "Vroue-Lewens Word Daagliks Bedreig," election advertisement for *The New National Party*, 1999 elections, *Huisgenoot*, May 27, 1999, 41.

10. Benedict Anderson's study of the role of literature in creating a national imaginary is obviously relevant here, though Anderson does not foreground race and gender. See:

Anderson: *Imagined Communities: Reflections on the Origin and Spread of Nationalism* (London: Verso, 1983). In my focus on gender, race, class, and the nation state within the literature of a country that has been through processes of colonization, I build on the foundation of work by scholars such as Meg Samuelson, Elleke Boehmer, Rajeswari Sunder Rajan, Gayatri Spivak, Jenny Sharpe, Florence Stratton, and Sangeeta Ray. See: Meg Samuelson, *Remembering the Nation/Dismembering Women? Stories of the South African Transition* (Scottsville: University of KwaZulu-Natal Press, 2007); Elleke Boehmer, *Stories of Women: Gender and Narrative in the Postcolonial Nation* (Manchester: Manchester University Press, 2005); Rajeswari Sunder Rajan, *Real and Imagined Women: Gender, Culture and Postcolonialism* (London: Routledge, 1993), and *Scandal of the State: Women, Law and Citizenship in Postcolonial India* (Durham: Duke University Press, 2003); Gayatri Spivak, "Women in Difference: Mahasweta Devi's Douloti the Bountiful," in *Nationalisms and Sexualities*, Andrew Parker et al. (eds.) (London: Routledge, 1992) 96–116; Jenny Sharpe, *Allegories of Empire: The Figure of Woman in the Colonial Text* (Minneapolis: University of Minnesota Press, 1993); Florence Stratton, *Contemporary African Literature and the Politics of Gender* (London: Routledge, 1994); and Sangeeta Ray, *En-gendering India: Women and Nation in Colonial and Postcolonial Narratives* (Durham: Duke University Press, 2000).

11. Fredric Jameson, *The Political Unconscious* (Ithaca: Cornell University Press, 1982), 9, 20.

12. J.M. Coetzee, "The Novel Today," *Upstream* (1988), 3. While my focus is on the literary field, there have been excellent sustained historical accounts of racism in South Africa, such as Saul Dubow's *Scientific Racism in South Africa* (New York: Cambridge University Press, 1995), and historians such as Charles van Onselen, Jonathan Hyslop, and Timothy Keegan have produced work that rigorously details the operation of sexuality and race in South Africa. See: Van Onselen, "The Witches of Suburbia," 45–54; Timothy Keegan, "Gender, Degeneration and Sexual Danger: Imagining Race and Class in South Africa, ca.1912," *Journal of Southern African Studies* 27.3 (September 2001), 459–477; Jonathan Hyslop, "White Working Class Women and the Invention of Apartheid: 'Purified' Afrikaner Nationalist Agitation for Legislation against 'Mixed' Marriages, 1934–9," *Journal of African History* 36.1 (1995), 57–81.

13. Mikhail Bakhtin, *The Dialogic Imagination: Four Essays*, trans. Caryl Emerson and Michael Holquist (Austin: University of Texas Press, 2004 edition), 259.

14. Ibid., 261.

15. Adorno argues that the increased commodification of the work of art in the past few centuries is the very condition of the artwork's autonomy, and art's social function (its ability to critique or uphold dominant ideological paradigms) arises precisely because of its autonomy: "art becomes social by its opposition to society, and it occupies this position only as autonomous art." See Theodor Adorno, *Introduction to the Sociology of Music*, trans. E. Ashton (New York: Continuum International, 1976) 209. For further reading on Adorno's sociology of art, see: Theodor Adorno, *Aesthetic Theory*, trans. R.Hullot-Kentor (London: Athlone, 1997).

16. Michel Foucault, *The Will to Knowledge: The History of Sexuality, Vol. I*, trans. Robert Hurley (London: Penguin 1998), 103. While I use Foucault's theories of sexuality, my approach counters his claim that "[rape] may be treated as an act of violence . . . of the same type as that of punching someone in the face." See: L. Kritzman (ed.), *Michel Foucault: Politics, Philosophy, Culture: Interviews and Other Writings* (London, Routledge, 1988), 201–202. Although Foucault is trying to resist cultural definitions that invest sexualized meaning in certain parts of the body, his statement does not take into account the fact that sexually

transmitted diseases (which may be fatal), as well as pregnancy, are high-risk factors for victims of sex crimes. Ironically, Foucault must have been unknowingly infected with HIV-AIDS when he made this claim.

17. Sharpe, *Allegories of Empire*, 128.

18. Judith Butler, "On Speech, Race and Melancholia," interview with Vicki Bell, *Theory, Culture and Society* 16. 2 (1999), 168.

19. Foucault has been accused of having little to say about race, but as Ann Laura Stoler has demonstrated, in the last section of *The History of Sexuality* (Vol 1.), and in the last chapter of *Society Must be Defended*, Foucault outlines the emergence of modern, biologizing ideas of race, and describes the workings of state racism. See: Ann Laura Stoler, *Race and the Education of Desire: Foucault's History of Sexuality and the Colonial Order of Things*, (Durham: Duke University Press, 1995,) and "A Colonial Reading of Foucault," in *Carnal Knowledge and Imperial Power: Race and the Intimate in Colonial Rule* (Berkeley: University of California Press, 2002), 140–161.

20. Foucault, *The Will to Knowledge*, 139.

21. Michel Foucault, *Society Must be Defended: Lectures at the Collège de France 1975–1976*, trans. David Macey (New York: Picador, 2003), 250.

22. Foucault, *The Will to Knowledge*, 139.

23. Ibid., 147.

24. Ibid., 149.

25. Ibid., 141. Previous commentators have applied Foucault's notion of biopower in analyses of the workings of power in the South African state. In his essay "Necropolitics," Achille Mbembe has in mind Foucault's analysis of biopower in the grid-like arrangement of the working-class estate when he proposes that the black "township" was "a peculiar spatial institution scientifically planned for the purposes of control." See: Achille Mbembe, "Necropolitics" (trans. Libby Meintjes), *Public Culture* 15.1 (2003), 26. Yet Mbembe has nothing to say here about the instrumentality of sexuality in the reterritorialization and mechanisms of control that characterized segregation and apartheid. Alexander Butchart's study *The Anatomy of Power* attempts to use Foucault's ideas about power, knowledge, and the body to trace the ways in which the African body was perceived in the colonial era and under apartheid. However, his rejection of historical studies is problematic. See: Alexander Butchart, *The Anatomy of Power* (London: Zed Books, 1998).

26. Foucault, *The Will to Knowledge*, 125.

27. Ibid., 127.

28. Ibid., 124.

29. Tanya Horeck, *Public Rape: Representing Violation in Fiction and Film* (London: Routledge, 2004).

30. Judith Butler, "On Speech, Race and Melancholia," 170. Butler's speculations on melancholia extend and complicate the ideas in Freud's "Mourning and Melancholia." For Freud, mourning is what happens with loss that is conscious, and melancholia results from a loss that has not been acknowledged. Butler uses melancholia to understand the ways in which homosexual desire is rendered unthinkable in heterosexual society, and in this interview she extends the notion of melancholia to thinking about race.

31. J.M. Coetzee, "Jerusalem Prize Acceptance Speech" in *Doubling the Point: Essays and Interviews*, David Attwell (ed.) (Cambridge, Massachusetts: Harvard, 1992), 97.

32. Vicki Bell, in Judith Butler, "On Speech, Race and Melancholia," 169.

33. Judith Butler, "On Speech, Race and Melancholia," 170.

34. Ibid., 170.

35. Ibid., 170.

36. J.M. Coetzee, "Jerusalem Prize Acceptance Speech," *Doubling the Point: Essays and Interviews*, David Attwell (ed.) (Cambridge, Massachusetts: Harvard, 1992), 96.

37. Ibid., 97.

38. For an account of Lewis Nkosi's representation of interracial desire, including the ways in which Nkosi plays with "black peril" stereotypes, see Lucy Valerie Graham, "'Bathing Area—For Whites Only': Reading Prohibitive Signs and 'Black Peril' in Nkosi's *Mating Birds*," in *Critical Perspectives on Lewis Nkosi*, eds. Liz Gunner and Lindy Stiebel (Johannesburg: Wits University Press, 2006), 147–166.

39. See: Pumla Dineo Gqola, "The Difficult Task of Normalizing Freedom: Spectacular Masculinities, Ndebele's Literary/Cultural Commentary and Post-Apartheid Life," *English in Africa* 36.1 (May 2009), 61–76; and Thembinkosi Goniwe, "Goodbye Post-Colonialism and Post-Apartheid." Division of Visual Arts Talks. University of the Witwatersrand, September 11, 2008, Johannesburg.

40. Butler, "On Speech, Race and Melancholia," 166.

41. Ibid., 168.

42. Here I take a cue from recent seminal studies such as *South African Textual Cultures* by Andrew van der Vlies and *The Literature Police* by Peter McDonald. See Andrew van der Vlies, *South African Textual Cultures: Black, White, Read All Over* (Manchester: Manchester University Press, 2007); and Peter D. McDonald, *The Literature Police: Apartheid Censorship and its Cultural Consequences* (Oxford: Oxford University Press, 2009).

43. In his 1911 letter to Lord Harcourt, Lord Gladstone accused the Afrikaner politicians Louis Botha and Jan Smuts of "laughing . . . to scorn" a prominent case of "black peril" (Lord Gladstone, Governor General, South Africa, to Lewis Harcourt, Colonial Secretary, London, February 1911, Harcourt Papers, Bodleian Library, Oxford), and in the same year, during debates of the first session of the parliament of the House of Assembly, the Minister of Justice, General J.B.M. Hertzog (who was to found the Afrikaner National Party in 1914), claimed that newspaper reports about "black peril" cases were greatly exaggerated (Debates of the First Session of the First Parliament of the House of Assembly, February 7, 1911, column 1021: "Outrages by Natives").

44. Bloke Modisane, *Blame Me on History* (London: Thames & Hudson, 1963), 214.

45. Sabine Sielke, *Reading Rape: The Rhetoric of Sexual Violence in American Literature and Culture, 1790–1990* (Princeton: Princeton University Press, 2002), 38.

46. See: Gareth Cornwell, "George Webb Hardy's *The Black Peril* and the Social Meaning of 'Black Peril' in Early Twentieth Century South Africa," *Journal of Southern African Studies* 22.3 (1996), 441–453; and Gareth Cornwell, "Francis Bancroft's *Of Like Passions and the Politics of Sex in Early Twentieth Century South Africa*," *English in Africa* 25.2 (October 1998), 1–36.

Chapter 1

1. Nancy Armstrong, "Captivity and Cultural Capital in the English Novel," *Novel: A Forum in Fiction* 31. 3 (1998), 373–399.

2. *The London Advertiser*, April 22, 1783. Quoted in Stephen Taylor, *The Caliban Shore: The Fate of the Grosvenor Castaways* (London: Faber & Faber, 2004), 181.

3. In 1810 Sarah Baartman, the "Hottentot Venus," had been taken from South Africa to England where she was displayed to the British public. The image of her physique has clearly influenced Cruikshank.

4. See: Norman Etherington, "Natal's Black Rape Scare of the 1870s," *Journal of Southern African Studies* 15. 1 (1988), 36–53; Jeremy C. Martens, "Settler Homes, Manhood and 'Houseboys': An Analysis of Natal's Rape Scare of 1886," *Journal of Southern African Studies* 28.2 (June 2002), 379–400; van Onselen, "The Witches of Suburbia," 45–54; and Keegan, "Gender, Degeneration and Sexual Danger," 459–477.

5. Foucault, *Society Must be Defended*, 243.

6. Achille Mbembe, *On the Postcolony* (Berkeley: University of California Press, 2001), 3.

7. John Purves, "Camoens and the Epic of Africa," *The State* 2.11 (November 1909), 543.

8. See: Stephen Gray, "The White Man's Creation Myth of South Africa," *South African Literature: An Introduction* (Cape Town: David Philip, 1979), 25.

9. Carmen Nocentelli Truett, *Islands of Love: Europe, "India" and Interracial Romance, 1572–1673*, PhD Dissertation, Stanford, 2004, 5.

10. Peter Fryer, *Staying Power: The History of Black People in Britain* (London: Pluto Press, 1984), 7.

11. Ania Loomba, *Shakespeare, Race and Colonialism* (Oxford: Oxford University Press, 2002), 22.

12. Camões, *Os Lusíadas*, Canto V, stanza 39.

13. Ania Loomba, *Gender, Race and Renaissance Drama* (Manchester: Manchester University Press, 1989), 7.

14. Dorothy Driver claims that Adamastor's story "has always been taken to be about race, and specifically about the black man's frustrated desire for the white woman." Dorothy Driver, "Women and Nature, Women as Objects of Exchange: Towards a Feminist Analysis of South African Literature," *Perspectives on South African English Literature*, Michael Chapman, Colin Gardner and Es'kia Mphahlele (eds.) (Johannesburg: Ad. Donker, 1992), 455. While Adamastor is generally seen by contemporary Portuguese people simply as a mythological Titan, in twentieth-century South Africa Adamastor becomes increasingly raced. In an introductory essay to the 1965 edition of William Plomer's *Turbott Wolfe*, Laurence van der Post describes Adamastor as "a gigantic black shape with negroid features" who has "dared to love a white nymph," and reads Adamastor's attempted rape of Tethys as an allegory for African history: "The black man received from the European the many gifts resulting from his Roman virtues; but just as the Roman denied the Etruscan, so the black man was denied the white love of which Camões's nymph is the image, and in the process his heart was turned to stone." Laurens van der Post, "The Turbott Wolfe Affair," introduction to William Plomer, *Turbott Wolfe*, (London: Hogarth Press, 1965), 51. In 1999, a large painting with the title "T'Kama Adamastor," by South African artist Cyril Coetzee, was hung in the Cullen Library at the University of the Witwatersrand. The painting is based on Brink's novel, *Cape of Storms: The First Life of Adamastor* (1993). Claiming that Camões' Adamastor is a "great, black, brooding figure" whose "Negroid characteristics are unmistakeable," Brink casts him in this novel as an African male with a massive penis. See: André Brink, "Reimagining the Past: André Brink in conversation with Reingard Nethersole," in *T'Kama Adamastor: Inventions of Africa in a South African Painting*, Ivan Vladislavic (ed.), (Johannesburg: University of Witwatersrand Press, 2000); and André Brink, *Cape of Storms: The First Life of Adamastor* (London: Secker and Warburg, 1993).

15. Landeg White (trans.), *Luiz Vaz de Camões: The Lusiads* (Oxford: Oxford University Press, 1997): Canto IX, stanza 59, lines 1–2.

16. Ibid., Canto IX, stanza 68, line 5.

17. Nocentelli Truett, *Islands of Love,* 27.

18. Josiah Blackmore, *Moorings: Portuguese Expansion and the Writing of Africa* (Minneapolis: University of Minnesota Press, 2009).

19. See: Anne McClintock, *Imperial Leather: Race, Gender and Sexuality in the Colonial Contest* (New York: Routledge, 1998), 2–3.

20. Jenny Sharpe, *Allegories of Empire: The Figure of Woman in the Colonial Text* (Minneapolis: University of Minnesota Press, 1993), 5, 61–73.

21. Nancy Paxton, *Writing Under the Raj: Gender, Race and Rape in the British Colonial Imagination,* 1830–1947 (Piscataway: Rutgers University Press, 1999), 4.

22. Ibid., 1–2.

23. Stephen Taylor, *The Caliban Shore* (London: Faber, 2004), 181.

24. Ian Glenn, "The *Wreck of the Grosvenor and the Making of South African Literature,*" *English in Africa* 22. 2 (1995), 1–3.

25. Taylor, *The Caliban Shore,* 225.

26. Captain F. Marryat, *The Mission: Or Scenes in Africa* (Leipzig: Bernhard Tauchnitz, 1845), 5.

27. Ibid., 282.

28. Edward Money, *The Wife and Ward: Or, A Life's Error* (London: Routledge, 1859), 371.

29. Elizabeth Thornberry, "History Helps Find Better Ways of Talking About Rape in South Africa", Gender News from the Clayman Institute for Gender Research. http://gender.stanford.edu/news/2011/history-helps-find-better-ways-talk-about-rape-south-africa.

30. Pamela Scully, "Rape, Race and Colonial Culture: The Sexual Politics of Identity in the Nineteenth Century Cape Colony, South Africa," *American Historical Review* 100. 2 (1995), 343.

31. Quoted in Scully, "Rape, Race and Colonial Culture," 343, from Johannes van der Linden, *Institutes of Holland, or Manuel of Law, Practice, and Mercantile Law . . .,* 5th edn. (Cape Town, 1906), 232.

32. Scully, "Rape, Race and Colonial Culture," 343.

33. Quoted in Scully, "Rape, Race and Colonial Culture," 343.

34. Scully, "Rape, Race and Colonial Culture," 340.

35. See: Vron Ware, *Beyond the Pale: White Women, Racism and History* (London: Verso, 1992), 42.

36. See: Etherington, "Natal's Black Rape Scare," 36–53; Martens, "Settler Homes, Manhood and 'Houseboys,'" 381; and van Onselen, "The Witches of Suburbia," 45–54.

37. Robert Young, *Colonial Desire: Hybridity in Theory Culture and Race* (London: Routledge, 1995), 92.

38. Dorothy Driver, "'Woman' as Sign in the South African Colonial Enterprise," *Journal of Literary Studies* 4.1 (March 1988), 3, 7.

39. For a graph detailing the incidence of southern African travel narratives by white women, see Margaret Hanzimanolis, "Ultramarooned: Gender and Empire in Early Southern African Travel Narratives," doctoral dissertation, University of Cape Town, 2005.

40. For detailed analyses of gendered imagery in Haggard's novel, see Rebecca Stott, "The Dark Continent: Africa as Female Body in Haggard's Adventure Fiction," *Feminist Review* 32 (1989), 69–89; and Anne McClintock, *Imperial Leather*, 1–4.

41. Patrick Brantlinger, *Rule of Darkness: British Literature and Imperialism, 1830–1914* (Ithaca: Cornell University Press, 1988), 135–172; Martin Green, *Dreams of Adventure, Deeds of Empire* (New York: Basic Books, 1970); John McClure, *Late Imperial Romance* (London: Verso, 1994).

42. Jawaharlal Nehru, *Towards Freedom: The Autobiography of Jawaharlal Nehru* (Boston: Beacon Press, 1967), 272.

43. Edward Said, *Orientalism* (New York: Random House, 1978), 44.

44. Sara Suleri, *The Rhetoric of English India* (Chicago: University of Chicago Press, 1992), 17.

45. Olive Schreiner, *Trooper Peter Halket of Mashonaland* (London: T. Fisher Unwin, 1897), 41. All subsequent references are to this edition.

46. Hazel Carby, "'On the Threshold of Woman's Era': Lynching, Empire and Sexuality in Black Feminist Theory," in Henry Louis Gates and Kwame Anthony Appiah, *"Race," Writing and Difference* (Chicago: University of Chicago Press, 1986), 311.

47. Pauline Hopkins, *Contending Forces: A Romance Illustrative of Negro Life North and South* (Carbondale, Ill., 1978, first edition, 1900), 261.

48. Robert Rotberg, *The Founder: Cecil Rhodes and the Pursuit of Power* (New York: Oxford University Press, 1988), 550.

49. Ibid., 552.

50. Ibid., 557.

51. Olive Schreiner, *Trooper Peter Halket of Mashonaland* (London: T. Fisher Unwin, 1897). Only in two editions, both published by the South African publisher Ad. Donker, one in 1974 and the other in 1992, has the photograph been reproduced since the novel's first publication. Stephen Gray notes that in the 1974 edition "the photo is tipped in so that should the book yet again run into censorship problems, the photo can discreetly be removed." Stephen Gray, "Schreiner's Trooper at the Hanging Tree," *English Studies in Africa* 2.2 (1975), 24.

52. Quoted in Marion Friedmann, introduction to Olive Schreiner, *Trooper Peter Halket of Mashonaland* (Johannesburg: Ad. Donker, 1974), 27–28.

53. Paul Walters and Jeremy Fogg note that Schreiner's husband, Samuel Cronwright, found the photograph in the window of a barber shop in Kimberley. Cronwright wrote on the title page of his Dutch first edition: "The photograph of this frontispiece, 3 or 4 times as large, was displayed in a shop window (a hairdressers, I think) in Du Toit's Pan Road, Kimberley, where I saw it and bought it for 3/- [sic] [adding, in a lighter shade, possibly at a later date] I was alone at the time." Unfortunately, since Cronwright does not give a date for his purchase, it is not clear as to whether it inspired Schreiner to write *Trooper Halket*, or whether she added Halket's reference to the photograph after most of the novel was written. It is also possible that more than one reproduction of the photograph existed, and that Cronwright found the reproduction he mentions after *Trooper Halket* was published. See: Paul Walters and Jeremy Fogg, introduction to reprint of S.C. Cronwright-Schreiner, *Olive Schreiner: Her Re-interment on Buffelskop* (Grahamstown: NELM, 2005), 5.

54. Patricia Schechter, *Ida B. Wells-Barnett and American Reform, 1880–1930* (Chapel Hill: University of North Carolina University Press, 2001), 82.

55. *The Times*, August 1, 1894.

56. Images of the suffering inflicted upon black bodies by Boers, rather than British soldiers, were later to become points of reference in the public discourse that justified the South African War, and suffragists in Britain were particularly vocal in this regard. Josephine Butler, for instance, argued for the invasion into the Transvaal on the grounds of alleviating the suffering of black servants at the hands of racist Boers.

57. Ware, *Beyond the Pale*, 72.

58. Carby, "'On the Threshold of Woman's Era'," 301–302.

59. Ibid., 302.

60. *The Speaker*, April 3, 1897.

61. Quoted in Sandra Gunning, *Race, Rape and Lynching: The Red Record of American Literature, 1890–1912* (New York: Oxford University Press, 1996), 5.

62. *Standard and Diggers News*, February 27, 1897.

63. See: Charles van Onselen "The Witches of Suburbia: Domestic Service on the Witwatersrand 1890–1914," in *Studies in the Social and Economic History of the Witwatersrand, 1890–1914*, Volume 2, *New Nineveh* (London: Longmans, 1982), 49.

64. See: Ida B. Wells-Barnett, *Crusade for Justice* (Chicago: University of Chicago Press, 1970), 122–123.

65. *Review of Reviews*, April 1897.

66. See: Laura Chrisman, *Re-reading the Imperial Romance: British Imperialism and South African Resistance in Haggard, Schreiner, and Plaatje* (Oxford: Oxford University Press, 2000).

67. Schreiner, *Trooper Peter Halket of Mashonaland*, 39–40.

68. Ibid., 55–58.

69. Paula Krebs, *Gender, Race and the Writing of Empire: Public Discourse and the Boer War* (Cambridge: Cambridge University Press, 2004), 136.

70. McClintock, *Imperial Leather*, 270.

71. Ibid., 106–107.

72. Ibid., 108.

73. Peter Wilhelm, "Peter Halket, Rhodes and Colonialism," in Cherry Clayton (ed.), *Olive Schreiner* (Johannesburg: McGraw-Hill, 1983), 210.

74. A particularly damning review in *Blackwoods Magazine* (April 1897) stated that *Trooper Halket* "is a political pamphlet of great bitterness, linked on to the very smallest thread of a story that ever carried red-hot opinions and personal abuse of the fiercest kind into the world." A commentator for *The Illustrated London News* (6 March 1897) similarly claimed: "Those whose sympathies are strongly against Mr Rhodes in the discussion of the South African problem will see in "Peter Halket" a very excellent pamphlet on their side; but there have been much cleverer pamphlets and they are not literature."

75. *Rhodesia Herald*, April 7, 1897.

76. *Cape Argus*, March 10, 1897.

77. Laura Chrisman, *Rereading the Imperial Romance: British Imperialism and South African Resistance in Haggard, Schreiner and Plaatje* (Oxford: Oxford University Press, 2000).

78. As I point out in the following chapter, in Millin's novels *God's Step-Children* (1924) and *King of the Bastards* (1949), white men's desire for black women is represented as abhorrent.

79. Ian Glenn, "Legislating Women," *Journal of Literary Studies* 12.1–2 (1996), 145.

80. Olive Schreiner, "The Problem of Slavery," *Thoughts on South Africa* (London: Fisher Unwin, 1923), 146.

81. In unusual cases where mixing of the black and white races was advocated, this was presented as a white sacrifice to be offered for the betterment of "the negro races." An example of this is *The Negro Question; Or Hints for the Physical Improvement of the Negro Race* (1892), by Joseph Renner Maxwell, from the Gold Coast, who was in 1876 one of the first African men admitted to Oxford University.

82. Stead, *Review of Reviews*, April 1897, 286.

83. Marcus Garvey, *Tragedy of White Injustice*, Stanza 54, published privately in 1927 in New York by Amy Jacques Garvey, but written during the First World War or soon after it.

84. Frans Johan Pretorius, *Life on Commando during the Anglo-Boer War, 1899–1902* (Cape Town: Human & Rousseau, 1999), 267; B. Nasson, *The South African War 1899–1902* (London: Arnold, 1999).

85. W. K. Hancock and J. van der Poel, *Selections from the Smuts Papers, June 1886– May 1902* (Cambridge: Cambridge University Press, 1966), J. Smuts to W.T. Stead, January 4, 1902, 482.

86. Shula Marks, "White Masculinity: Jan Smuts, Race and the South African War," *Proceedings of the British Academy* 111 (2001), 219.

87. Arthur Conan Doyle, *The Great Boer War* (London: Smith, Elder & Co, 1900), 11.

88. Rudyard Kipling, "A Sahib's War," in *A Century of Anglo-Boer War Stories*, selected and introduced by Chris N. van der Merwe and Michael Rice (Johannesburg: Jonathan Ball, 1999), 111.

89. Ibid., 118–199.

90. Ibid., 121.

91. Ibid., 124.

92. Ibid.

93. Similar anger and anxiety surfaced in Europe after the First World War, when the French stationed black troops in Germany, and in the latter stages of the Second World War, when the American troops, many of whom were black, arrived in Europe. Popular representations of the day showed images of naked European women under threat from lewd, gigantic, and rapacious black soldiers. For two illustrative posters, see Klaus Theweleit, *Male Fantasies*, vol.1 (Cambridge: Polity Press, 1987), 94, 96.

94. Krebs, *Gender, Race and the Writing of Empire*, 89–101.

95. W. T. Stead, *How Not to Make Peace* (London: Review of Reviews, 1900), 88.

96. Ibid., 89.

97. Ibid.

98. W. T. Stead, *Methods of Barbarism* (London: Review of Reviews, 1901), 89–90.

99. The testimonies in *Vroueleed* corroborate that rape of Boer women and children by British soldiers did occur during the war. A.W.G. Raath, and R.M. Louw, *Vroueleed* [Women's Sorrow] (Bloemfontein: Oorlogsmuseum, 1993).

100. Arthur Conan Doyle, *The War in South Africa: Its Cause and Conduct* (London: Smith, Elder and Company, 1902).

101. Krebs, *Gender, Race and Writing Empire*, 6.

102. This was by no means exclusive to South Africa. As Nancy Paxton points out in a chapter entitled "Mobilising Chivalry," ideas about male honor and the vulnerability of white women to sexual assault by Indian men were an integral part of English narratives on the Indian Mutiny of 1857. See: Paxton, *Writing Under the Raj*, 109–136. Similarly, in the United States following Reconstruction, the notion of the black rapist presented a useful fantasy for white southerners who were struggling to resolve anxieties in the period of Reconstruction. See: Sandra Gunning, *Race, Rape and Lynching*, 6.

103. John Dickson Carr, *The Life of Sir Arthur Conan Doyle* (London: John Murray, 1949), 285.

104. Stowell Kessler, "The Black Concentration Camps of the South African War 1899–1902," doctoral dissertation, University of Cape Town, 2003.

105. Charlotte Moor, "Colonia," *Marina de la Rey* (London: Digby, Long and Company, 1903), 309.

106. Ibid., 285.

107. Michael Rice, *From Dolly Gray to Sarie Marais: A Survey of Fiction from the First and Second Anglo-Boer Conflicts* (Noordhoek: Fischer Press, 2004), 69.

108. Gustav Preller, "Lettie" (trans. Madeline van Biljon), in C. N. van der Merwe and M. Rice (eds.) *A Century of Anglo-Boer War Stories* (Johannesburg: Jonathan Ball, 1999), 51.

109. Ibid., 52.

Chapter 2

1. George Heaton Nicholls, *Bayete! "Hail to the King"* (London: George Allen & Unwin, 1923), 239.

2. Anderson, *Imagined Communities*, 32.

3. Cornwell, "George Webb Hardy's *The Black Peril*," 441.

4. Isabel Hofmeyr, "Gandhi's Printing Press: Print Cultures of the Indian Ocean," unpublished conference paper, 2009.

5. Jeff Peires, "Lovedale and Literature for the Bantu Revisited," *English in Africa*, 7.1 (1980), 158.

6. Van Onselen, "The Witches of Suburbia," 51.

7. Ibid., 45.

8. Jack and Ray Simons, *Class and Colour in South Africa 1850–1950* (London: International Defence and Aid Fund for Southern Africa, 1983 (first published in 1969)), 97.

9. The *Star* (established in 1889) and the *Rand Daily Mail* (established in 1903) were both Johannesburg-based papers that catered predominantly for white working-class readers in this mining city. The white Labour Party ran a weekly paper from 1908–12 called *The Voice of Labour*, and the International Socialist League (predecessor of the Communist Party) published *The International* as a weekly from 1915.

10. Grahamstown: Rhodes University, Cory History Library: General Missionary Conference commission on "the so-called Black Peril," 1912, MS 14847, folder 18, undated newspaper clipping.

11. *Report of the Commission of Enquiry to Report on Assaults on Women*, 1913.

12. Grahamstown, Cory Library, General Missionary Conference papers, MS 14847.

13. The Entertainments (Censorship) Act No 29 of 1931, House of Assembly of the Union of South Africa.

14. See: David Attwell, *Rewriting Modernity: Studies in Black South African Literary History* (Pietermaritzburg: University of KwaZulu-Natal Press, 2005), 55.

15. Paxton, *Writing Under the Raj*: Mikhail Bakhtin, "Discourse in the Novel," *The Dialogic Imagination: Four Essays*, Michael Holquist (ed.), Caryl Emerson and Michael Holquist (trans.) (Austin: University of Texas at Austin, 1981), 291.

16. While white readers saw the novel as confronting "the Native question" and warning about threats to white supremacy, black readers such as H. Selby Msimang and Clements

Kadalie read it as a call to political action. In *The Crisis*, a pamphlet published in 1936, which deals with Hertzog's "Native Bills" and the abolition of the common roll franchise for Africans in the Cape, Msimang, who was a long-time leader of the ANC and a co-founder of the ICU with Kadalie, ironically thanks Heaton Nicholls for showing that Africans had to choose between segregation or liberation, and for implying that they would prefer the latter:

> Another alternative is contained in the book "Bayete," by the distinguished champion of the Native Bills, Chairman of the Native Affairs Commission, and Honourable Member for Zululand, Mr. G. Heaton Nicholls, M.P., to whom we owe an irredeemable debt of gratitude for this book. In this book Mr. Nicholls indicates to us the way and method that we should adopt to seize the reins of government and to regain all the freedom we have lost since the advent of white men in this country. It is the only way short of a creation of two States. It calls for no machine guns, no bombs nor aeroplanes. The weapon is a power in itself in that it is the power of the soul . . . the will and determination to be free, the ineradicable craving of human nature, without which we must certainly agree to perish or be made slaves.

Quoted in Tim Couzens, *The New African, a Study of the Life and Work of H.I.E. Dhlomo* (Johannesburg: Ravan Press, 1985), 142.

17. Francis Bancroft, Author's note (London, April 1907), *Of Like Passions* (London: Sisley's, 1907).

18. Review of Francis Bancroft's *Of Like Passions*, *Times Literary Supplement*, June 14, 1907, 18.

19. Bancroft, *Of Like Passions*, 211.

20. Thomas Dixon, *The Clansman*, quoted in Sielke, *Reading Rape*, 38.

21. Ibid.

22. Bancroft, *Of Like Passions*, 212–213.

23. Cornwell, "Francis Bancroft's *Of Like Passions*," 1–36.

24. Francis Bancroft, "White Women in South Africa," *The Englishwoman* 9 (January–March 1911), 267–268. As Cornwell points out, this article was translated and published in the very first issue of the Paris journal *Le Monde* 1.1 (1911), 75–81.

25. George Webb Hardy, *The Black Peril* (London: Holden & Hardingham, 1912), 147.

26. Ibid., 208, 213.

27. Cornwell, "George Webb Hardy's *The Black Peril*," 441–453.

28. Hardy, *The Black Peril*, 143–144.

29. Ibid., 147.

30. Oxford: Bodleian Library, Harcourt Papers, Lord Gladstone to Lewis ("Lulu") Harcourt, London, February 8, 1911.

31. Neil Roberts, "Native Education from an Economic Point of View," *South African Journal of Science* 14 (1917), 99.

32. Hardy, *The Black Peril*, 163.

33. Ibid., 178–179.

34. Sielke, *Reading Rape*, 37.

35. Hardy, *The Black Peril*, 179.

36. George Webb Hardy, "The Black Peril," *The Prince*, October 7, 1904, 607, 609.

37. Hardy, *The Black Peril*, 138.

38. John Shepstone (1827–1916) was the younger brother of Sir Theophilus Shepstone, Diplomatic Agent to the Native Tribes and Secretary for Native Affairs in Natal between

1845 and 1875. Like his brother Theophilus, John believed in maintaining separate racial development by encouraging "a tribal system" for Africans and opposing the African franchise. He was involved in drawing up the Natal Penal Code and helped in the break-up of Zululand after the war of 1879. See: Shula Marks, *Reluctant Rebellion: the 1906-8 Disturbances in Natal* (Oxford: Clarendon Press, 1970), 14, and E. H. Brookes and C. De B. Webb, *A History of Natal* (Pietermaritzburg: University of Natal Press, 1967), 217.

39. Hardy, *The Black Peril*, 196.

40. Ibid., 83.

41. Ibid., 109–110.

42. Ibid., 119.

43. Ibid., 164.

44. Shula Marks, "Natal, the Zulu Royal Family and the Ideology of Segregation," in W. Beinart and S. Dubow (eds.), *Segregation and Apartheid in Twentieth Century South Africa* (London: Routledge, 1995), 98.

45. Susanna Glouwdina Bekker, "George Heaton Nicholls and the Formulation of 'Native Policy,' 1927 to 1936," Master of Arts dissertation in History at the University of Natal, Durban, 1987, ii.

46. Couzens, *The New African*, 140.

47. C.M. Tatz, *Shadow and Substance in South Africa: A Study in Land and Franchise Policies Affecting Africans 1910–1960* (Pietermaritzburg: University of Natal Press, 1962), 3–5.

48. Following Hannah Arendt, Paul Gilroy claims that "Boer settlers at the Cape were the original architects of a ruthless and practical racism that would supply new social and political views for colonial organization elsewhere." See: Gilroy, *After Empire: Melancholia or Convivial Culture?* (Abingdon: Routledge, 2004), 17. However, as historians such as Beinart and Dubow point out, the idea that apartheid stemmed merely from the "ruthless and practical racism" of "Boers" has largely been discredited, and continuity has been shown between policies of segregation in British South Africa and apartheid. See: Beinart and Dubow, "Introduction," *Segregation and Apartheid*, 4–8.

49. Helen Bradford, *A Taste of Freedom, the ICU in Rural South Africa, 1924–30* (New Haven: Yale University Press, 1987), 97–101.

50. Nicholls, *Bayete!*, 5.

51. Ibid., 222–224.

52. James T. Campbell, *Songs of Zion: The African Methodist Episcopal Church in the United States and South Africa* (New York: Oxford University Press, 1995), *passim*.

53. Nicholls, *Bayete!*, 5, and Nicholls, *South Africa in My Time* (London: George Allen & Unwin, 1961), 93–94.

54. Nicholls, *Bayete!*, 6.

55. Ibid., 5.

56. Nicholls, *Bayete!*, 222.

57. Nicholls, *Bayete!*, 13, 74.

58. Carby, "'On the Threshold of Woman's Era,'" 301–302.

59. Cape Town, National Archives, 2/SPT/17/1/15/4, report of meeting with secretary for Native Affairs, June 24, 1926, and with resident magistrate, September 15, 1926. See also William Beinart, "*Amafeladawonye* (the Die-hards), Popular Protest and Women's Movements in Herschel District in the 1920s," in W. Beinart and C. Bundy (eds.), *Hidden Struggles in Rural South Africa: Politics and Popular Movements in the Transkei and Eastern Cape, 1890–1930* (Johannesburg: Ravan Press, 1987), 233–250.

60. Nicholls, *Bayete!*, 134.

61. Ibid., 253.

62. Ibid., 345.

63. Ibid., 359.

64. Ibid., 278.

65. Whereas *Bayete!* damns physical attraction between Olive and Nelson by finally reducing their relationship to an image of "black peril," interracial desire between a white man and a black woman is treated more sympathetically in the novel. When Lionel, Olive's younger brother, falls for the charms of a black servant named Martha, their relationship is linked to settler counter-insurgency, since it is Martha who tells Lionel of a local chief's plan for an armed uprising. While sexual relationships between black men and white women had been outlawed as early as 1902, sex and co-habiting between white men and black women (which was often, as Sol Plaatje points out in *The Mote and the Beam*, based on the exploitation of the black woman) was legislatively tolerated until the late 1920s.

66. Nicholls, *Bayete!*, 112–113.

67. Ibid. The "black peril" was used in arguments against black access to liquor and the Liquor Act of 1928 applied the prohibition to Africans only. See: Eugene P. Dvorin, *Racial Separation in South Africa* (Chicago: University of Chicago Press, 1952), 28–29. Apart from the New Woman, another class of white women in South Africa was also perceived as endangering the white social cell. In *Bayete!*, an assault on a white women is provoked when Mukwasi sees white women prostitutes, lubricated by "illicit liquor," mixing with black men on the Witwatersrand. As in other colonial contexts, in South Africa the obsession with protecting white women from ravishment at the hands of "native" men was linked to a biopolitical system of gender and class-based regulation that sought to demarcate the boundaries of white bourgeois sexuality.

68. Nicholls, *Bayete!*, 239.

69. Ibid., 27, 29, 47–48, 52.

70. Ibid., 136, 222, 287.

71. Ibid., 96, 137.

72. Ibid., 52, 224.

73. Ibid., 35–36.

74. Ibid., 287.

75. Ibid., 212.

76. Ibid., 232.

77. Schechter, *Ida B. Wells and American Reform*, 93.

78. In their preoccupation with voice, and particularly in their ambivalence towards the New Woman, "black peril" novels such as *The Black Peril* by Webb Hardy and *Bayete!* by Heaton Nicholls could provide an interesting transnational historical backdrop for reading E.M. Forster's *A Passage to India* (1924), which was also written by a white male author, similarly focuses on the question of interracial rape in a colonial setting, and was published a year after *Bayete!* Like Mary Roseberry in Webb Hardy's novel, whose outspoken liberal views and smoking of a cigarette "like a practised hand" mark her as a New Woman, it is her oral symptoms that signify Adela Quested's status as a New Woman in *A Passage to India*. Although the published novel famously elides any scene of rape, rendering doubtful Adela's claim that she was assaulted in the caves, in a manuscript version Forster scripted a scene of attempted rape that focuses on organs of speech:

At first she thought that <she was being robbed,> . . . then she realized and shrieked at the top of her voice. Boum <went>\ shrieked [?] the echo. She struck out and he got hold of her other hand and forced her against the wall, he got both of her hands in one of his, then felt at her <dress>\ breasts\. "Mrs. Moore," she yelled. "Ronny—don't let him, save me." The strap of her Field Glasses, tugged suddenly, *was drawn across her throat*. She understood—*it was to be passed around her neck*, <it was to> *she was to be throttled as far as necessary and then* . . . [Forster's ellipsis] Silent, though the echo still raged up and down, she waited and when the breath was on her wrenched a hand free, got hold of the glasses and pushed them at*into her assailant's mouth*.

See: Paxton, *Writing Under the Raj*, 233–4. As with South African "black peril" novels, what is dramatized here is precisely a contest over voice. Adela's assailant first tries to silence her by drawing a strap "across her throat," while she thrusts her field glasses "into her assailant's mouth," and thus, like Bancroft, Forster places the vocalization of the New Woman and the "native" in opposition. Adela is silenced by Forster as her testimony at the trial is elided, left off-stage, and her aphasia results in the proceedings against Aziz. Unlike classic "black peril" novels, however, because the scene of rape is elided in the published version of the novel, the reader is led by Forster to question whether Adela's hysteria and sexual repression made her fall prey to hallucinations, and whether any attempted rape has taken place at all. Modernist uncertainty in this novel could be read as a symptom of male fear that rape is a female fiction. On the other hand, the fact that it is elided in the published version suggests that Forster decided to treat the question of interracial rape with self-reflexivity and critical distance.

79. Homi K. Bhabha, "Signs Taken for Wonders: Questions of Ambivalence and Authority under a Tree outside Delhi, May 1817," in Bhabha, *The Location of Culture*, 102–122.

Chapter 3

1. *Parliamentary Debates, Official Reports*, 5th Series, House of Commons, July 28, 1914, columns 1194–1197. According to Leo McKinstry, Harcourt's "most notable characteristic was his sexual craving for adolescents," and it was said that during his lifetime Harcourt amassed the largest collection of child pornography in Britain. He met with his downfall after an attempted sexual assault on a young boy in 1921. See: Leo McKinstry, *Rosebery: Statesman in Turmoil* (London: John Murray, 2005), 275–276. Plaatje knew of the scandal when he claimed in 1921 that "in the opinion of the South African Natives" Harcourt was "the weakest colonial secretary that ever succeeded Joseph Chamberlain at Downing Street." See: Sol Plaatje, *The Mote and the Beam*, 283.

2. See: Sol Plaatje, *Native Life in South Africa* (London: P.S. King & Son, 1916), 200.

3. Plaatje, *Native Life in South Africa*, 17.

4. Hyslop, "White Working-Class Women and the Invention of Apartheid," 57–81.

5. I. D. MacCrone, *Race Attitudes in South Africa: Historical, Experimental, and Psychological Studies* (Johannesburg: Oxford University Press, 1937), 254.

6. Ibid., 5.

7. Ibid., 278–279.

8. Frantz Fanon, *Black Skin, White Masks* (New York: Grove, 1967), 166, 183.

9. Ibid., 155.

10. See: Sandra Gunning, *Race, Rape and Lynching: The Red Record of American Literature, 1890–1912,* (New York: Oxford University Press, 1996), vii. A decade later, Plaatje was to publish in the black South African newspaper, *Umteteli wa Bantu*, a review of *Birth of a*

Nation in which he declared of the film: "Ugly black peril scenes are shown until the emotions of white people are worked up to fever heat." Brian Willan, *Sol Plaatje: South African Nationalist 1876–1932* (London: Heinemann, 1984), 271.

11. Plaatje, *The Mote and the Beam*, 280.

12. Ibid., 277.

13. Willan, *Sol Plaatje: South African Nationalist*, vi.

14. Ibid., 279.

15. Ibid., 269–270.

16. Ibid., 274.

17. Defending the price of the pamphlet, Plaatje noted that "members of the other race pay 25 cents for *The Mote and the Beam* as cheerfully as my Negro readers." See: "Mr. Sol T. Plaatje explains his mission," letter to the editor, *Negro World*, June 18, 1921, in Willan (ed.), *Sol Plaatje: Selected Works*, 285.

18. Hubert Harrison, *Negro World*, April 23, 1921. He states that pamphlets of 24 to 48 pages usually sold for 10 cents and those of 64 to 100 pages for 25 cents.

19. *Journal of Southern African Studies* 30.1 (2004).

20. Linda McMurry, *To Keep the Waters Troubled: The Life of Ida B. Wells* (New York: Oxford University Press, 1998), xiv.

21. Plaatje, *The Mote and the Beam*, 274.

22. Ida B. Wells, *Southern Horrors: Southern Lynch Law in All Its Phases* (1892), in *Southern Horrors and Other Writings: The Anti-Lynching Campaign of Ida B. Wells 1892–1900*, Jacqueline Jones (ed.) (Boston: Bedford, 1997) 50.

23. Patricia Schechter, *Ida B. Wells-Barnett and American Reform, 1880–1930* (Chapel Hill: University of North Carolina University Press, 2001), 85.

24. Plaatje, *The Mote and the Beam*, 278.

25. Trudier Harris (ed.), Introduction, *Selected Works of Ida B. Wells-Barnett* (New York: Oxford University Press, 1991), 8.

26. Ibid., 282.

27. Harrison, *Negro World*, April 23, 1921.

28. Joel Augustus Rogers, *As Nature Leads: An Informal Discussion of the Reason Why Negro and Caucasian are Mixing in Spite of Opposition* (Chicago: M.A. Donohue, 1919), 23.

29. Plaatje, *The Mote and the Beam*, 279.

30. Rogers, *As Nature Leads*, 29.

31. William Plomer, "Black Peril," in Stephen Gray (ed.), *William Plomer, Selected Stories* (Cape Town: David Philip, 1984), 88.

32. Judith Butler, "On Speech, Race and Melancholia," 170.

33. Laurens van der Post, "Introduction," Plomer, *Turbott Wolfe*, 13.

34. Ibid., 19.

35. Peter Blair, "'That Ugly Word: Miscegenation and the Novel in Preapartheid South Africa," *Modern Fiction Studies* 49.1 (2003), 592.

36. William Plomer, *Turbott Wolfe* (London: Hogarth Press, 1965 (first published by Hogarth Press, 1925)), 142.

37. Fanon, *Black Skin, White Masks*, 46.

38. Plaatje, *The Mote and the Beam*, 278.

39. Sarah Gertrude Millin, *The Night is Long* (London: Faber & Faber, 1941), 55, 61.

40. Ibid., 27, 29.

41. E.T.A. Hoffman, "The Sandman," trans. R.J. Hollingdale, in *The Tales of Hoffman* (London: Penguin, 1982), 85–126. Sigmund Freud, *The Uncanny*, trans. David McLintock (London: Penguin, 2003).

42. Quoted from Hitler's *Mein Kampf* in J. M. Coetzee, "Blood, Flaw, Taint, Degeneration: the Case of Sarah Gertrude Millin," in *White Writing: on the Culture of Letters in South Africa* (New Haven: Yale University Press, 1988), 137.

43. Tony Voss, introduction to S. G. Millin, *God's Stepchildren* (Craighall: Ad. Donker, 1986, first published in 1924), 8. All subsequent references are to this edition.

44. Sarah Gertrude Millin, *The South Africans* (London: Constable, 1926), 195–209.

45. Sarah Gertrude Millin, "Why Adonis Laughed," *The New Adelphi*, June–August, 1929, 255–256.

46. Millin, *God's Stepchildren*, 171.

47. Ibid.

48. Sarah Gertrude Millin, *King of the Bastards* (London: Heinemann, 1950), vi. (Quotation is from introduction by General J. C. Smuts).

49. Ibid., 178.

50. Ibid., 187.

51. Sarah Gertrude Millin, *The Burning Man* (London: Heinemann, 1952).

52. Ibid., 297.

53. Ibid., 136.

54. Ibid., 137.

55. See: Gayatri Chakravorty Spivak, "Can the Subaltern Speak?" in Cary Nelson and Larry Grossberg (eds.), *Marxism and the interpretation of Culture* (Chicago: Uni of Illinois Press, 1988), 271–313; and Robert Young, *Colonial Desire*, 108.

56. Lavinia Braun, "Not Gobineau but Heine: Not Racial Theory but Biblical Theme: the Case of Sarah Gertrude Millin," *English Studies in Africa* 34.1 (1991), 27–38; Marcelle Leveson, *People of the Book: Images of the Jew in South African English Fiction* (Johannesburg: University of the Witwatersrand Press, 2001).

57. Quoted in Ronald Suresh Roberts, *Fit to Govern: The Native Intelligence of Thabo Mbeki* (Johannesburg: Ste Publishers, 2006), 292.

58. Millin, *The Night is Long*, 253.

59. Millin's attempt to trace a history of "miscegenation" through relationships between colonizing men and colonized women may be contrasted with that of her contemporary, Marie Kathleen Jeffreys (1883–1968), a writer and also an ambiguously "white" woman, who published articles and poems in national periodicals around the same time as the publication of *King of the Bastards* and *The Burning Man*. While Millin damns interracial sex, Jeffreys celebrates the hybrid identity of the South African nation.

60. Michael Wade, "Myth, Truth and the South African Reality in the Fiction of Sarah Gertrude Millin," *Journal of Southern African Studies* 1.1 (1974), 81–108.

61. Dora Taylor, "Sarah Gertrude Millin, South African Realist," *Trek*, May 21, 1943.

62. Millin, *The Night is Long*, 269.

63. Ibid., 161–162.

64. Foucault, *The Will to Knowledge: The History of Sexuality, Volume I*, 118.

65. Quoted in J. M. Coetzee, *Giving Offense: Essays on Censorship* (Chicago: University of Chicago Press, 1996), 172.

66. Foucault, *Society Must be Defended*, 259.

67. Foucault, *The Will to Knowledge: The History of Sexuality, Volume I*, 149. While Foucault claims that "the bourgeoisie's blood" became "its sex," in the writings of Millin an obsession with sex coalesces with, rather than replaces, the notion of "pure blood," suggesting that Foucault may have underestimated the ways in which ideas about blood continued to function within discourses on race.

68. J. M. Coetzee, "Blood, Flaw, Taint," 137.

69. Milton Shain, *The Roots of Anti-Semitism in South Africa* (Johannesburg: Witwatersrand University Press, 1994), 32.

70. Quoted in Charles van Onselen, *The Fox and the Flies: the World of Joseph Silver, Racketeer and Psychopath* (London: Jonathan Cape, 2007), 192.

71. Millin, *The Night is Long*, 191.

72. Ibid., 76.

73. Ibid., 76–77.

74. Sarah Gertrude Millin, *The Wizard Bird* (London: Heinemann, 1962), 201.

75. Ibid., 9. Millin must have known that Kenyatta had a white wife and a bi-racial son.

76. Ibid., 190, 218.

77. Dora Taylor, "To Tell my Story," in *Don't Tread on my Dreams*, ed. Sheila Belshaw and Michael Muskett (eds.) with an afterword by Dorothy Driver (Cape Town: Penguin 2008), 1–55.

78. Ibid., 19, 6, 11.

79. Ibid., 6.

80. Ibid., 37.

81. Ibid., 36.

82. Ibid., 55.

83. Coetzee, "Jerusalem Prize Acceptance Speech," 97.

84. Taylor, "To Tell My Story," 46.

85. Ibid., 48.

86. Coetzee, "Blood, Flaw, Taint," 150.

87. *Mittee* was also translated into a number of languages and circulated in Europe and Latin America.

88. "Transvaal Tangle," review of Rooke's *Mittee*, *Time Magazine*, February 18, 1952.

89. "What America is reading," *New York Herald Tribune Book review*, May 4, 1952, and Frank O'Neill, "Two Daphnes write heady novels of romance and suspense," Review of Rooke's *Mittee*, *Cleveland News*, February 12, 1952.

90. Ian Glenn, Introduction, *Mittee* (Cape Town: Chameleon Press), 1987, 3, and J.M. Coetzee, Afterword, *Mittee*, (London: Penguin, 1991), 205.

91. No previous criticism has yet examined this discrepancy, though the difference between the editions is noted in an interview with Rooke by Ian Glenn. See: Ian Glenn, "The production and prevention of a colonial author—the case of Daphne Rooke," *New Contrast* 22.1 (1984), 78–85.

92. Coetzee, Afterword, *Mittee* (London: Penguin, 1991), 205.

93. Ibid., 207.

94. See: Lucy Graham, "Reading the Unspeakable: Rape in J.M. Coetzee's *Disgrace*," *Journal of Southern African Studies* 29.1 (2003), 433–444.

95. Daphne Rooke, *Mittee* (New Milford, USA: Toby Press, 2007).

96. Doris Lessing, *Walking in the Shade: Volume Two of my Autobiography 1949–1962* (London: Harper Collins, 1997), 7–8.

97. Victor Gollancz Ltd. archive, by permission of the Orion Publishing Group, London: Sheila Hodges to Margaret Macpherson, May 15, 1951.

98. Gollancz archive, Hodges to Macpherson, June 7, 1951.

99. Gollancz archive, Edwin Lamberth to John Bush, May 19, 1951.

100. *Time Magazine*, January 24, 1938.

101. Black men who wrote about black-on-white rape risked censorship in South Africa. This is evidenced by the banning in 1976 of Arthur Maimane's *Victims*. In 1986 Lewis Nkosi's *Mating Birds*, which questions rather than simply reproduces "black peril" stereotypes, was embargoed, though not banned.

102. Gollancz archive, Margaret Macpherson to Sheila Hodges, May 17, 1951.

103. In 1962 *The Greyling* was banned before its publication by the censors for being "a most undesirable publication about the love-relationship between a non-white—the child of a white man and a Bantu—on a farm and the son of the white farm owner. They have sexual intercourse, a child is born and the consequences are sketched." The reader's report is missing in this file. See: Cape Archives, BCS 2654/13/32, vol. 9, No. 83. The novel was only unbanned in 1991 following an appeal. The reader in this case, Mrs. Giannelos, declared that during the thirty years since the novel was banned "race relations have undergone a tremendous change" and motivated for its unbanning. See: Cape Archives BCS P91/10/112.

104. Gollancz archive, Sheila Hodges to Daphne Rooke, May 31, 1951.

105. Gollancz archive, Rooke to Hodges, June 11, 1951.

106. Ibid.

107. Rooke, *Mittee* (Houghton Mifflin edition, 1952), 245.

108. Ibid., 246.

109. Rooke, *Mittee* (Gollancz edition, 1951), 167.

110. Ibid., 165–166.

111. R. K. Cope, "Young Writer," *Cape Times*, March 13, 1952.

112. Tanya Horek, *Public Rape: Representing Violation in Fiction and Film* (London: Routledge, 2003), 140.

113. Ibid., 140–141.

114. Judith Butler, "On Being Beside Oneself," in Nicholas Bamforth (ed.), *Sex Rights: the Oxford Amnesty Lectures, 2002* (Oxford: Oxford University Press, 2005), 48, 58.

115. Achille Mbembe (trans. L. Meintjies), "Necropolitics," *Public Culture* 15.1, 21.

116. "European Gaoled for Raping Native Child," *Rand Daily Mail*, April 24, 1946.

117. "Native Sentenced to Death for Rape," *Rand Daily Mail*, April 24, 1946.

118. "Racial Conflict," review in *Times Literary Supplement*, December 21, 1952.

119. Rooke, *Mittee* (Gollancz edition, 1951), 81.

120. Lynn A. Higgins and Brenda R. Silver, *Rape and Representation* (New York: University of Columbia Press, 1991).

121. Daphne Rooke, *Diamond Jo* (London: Gollancz, 1965). Tanguy is then killed by the white woman protagonist, Jo, who commits suicide in prison. This novel by Rooke resonates uncannily with Plaatje's story, in *The Mote and the Beam*, of a white woman who was "unmolested by the thousands of Natives surrounding her," but when "already married . . . was outraged by a white traveling trader." Rooke's story echoes Plaatje's claim that "the first authenticated cases of rape, murder and suicide . . . were the work of a white man" (Plaatje, *The Mote and the Beam*, 283).

122. Rooke, *Mittee* (Gollancz edition, 1951), 180.

123. Rooke, *Mittee* (Houghton Mifflin edition, 1952), 266.

124. Rooke, *Mittee* (Gollancz edition, 1951), 180 and (Houghton Mifflin edition, 1952), 226.

125. Rooke, *Mittee* (Gollancz edition, 1951), 123.

126. Ibid., 66.

127. Coetzee, Afterword in Rooke, *Mittee* (London: Penguin, 1991), 262–263.

128. Butler, "On Speech, Race and Melancholia," 170.

129. Young, *Colonial Desire*, 115.

130. Rooke, *Mittee* (Gollancz edition, 1951), 26.

131. Ibid., 37.

132. Daphne Rooke, *The Greyling* (London: Gollancz, 1962), 93.

133. Ibid., 165.

134. Ibid., 134.

135. This difference in punitive measures was reflected in reality: while a white man was reprimanded in 1946 as a "disgrace to his European race" and given seven years imprisonment and six strokes for raping "a native child nine years old," in the same year a "European" was given only four years hard labor and six cuts for the violation of "a European child less than 12 years old." See: "European gaoled for raping native child," *Rand Daily Mail*, April 24, 1946 and "European convicted of raping child," *The Star*, December 13, 1945.

136. Lucy Graham, interview with Daphne Rooke, Cambridge, November 24, 2005.

137. Slavoj Žižek, *The Art of the Ridiculous Sublime: on David Lynch's Lost Highway* (Seattle: University of Washington Press, 2000), 19, 34–35.

138. In Rooke's memoir, *Three Rivers: A Memoir* (Cambridge: Daffodil Press, 2003), she writes that: "Ours was a feminine household. My father had been killed in the Great War: and my brothers and elder sister were in Johannesburg." (6). Although this does not excuse white women from complicity in racial oppression, the "excessive phallic 'life power'" and unconditional "Life-Assertion" of the violent white men in Rooke's novels can be read as mirroring the very maximization of life towards which the biopolitical state violently strains. The violence of these men, and their emphasis on maintaining patriarchal order echoes that of the authoritarian apartheid state, but Rooke reveals that they also break the rules through their sexual relationships with "coloured" women.

139. Rooke, *Mittee* (Gollancz edition, 1951), 20.

140. Daphne Rooke, *Three Rivers*, 6.

141. Zoë Wicomb, "Classics," *Southern African Review of Books* 2.4 (1989), 17.

Chapter 4

1. Butler, "On Speech, Race and Melancholia," 166.

2. Meg Samuelson "The Rainbow Womb: Race and Rape in South African Fiction of the Transition," *Kunapipi* 14.1 (2002), 89.

3. Bloke Modisane, *Blame Me on History* (London: Thames & Hudson, 1963), 214.

4. Janice Harris, "On Tradition, Madness, and South Africa: an Interview with Lewis Nkosi," *Weber Studies* 11. 2 (Spring/Summer, 1994), 23.

5. For an analysis of the ways in which *Mating Birds* parodies "black peril" stereotypes see: Lucy Graham, "'Bathing Area—For Whites Only': Reading 'Black Peril' and Prohibitive Signs in Lewis Nkosi's *Mating Birds*," in *Still Beating the Drum: Critical Perspectives on Lewis Nkosi*, Liz Gunner and Lindy Stiebel (eds.) (Amsterdam: Rodopi, 2006), 147–164.

6. Njabulo Ndebele, The *Rediscovery of the Ordinary: Essays in South African Culture and Literature* (Johannesburg: Cosaw, 1991), 46.

7. Ibid., 40.

8. With the exceptions of Sheila Fugard (whose novel, *A Revolutionary Woman* (1983), deals with "black peril" rape), André Brink and J.M. Coetzee, white novelists of the 1970s and 1980s generally avoided confronting the topic of rape.

9. The Publications Amendment Act, No 109 of 1978. For an in-depth study of censorship and South African literature, see: McDonald, *The Literature Police*.

10. J.C.W. van Rooyen, *Censorship in South Africa* (Juta, Cape Town, 1987), 21.

11. Arthur Maimane, *Victims* (London: Alison & Busby, 1976), 8.

12. Cape Town: National Archives, IDP P77/3/104, Arthur Maimane, *Victims* file, 1977, reader's report by Professor H. van der Merwe Scholtz.

13. Meredith Goldsmith, "Of Masks, Mimicry, Misogyny and Miscegenation: Forging Black South African Masculinity in Bloke Modisane's *Blame me on History*," *The Journal of Men's Studies* 10. 3 (2002), 292. Maimane went to work for a newspaper in Ghana in 1958 and from there to London in 1961. Unlike his contemporaries, such as Lewis Nkosi and Nat Nakasa, who applied later and had to leave the country as exiles on one-way exit permits in 1961, Maimane, like Ezekiel Mphahlele, left the country on a South African passport. He was able to visit South Africa in 1983 on a British passport.

14. Mark Gevisser, *Thabo Mbeki: the Dream Deferred* (Johannesburg: Jonathan Ball, 2007), 140.

15. Cape Town: University of the Western Cape, Mayibuye Archives: International Defence and Aid Fund (IDAF) papers, Arthur Maimane, unpublished memoir, "One of Us," f. 17.

16. Notes of interview with Jenny Maimane by Hugh Macmillan, London, December 20, 2008.

17. Cape Archives, IDP, P77/3/104, *Victims* file, 1977, reader's report by Professor H. van der Merwe Scholtz.

18. Samuelson, "The Rainbow Womb," 89.

19. Cape Archives, IDP, P84/12/53, *Victims* file, resubmission to the censorship board by the Public Library of South Africa, Cape Town.

20. Johannesburg: Kwela Books, Annari van der Merwe to Arthur Maimane, e-mail correspondence, August 31, 1999, by courtesy of Annari van der Merwe.

21. Maimane, *Victims*, 57.

22. Fanon, *Black Skin, White Masks*, 8, 139, 11.

23. Maimane, *Victims*, 57.

24. Fanon, *Black Skin, White Masks*, 140.

25. T. Denean Sharpley-Whiting, *Fanon: Conflicts and Feminisms* (Lanham, USA: Rowman & Littlefield, 1997), 14.

26. Fanon, *Black Skin, White Masks*, 166.

27. Arthur Maimane, *Hate No More* (Johannesburg: Kwela Books, 2000), 188.

28. Sharpley-Whiting, *Fanon: Conflicts and Feminisms*, 14.

29. Maimane, *Victims*, 58.

30. Maimane, *Hate No More*, 74.

31. Samuelson, "The Rainbow Womb," 89.

32. Maimane, *Hate No More*, 23.

33. Ibid., 88–89.

34. C. J. Driver, "Sincere but Wrong" (review of Maimane, *Victims* and other books), *Guardian*, May 5, 1977.

35. Maimane, "One of Us," f. 26

36. Maimane, *Hate No More*, 289.

37. Ibid., 290.

38. Ibid., 24.

39. Maimane, "One of Us," f. 255.

40. Ibid., ff. 254–255.

41. ANC, Statement of the ANC at the Human Rights Commission Hearings on Racism in the Media, paragraphs 72–74. http://www.anc.org.za/ancdocs/misc/2000/sp0405.html.

42. Joan Brickhill, "Self-indulgent, Unrealistic: *Victims* by Arthur Maimane," *Africa Magazine*, December 1976.

43. Fanon, *Black Skin, White Masks*, 63.

44. Ibid., 17–18.

45. Homi K. Bhabha, *The Location of Culture* (London: Routledge, 1994), 85–86.

46. Ibid., 81.

47. Ibid., 113.

48. Dr T.E. Dönges, in *Hansard* [1949] 1968: 6167–6168, quoted in Ian Glenn, "Legislating Women," *Journal of Literary Studies* 12. 1 and 2 (1996), 135–170.

49. Glenn, "Legislating Women," *Journal of Literary Studies* 12. 1 and 2 (1996), 145–46.

50. Miriam Tlali, whose *Muriel at Metropolitan* (Johannesburg: Ravan Press, 1975) is credited as being the first novel published by a black woman in South Africa, has written a play entitled *Crimen Injuria*, depicting a "white peril" encounter where a white soldier rapes his black childhood friend in the servants' quarters. Despite being performed in Europe in 1986, however, the play has not so far been published. See: Christina Cullhed, "Grappling with Patriarchies: Narrative Strategies of Resistance in Miriam Tlali's Writings," doctoral dissertation, Uppsala University, 2006, 45.

51. Matthew Krouse, "Bella," in C. Doherty (ed.) *Porno* (Grahamstown: Bobbejaan Press, 1989).

52. Donald Barthelme, "Manual for Sons," *Sixty Stories*, Penguin Classics, first edition 1981.

53. Krouse, "Bella," 30.

54. Notes of interview with Matthew Krouse by Lucy Graham, Cape Town, February 25, 2009.

55. Krouse, "Bella," 31.

56. Samuelson, "The Rainbow Womb," 88. As evidence of this, Samuelson cites a 1992–1996 study that records the rate of interracial rape in South Africa as only 1.65 per cent of recorded rapes, and cites a "U.S. statistic" as evidence of the "comparably" low rate of "conception" in cases of rape. I find the inference that rape would result in a "comparably" lower rate of "conception" than normal sexual intercourse misleading and problematic. As Sabine Sielke points out, disassociation between rape and conception retrogressively evokes an old belief that conception "requires orgasm or heat, and the involvement of bodily fluids from both partners," as expressed, for instance, in Laqueur's *Making Sex* (quoted in Sielke, *Reading Rape*, 193). In reality, the rate of *conception* for rape victims should be comparable to that for any single sexual act of sexually-active women in the general population. The rate of *pregnancy* in the post-apartheid period, on the other hand, is indeed likely to be lower in cases of rape due to the victim's access to legal abortion.

57. Farida Karodia, *Daughters of the Twilight* (London: the Women's Press, 1986), 134.

58. Sharon Pillai's article "Remarkable Coincidence or what? A comparison of Karmala Markandaya's *Two Virgins* and Farida Karodia's *Daughters of the Twilight*," *Journal of the*

School of Languages, Literature and Culture Studies, New Series, 5 (2004), 36–47, appears to suggest a questionable relationship between the two novels.

59. Karodia, *Daughters of the Twilight*, 1.

60. Karmala Markandaya, *Two Virgins* (London: Chatto & Windus, 1974 (first published in USA in 1973)), 84.

61. Karodia, *Daughters of the Twilight*, 5–6.

62. Ibid., 119.

63. Ibid., 121.

64. Ibid., 136.

65. Farida Karodia, *Other Secrets* (Johannesburg: Penguin, 2000). This lapse of more than a decade in negotiating a South African publisher suggests a concern that the novel would be banned by the apartheid regime.

66. Samuelson, "The Rainbow Womb," 96.

67. Karodia, *Other Secrets*, 139.

68. Ibid., 142.

69. M. J. Daymond, afterword in Lauretta Ngcobo, *And They Didn't Die* (New York: Feminist Press at CYNU, 1999), 247.

70. Ibid., 253.

71. Ibid.

72. Grahamstown: Rhodes University, Cory Library, General Missionary Conference, Commission on Assaults on Women, MS 14847, Olive Schreiner to James Henderson, December 26, 1911.

73. Olive Schreiner, *From Man to Man*, (London: T. Fisher Unwin, 1926), 301.

74. Ibid. This was possibly added by Cronwright Schreiner, who edited the unfinished novel for publication after Schreiner's death.

75. Schreiner, *From Man to Man*, 307.

76. In a note where the story of *From Man to Man* finally breaks off, Cronwright Schreiner attests to the endings that Schreiner discussed with him regarding the novel's two white woman protagonists.

77. Schreiner, *From Man to Man*, 411.

78. Ngcobo, *And They Didn't Die* (London: Virago Press, 1990), 205–206.

79. Ibid., 101.

80. Ibid., 207.

81. Ibid., 228.

82. Ibid., 229.

83. Frantz Fanon, *The Wretched of the Earth* (Harmondsworth: Penguin, 1967), 200.

84. Ibid., 204–205.

85. Ibid., 203.

86. Ibid., 208.

87. Ngcobo, *And They Didn't Die*, 242.

88. Ibid., 245.

89. Valerie Smith, "Split Affinities: The Case of Interracial Rape" in Marianne Hirsch and Evelyn Fox-Keller (eds.), *Conflicts in Feminism* (London: Routledge, 1990), 275.

90. Ngcobo, *And They Didn't Die*, 193.

91. Njabulo S. Ndebele, *Fools and Other Stories* (Johannesburg: Ravan Press, 1983), 277–278.

92. Ibid., 160.

93. Ibid., 164.

94. During his MA studies at Cambridge, Ndebele "delved into Soviet writing and the great tradition of Russian literature." See: Njabulo Ndebele, Interview with Andries Walter Olifant, "The Writer as Critic and Interventionist," *Staffrider* 7.3–4 (1988), 342.

95. Fanon, *Black Skin, White Masks*, 14.

96. Ndebele, *Fools*, 205.

97. Ibid., 164.

98. Ibid., 189.

99. Ibid., 23.

100. Ndebele, "The Rediscovery of the Ordinary," in *The Rediscovery of the Ordinary: Essays in South African Culture and Literature* (Johannesburg: Cosaw, 1991), 47, 57.

101. Ndebele, *Fools*, 217.

102. Ibid., 275.

103. Ibid., 161.

104. Ibid., 160.

105. Ibid., 226.

106. Ibid., 229.

107. Ibid., 202.

108. Ibid., 193.

109. Ibid., 194–195.

110. Ibid., 195.

111. Ibid., 138.

112. Ibid., 194.

113. Ibid., 168.

114. Higgins and Silver, *Rape and Representation*, 5–6.

115. Conversation with Ramadan Suleman in Nwachukwu Frank Ukadike, *Questioning African Cinema: Conversations with Filmmakers* (Minneapolis: University of Minnesota, 2002), 294.

116. Lindiwe Dovey, "Engendering Gender Discourses through African Cinema: The Case of *Fools* (1998) and *Karmen Gei* (2001)," unpublished paper presented at *Writing African Women: The Poetics and Politics of African Gender Research*, Conference at the University of the Western Cape, 19–22 January 2005, f. 10.

117. Cape Town: National Archives, Njabulo S. Ndebele, *Fools and Other Stories*, IDP 3/225 P88/3/23.

118. Ndebele, *Fools*, 220.

119. Gcina Mhlophe, "Nokulunga's Wedding," in Annemarie van Niekerk (ed.), *The Torn Veil: Women's Stories from the Continent of Africa* (Cape Town: Queillerie, 1998), 123.

120. Ibid., 124.

121. Ibid.

122. Ibid., 127.

123. Ibid., 127.

124. Mahmood Mamdani, "Amnesty or Impunity? A Preliminary Critique of the Report of the Truth and Reconciliation Commission," *Diacritics* 32.3–4 (2002), 50.

125. Mhlophe, "Nolukunga's Wedding," 129.

126. Ama Ata Aidoo, *Changes: A Love Story*, New York: Feminist Press, 1991, 9.

127. Mhlophe, "Nolukunga's Wedding." 129.

128. Baleka Kgositsile, "In the Night," *Rixaka* (Lusaka: ANC, 1988), 43.

129. Ibid., 40.

130. Ibid., 42.

131. Ibid., 43.

132. Ibid.

133. Sielke, *Reading Rape*, 151.

134. Interview with Ramadan Suleman in Nwachukwu Frank Ukadike, *Questioning African Cinema: Conversations with Filmmakers* (Minneapolis: University of Minnesota Press, 2002), 293.

Chapter 5

1. J.M. Coetzee, *Disgrace*, 156.

2. Achmat Dangor, *Bitter Fruit* (Cape Town: Kwela Books, 2001), 32.

3. Interview with Fred de Vries, quoted in Sam Raditlhalo, "'The Travelling Salesman': a tribute to K. Sello Duiker, 1974–2005," *Feminist Africa*, 11, 2008. http://www.feministafrica.org/index.php/k-sello-duiker.

4. Lisa Vetten, "Violence against Women in South Africa," in S. Buhlungu and others (eds.), *State of the Nation, South Africa, 2007* (Cape Town: HSRC Press, 2007) 425.

5. Lillian Artz, "The Weather Watchers: Gender, Violence and Social Control in South Africa," in *The Prize and the Price: Shaping Sexualities in South Africa* (HSRC Press, 2009), 175.

6. Helen Moffett, "'These Women, They Force Us to Rape Them: Rape as Narrative of Social Control in Post-Apartheid South Africa," *Journal of Southern African Studies* 32.1 (March 2006), 129.

7. Gayatri Chakravorty Spivak, "Woman in Difference: Mahasweta Devi's 'Douloti the Bountiful,'" in Andrew Parker, Mary Russo, Doris Sommer, and Patricia Yaeger (eds.), *Nationalisms and Sexualities* (New York: Routledge, 1992), 97–98.

8. The texts chosen for analysis in this chapter are by no means the only literary representations of sexual violation in post-apartheid fiction. Some of the texts not discussed include the post-apartheid novels of André Brink, many of which deal with gender violence; Jo-Anne Richard's *The Innocence of Roast Chicken*; Zakes Mda's *The Madonna of Excelsior* and Rachel Zadok's *Gem-Squash Tokoloshe*, (both of which center on "white peril" incidents); and Megan Voysey-Braig's *Till We Can Keep an Animal*.

9. Zoë Wicomb, "To Hear the Variety of Discourses," *Current Writing* 2 (October 1990), 54.

10. Cherryl Walker, *Women and Resistance in South Africa* (London: Onyx Press, 1982), preface to the 1991 edition, xi, xiii-xiv.

11. Vetten, "Violence against Women in South Africa," 435.

12. Charlene Smith, "Keeping It in Their Pants: Politicians, Men and Sexual Assault in South Africa," paper presented in the Harold Wolpe Lecture Series, University of KwaZulu Natal, March 17, 2005. http://www.wolpetrust.org.za/dialogue2005/DN032005smith_paper.htm.

13. Meg Samuelson claims that violence against women is "ascendant" (Meg Samuelson, "The Rainbow Womb: Race and Rape in South African Fiction of the Transition," *Kunapipi* 24.1&2 (2003), 88). Helen Moffett states that sexual violence has "spiralled" and reached "epidemic proportions" (Helen Moffett, "These Women," 129). Similarly, Lisa Vetten says that rape figures showed "an upward trend" between 1994–1995 and 2004–2005 (Vetten, "Violence

against Women in South Africa," 430). While she looks at available statistics, Vetten does not take into account population increase, nor was she aware of later figures that actually show a decrease in reported rape. Taking into account population increase, and thus measuring reported rape by cases per 100,000 population, according to the *South Africa Survey* from there has been no significant increase in reported rapes from 1994 to 2008 (*South Africa Survey 2007–8*, Johannesburg: Institute of Race Relations, 556, 570, 1995–2008).

14. Veena Das, "Language and Body: Transactions in the Construction of Pain," in Veena Das, Arthur Kleinman and Margaret Lock (eds.), *Social Suffering* (Berkeley: University of California Press, 1997), 34.

15. Njabulo Ndebele, "Why Zuma's Bravado is Brutalising the Public," *Sunday Times*, South Africa, March 5, 2006.

16. Ibid.

17. Pumla Dineo Gqola, "The Difficult Task of Normalizing Freedom: Spectacular Masculinities, Ndebele's Literary/Cultural Commentary and Post-Apartheid Life," *English in Africa* 36 No. 1 (May 2009), 61.

18. Part of a series entitled "Disasters of Peace," Victor's etching was made before the Zuma rape trial or Zuma's prosecution for corruption.

19. Pierre de Vos, "Constitutionally Speaking: On Zuma, Zapiro and that Cartoon," September 8, 2008. http://constitutionallyspeaking.co.za/?p=658.

20. Christopher Warnes, "Writing Crime in the New South Africa: Negotiating Threat in the Novels of Deon Meyer, Margie Orford, and Andrew Brown," unpublished paper, 2011.

21. J.M. Coetzee, *Stranger Shores: Essays 1986–1999* (London: Secker & Warburg, 2001), 259. As I demonstrate in chapter 3, Coetzee must have read the Gollancz or Chameleon Press edition of *Mittee*, because Rooke did in fact originally script a "black peril" rape, which is retained in the American first edition and in the recent Toby Press edition.

22. Sol Plaatje, *The Mote and the Beam*, 283.

23. J.M. Coetzee, *Disgrace* (London, Secker and Warburg, 1999), 110. All further references to *Disgrace* will be to this edition.

24. Ibid., 25.

25. Ibid., 50.

26. Ibid., 99.

27. Ibid., 107.

28. Ibid., 134.

29. Ibid., 140.

30. Ibid., 158.

31. Higgins and Silver (eds.), *Rape and Representation*, 3.

32. Ibid., 6.

33. Ibid.

34. Michael Marais, "Self-fulfilling Racism," letter, *Mail & Guardian* (April 28—May 4, 2000), 27.

35. Coetzee, *Disgrace*, 112.

36. Ibid., 112.

37. Michael Marais, "Very Morbid Phenomena: 'Liberal Funk', the 'Lucy-Syndrome' and JM Coetzee's *Disgrace*," *Scrutiny2* 6.1 (2001), 32.

38. Gayatri Spivak, "Ethics and Politics in Tagore, Coetzee and Certain Scenes of Teaching," *Diacritics* 32.3–4 (Fall-Winter 2002), 21; Ian Glenn, "Gone for Good: Coetzee's *Disgrace*," *English in Africa* 36.2 (October 2009), 88.

39. Spivak, "Ethics and Politics," 22–23.

40. Lucy Hughes-Hallett writes that Lurie "seduces a young female student," and other reviewers represent his abuse of Melanie as an "affair." Overlooking the violation entirely, Albert du Toit explains that the "affair" between Lurie and Melanie "blossoms but soon sours." Even an astute critic such as Derek Attridge describes what transpires between David and Melanie as "an affair." See: Lucy Hughes-Hallett, "Coetzee Triumphs in Description of Fall from Grace," *Saturday Argus: The Good Weekend*, August 7, 1999, 5; Michael Morris, "Coetzee Thinks Publicly about New SA," *Cape Argus*, August 10, 1999; 16; Toni Younghusband, review of *Disgrace*, *Femina*, September 1999, 148; Max Du Preez "It's a disgrace, but the truth is . . . ," *The Star*, January 27, 2000, 18; Albert du Toit, "Finely Tuned Novel Set in New SA," *Eastern Province Herald*, August 11, 1999, 4; Derek Attridge, "*Age of Bronze*, State of Grace: Music and Dogs in Coetzee's *Disgrace*," *Novel: A Forum on Fiction* 34.1 (2000), 98–121.

41. Meg Samuelson, "Writing Rape 'in this Place at this Time': J.M. Coetzee's *Disgrace*," in Samuelson, *Remembering the Nation, Dismembering Women*, 140–153.

42. Elizabeth Lowry, "Like a Dog," *London Review of Books*, October 14, 1999, 12.

43. Coetzee, *Disgrace*, 16.

44. Ibid., 91.

45. Ibid., 24.

46. Lawrence Venuti, "Translation, Interpretation, Canon Formation," in *Translation and the Classic,* eds. Alexandra Lianeri and Vanda Zajko (Oxford University Press, 2008), 27, 34–35.

47. Ibid., 18.

48. Plaatje, *The Mote and the Beam*, 277.

49. Dorothy Driver, "'Woman' as Sign in the South African Colonial Enterprise," *Journal of Literary Studies* 4.1 (March 1988), 16.

50. Coetzee, *Disgrace*, 156.

51. Ibid., 53.

52. Ibid., 53, my emphasis, 112.

53. Coetzee, *Disgrace*, p.3.

54. Ibid., 2, 10.

55. Andrew van der Vlies, *J.M. Coetzee's Disgrace: A Reader's Guide* (London: Continuum, 2010), 86.

56. Coetzee, *Disgrace*, 11.

57. Ibid., 19.

58. Ibid., 24–25.

59. Ibid.

60. Ibid.

61. Coetzee, *Disgrace*, 29.

62. This is in direct contrast with the representation of Lucy's body. When, in the film, Lucy's dressing gown falls open in front of her father and a young black man, there is a sense of shock, her naked breasts are distinctly un-erotic, the very epitome of the sacrosanct aspect of the white female body.

63. Coetzee, *Disgrace*, 43.

64. Jacques Derrida, "On Forgiveness," trans. Simon Critchley, in Jacques Derrida, *On Cosmopolitanism and Forgiveness* (London: Routledge, 2001), 45.

65. Jacques Derrida, *The Gift of Death* (Chicago: University of Chicago Press, 1995), 64.

66. Ibid., 66.

67. Ibid., 67.

68. Coetzee, *Disgrace*, 158.

69. Ibid., 52.

70. Ibid., 166.

71. Derrida, *The Gift of Death*, 76.

72. Coetzee, *Disgrace*, 133.

73. J.M. Coetzee, *Foe* (London: Penguin, 1986), 122.

74. Coetzee, *Disgrace*, 155.

75. Plaatje, *The Mote and the Beam*, 283.

76. J.M. Coetzee, *White Writing: On the Culture of Letters in South Africa* (New Haven, Yale University Press, 1988).

77. Ibid., 13.

78. See: Susan Brownmiller, *Against our Will: Men, Women and Rape* (New York, Fawcett Columbine, 1975), 24.

79. J.M. Coetzee, *Dusklands* (Johannesburg: Ravan Press, 1974), 18.

80. Ibid., 61.

81. Ibid., 33.

82. Derek Attridge, *J. M. Coetzee and the Ethics of Reading: Literature in the Event* (Chicago: University of Chicago Press, 2004), 28.

83. Ibid., 28.

84. Coetzee, *White Writing*, 9.

85. Coetzee, *Disgrace*, 105.

86. Cape Town: National Archives, Publications Control Board, BCS 26963, file on Daphne Rooke, *The Greyling*.

87. National Archives, Cape Town, IDP P77/09/103, Coetzee, *Heart of the Country* file.

88. See: Peter McDonald, "Not Undesirable: How J.M. Coetzee Escaped the Censor," *Times Literary Supplement* (May 19, 2000), 14–15.

89. J.M. Coetzee, "Autobiography and Confession," interview with David Attwell, in David Attwell (ed.), *Doubling the Point: Essays and Interviews* (Cambridge, Massachusetts, Harvard, 1992), 248.

90. Ibid.

91. Coetzee, *Disgrace*, 133.

92. Coetzee, "The Harms of Pornography," 80; emphasis added.

93. Coetzee, *Disgrace*, 115.

94. Ibid., 34.

95. Ibid., 158.

96. Amina C. Mama, "Sheroes and Villains: Conceptualising Colonial and Contemporary Violence Against Women in Africa," in Jacqueline Alexander and Chandra Mohanty (eds.), *Feminist Genealogies, Colonial Legacies, Democratic Futures* (London, Routledge, 1997), 47–62.

97. Coetzee, "The Harms of Pornography," 75.

98. For discussion of rape in Western art, see: Diane Wolfthal, *Images of Rape: The Heroic Tradition and Its Alternatives* (Cambridge: Cambridge University Press, 2000).

99. Coetzee, *Disgrace*, 160.

100. Ibid., 160.

101. Ibid., 52.

102. Ibid., 25.

103. Ibid., 21–22, emphasis added.

104. Ibid., 25.

105. Coetzee, "The Harms of Pornography," 74.

106. Coetzee, "The Harms of Pornography," 72.

107. Ibid., 73–74.

108. Coetzee, *Disgrace*, 64.

109. Ibid., 146.

110. Ibid.

111. Ibid., 90.

112. Ibid., 159.

113. Ibid., 160.

114. Coetzee, *Stranger Shores*, 40.

115. The opera and its revisions are elided in the film of *Disgrace*.

116. Ibid., 182.

117. Ibid., 215.

118. There is also an incident of gender violence, though not specifically rape, in *Elizabeth Costello*, when Elizabeth narrates how she was once attacked by a sailor. J.M. Coetzee, *Elizabeth Costello* (London: Secker & Warburg, 2003) 165. Jacqueline Rose has berated Coetzee for scripting this scene. Jacqueline Rose, "Coetzee's Women," paper delivered at the conference Making Waves: Literary Studies in an Interdisciplinary Frame, Robinson College, Cambridge, July 2003.

119. J.M. Coetzee, *Diary of a Bad Year*, 97.

120. J.M. Coetzee, *Summertime*, 72.

121. For instance, in *Age of Iron* Elizabeth Curren mentions both menstruation and childbirth, and images of defecation and imagined childbirth appear in *In the Heart of the Country*. In *Foe* Susan Barton describes sexual intercourse with Cruso and Foe.

122. Coetzee, *Diary of a Bad Year*, 92.

123. Tessa Hadley, "J. M. Coetzee, *Disgrace*," in Liam McIlvanney and Ray Ryan (eds.), *The Good of the Novel* (London: Faber & Faber, 2011), 57.

124. Coetzee, *Disgrace*, 160.

125. Spivak, "Ethics and Politics," 23.

126. Beth Goldblatt and Sheila Meintjes, "Dealing with the aftermath—sexual violence and the Truth and Reconciliation Commission," *Agenda*, 36 (1999), 7.

127. Binaifer Nowrojee and Bronwen Manby, *Violence against Women in South Africa* (New York: Human Rights Watch, 1995), 21.

128. Quoted in Goldblatt and Meintjes, "Dealing with the Aftermath," 11.

129. *Report of the Truth and Reconciliation Commission*, Volume 4, chapter 10.

130. Dangor, *Bitter Fruit*, 59.

131. Ibid., 117.

132. Ibid., 18.

133. Meg Samuelson, "Speaking Rape 'Like a Man': Achmat Dangor's *Bitter Fruit*," 2004. http://web.uct.ac.za/depts/religion/documents/ARISA/2004_AL4.pdf.

134. Dangor, *Bitter Fruit*, 115.

135. Ibid., 32.

136. Achmat Dangor, interview with Audrey Brown, *Insig*, January/February 2002, 70.

137. See Fanon, *Wretched of the Earth* (Harmondsworth: Penguin, 1967), 204–208. There was no Truth Commission after Algeria attained independence in 1962, and Fanon's case studies are to my knowledge the only published record of "the talking cure" as a treatment for trauma resulting from political crimes in the French-Algerian conflict. Notably, in Fanon's publication the speakers remain anonymous and their testimonies are only available in the public sphere through Fanon's case studies.

138. Dangor, *Bitter Fruit*, 16.

139. Ibid., 115.

140. Ibid., 115.

141. Ibid., 114.

142. Ibid., 115.

143. The Centre for Applied Legal Studies' submission, "Gender and the Truth and Reconciliation Commission," drafted by Sheila Meintjes and Beth Goldblatt, is available online at: http://www.truth.org.za/submit/gender.htm. (See also *Report of the Truth and Reconciliation Commission*, Volume 4, 288–289).

144. Mark Sanders, "Extraordinary Violence," *Interventions: International Journal of Postcolonial Studies* 3.2 (2001), 246.

145. Dangor, *Bitter Fruit*, 111.

146. According to the mandate of the TRC, "gross violation of human rights" meant "the violation of human rights through (a) the killing, abduction, torture, or severe ill-treatment of any person; or (b) any attempt, conspiracy, incitement, instigation, command, or procurement to commit an act referred to in paragraph (a), which emanated from conflicts of the past and which was committed during the period 1 March 1960 to 10 May 1994 within or outside the Republic, and the commission of which was advised, planned, directed, commanded or ordered, by any person acting with a political motive" (section l(l)(ix)). [TRC Report, 1: 60.]

147. Shane Graham, "The Truth Commission and Post-Apartheid Literature in South Africa," *Research in African Literatures* 34.1 (2003), 12.

148. Mahmood Mamdani, "Amnesty or Impunity? A Preliminary Critique of the Report of the Truth and Reconciliation Commission," *Diacritics* 32.3–4 (2002), 33.

149. See: Mark Sanders, *Ambiguities of Witnessing: Law and Literature in the Time of a Truth Commission* (Stanford: Stanford University Press, 2007).

150. Jacques Derrida, *On Cosmopolitanism and Forgiveness* (London: Routledge, 2002), 45.

151. Ariel Dorfman, "A Vicious Circle," *The Guardian*, January 17, 2008. http://www.guardian.co.uk/world/2008/jan/17/chile.theatre.

152. Dangor, *Bitter Fruit*, 19.

153. Ibid., 108.

154. Ibid., 188.

155. Ibid., 156.

156. Ibid., 182–183.

157. Ibid., 91.

158. *Report of the Truth and Reconciliation Commission*, Volume 4, chapter 10. http://www.nelsonmandela.org/omalley/index.php/site/q/03lv02167/04lv02264/05lv02335/06lv02357/07lv02387/08lv02397.htm.

159. Ampie Coetzee and James Polley (eds.) *Crossing Borders: Writers Meet the ANC* (Bramley: Taurus, 1990), 150.

160. *Report of the Truth and Reconciliation Commission*, Volume 4, chapter 10, paragraph 50 http://www.nelsonmandela.org/omalley/index.php/site/q/03lv02167/04lv02264/05lv02335/06lv02357/07lv02387/08lv02397.htm.

161. Ingrid Sinclair (director), *Flame* (1996).

162. Media Rights website—Films, FLAME. http://www.mediarights.org/film/flame.

163. Zoë Wicomb, *David's Story* (Cape Town: Kwela Books, 2000), 178.

164. Meg Samuelson, *Remembering the Nation: Dismembering Women?* (Pietermaritzburg: University of Kwazulu-Natal Press, 2007), 128.

165. Wicomb, *David's Story*, 123.

166. Thenjiwe Mtintso, quoted in Truth and Reconciliation Commission, Special Hearings, Chapter 10.

167. Wicomb, *David's Story*, 35.

168. Ibid.

169. Stephan Meyer and Thomas Olver, "Zoë Wicomb Interviewed on Writing and Nation," *Journal of Literary Studies* 18.1 (2002), 182–198.

170. Ibid.

171. Ibid., 35.

172. Ibid., 78.

173. Ibid., 192–193.

174. Spivak, translator's preface in Derrida, *Of Grammatology*, xv.

175. Ibid., xvii.

176. Wicomb, interview with Meyer and Olver.

177. Wicomb, *David's Story*, 124.

178. Wicomb, interview with Meyer and Olver.

179. Wicomb, *David's Story*, 117.

180. Ibid., 135.

181. Ibid., 150–151.

182. Ibid., 184. The only definitive indication that Dulcie has been tortured by the proponents of freedom lies outside of the text, in an interview with Wicomb, where the mode of the authorial interview shuts down ambiguity, even as Wicomb speaks about "unknowableness":

> . . . . a liberation movement, driven to taking up arms, necessarily adopts the tactics of the enemy. My novel does assert that abominable things happen in the name of freedom—take the torturing of Dulcie—but it also at the same time casts her in mythological terms, hopefully to open up the idea of truth, to wrest it from the pieties of liberal humanism, and to assert a measure of unknowableness about that past. (Wicomb, interview with Meyer and Olver).

183. Wicomb, *David's Story*, 115.

184. Ibid., 82.

185. Ibid., 83.

186. Ibid., 179.

187. Ibid., 136.

188. Dangor, *Bitter Fruit*, 115.

189. K. Sello Duiker, *The Quiet Violence of Dreams* (Cape Town: Kwela Books, 2001), 139.

190. Joseph Slaughter *Human Rights Inc.: The World Novel, Narrative Form and International Law* (New York: Fordham University Press, 2007), 4.

191. Ibid., 5.

192. Ibid., 38.

193. Ibid.

194. Mark Behr, *Die Reuk van Appels* (Strand: Queillerie, 1993).

195. Tony Morphet, cited in Rita Barnard, "*The Smell of Apples, Moby Dick* and Apartheid Ideology," *Modern Fiction Studies* 46.1 (Spring 2000), 207. Behr's novel won the M-Net literary award, the Eugene Marais Prize, the CNA literary debut award, the Betty Trask award in the United Kingdom, and the *Los Angeles Times* Art Seidenbaum award.

196. Mark Behr, "South Africa: Living in the Fault Lines, Cape Town, July 4, 1996," *Common Sense*, October 14, 1996.

197. Cheryl Stobie bases her discussion of bisexuality in Behr's novel around her claim that the author was a "double agent." Given the details of his confession, however, it is by no means clear that Behr was a "double agent," and moreover it seems that he is gay, rather than bisexual. Stobie also problematically claims that Marnus's father in *The Smell of Apples* is "bisexual." See Cheryl Stobie, *Somewhere in the Double Rainbow: Representations of Bisexuality in Post-Apartheid Novels* (Pietermaritzburg: University of KwaZulu-Natal Press, 2007).

198. Behr, "South Africa: Living in the Fault Lines," 13.

199. Mark Behr, *The Smell of Apples* (London: Abacus, 1995), 67.

200. Ibid., 45.

201. Ibid., 171–172.

202. Published in the same year as the Afrikaans edition of *The Smell of Apples*, Elleke Boehmer's *An Immaculate Figure* similarly uses an intraracial sexual violation (though not male rape) in order to draw attention to the corruption within white society. In Boehmer's novel, a white beauty queen Rosandra narrates to her friend Jem how the powerful and charismatic Thony, "the man who built the star palace", entered her bedroom and forced himself upon her while she slept. See: Elleke Boehmer, *An Immaculate Figure* (London: Bloomsbury, 1993), 110–112.

203. Ibid., 175–177.

204. Rita Barnard claims that "[Behr's] revelation of a homosexual act at the very heart of apartheid's darkness flirts with a sensationalism similar to that deployed by the government itself." See Barnard, "*The Smell of Apples, Moby Dick* and Apartheid Ideology," *Modern Fiction Studies* 46.1 (2000). In her account of bisexuality in South African fiction, Cheryl Stobie claims that the rape of Frikkie makes Marnus's father bisexual.

205. Notes of informal discussion with Mark Behr by Lucy Graham, Stellenbosch, May 21, 2009.

206. Behr, *The Smell of Apples*, 179.

207. Ibid., 116.

208. Ibid., 179.

209. Ibid., 178.

210. Barnard, "*The Smell of Apples, Moby Dick* and Apartheid Ideology," 212.

211. Ibid., 219

212. Behr, *The Smell of Apples*, 180.

213. Slaughter, *Human Rights Inc.*, 32.

214. Behr, *The Smell of Apples*, 151.

215. Herman Melville, *Moby Dick* (Ware: Wordsworth Classics, 1992, first edition, 1851), chapters 4, 72.

216. Foucault, *Society Must be Defended*, 259–260.

217. K. Sello Duiker, *Thirteen Cents* (Cape Town: David Philip, 2000), 1.

218. Ibid., 142.

219. K. Sello Duiker, "The Streets and the Gods of Truth," *Rhodes Journalism Review*, September 2004. http://www.rjr.ru.ac.za/rjrpdf/rjr_no24/streets_gods_truth.pdf.

220. According to Roslyn Mickelson in a recent book, *Children on the Streets: Globalization, Homelessness, and Education in the United States, Brazil and Cuba* (London: Routledge, 2000), unlike the US and Brazil, Cuba has demonstrated a willingness to provide for the social welfare of its children, despite the fact that it is not a wealthy country. Noting, however, that with the recent opening of the market in Cuba street children are beginning to appear, Mickleson argues that the presence of homeless children is related to globalization and the emergence of free trade. As noted by José Álvarez Blanco, President of the NGO "Voices for Latin America," the issue of street children is a global problem directly related to the effects of capitalism and neoliberalism, which accentuate dire poverty, leading among the poor to the breakdown of the family and the formation of sub-cultures such as gangs and prostitution circles. Alvarez Blanco speaks on street children, *The Carletonian*, May 30, 2008.

221. Hans Bergmann, *The God in the Street: New York Writing from the Penny Press to Melville* (Philadelphia: Temple University Press, 1995), 95.

222. Ibid., 98.

223. Duiker, *Thirteen Cents*, 30.

224. Ibid., 52, 54.

225. Ibid., 43.

226. Ibid.

227. Ibid., 41.

228. Ibid., 53.

229. E-mail correspondence in possession of Lucy Graham, 2009.

230. Cited in Chris MacGreal, "Reality TV," *The Guardian*, January 22, 2002. However, while *Yizo Yizo* openly criticizes the conditions in government schools, its attitude to the prison environment is more ambiguous. The show suggests that Chester, who himself is a rapist, deserves his treatment in prison, and thus any real criticism of the prison system is actually avoided. Young viewers saw the message of the incident not as being that South African disciplinary modes need to be rethought, but rather that viewers should take care to avoid going to jail where they would be forced to have "that kind of sex."

231. Sasha Gear, "Sex, Sexual Violence and Coercion in Men's Prisons," paper presented at *AIDS in Context* conference, University of the Witwatersrand, 2001. http://www.csvr.org.za/wits/papers/papgear1.htm.

232. Duiker, *Quiet Violence*, 41.

233. Ibid., 42.

234. Ibid., 139.

235. Interview with de Vries, quoted in Raditlhalo, "The Travelling Salesman," 184.

236. Duiker, *Quiet Violence*, 184.

237. Ibid., 212.

238. Ibid., 213.

239. Ibid., 197.

240. Foucault, *Discipline and Punish*, 168.

241. Duiker, *Quiet Violence*, 214.

242. Ibid., 343.

243. The mythology of Horus (Egyptian god of the Lower Kingdom) includes a narrative of male rape in that Horus's enemy Set (god of the Upper Kingdom) tries to rape Horus in order to show his dominance over him, but Horus outwits Set by tricking him into ingesting Horus's semen instead.

244. Duiker, *Quiet Violence*, 445.

245. Ibid., 454.

246. Duiker, *Quiet Violence*, 454.

247. Slaughter, *Human Rights Inc.*, 182.

248. Ibid.

249. Ibid., 25.

250. Encounters: South African International Documentary Film Festival, 2002, blurb for "The Dark Heart," directed by Clifford Bestall. http://www.encounters.co.za/archive/2002/films.html.

251. Achille Mbembe, "What is Postcolonial Thinking? An Interview with Achille Mbembe," *Eurozine*, January 9, 2008. http://www.eurozine.com/articles/2008-01-09-mbembe-en.html.

252. Deborah Posel, "The Scandal of Manhood: 'Baby Rape' and the Politicization of Sexual Violence in Post-Apartheid South Africa," *Culture, Health and Sexuality*, 7, 3 (2005), 239–252.

253. Lara Foot-Newton, *Tshepang: The Third Testament* (Johannesburg: Wits University Press, 2005).

254. Hugh Kirkegaard & Wayne Northey, *The Sex Offender as Scapegoat: Vigilante Violence and a Faith Community Response.* http://www.religion.emory.edu/faculty/smith/vr/wayne.html.

255. René Girard, *Violence and the Sacred*, trans. Patrick Gregory (London: Continuum, 2005), 7.

256. Ibid., 2.

257. Leo Lefebure, "Victims, Violence and the Sacred: the Thought of René Girard," 1996. http://lonestar.texas.net/~mseifert/girard.html2.

258. Nicky Naylor, "Sexism in the Media," *Rhodes Journalism Review*, 24 (2004), 57.

259. Lara Foot-Newton, cited in LSM Newswire, "Tshepang, Theatre La Chapelle & Maurice Podrey's Mopo Productions," February 4, 2009. http://www.scena.org/blog/newswire/2009/02/tshepang-theatre-la-chapelle-maurice.html.

260. Gerhard Marx, "Designer's Note," in Lara Foot-Newton, *Tshepang: The Third Testament* (Johannesburg: Wits University Press, 2005), x.

261. Lara Foot-Newton and Gerhard Marx (film directors), *And There in the Dust*, 2005.

262. Historically South African cinema has focused on white protagonists as registers for the drama depicted on screen. An example would be *Cry Freedom*, which places Donald Woods at the center of a story about Steve Biko.

263. Foot-Newton, *Tshepang: The Third Testament*, 38–39.

264. Lara Foot-Newton, quoted in *Tshepang: the Third Testament*, 2009. http://www.scena.org/blog/newswire/2009/02/tshepang-theatre-la-chapelle-maurice.html.

265. Lara Foot-Newton, quoted in *Tshepang: the Third Testament*, 2009. http://www.scena.org/blog/newswire/2009/02/tshepang-theatre-la-chapelle-maurice.html.

266. Foot-Newton, *Tshepang: The Third Testament*, 40.

267. Lara Foot-Newton, quoted in Carolyn Dempster, "South African Trial Brings Rape into Public View," *News from Africa*, 2006. http://www.newsfromafrica.org/newsfromafrica/articles/art_10669.html.

The figure that Foot-Newton cites here comes from police statistics, and refers to figures of both rape and attempted rape of those under the age of 18 (National Department of Health, 2004).

268. Suzannne Leclerc-Madlala, quoted in Charlene Smith, "The Relation between HIV-Prevalence and Virgin Rape," *News from the Nordic Africa Institute*, No. 2, 2003. http://www.nai.uu.se/publications/news/archives/203smith/.

269. Charlene Smith, "The Relation between HIV-Prevalence and Virgin Rape," *News from the Nordic Africa Institute*, No. 2, 2003. http://www.nai.uu.se/publications/news/archives/203smith/.

270. R. Jewkes, L. Martin, and L. Penn-Kekana, "The Virgin Cleansing Myth: Cases of Child Rape are not Exotic," *The Lancet* 359 (2001), 9307: 711.

271. G. Pitcher, and D. Bowley, "Infant Rape in South Africa," *The Lancet* 359 (2002), 9303: 274–275.

272. Marianne Merten, "MPs Give Baby Rape Documentary the Thumbs up," *Mail & Guardian*, September 9, 2002.

273. Oprah Winfrey, *The Oprah Winfrey Show*, "Children at Risk: South African Baby Raping," July 15, 2004. http://www2.oprah.com/tows/slide/200407/20040715/tows_slide_20040715_01.jhtml.

274. Alan Little, "AIDS: A South African Horror story," BBC News, 2002. http://news.bbc.co.uk/1/hi/programmes/correspondent/2311067.stm.

275. Fred Rundle, "961 Child Rapes a Day in South Africa," *Jeff Rense Program*, 2004. http://www.rense.com/general56/RAPES.HTM.

276. Matthew Lewin, "Bring me my Assegai," review of Deon Meyer's *Devil's Peak*, *The Guardian*, Saturday July 21, 2007. http://books.guardian.co.uk/review/story/0,,2131078,00.html.

277. David Hickson (director), *Beat the Drum*, 2006.

278. Achille Mbembe, "What is Postcolonial Thinking? An Interview with Achille Mbembe," *Eurozine*, January 9, 2008, trans. John Fletcher. http://www.eurozine.com/articles/2008-01-09-mbembe-en.html.

279. Foot-Newton, *Tshepang*, 28.

280. Ibid., 45.

281. Lara Foot-Newton and Gerhard Marx (directors), *And There in the Dust*, 2005.

282. Foot-Newton, *Tshepang*, 37.

283. Deborah Posel, "The Scandal of Manhood: 'Baby Rape' and the Politicization of Sexual Violence in South Africa", *Culture, Health and Sexuality* 7.3 (May 2005), 240–241.

284. Ibid., 247.

285. Ibid., 248–249.

286. Ibid., 249.

287. Ibid., 247.

288. Gavin Hood (director), *Tsotsi*, 2005.

289. Athol Fugard, *Tsotsi* (Johannesburg: Ad. Donker, 1980).

Conclusion

1. Jonny Steinberg, "Of Blocked Paths, Borrowed Dreams and Zuma's appeal," *Open Society Foundations*. http://www.soros.org/initiatives/fellowship/articles_publications/articles/steinberg_20090518.

{ BIBLIOGRAPHY }

Printed Sources
PRIMARY

Aidoo, Ama Ata, *Changes: A Love Story* (New York: Feminist Press, 1991).

Bancroft, Francis, *Of Like Passions* (London: Sisley's Ltd., 1907).

Barter, Charlotte [published as by "A Plain Woman"], *Alone among the Zulus, the Narrative of a Journey through the Zulu Country* (London: Society for the Propagation of Christian Knowledge (n.d., [c.1866]).

Behr, Mark, *Die Reuk van Appels* (Strand: Queillerie, 1993).

———, *The Smell of Apples* (London: Abacus, 1995).

Boehmer, Elleke, *An Immaculate Figure* (London: Bloomsbury, 1993).

Brink, André, *Cape of Storms: The First Life of Adamastor* (New York: Simon & Schuster, 1997).

Camões, Luiz Vaz de, *The Lusíads*, trans. Landeg White (Oxford: Oxford University Press, 1997).

Cloete, Stuart, *Turning Wheels* (London: Collins, 1937).

Coetzee, J.M., *Age of Iron* (London: Secker & Warburg, 1990).

———, *Diary of a Bad Year* (London: Secker & Warburg, 2007).

———, *Disgrace* (London: Secker & Warburg, 1999).

———, *Dusklands* (Johannesburg: Ravan Press, 1974).

———, *Elizabeth Costello* (London: Secker & Warburg, 2003).

———, *Foe* (London: Penguin, 1986).

———, *In the Heart of the Country* (London: Secker & Warburg, 1977).

———, *Summertime* (London: Secker & Warburg, 2009).

———, *The Lives of Animals* (Princeton: Princeton University Press, 1999).

Dangor, Achmat, *Bitter Fruit* (Cape Town: Kwela Books, 2000).

Doherty, C. (ed.), *Porno* (Grahamstown: Bobbejaan Press, 1989).

Duiker, K. Sello, *The Quiet Violence of Dreams* (Cape Town: Kwela Books, 2001).

———, *Thirteen Cents* (Cape Town: David Philip, 2000).

Foot-Newton, Lara, *Tshepang: The Third Testament* (Johannesburg: Witwatersrand University Press, 2005).

Fugard, Athol, *Tsotsi* (Johannesburg: Ad. Donker, 1980).

Garvey, Marcus, *The Tragedy of White Injustice* (New York: Amy Jacques Garvey, 1927).

Hardy, George Webb, *The Black Peril* (London: Holden & Hardingham, 1912).

———, "The Black Peril," *The Prince* (October 7, 1904).

Harris, Trudier (ed.), *Selected Works of Ida B. Wells-Barnett* (New York: Oxford University Press, 1991).

Hoffman, E.T.A., "The Sandman," trans. R.J. Hollingdale, in *The Tales of Hoffman* (London: Penguin, 1982).

Karodia, Farida, *Daughters of the Twilight* (London: The Women's Press, 1986).

——, *Other Secrets* (Johannesburg: Penguin, 2000).

Kgositsile, Baleka, "In the Night," *Rixaka: Cultural Journal of the African National Congress*, special issue, "Culture in Another South Africa" (Lusaka: ANC, 1988).

Kipling, Rudyard, "A Sahib's War," in *A Century of Anglo-Boer War Stories*, selected and introduced by Chris N. van der Merwe and Michael Rice (Johannesburg: Jonathan Ball, 1999).

Krouse, Matthew, "Bella," in C. Doherty (ed.) *Porno* (Grahamstown: Bobbejaan Press, 1989).

Maimane, Arthur, *Hate No More* (Johannesburg: Kwela Books, 2000).

——, *Victims* (London: Alison & Busby, 1976).

Markandaya, Karmala, *Two Virgins* (London: Chatto & Windus, 1974 (first published in USA in 1973)).

Marryat, F., *The Mission: Or Scenes in Africa* (Leipzig: Bernhard Tauchnitz, 1845).

Mda, Zakes, *Ways of Dying* (Cape Town: Oxford University Press, 1997).

Melville, Herman, *Moby Dick* (Ware: Wordsworth Classics, 1992, first edition, 1851).

Mhlophe, Gcina, "Nokulunga's Wedding," in Annemarie van Niekerk (ed.) *The Torn Veil: Women's Stories from the Continent of Africa* (Cape Town: Queillerie, 1998).

Millin, Sarah Gertrude, *God's Stepchildren* (Craighall: Ad. Donker, 1986 (first published, 1924)).

——, *King of the Bastards* (London: Heinemann, 1950).

——, *The Burning Man* (London: Heinemann, 1952).

——, *The Wizard Bird* (London: Heinemann, 1962).

——, "Why Adonis laughed," *New Adelphi*, June-August, 1929, 255–259.

Modisane, Bloke, *Blame Me on History* (London: Thames & Hudson, 1963).

Money, Edward, *The Wife and Ward; Or, A Life's Error* (London: Routledge, 1859).

Moor, Charlotte, "Colonia," *Marina de la Rey* (London: Digby, Long and Co., 1903).

Morrison, Toni, *The Bluest Eye* (London, Vintage, 1999), first published 1970.

Ndebele, Njabulo S., *Fools and Other Stories* (Johannesburg: Ravan Press, 1983).

Ngcobo, Lauretta, *And They Didn't Die* (London: Virago Press, 1990).

——, *And They Didn't Die* (Johannesburg: Skotaville, 1990).

——, *And They Didn't Die* (New York: Feminist Press at CUNY, 1999).

Nicholls, George Heaton, *Bayete! Hail to the King* (London: George Allen & Unwin, 1923).

Nkosi, Lewis, *Home and Exile* (London: Longman, 1965).

——, *Mating Birds* (Nairobi: East African Publishing House, 1983).

——, *Mating Birds* (New York: St Martin's Press, 1986).

——, "The Black Psychiatrist," *Weber Studies* 13. 2 (1994), 5–24.

Page, Thomas Nelson, *Red Rock: A Chronicle of Reconstruction* (Albany: N.C.U.P., 1991), first published 1898.

Plaatje, Sol, *The Mote and the Beam: An Epic on Sex-Relationship 'twixt White and Black in British South Africa* in Brian Willan (ed.), *Sol Plaatje: Selected Writings* (Johannesburg: University of the Witwatersrand Press, 1996), first published 1921.

——, *Native Life in South Africa* (London: P.S. King & Son, 1916).

Plomer, William, "Black Peril," in Stephen Gray (ed.) *William Plomer, Selected Stories* (Cape Town: David Philip, 1984).

——, *Turbott Wolfe* (London: Hogarth Press, 1965), first published 1925.

Preller, Gustav, "Lettie," trans. Madeline van Biljon, in Chris N. van der Merwe and Michael Rice (eds.), *A Century of Anglo-Boer War Stories* (Johannesburg: Jonathan Ball, 1999).

Rogers, Joel Augustus, *As Nature Leads: An Informal Discussion of the Reason Why Negro and Caucasian are Mixing in Spite of Opposition* (Chicago: M.A. Donahue, 1919).

Rooke, Daphne, *Diamond Jo* (London: Gollancz, 1965).

——, *The Greyling* (London: Gollancz, 1962).

——, *The Greyling* (New York: Reynal, 1963).

——, *Mittee* (London: Victor Gollancz, 1951).

——, *Mittee* (Boston: Houghton, Mifflin, 1952).

——, *Mittee*, with an introduction by Ian Glenn (Cape Town, Chameleon Press, 1987).

——, *Mittee*, with an afterword by J.M. Coetzee, (London: Penguin, 1991).

——, *Mittee*, with an afterword by J.M. Coetzee (New Milford, USA: Toby Press, 2007).

——, *Three Rivers: a Memoir* (Cambridge: Daffodil Press, 2003).

Schreiner, Olive, *From Man to Man* (London: T. Fisher Unwin, 1926).

——, *Trooper Peter Halket of Mashonaland* (London: T. Fisher Unwin, 1897).

——, *Trooper Peter Halket of Mashonaland*, with introduction by Marion Friedmann (Johannesburg: Ad. Donker, 1974).

Stead, W.T., *If Christ Came to Chicago* (Chicago: Laird & Lee, 1894).

——, *Methods of Barbarism* (London: Review of Reviews, 1901).

——, *How Not to Make Peace* (London: Review of Reviews, 1900).

Taylor, Dora, *Don't Tread on My Dreams*, Sheila Belshaw and Michael Muskett (eds.) with afterword by Dorothy Driver (Johannesburg: Penguin, 2008).

——, "To Tell my Story," in *Don't Tread on my Dreams*, 1–55.

Tlali, Miriam, *Muriel at Metropolitan* (Johannesburg: Ravan Press, 1975).

Van Niekerk, Annemarie (ed.), *The Torn Veil: Women's Stories from the Continent of Africa* (Cape Town: Queillerie, 1998).

Wells-Barnett, Ida B., *Crusade for Justice* (Chicago: University of Chicago Press, 1970).

Wicomb, Zoë, *David's Story* (Cape Town: Kwela Books, 2000).

Willan, Brian (ed.) *Sol Plaatje: Selected Writings* (Johannesburg: Witwatersrand University Press, 1996).

Printed Sources
SECONDARY

Adorno, Theodor, *Aesthetic Theory*, trans. R.Hullot-Kentor (London: Athlone Press), 1997.

——, *Introduction to the Sociology of Music*, trans. E. Ashton (New York, Continuum International, 1976).

Agamben, Giorgio, *Homo Sacer* (Stanford: Stanford University Press, 1998).

Alexander, Jacqueline, and Chandra Talpade Mohanty (eds.), *Feminist Genealogies, Colonial Legacies, Democratic Futures* (New York: Routledge, 1997).

ANC News Briefing, "Mediaracism-ANC," South African Press Association, Johannesburg, April 5, 2000.

Anderson, Benedict, *Imagined Communities: Reflections on the Origin and Spread of Nationalism* (London: Verso, 1983).

Armstrong, Nancy, "Captivity and Cultural Capital in the English Novel," *Novel: A Forum on Fiction* 31.3 (1998), 373–398.

Artz, Lillian, "The Weather Watchers: Gender Violence and Social Control," in *The Prize and the The Price: Shaping Sexualities in South Africa* (HSRC Press, 2009), 169–191.

Ashcroft, Bill, Gareth Griffiths and Helen Tiffin, *The Empire Writes Back: Theory and Practice in Post-Colonial Literatures* (London: Routledge, 1989).

Athenaeum, anonymous review of Schreiner, *Trooper Peter Halket*, February 27, 1897.

Attridge, Derek, "Age of Bronze, State of Grace: Music and Dogs in Coetzee's *Disgrace*," *Novel: A Forum on Fiction* 34.1 (2000), 98–121.

——, *J.M. Coetzee and the Ethics of Reading: Literature in the Event* (Chicago: University of Chicago Press, 2004).

Attridge, Derek, and Rosemary Jolly, *Writing South Africa: Literature, Apartheid and Democracy, 1970–1995* (Cambridge: Cambridge University Press, 1998).

Attwell, David, and Barbara Harlow, "Introduction: South African Fiction After Apartheid," *Modern Fiction Studies* 6.1 (2000), 1–9.

Aubertin, J.J., *Introduction, The Lusíads of Camões* (London: Kegan Paul, 1878).

Baines, Barbara, "Effacing Rape in Early Modern Representation," *English Literary History* 65.1 (Spring 1998), 69–98.

Bakhtin, Mikhail, "Discourse in the Novel," *The Dialogic Imagination: Four Essays*, Michael Holquist, (ed.) Caryl Emerson and Michael Holquist (trans.) (Austin: University of Texas at Austin, 1981).

——, "Dostoevsky's Polyphonic Novel and its Treatment in Critical Literature" in *Problems of Dostoevsky's Poetics*, Caryl Emerson ed. and trans. (Minneapolis: University of Minnesota Press, 1984).

Bakker, Dirk, "Vroue-lewens word daagliks bedreig," election advertisement for The New National Party, 1999 elections, *Huisgenoot*, May 27, 1999, 41.

Bal, Meike, 1986, "The Rape of Narrative and the Narrative of Rape: Speech Acts and Body Language in Judges," in Elaine Scarry (ed.) *Language and the Body: Essays on Populations and Persons* (Baltimore: John Hopkins University Press, 1986).

Bamforth, Nicholas (ed.), *Sex Rights: the Oxford Amnesty Lectures, 2002* (Oxford: Oxford University Press, 2005).

Barnard, Rita, "*The Smell of Apples, Moby Dick* and Apartheid Ideology," *Modern Fiction Studies* 46.1 (2000), 207–226.

Barthelme, Donald, "Manual for Sons," in *Sixty Stories* (London: Penguin, 2003), first published in 1981.

Behr, Mark, "South Africa: Living in the Fault Lines, Cape Town, July 4, 1996," *Common Sense*, October 1996.

Beinart, William, "*Amafelandawonye* (the Die-hards): Popular Protest and Women's Movements in Herschel District in the 1920s," in W. Beinart and C. Bundy (eds.), *Hidden Struggles in Rural South Africa: Politics and Popular Movements in the Transkei and Eastern Cape, 1890–1930* (Johannesburg: Ravan Press, 1987), 222–269.

Bergmann, Hans, *The God in the Street: New York Writing from the Penny Press to Melville* (Philadelphia: Temple University Press, 1995).

Bhabha, Homi K. *The Location of Culture* (London: Routledge, 1994).

———, "Signs Taken for Wonders: Questions of Ambivalence and Authority under a Tree outside Delhi, May 1817," in Bhabha, *The Location of Culture*, 102–122.

Blackwood's Magazine, anonymous review of Olive Schreiner, *Trooper Peter Halket*, April 1897.

Blackmore, Josiah, *Moorings: Portuguese Expansion and the Writing of Africa* (Minneapolis: University of Minnesota Press, 2009).

Blair, Peter, "That Ugly Word: Miscegenation and the Novel in Preapartheid South Africa," *Modern Fiction Studies* 49.3 (2003), 581–613.

Boehmer, Elleke, *Stories of Women: Gender and Narrative in the Postcolonial Nation* (Manchester: Manchester University Press, 2005).

Bradford, Helen, *A Taste of Freedom: The ICU in Rural South Africa, 1924–30* (New Haven: Yale University Press, 1987).

Brantlinger, Patrick, *Rule of Darkness: British Literature and Imperialism, 1830–1914* (Ithaca: Cornell University Press, 1988).

Braun, Lavinia, "Not Gobineau but Heine: Not Racial Theory but Biblical Theme: the Case of Sarah Gertrude Millin," *English Studies in Africa* 34.1 (1991), 27–38.

Brickhill, Joan, "Self-indulgent, Unrealistic: *Victims* by Arthur Maimane," *Africa Magazine*, December 1976.

Brink, André, "A Myth of Origin," in Ivan Vladislavic (ed.), *T'kama-Adamastor: Inventions of Africa in a South African Painting* (Johannesburg: University of Witwatersrand Press), 41–48.

———, "Reimagining the Past: André Brink in Conversation with Reingard Nethersole," in Vladislavic (ed.),*T'Kama Adamastor*, 49–57.

———, *Cape of Storms: The First Life of Adamastor* (New York: Simon & Schuster, 1997).

Brookes, Edgar H., and Colin de B. Webb, *A History of Natal* (Pietermaritzburg: University of Natal Press, 1967).

Brownmiller, Susan, *Against Our Will: Men, Women and Rape* (New York: Fawcett Columbine, 1975).

Butler, Judith, *Gender Trouble* (London, Routledge, 1999).

———, "On Being Beside Oneself," in N. Bamforth (ed.), *Sex Rights: the Oxford Amnesty Lectures, 2002* (Oxford: Oxford University Press, 2005).

———, "On Speech, Race and Melancholia," interview with Vicki Bell, *Theory, Culture and Society* 16.2 (1999).

Campbell, James T., *Songs of Zion: The African Methodist Episcopal Church in the United States and South Africa* (New York: Oxford University Press, 1995).

Cape Argus, anonymous review of Olive Schreiner, *Trooper Peter Halket*, March 10, 1897.

Carby, Hazel, "'On the Threshold of Woman's Era': Lynching, Empire and Sexuality in Black Feminist Theory," in Henry Louis Gates and Kwame Anthony Appiah (eds.) *"Race," Writing and Difference* (Chicago: University of Chicago Press, 1986).

Carr, John Dickson, *The Life of Sir Arthur Conan Doyle* (London: John Murray, 1949).

Cell, John, *The Highest Stage of White Supremacy: The Origins of Segregation in South Africa and the American South* (Cambridge: Cambridge University Press, 1982).

Chait, Sandra, "Mythology, Magic Realism, and White Writing after Apartheid," *Research in African Literatures* 31.2 (2000), 17–28.

Chapman, Michael, Colin Gardner and Es'kia Mphahlele (eds.), *Perspectives on South African English Literature* (Johannesburg: Ad. Donker, 1992).

Chrisman, Laura, *Rereading the Imperial Romance: British Imperialism and South African Resistance in Haggard, Schreiner and Plaatje* (Oxford: Oxford University Press, 2000.

Coetzee, Ampie, and James Polly, *Crossing Borders: Writers Meet the ANC* (Bramley: Taurus, 1990).

Coetzee, J.M., afterword in Daphne Rooke, *Mittee* (New Milford, USA: Toby Press, 2007).

———, "Autobiography and Confession," interview with David Attwell, in David Atwell (ed.) *Doubling the Point: Essays and Interviews* (Cambridge, Massachusetts: Harvard University Press, 1992).

———, "Blood, Flaw, Taint, Degeneration: the Case of Sarah Gertrude Millin," in *White Writing: On the Culture of Letters in South Africa* (New Haven: Yale University Press, 1988), 136–162.

———, *Doubling the Point: Essays and Interviews*, David Attwell (ed.) (Cambridge, Massachusetts: Harvard University Press, 1992).

———, *Giving Offense: Essays on Censorship* (Chicago: University of Chicago Press, 1996).

———, "The Harms of Pornography," in *Giving Offense: Essays on Censorship*, 61–82.

———, "Jerusalem Prize Acceptance Speech," in Coetzee, *Doubling the Point: Essays and Interviews*, 96–99.

———, "The Novel Today," *Upstream* (1988), 2–5.

———, *Stranger Shores: Essays 1986–1999* (London: Secker and Warburg, 2001).

———, *White Writing: On the Culture of Letters in South Africa* (New Haven: Yale University Press, 1988).

Cope, R.K., "Young Writer Produces a Bestseller," review of Daphne Rooke, *Mittee, Cape Times*, March 13, 1952.

Cornwell, Gareth, "Always Somewhere Else," *Southern African Review of Books* (March-April, 1996).

———, "Francis Bancroft's *Of Like Passions* and the Politics of Sex in Early Twentieth Century South Africa," *English in Africa* 25.2 (October 1998), 1–36.

———, "George Webb Hardy's *The Black Peril* and the Social Meaning of 'Black Peril' in Early Twentieth Century South Africa," *Journal of Southern African Studies* 22.3 (1996), 441–453.

Couzens, Tim, *The New African, a Study of the Life and Work of H.I.E. Dhlomo* (Johannesburg: Ravan Press, 1985).

Critchley, Simon, *Very Little . . . Almost Nothing: Death, Philosophy, Literature* (London: Routledge, 1997).

Cronwright Schreiner, S.C., *Olive Schreiner: Her Re-intermennt on Buffelskop*, with introduction by Paul Walters and Jeremy Fogg (Grahamstown: NELM, 2005).

Cuklanz, Lisa M., "The Masculine Ideal: Rape on Prime-Time Television," *Critical Studies in Mass Communication* 15.4 (1998), 423–449.

Daalder, Joost, "Shakespeare's "The Rape of Lucrece," *Explicator* 55.4 (Summer 1997), 195–197.

Danby, Frank, "The Case of Olive Schreiner," review of *Trooper Peter Halket, Saturday Review*, April 10, 1897.

Dangor, Achmat, interview with Audrey Brown, *Insig*, January/February 2002.

Das, Veena, "Language and Body: Transactions in the Construction of Pain," in Veena Das, Arthur Kleinman and Margaret Lock (eds.), *Social Suffering* (Berkeley: University of California Press, 1997).

Daymond, Margaret J. afterword in L. Ngcobo, *And They Didn't Die* (New York: Feminist Press at CUNY, 1999).

Daymond, Margaret J (ed.), *South African Feminisms* (New York: Garland, 1996).

Derrida, Jacques, *Of Grammatology* (Baltimore: Johns Hopkins University Press, 1976).

———. *On Cosmopolitanism and Forgiveness* (London: Routledge, 2002).

———, "Plato's Pharmacy" in *Dissemination*, trans. Barbara Johnson (Chicago: Chicago University Press, 1981), 63–171.

———. *The Gift of Death* (Chicago: University of Chicago Press, 1995).

Dodd, Josephine, "The South African Literary Establishment and the Textual Production of 'Woman': J.M. Coetzee and Lewis Nkosi," *Current Writing: Text and Reception in Southern Africa* (October 1990), 117–129.

Dovey, Teresa, *The Novels of J.M. Coetzee: Lacanian Allegories* (Johannesburg: Ad. Donker, 1988).

Doyle, Arthur Conan, *The Great Boer War*, Revised and Enlarged Edition (New York: McClure, Philips and Company), 1902.

———, *The War in South Africa: Its Cause and Conduct* (London: Smith, Elder and Company, 1902).

Driver, C.J., "Sincere but Wrong," review of Maimane, *Victims* and other books, *Guardian*, May 5, 1977.

Driver, Dorothy, "'Woman' as Sign in the South African Colonial Enterprise," *Journal of Literary Studies* 4.1 (1988), 3–20.

———, "Women as Objects of Exchange: Towards a Feminist Analysis of South African Literature," in Michael Chapman, Colin Gardner, and Es'kia Mphahlele (eds.), *Perspectives on South African English Literature* (Johannesburg: Ad. Donker, 1992).

Duiker, K. Sello, "The Streets and the Gods of Truth," *Rhodes Journalism Review*, September 2004.

Du Preez, Max, "It's a Disgrace, but the Truth is. . . . ," *The Johannesburg Star*, January 27, 2000.

Du Toit, Albert, "Finely Tuned Novel Set in the New SA," *Eastern Province Herald*, August 11, 1999.

Dvorin, Eugen P., *Racial Separation in South Africa* (Chicago: University of Chicago Press, 1952).

Eagleton, Terry, *The Rape of Clarissa: Writing, Sexuality and Class Struggle in Samuel Richardson* (Oxford: Blackwell, 1998).

———, *Sweet Violence: The Idea of the Tragic* (Oxford: Blackwell, 2003).

Elia, Nada, "'To be an African Working Woman': Levels of Feminist Consciousness in Ama Ata Aidoo's *Changes*," *Research in African Literatures* 30.2 (1999), 136–147.

Ellmann, Maud, "The Power to Tell: Rape, Race and Writing in Afro-American Women's Fiction," *An Introduction to Contemporary Fiction: International Writing in English Since 1970*, Rod Mengham (ed.) (Cambridge: Polity Press, 1999).

Etherington, Norman, "Natal's Black Rape Scare of the 1870s," *Journal of Southern African Studies* 15.1 (1988), 36–53.

Fanon, Frantz, *Black Skin, White Masks* (New York: Grove, 1967).

——— *The Wretched of the Earth* (Harmondsworth: Penguin, 1967).

Film and Publications Board, *From Censorship to Classification* (Cape Town: The Film and Publications Board, no date).

First, Ruth, and Ann Scott, *Olive Schreiner* (London: André Deutsch, 1980).

Foucault, Michel, *Michel Foucault: Politics, Philosophy, Culture. Interviews and Other Writings*, L. Kritzman (ed.) (London: Routledge, 1988).

——, *Society Must Be Defended, Lectures at the Collège de France, 1975–6*, trans. David Macey (New York: Picador, 2003).

——, *The Will to Knowledge: The History of Sexuality Vol. I*, trans. Robert Hurley (London: Penguin 1998).

Frederickson, George, *White Supremacy: A Comparative Study on American and South African History* (New York and Oxford: Oxford University Press, 1981)

Freud, Sigmund, *The Uncanny*, trans. David McLintock (London: Penguin, 2003).

Fryer, Peter, *Staying Power: The History of Black People in Britain* (London: Pluto Press, 1984).

Gates, Henry Louis, and Kwame Anthony Appiah (eds.) *"Race," Writing and Difference* (Chicago: University of Chicago Press, 1986).

Gevisser, Mark, *Thabo Mbeki: The Dream Deferred* (Johannesburg: Jonathan Ball, 2007).

Gilroy, Paul, *After Empire: Melancholia or Convivial Culture?* (Abingdon: Routledge, 2004).

Girard, René, *Violence and the Sacred*, trans. Patrick Gregory (London: Continuum Books, 2005).

Glenn, Ian, "Gone for Good: Coetzee's *Disgrace*," *English in Africa* 36.2 (October 2009), 79–98.

——, "Legislating Women," *Journal of Literary Studies* 12.1 & 2 (1996), 135–170.

——, "The Production and Prevention of a Colonial Author—the Case of Daphne Rooke," *New Contrast* 22.1 (1984), 78–85

——, "The Wreck of the Grosvenor and the Making of South African Literature," *English Studies in Africa* 22. 2 (1995), 1–18.

Goldblatt, Beth, and Sheila Meintjes, "Dealing with the Aftermath—Sexual Violence and the Truth and Reconciliation Commission," *Agenda* 36 (1999), 7–18.

Goldsmith, Meredith, "Of Masks, Mimicry, Misogyny and Miscegenation: Forging Black South African Masculinity in Bloke Modisane's Blame me on History," *The Journal of Men's Studies* 10.3 (2002), 291–307.

Gqola, Pumla Dineo, "'The Difficult Task of Normalizing Freedom': Spectacular Masculinities, Ndebele's Literary/Cultural Commentary and Post-Apartheid Life," *English in Africa* 36.1 (May 2009), 61–76.

Graham, Lucy Valerie, "'A Hidden Side to the Story': Reading Rape in Recent South African Literature," *Kunapipi* 24.1 & 2 (2003), 105–125.

——, "'Bathing Area—For Whites Only': Reading Prohibitive Signs and 'Black Peril' in Lewis Nkosi's *Mating Birds*," in Lindy Stiebel and Liz Gunner (eds.), *Still Beating the Drum, Critical Perspectives on Lewis Nkosi* (Amsterdam: Rodopi, 2005), 147–164.

——, "'Consequential Changes': Daphne Rooke's *Mittee* in America and South Africa," *Safundi: The Journal of South African and American Studies* 10.1 (2009), 43–58.

——, "Reading the Unspeakable: Rape in J.M. Coetzee's *Disgrace*," *Journal of Southern African Studies* 29.2 (2003), 433–444.

——, "Re-imagining the Cave: Gender, Land and Imperialism in Olive Schreiner's *Trooper Peter Halket of Mashonaland* (1897)," *English Studies in Africa* 50.1(2007), 25–40.

——, "Save Us All: 'Baby Rape' and Post-apartheid Narratives," *Scrutiny2* 13.1 (2008), 105–119.

———, "'Yes, I am giving him up': Sacrificial Responsibility and Likeness with Dogs in J M Coetzee's Recent Fiction," in *Scrutiny2* 7.1 (2002), 4–15.

Graham, Shane, "The Truth Commission and Post-Apartheid Literature in South Africa," *Research in African Literatures* 34.1 (2003), 11–30.

Gravdal, Kathryn, *Ravishing Maidens: Writing Rape in Medieval French Literature and Law* (Philadelphia: University of Pennsylvania Press, 1991).

Gray, Stephen, "Nkosi-roman" (review of Nkosi, *Mating Birds*), *Insig*, August 1987.

———, "Schreiner's Trooper at the Hanging Tree," *English in Africa* 2.2 (1975), 23–37.

———, Southern African Literature: An Introduction (Cape Town: David Philip, 1979).

Green, Martin, *Dreams of Adventure, Deeds of Empire* (New York: Basic Books, 1970).

Greenberg, Stanley, *Race and State in Capitalist Development* (New Haven: Yale University Press, 1980).

Gunning, Sandra, *Race, Rape and Lynching: The Red Record of American Literature, 1890–1912* (New York: Oxford University Press, 1996).

Hadley, Tessa, "J.M. Coetzee, *Disgrace*," in Liam McIlvanney and Ray Ryan (eds.), *The Good of the Novel* (London: Faber & Faber, 2011), 42–59.

Halttunen, Karen, "Humanitarianism and the Pornography of Pain in Anglo-American Culture," *American Historical Review* 100.2 (1996), 303–334.

Hancock, W.K., and J. van der Poel (eds.), *Selections from the Smuts Papers, June 1886-May 1902* (Cambridge: Cambridge University Press, 1966).

Hardt, Michael and Antonio Negri, *Multitude* (London: Penguin, 2006).

Harris, Janice, "On Tradition, Madness, and South Africa: an Interview with Lewis Nkosi," *Weber Studies* 11.2 (Spring/Summer, 1994), 25–37.

Harrison, Hubert, review of Plaatje, *The Mote and the Beam*, *Negro World*, April 23, 1921.

Heyns, Michiel, "Fathers and Sons: Structures of Erotic Patriarchy in Afrikaans Writing of the Emergency," *Ariel* 27.1 (January 1996), 81–104.

Higgins, Lynn A., and Brenda R. Silver, *Rape and Representation* (New York: Columbia University Press, 1991).

Hirsch, Marianne, and Evelyn Fox-Keller (eds.), *Conflicts in Feminism* (London: Routledge, 1990).

Hirshowitz, Ros, Sebele Worku, and Mark Orkin, Quantitative Research Findings on Rape in South Africa (Pretoria: Statistics South Africa, 2000).

Hopkins, Pauline, *Contending Forces: a Romance Illustrative of Negro Life North and South* (Carbondale: Southern Illinois University Press, 1978 (first published 1900)).

Horek, Tanya, *Public Rape: Representing Violation in Fiction and Film* (London: Routledge, 2003).

Hughes-Hallett, Lucy, "Coetzee Triumphs in Description of Fall from Grace," *Saturday Argus: The Good Weekend*, August 7, 1999.

Hyslop, Jonathan, "White Working-class Women and the Invention of Apartheid: 'Purified' Afrikaner Nationalist Agitation against 'Mixed' Marriages, 1934–9," *Journal of African History* 36.1 (1995), 57–81.

Illustrated London News, anonymous review of Schreiner, *Trooper Peter Halket*, March 6, 1897.

Institute of Race Relations, *South Africa Survey, 2007–8* (Johannesburg: Institute of Race Relations, 2008).

Jameson, Frederic, *The Political Unconscious* (Ithaca: Cornell University Press, 1982).

Jed, Stephanie, *Chaste Thinking: The Rape of Lucretia and the Birth of Humanism* (Bloomington: Indiana University Press, 1989).

Jewkes, Rachel, Lorna Martin and Loveday Penn-Kekana, "The Virgin-Cleansing Myth: Cases of Child Rape are not Exotic," *The Lancet* (2002) 359: 711.

Jolly, Rosemary, "Gun as Copula: Colonisation, Rape, and the Question of Pornographic Violence in J.M. Coetzee's Dusklands," *World Literature Written in English 32.2 & 33.1 (1992/1993)*, 44–55.

Keegan, Timothy, "Gender, Degeneration and Sexual Danger: Imagining Race and Class in South Africa, ca. 1912," *Journal of Southern African Studies* 27.3 (2001), 459–447.

Kelly, Amy, *Eleanor of Aquitaine and the Four Kings* (New York: Random House, 1959).

Krebs, Paula, *Gender Race and the Writing of Empire: Public Discourse and the Boer War* (Cambridge: Cambridge University Press, 2004).

Kritzman, L. (ed.), *Michel Foucault: Politics, Philosophy, Culture, Interviews and Other Writings* (London: Routledge, 1988).

Lessing, Doris, *Walking in the Shade: Volume Two of my Autobiography 1949–1962* (London: Harper Collins, 1997).

Leveson, Marcelle, *People of the Book: Images of the Jew in South African English Fiction* (Johannesburg: University of the Witwatersrand Press, 2001).

Loomba, Ania, *Gender, Race, Renaissance Drama* (Manchester: Manchester University Press, 1989).

——, *Shakespeare, Race and Colonialism* (Oxford: OUP, 2002).

Lowry, Elizabeth, "Like a Dog," *London Review of Books*, October 14, 1999, 12–14.

McClintock, Ann, *Imperial Leather: Race, Gender and Sexuality in the Colonial Contest* (London: Routledge, 1995).

McClure, John, *Late Imperial Romance* (London: Verso, 1994).

MacCrone, I.D., *Race Attitudes in South Africa: Historical, Experimental, and Psychological Studies* (Johannesburg: Oxford University Press, 1937).

McDonald, Peter, "Not Undesirable: How J.M. Coetzee Escaped the Censor," *Times Literary Supplement*, May 19, 2000.

——, *The Literature Police: Apartheid Censorship and its Cultural Consequences* (Oxford: Oxford University Press, 2009).

McGreal, Chris, "Reality TV," *The Guardian*, January 22, 2002.

McKinstry, Leo, *Rosebery: Statesman in Turmoil* (London: John Murray, 2005).

McMurry, Linda, *To Keep the Waters Troubled: The Life of Ida B. Wells* (New York: Oxford University Press, 1998).

Mama, Amina C., "Sheroes and Villains: Conceptualising Colonial and Contemporary Violence against Women in Africa," in Jacqueline Alexander and Chandra Talpade Mohanty (eds.), *Feminist Genealogies, Colonial Legacies, Democratic Futures* (New York: Routledge, 1997), 46–62.

Mamdani, Mahmood, "Amnesty or Impunity? A Preliminary Critique of the Report of the Truth and Reconciliation Commission," *Diacritics* 32.3–4 (2002).

Mann, Harveen Sachdeva, "Woman in Decolonisation: The National and Textual Politics of Rape in Saadat Hasan Manto and Mahasweta Devi," *Journal of Commonwealth Literature* 33.2 (1998), 127–141.

Marais, Mike, "'Little Enough, Less than Little, Nothing': Ethics, Engagement, and Change in the Fiction of J.M. Coetzee," *Modern Fiction Studies* 46.1 (Spring 2000), 159–182.

——, "Self-fulfilling Racism," *Mail & Guardian*, April 28, 2000.

——, "Very Morbid Phenomena: 'Liberal Funk', the 'Lucy-Syndrome' and J.M. Coetzee's *Disgrace*," *Scrutiny2* 6.1 (2001), 32–38.

Marks, Shula, "Natal, the Zulu Royal Family and the Ideology of Segregation," in William Beinart and Saul Dubow (eds.) *Segregation and Apartheid in Twentieth Century South Africa* (London: Routledge, 1995).

——, *Reluctant Rebellion: the 1906–8 Disturbances in Natal* (Oxford: Clarendon Press, 1970).

——, "White Masculinity: Jan Smuts, Race and the South African War," *Proceedings of the British Academy* 111 (2001), 199–223.

Martens, Jeremy C., "Settler Homes, Manhood and 'Houseboys': An Analysis of Natal's Rape Scare of 1886," *Journal of Southern African Studies* 28.2 (2002), 379–400.

Marx, Gerhard, "Designer's Note," in Lara Foot-Newton, *Tshepang: The Third Testament* (Johannesburg: University of Witwatersrand Press, 2005).

Masson, Madeline, *Lady Anne Barnard: The Court and Colonial Service under George III and the Regency* (London: George Allen and Unwin, 1948).

Mbeki, Thabo, "AIDS: Mbeki vs. Leon," *The Sunday Times, South Africa*, July 1, 2000.

Mbembe, Achille, (trans. L. Meintjies), "Necropolitics," *Public Culture* 15.1 (2003), 11–40.

——, *On the Postcolony* (Berkeley: University of California Press, 2001).

Merten, Marianne, "MPs Give Baby Rape Documentary the Thumbs up," *Mail & Guardian*, September 9, 2002.

Mickelson, Roslyn, *Children on the Streets: Globalization, Homelessness, and Education in the United States, Brazil and Cuba* (London: Routledge, 2000).

Millin, Sarah Gertrude, *The Night is Long* (London: Faber & Faber, 1941).

——, *The South Africans* (London: Constable, 1926).

Morris, Michael, "Coetzee Thinks Publicly about New South Africa," *Cape Argus*, August 10, 1999.

Nasson, B., *The South African War 1899–1902* (London: Arnold, 1999).

Naylor, Nicky, "Sexism in the Media," *Rhodes Journalism Review* 24 (2004), 57–58.

Ndebele, Njabulo S., interview with Andries Walter Olifant, "The Writer as Critic and Interventionist," *Staffrider* 7. 3 & 4. (1988), 341–346.

——, *The Rediscovery of the Ordinary: Essays in South African Culture and Literature* (Johannesburg: Cosaw, 1991).

——, "Why Zuma's Bravado is Brutalising the Public," *Sunday Times*, March 5, 2006.

Nehru, Jawaharlal, *Towards Freedom: The Autobiography of Jawaharlal Nehru* (Boston: Beacon Press, 1967).

New York Herald Tribune Book Review, "What America is Reading," anonymous review of Daphne Rooke's *Mittee*, May 4, 1952.

Nicholls, George Heaton, *South Africa in My Time* (London: George Allen & Unwin, 1961).

Nkosi, Lewis, "Postmodernism and Black Writing in South Africa," in Derek Attridge and Rosemary Jolly (eds.), *Writing South Africa: Literature, Apartheid and Democracy, 1970–95* (Cambridge: Cambridge University Press, 1998), 75–90.

——, "On Tradition, Madness, and South Africa," interview with Janice Harris, *Weber Studies* 11.2 (Spring/Summer, 1994), 25–37.

——, *Tasks and Masks: Themes and Styles of African Literature* (Harlow, Essex: Longman, 1981).

Nowrojee, Binaifer, and Bronwen Manby, Violence against Women in South Africa: The State Response to Domestic Violence and Rape (New York: Human Rights Watch/Africa and Human Rights Watch Women's Project, 1995).

Nuttall, Sarah, "Girl Child," *Social Text* 22.1 (2004), 17–33.

Nuttall, Sarah, and Carli Coetzee (eds.), *Negotiating the Past: The Making of Memory in South Africa* (Oxford: Oxford University Press, 1998).

O'Neill, Frank, "Two Daphnes Write Heady Novels of Romance and Suspense," review of Daphne Rooke, *Mittee, Cleveland News*, February 12, 1952.

Paxton, Nancy, *Writing Under the Raj: Gender, Race and Rape in the British Colonial Imagination, 1830–1947* (Piscataway: Rutgers University Press, 1999).

Peires, Jeff, "Lovedale and Literature for the Bantu Revisited," *English in Africa* 7.1 (1980), 71–85.

Pillai, Sharon, "Remarkable Coincidence or What? A Comparison of Karmala Markandaya's Two Virgins and Farida Karodia's Daughters of the Twilight," *Journal of the School of Languages, Literature and Culture Studies, New Series* 5 (2004), 36–47.

Pitcher, G., and D. Bowley, "Infant Rape in South Africa," *The Lancet* 359 (2002), 9303: 274–275.

Posel, Deborah, "The Scandal of Manhood: 'Baby Rape' and the Politicization of Sexual Violence in Post-apartheid South Africa," *Culture, Health and Sexuality* 7.3 (2005), 239–252.

Pretorius, F., *Life on Commando during the Anglo-Boer War, 1899–1902* (Cape Town: Human & Rousseau, 1999).

Punch, anonymous review of Olive Schreiner, *Trooper Peter Halket*, March 6, 1897.

Pursell, Tim, "Queer Eyes and Wagnerian Guys: Homoeroticism in the Art of the Third Reich," *Journal of the History of Sexuality* 17.1 (2008), 110–137.

Purves, John, "Camões and the Epic of Africa," *The State* 2.11, (November 1909), 542–555 and 2.12 (December 1909), 734–745.

Quiller-Couch, Arthur, review of *Trooper Peter Halket, The Speaker*, April 3, 1897.

Raath, A.W.G. and R.M. Louw, *Vroueleed* [Women's Sorrow] (Bloemfontein: Oorlogsmuseum, 1993).

"Racial Conflict," anonymous review of Daphne Rooke, *Mittee, Times Literary Supplement*, December 21, 1952.

Radziwill, Princess Catherine, *The Resurrection of Peter: A Response to Olive Schreiner* (London: Hurst & Blackett, 1900).

Rajan, Rajeswari Sunder, *Real and Imagined Women: Gender, Culture and Postcolonialism* (London: Routledge, 1993).

———, *Scandal of the State: Women, Law and Citizenship in Postcolonial India* (Durham, Duke University Press, 2003).

Ray, Sangeeta, *En-gendering India: Women and Nation in Colonial and Postcolonial Narratives* (Durham: Duke University Press, 2000).

Rhodesia Herald, anonymous review of Olive Schreiner, *Trooper Peter Halket*, April 7, 1897.

Rice, Michael, *From Dolly Gray to Sarie Marais: A Survey of Fiction from the First and Second Anglo-Boer Conflicts* (Noordhoek: Fischer Press, 2004).

Roberts, Neil, "Native Education from an Economic Point of View," *South African Journal of Science* 14 (1917).

Roberts, Ronald Suresh, *Fit to Govern: The Native Intelligence of Thabo Mbeki* (Johannesburg: Ste Publishers, 2006).

Rose, Gillian, *The Melancholy Science: An Introduction to the Thought of Theodor W. Adorno* (London: Macmillan, 1978).

Rose, Jacqueline, *States of Fantasy* (Oxford: Clarendon Press, 1995).

Said, Edward, *Orientalism* (New York: Random House, 1978).

Samuelson, Meg, "The Rainbow Womb: Race and Rape in South African Fiction of the Transition," *Kunapipi* 24.1 & 2 (2003), 88–100.

——, *Remembering the Nation: Dismembering Women?* (Pietermaritzburg: University of Kwazulu-Natal Press, 2007).

Sanders, Mark, "Extraordinary Violence," *Interventions: International Journal of Postcolonial Studies* 3. 2 (2001), 239–247.

——, *Ambiguities of Witnessing: Law and Literature the Time of a Truth Commission* (Stanford: Stanford University Press, 2007).

Schechter, Patricia, *Ida B. Wells-Barnett and American Reform, 1880–1930* (Chapel Hill: University of North Carolina University Press, 2001).

Scully, Pamela, "Rape, Race and Colonial Culture: The Sexual Politics of Identity in the Nineteenth Century Cape Colony, South Africa," *American Historical Review* 100.2 (1995), 335–359.

Shain, Milton, *The Roots of Anti-Semitism in South Africa* (Charlottesville, University of Virginia University Press, 1994).

Sharpe, Jenny, *Allegories of Empire: The Figure of Woman in the Colonial Text* (Minneapolis: University of Minnesota Press, 1993).

Sharpley-Whiting, T. Denean, *Fanon: Conflicts and Feminisms* (Lanham, Md., USA: Rowman & Littlefield, 1997).

Sielke, Sabine, *Reading Rape: the Rhetoric of Sexual Violence in American Literature and Culture, 1790–1990* (New Haven: Princeton University Press, 2002).

Simons, H.J. and R.E., *Class and Colour in South Africa 1850–1950* (London: International Defence and Aid Fund, 1983 (first published 1969)).

Slaughter, Joseph, *Human Rights Inc.: The World Novel, Narrative Form and International Law* (New York: Fordham University Press, 2007).

Smart, Barry, "Facing the Body—Goffman, Levinas and the Subject of Ethics," *Body and Society* 2.2 (1996), 67–78.

Smith, Charlene, "Rape Victims are not just Statistics: We are People too," *Mail & Guardian*, April 9, 1999.

——, "Their Deaths, His Doubts, My Fears," *Washington Post*, June 4, 2000.

Smith, Valerie, "Split Affinities: The Case of Interracial Rape," in Marianne Hirsch and Evelyn Fox-Keller (eds.), *Conflicts in Feminism*, (London: Routledge, 1990), 271–287.

Spivak, Gayatri Chakravorty, "Ethics and Politics in Tagore, Coetzee and Certain Scenes of Teaching," *Diacritics* 32.3–4 (fall-winter 2002), 17–31.

——, "Can the Subaltern Speak?" in Cary Nelson and Larry Grossberg (eds.), Marxism and the interpretation of Culture (Chicago: Uni of Illinois Press, 1988), 271-313.

——, translator's preface, in J. Derrida, *Of Grammatology* (Baltimore: Johns Hopkins University Press: 1976).

——, "Woman in Difference: Mahasweta Devi's 'Douloti the Bountiful'," in Andrew Parker and others (eds.), *Nationalisms and Sexualities* (New York: Routledge, 1992), 96–116.

Standard and Diggers News, anonymous review of Olive Schreiner, *Trooper Peter Halket*, February 27, 1897.

Stead, W.T., review of Olive Schreiner, *Trooper Peter Halket*, in *Review of Reviews*, April 1897.

Stiebel, Lindy, and Liz Gunner (eds.), *Still Beating the Drum, Critical Perspectives on Lewis Nkosi* (Amsterdam: Rodopi, 2005).

Stobie, Cheryl, *Somewhere in the Double Rainbow: Representations of Bisexuality in Post-Apartheid Novels* (Pietermaritzburg: University of KwaZulu-Natal Press, 2007).

Stoler, Ann Laura, *Race and the Education of Desire: Foucault's History of Sexuality and the Colonial Order of Things* (Durham: Duke University Press, 1995).

——, "A Colonial Reading of Foucault," in Ann Stoler, *Carnal Knowledge and Imperial Power: Race and the Intimate in Colonial Rule* (Berkeley: University of California Press, 2002).

Stott, Rebecca, "The Dark Continent: Africa as Female Body in Haggard's Adventure Fiction," *Feminist Review* 32 (1989), 69–89.

Stratton, Florence, *Contemporary African Literature and the Politics of Gender* (London: Routledge, 1994).

Suleri, Sara, *The Rhetoric of English India* (Chicago: University of Chicago Press, 1992).

Sunder Rajan, Rajeswari, *Real and Imagined Women: Gender, Culture and Postcolonialism* (London: Routledge, 1993).

Ukadike, Nwachukwu Frank, *Questioning African Cinema: Conversations with Filmmakers* (Minneapolis: University of Minnesota Press, 2002).

Tanner, Laura, *Intimate Violence: Reading Rape and Torture in Twentieth Century Fiction* (Bloomington: Indiana University Press, 1994).

Tatz, C.M., *Shadow and Substance in South Africa: A Study in Land and Franchise Policies Affecting Africans 1910–1960* (Pietermaritzburg: University of Natal Press, 1962).

Taylor, Dora, "Sarah Gertrude Millin, South African Realist," *Trek*, May 21 and June 4, 1943.

Taylor, Stephen, *The Caliban Shore: The Fate of the Grosvenor Castaways* (London: Faber & Faber, 2004).

Theweleit, Klaus, *Male Fantasies*, 2 volumes (Cambridge: Polity Press, 1987).

Times Literary Supplement, anonymous review of Francis Bancroft, *Of Like Passions*, June 14, 1907.

"Transvaal Tangle," anonymous review of Daphne Rooke, *Mittee, Time Magazine*, February 18, 1952.

Truth and Reconciliation Commission, *Report of the Truth and Reconciliation Commission* (Johannesburg: Truth and Reconciliation Commission, 1998).

Van der Merwe, C.N. and M. Rice (eds.), *A Century of Anglo-Boer War Stories* (Johannesburg: Jonathan Ball, 1999).

Van der Post, Laurens, "The Turbott Wolfe Affair," introduction to William Plomer, *Turbott Wolfe*, (London: Hogarth Press, 1965), 9–55.

Van der Vlies, Andrew, *J.M. Coetzee's Disgrace* (London: Continuum, 2010).

——, *South African Textual Cultures: Black, White, Read All Over* (Manchester University Press, 2007).

Van Onselen, Charles, *The Fox and the Flies: The World of Joseph Silver, Racketeer and Psychopath* (London: Jonathan Cape, 2007).

——, "The Witches of Suburbia: Domestic Service on the Witwatersrand 1890–1914," in *Studies in the Social and Economic History of the Witwatersrand, 1890–1914*, Vol. 2, New Nineveh (London: Longmans, 1982), 45–54.

Van Reenen, R., (ed.), *Emily Hobhouse: Boer War Letters* (Cape Town: Human & Rousseau, 1984).

Venuti, Lawrence, "Translation, Interpretation, Canon Formation," in *Translation and the Classic*, eds. Alexandra Lianeri and Vanda Zajko (Oxford University Press, 2008), 27–51.

Vetten, Lisa, "Violence against Women in South Africa," in S. Buhlungu and others, *State of the Nation, South Africa*, 2007 (Cape Town: HSRC Press, 2007), 425–447.

Vladislavic, Ivan (ed.) *T'kama-Adamastor: Inventions of Africa in a South African Painting* (Johannesburg: University of Witwatersrand Press, 2000).

Wade, Michael, "Myth, Truth and the South African Reality in the Fiction of Sarah Gertrude Millin," *Journal of Southern African Studies* 1. 1 (1974), 81–108.

Walker, Cherryl, *Women and Resistance in South Africa* (London: Onyx Press, 1982).

Ware, Vron, *Beyond the Pale: White Women, Racism and History* (London: Verso, 1992).

Wicomb, Zoë, "Classics," *Southern African Review of Books* 2.4 (1989), 16–17.

———, "Zoë Wicomb Interviewed on Writing and Nation," by Stephan Meyer and Thomas Olver, *Journal of Literary Studies* 18.1 (2002), 182–198.

———, "To Hear the Variety of Discourses," *Current Writing* 2 (October 1990), 35–44.

Wilhelm, Peter, "Peter Halket, Rhodes and Colonialism," in Cherry Clayton (ed.), *Olive Schreiner* (Johannesburg: McGraw-Hill, 1983), 208–212.

Willan, Brian, *Sol Plaatje: South African Nationalist 1876–1932* (London: Heinemann, 1984).

Wolfthal, Diane, *Images of Rape: The Heroic Tradition and its Alternatives* (Cambridge: Cambridge University Press, 2000).

Young, Robert, *Colonial Desire: Hybridity in Theory, Culture, and Race* (London: Routledge), 1995.

———, *Postcolonialism: An Historical Introduction* (Oxford: Blackwell, 2001).

Younghusband, Toni, review of Coetzee's *Disgrace, Femina* (September 1999), 148.

Yusuf, Yisa Kehinde, "Rape-related English and Yoruba Proverbs," *Women and Language* 21.2 (1998), 39–43.

Žižek, Slavoj, *The Art of the Ridiculous Sublime: On David Lynch's Lost Highway* (Seattle: University of Washington Press, 2000).

Archival Sources
PUBLIC ARCHIVES

Cape Town, National Archives:

BCS 2654/13/32 vol. 9 No. 83, Daphne Rooke, *The Greyling.*

BCS 26963, Daphne Rooke, *The Greyling.*

BCS P91/10/112, Daphne Rooke, *The Greyling.*

IDP P77/3/104 and IDP P84/12/53, Arthur Maimane, *Victims.*

IDP P77/09/103, J. M. Coetzee, *Heart of the Country.*

IDP P88/3/23, Njabulo S. Ndebele, *Fools and Other Stories.*

Cape Town, University of the Western Cape, Mayibuye Archives:

IDAF papers, Arthur Maimane, unpublished memoir, "One of Us."

Grahamstown, Rhodes University, Cory Library:

MS 14847, General Missionary Conference, Commission on Assaults on Women.

Oxford, Oxford University, Bodleian Library:

Lord Harcourt papers, correspondence with Lord Gladstone on "black peril."

Private Archives

Cape Town: Lucy Graham, e-mail correspondence with Lewis Nkosi, 2002.

Cape Town: Lucy Graham, e-mail correspondence with parents of students of English Department, University of Stellenbosch, concerning suitability as first-year text of K. Sello Duiker *Thirteen Cents.*

Johannesburg: Kwela Books archive, by courtesy of Annari van der Merwe.

London: Victor Gollancz Ltd archive, by permission of the Orion Publishing Group.

London: Jenny Maimane, papers of Arthur Maimane, by courtesy of Jenny Maimane.

Oral Sources

Notes of informal discussion with Mark Behr by Lucy Graham, Stellenbosch, May 21, 2009.
Notes of interview with Matthew Krouse by Lucy Graham, Cape Town, February 25, 2009.
Notes of interview with Jenny Maimane by Hugh Macmillan, London, December 20, 2008.
Notes of interview with Daphne Rooke by Lucy Graham, Cambridge, November 24, 2005.

Films and Dramatic Productions

Bestall, Clifford (director), *The Dark Heart*, 2002.
Cavani, Liliana (director), *Night Porter*, 1974.
Foot-Newton, Lara, and Gerhard Marx (directors), *And There in the Dust*, 2005.
Greene, Tim (director), *Boy Called Twist*, 2004.
Hermanus, Oliver (director), *Skoonheid*, 2011.
Hickson, David (director), *Beat the Drum*, 2003.
Hood, Gavin (director), *Tsotsi*, 2005.
Jacobs, Steve (director), *Disgrace*, 2008.
Kaplan, Jonathan (director), *The Accused*, 1988.
Ngakane, Lionel (director), *Jemima and Johnny*, 1966.
Sinclair, Ingrid (director), *Flame*, 1996.
Stopford, Clare (director), *Green Man Flashing*, 2004.
Suleman, Ramadan (director), *Fools*, 1997.
Valley, Yunus (director), *The Glow of White Women*, 2007.

Internet Sources

ANC, Statement of the ANC at the Human Rights Commission Hearings on Racism in the Media, April 2000, viewed September 29, 2000. http://www.anc.org.za/ancdocs/misc/2000/sp0405.html.

Centre for Applied Legal Studies, "Gender and the Truth and Reconciliation Commission," submission to the TRC, drafted by Sheila Meintjes and Beth Goldblatt, viewed September 29, 2000. http://www.truth.org.za/submit/gender.html.

Dempster, Carolyn, "South African Trial Brings Rape into Public View," *News from Africa*, 2006, viewed August 20, 2007. http://www.newsfromafrica.org/newsfromafrica/articles/art_10669.html.

De Vos, Pierre, "Constitutionally Speaking: On Zuma, Zapiro and that Cartoon," September 8, 2008, viewed December 2008. http://constitutionallyspeaking.co.za/?p=658.

Dorfman, Ariel, "A Vicious Circle," *The Guardian*, January 17, 2008, viewed January 18, 2008. http://www.guardian.co.uk/world/2008/jan/17/chile.theatre.

Eastern Cape News Agency, "Abusing Teacher Still at School," *The Daily Dispatch*, October 10, 2001, viewed September 30, 2003. http://www.dispatch.co.za/2001/10/10/easterncape/ABUSING.HTM.

Encounters: South African International Documentary Film Festival, 2002, blurb for *The Dark Heart*, directed by Clifford Bestall, viewed June 6, 2007. http://www.encounters.co.za/archive/2002/films.html.

Fisher, Phillip, Review of *Tshepang*, by Lara Foot-Newton, *British Theatre Guide*, 2004, viewed July 5, 2007. http://www.britishtheatreguide.info/reviews/tshepang-rev.htm.

Foot-Newton, Lara, cited in LSM Newswire, "*Tshepang*, Theatre La Chapelle & Maurice Podrey's Mopo Productions," February 4, 2009, viewed November 30, 2009. http://

www.scena.org/blog/newswire/2009/02/tshepang-theatre-la-chapelle-maurice.html.

Gear, Sasha, "Sex, Sexual Violence and Coercion in Men's Prisons," paper presented at AIDS in Context conference, University of the Witwatersrand, 2001, viewed October 25, 2008. http://www.csvr.org.za/wits/papers/papgear1.htm.

Govender, Pregs, "Child Rape: A Taboo within the AIDS Taboo," *Sunday Times,* South Africa, April 4, 1999, viewed July 5, 2007. http://www.aegis.com/news/suntimes/1999/ST990401.html.

King, Judith, "NU Medical Students Promote Abstinence," HIVAN: Centre for HIV-AIDS Networking, 2005, viewed June 5, 2007. http://www.hivan.org.za/campussupport/stories/abstain.asp.

Kirkegaard, Hugh, and Wayne Northey, "The Sex Offender as Scapegoat: Vigilante Violence and a Faith Community Response," viewed October 20, 2009. http://www.religion.emory.edu/faculty/smith/vr/wayne.html.

Lefebure, Leo, "Victims, Violence and the Sacred: the Thought of René Girard," 2006, viewed November 30, 2009. http://lonestar.texas.net/~mseifert/girard.html.

Lewin, Matthew, "Bring me my Assegai," review of Deon Meyer's *Devil's Peak, The Guardian,* Saturday July 21, 2007, viewed December 1, 2007. http://books.guardian.co.uk/review/story/0, 2131078,00.html.

Little, Alan, "AIDS: A South African Horror story," BBC news, 2002, viewed June 5, 2007. http://news.bbc.co.uk/1/hi/programmes/correspondent/2311067.stm.

McGreal, Chris, 2001, "Aids Myth Drives South African baby rape," *The Guardian,* Saturday November 3, 2001, viewed July 5, 2007. http://www.guardian.co.uk/aids/story/0, 7369, 587165,00.html.

Mbeki, Thabo, letter from Thabo Mbeki to Tony Leon, July 1, 2000, viewed September 20, 2007. http://www.insidepolitics.org.za/blog_details.aspx?EntryId=109&page=search.

——, "Thabo Mbeki Answers your Questions," live web cast, *BBC Talking Point,* June 6, 2000, viewed August 30, 2003. http://news.bbc.co.uk/1/hi/talking_point/forum/746464.stm.

Mbembe, Achille, "What is postcolonial thinking? An interview with Achille Mbembe," trans. John Fletcher, *Eurozine,* January 9, 2008, viewed August 7, 2008. http://www.eurozine.com/articles/2008-01-09-mbembe-en.html.

Media Rights Website—Films: Flame, viewed October 20, 2009. http://www.mediarights.org/film/flame.

National Department of Health, South Africa, "Research update," 2004, viewed August 20, 2007. http://www.doh.gov.za/docs/research/vol6-1rape.html.

Raditlhalo, Sam, "'The Travelling Salesman': a Tribute to K. Sello Duiker, 1974–2005," *Feminist Africa,* 11, 2008, viewed November 8, 2009. http://www.feministafrica.org/index.php/k-sello-duiker.

Rundle, Fred, "961 Child Rapes a Day in South Africa," *Jeff Rense Program,* 2004, viewed June 5, 2007. http://www.rense.com/general56/RAPES.HTM.

Samuelson, Meg, and Natasha Distiller, "Denying the Coloured Mother: Gender and Race in South Africa," *Eurozine,* March 2, 2006, viewed February 10, 2008. http://www.eurozine.com/articles/2006-03-02-distiller-en.html.

Smith, Charlene, "Keeping it in their pants: Politicians, men and sexual assault in South Africa," paper presented in the Harold Wolpe Lecture Series, University of KwaZulu Natal March 17, 2005, viewed July 10, 2006. http://www.wolpetrust.org.za/dialogue2005/DN032005smith_paper.htm.

———, "Rape Survivor Speaks Out," transcript of live interview on 20/20 Downtown, *ABC News*, February 8, 2001, viewed July 31, 2008. http://www.abcnews.go.com/onair/DailyNews/chat_CharleneSmith.html.

———, "The Relation between HIV-Prevalence and Virgin Rape," *News from the Nordic Africa Institute*, No. 2, viewed June 5, 2007. http://www.nai.uu.se/publications/news/archives/203smith/.

Steinberg, Jonny, "Of Blocked Paths, Borrowed Dreams and Zuma's appeal," *Open Society Foundations*, viewed 15 January 2011. http://www.soros.org/initiatives/fellowship/articles_publications/articles/steinberg_20090518.

Thornberry, Elizabeth, "History Helps Find Better Ways to Talk About Rape in South Africa," Gender News from the Clayman Institute for Gender Research, viewed 1 October 2011. http://www.stanford.edu/group/gender/cgi-bin/wordpressblog/2011/07/history-helps-find-better-ways-to-talk-about-rape-in-south-africa/.

Truth and Reconciliation Commission, Report of, volume 4, chapter 10, paras. 47–49, viewed May 8, 2011. http://www.nelsonmandela.org/omalley/index.php/site/q/03lv02167/04lv02264/05lv02335/06lv02357/07lv02387/08lv02397.htm.

Tshwete, Steve, interview, 2005, viewed March 30, 2008. http://www.wolpetrust.org.za/dialogue2005/DN032005smith_paper.htm.

Van Graan, Mike, "Crime the Beloved Country," Fleur de Cap Theatre Awards, 2006, viewed June 5, 2007. http://www.fdcawards.co.za/base.php?top_id=1&side_id=13&editorial_id=80&category_id=3&page=14.

Winfrey, Oprah, *The Oprah Winfrey Show*, "*Children at Risk: South African baby Raping*," July 15, 2004, viewed August 20, 2007. http://www2.oprah.com/tows/slide/200407/20040715/tows_slide_20040715_01.jhtml.

Official Publications

Great Britain:

Parliamentary Debates, Official Reports, 5th Series, House of Commons, 1914.

South Africa:

Debates of the First Session of the First Parliament of the House of Assembly, 1911.

Report of the Commission of Inquiry to Report on Assaults on Women, 1913.

Unpublished Sources

Bekker, Susanna, "George Heaton Nicholls and the Formulation of 'Native Policy', 1927 to 1936," Master of Arts dissertation in History, University of Natal, Durban, 1987.

Cullhed, Christina, "Grappling with Patriarchies: Narrative Strategies of Resistance in Miriam Tlali's Writings," doctoral dissertation, Uppsala University, 2006.

Dovey, Lindiwe, "Engendering Gender Discourses through African Cinema: The Case of *Fools* (1998) and *Karmen Gei* (2001)," unpublished paper presented at "Writing African Women: The Poetics and Politics of African Gender Research" Conference at the University of the Western Cape, January 19–22, 2005.

Goniwe, Thembinkosi, "Goodbye Post-Colonialism and Post-Apartheid," unpublished paper, Division of Visual Arts, University of the Witwatersrand, Johannesburg, September 11, 2008.

Hanzimanolis, Margaret, "Ultramarooned: Gender, Empire and Narratives of Travel in Southern Africa," doctoral dissertation, University of Cape Town, 2005.

Hofmeyr, Isabel, "Gandhi's Printing Press: Print Cultures of the Indian Ocean," unpublished conference paper, 2009.

Kessler, Stowell, "The Black Concentration Camps of the South African War 1899–1902," doctoral dissertation, University of Cape Town, 2003.

Rose, Jacqueline, "Coetzee's Women," paper delivered at the conference "Making Waves: Literary Studies in an Interdisciplinary Frame," Robinson College, Cambridge, July 2003.

Truett, Carmen Nocentelli, "Islands of Love: Europe, 'India' and Interracial Romance, 1572–1673," doctoral dissertation, Stanford University, 2004.

Warnes, Christopher, "Writing Crime in the New South Africa: Negotiating Threat in the Novels of Deon Meyer, Margie Orford and Andrew Brown," unpublished paper viewed with permission of the author, 2011.

{ INDEX }

CPSIA information can be obtained at www.ICGtesting.com
Printed in the USA

9 780190 256418